Disney INFINITY

PRIMA Official Game Guide

Table of Contents

Game Basics

Basics

Searching

Looking for missions is an easy process, since all Mission Givers for Main or Side Missions have a blue exclamation mark over their head and generate a blue beacon. After a mission is started the Mission Giver will have a blue question mark over them until the quest is completed. Challenges also give off a beacon as long as you have the correct character for that Challenge. Initially the beacon is yellow to represent the first level of difficulty, which is easy. As you complete a challenge the beacon will change to orange for medium and red for hard. When all three levels of difficulty are completed it will turn grey.

A lot of the guesswork is taken out of searching due to the green compass arrow built into the game. When in doubt, go into the mission log and make sure to activate a mission to get the helpful arrow to appear.

Show Me the Money

A lot of the destructible environment as well as enemies will drop coins, however you must actually run over the coins to collect them. It is easy to overlook this fact, so make sure not to miss out. If you are running low on funds, try completing some challenges on the higher levels or simply find a spot with a lot of destructible objects to smash and let them regenerate so you can do it again.

Moves/Movement

People

There are a large number of characters to play with in this game, and fortunately they all move in a similar fashion. You use one stick to move and the other to look around for all human and super-human characters. You also use the same buttons to jump, block, dodge, and activate the character's "powers", however each character from a Play Set is unique and has his or her own powers and methods of attack. They do all share a few common movements that are essential to platforming, as explained here.

Double Jump

The first common technique is the double jump, and while it is easy to do, there is more to it than merely pressing a button twice. Double jumps will allow you to jump higher, but they can also allow you to jump longer. The second jump can be done to extend the distance you cover, allowing you to jump across far ledges and buildings.

Climbing

Most of the platforming in the game will include plenty of climbing. This skill is easy to perform, but it can be tricky to know where you can actually climb. Always look for a ledge, edge, or ridge that has a yellow glow, which indicates you can grab on to it. Once you are hanging, there are a lot of options including jumping up or over to another grapple point, jumping down or off the structure, or following the hand hold to maneuver around the edge. Holding on to an edge and running or moving hand-over-hand is an important technique to get to through some tricky spots.

There are also other objects that can be climbed in various Play Sets such as poles, ropes, and drain pipes. These objects aren't highlighted in yellow all the time, but their narrow shape should give you a good idea that they are something to try out.

Dodge/Charge/Roll

Several characters have the ability to move in a quick fashion that can be used for defense or offense. A roll is a great way to dodge an attack (by holding block and pressing the control stick) and to maneuver when there is a lot of action on screen at once. Also available is a charge move (done by pressing the normal attack button) that can be used to cover ground quickly or simply to move faster or to avoid a bad situation. There are also characters like the ones from Monsters University that can use a charging move to break objects or stun enemies.

Vehicles

Cars

All vehicles move by using one stick to steer and the other to look around, and they all use the triggers to accelerate and brake/reverse. Cars can jump and, as you might guess, the faster it goes the farther it jumps—this is especially true when you hit a ramp. This is where two important features come in: drifting and turbo.

Drifting

Drifting is the process of holding both triggers while driving into a turn or even a circle. This maneuver is great for getting around corners when you are at top speeds, but more importantly it builds up the turbo meter. More turbo means more speed. Drift in any race or situation where you need to store up that potential boost.

Turbo

There is a meter under your vehicle that indicates how many bars of turbo you have. When you do a stunt or drift, the meter in one bar will fill until it is yellow, which means you can activate that boost. After one bar is yellow, the next gauge will start to fill and continue the process. Once all segments of the meter are yellow, you are wasting an effort to build turbo and should use a boost as soon as possible. To activate the turbo is a simple flick of the control stick and your vehicle will shoot flames showing you are boosting. Obviously it can be dangerous to boost at a turn, but a drift can help control that speed. A turbo assist is great any time you are in a straightaway, a close race to the finish, or when you want to hit a ramp at top speed to maximize your air time for stunts or tricks.

Stunts/Tricks

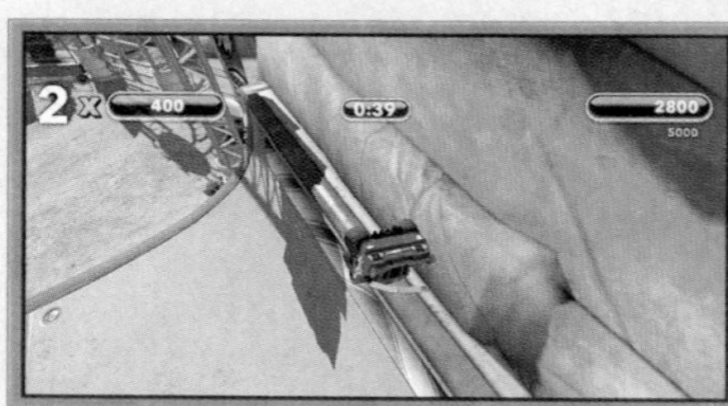

Probably the coolest thing about cars, besides high-speed driving, is the tricks you can pull off. After leaping in the air, pushing the right stick up, down, left, or right will trigger front or back flips, spins, or barrel rolls. Doing two of the same motions while in the air is considered a double trick. However, if you push in two different directions, the stunt is considered a combo and earns even more points. If you get enough height and speed, it is possible to pull off a triple combo for really big points. The key to chaining moves is to immediately flip the control stick when you are airborne and quickly press another direction as that move completes to perform the next trick.

Bikes

Two wheelers can perform stunts and tricks similar to cars, but they don't have a turbo gauge. Generally bikes are pretty slow, but to get a boost you need to do a trick that gives the bike a blue trail as it speeds along. This speed trail shows that the bike is going at top speed and it is the perfect time for hitting ramps to get big air and do tricks. A cool feature of bikes is that they can grind on rails and even build up a blue speed burst while doing so. One down side to bikes is that they are somewhat fragile. If you don't land well after even a short jump, that bike will break apart and you have to wait for it to reform.

Mounts

There are several unique animals to ride in the Play Sets, mostly in Lone Ranger. You can expect to find a bunch of horses, an elephant, and other critters in the Play Sets and Toy Box. Horses can run (accelerate) and turn, as they stand on their back legs and neigh, but they don't do stunts. However, unlike other rides, you can shoot while on horseback. That speed while shooting is a big advantage. As you might guess, an elephant doesn't run, but it can stomp and charge. Animal companions may not be as fast as other forms of transportation, but they are very fun to ride around and bring a lot of variety traveling throughout the worlds.

Ships

Found in the Pirates Play Set, ships are essential to the pirate theme and come in two types. There is a small dinghy, which is a tiny boat, but it still packs a cannon that can wipe out enemies and remove debris. The big ship is where you really get to act as a captain to customize, steer, and battle your boat on the open seas, however. Visually the ship can be customized like many buildings or NPCs, but the exciting part is changing the type of cannons it can fire and the type of power-ups it uses. These options make your ship the terror of the seas to anyone foolish enough to cross your path. It is literally a blast to sink other ships, especially when you can change views to see things from another angle and manually fire the final cannon to send them to the locker.

Flight

A few special methods allow a player to fly through the world, and some even come with weapons. It is pretty thrilling to fly over an entire map, but remember that these are not fighting jets and most modes of air travel are not very fast. These vehicles move in a similar way to others, but there is the added element of controlling elevation by going higher and lower.

Unique

There are many other modes of transportation that are unique to each Play Set and can appear in the Toy Box, such as the Hover Board and Glide Pack. Their special functionality determines how they are controlled and what they can do. These add a new experience in game play and can take a while to master.

Combat

Conflict is an essential part of any game, and in *Disney Infinity* it can take place on land, air, or sea. Each character has his or her own attacks, but these are further enhanced by Tools, Packs, and Vehicles. There are tons of variations, but here are a few tips to keep in mind when battling your way to victory.

On Foot

Characters like The Incredibles have unique superpowers that give them a big advantage in hand-to-hand combat, but most characters share some common moves. One move that is not very obvious is the ground slam, where a character jumps and attacks. This is useful when surrounded by enemies as it lifts your character out of danger for a second and delivers an attack with a small area of effect. On the other end of the spectrum is the defensive ability to block with a simple button press. This is often overlooked as players try to overpower enemies with combos, but it is probably one of the best options in a fight. Most attacks can be blocked, and while this doesn't get you any closer to defeating your enemy, it can set your enemy up to drop his or her guard. By blocking or absorbing an attack, it can create an opening for you to counter or avoid getting knocked out of range. This is a fallback move, so whenever you are not sure what to do in battle—block!

Cars

There are lots of options for vehicular combat, especially with the cars that have built-in guns. Also, vehicles from the Cars Play Set have a large variety of weapons including machine guns, mines, and missiles that only appear after they are unlocked

from side missions and purchased. All of these weapons are great for knocking the competition out of a race or destroying objects. Even without weapons, there is an overlooked ability for Cars characters to bump into other vehicles and knock them off balance. This isn't as powerful as a full-out weapon attack, but a hard hit could give the edge in a race.

Shooting

Numerous types of projectiles range from Toilet Paper Launchers to Tomahawks, but they are controlled in the same way. Gun-like toys can be fired from the hip and shot in the general direction the character is pointing. With enough firing of the toy, it will spread enough ammo to take out most targets. However, if you need precision, you can enter a zoomed in mode where you can place the aiming cursor over what you want to hit. The important thing to remember is that while the gun is locked in one position, you can still run and gun, allowing you to move quickly with the gun focused on a single point. This technique comes in handy when trying to shoot specific targets during Challenges. The Lone Ranger features some special projectile properties, because the shots all ricochet off of a target. Essentially a single shot can bounce and hit many targets, opening up lots of tricky shooting.

Big Guns

Many of the larger guns like the Gattling guns and cannons will change the perspective to first person. These powerful weapons can cover great distance, but they must be adjusted for height to lob and launch ammunition to reach the targets. Cannons are extremely damaging, but they track and move very slowly and have a slower rate of fire than most other guns. These are best for large and tough targets, otherwise use a Gattling gun to shoot lots of ammunition to track smaller and quicker targets.

On the Open Seas

Your main ship from the Pirates Play Set has several types of cannons to take out enemies. There is a lot of strategy in choosing what type of cannon due to their firing rate, range, and damage capabilities. Another factor is whether you fire the guns from the helm, shooting the side cannons from a few views, or if you want to manually use the cannon to personally target and fire away on ships. The other important option is that the Broadside cannons can fire a single shot if you press the fire button quickly. But if it is held to charge the cannons, several of them will fire at the same time. All of these options depend on the type and amount of ships that you are battling, but in a large sea battle it is probably best to stick to the helm and blast with full cannon fire when you can hit with all your cannons.

In addition to the variety of cannons, there are many power-ups that can speed up your ship, turn the sea against foes, and even summon the Kraken. Only a single power-up can be active at one time and each has a charge/recharge time before it can be used. These powerful weapons can quickly sink a single ship and can effectively turn the tide of battle.

Finish Them

Many enemies will fall down after taking some damage, but that doesn't mean they are defeated. A lot of them can be hit while they are down or trying to get up, so make sure to finish off a single enemy. Quickly switching enemies is a good tactic when you are surrounded, but it is always a good idea to reduce the number of foes you face as soon as possible.

Mission Types

Each Play Set has a variety of missions to keep you busy. There are missions that tell a story or provide optional side quests, and even repeatable missions. A blue exclamation mark over a character denotes that he or she has a mission to discuss with you. Also, the character sends out a blue beacon above that can be see from far away.

NOTE

It's important to note that some missions only become available after completing other tasks, after buying specific items, or at certain points in the game.

Main Missions

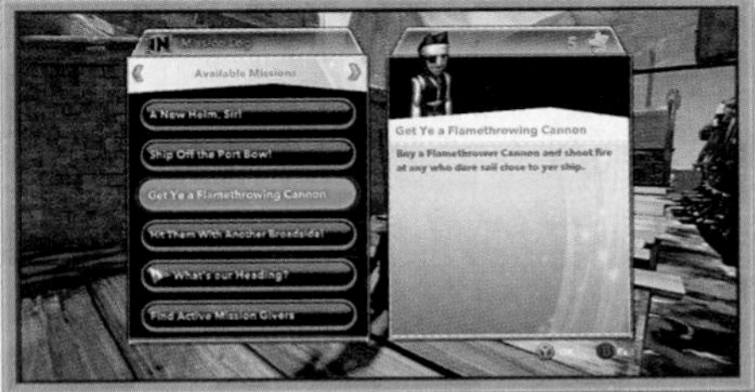

These are the primary quests where you will encounter many familiar characters from that Play Set's world. The story missions are considered Main Missions, as they complete an adventure centered around each unique world. All of the Main Missions combine to tell a complete tale from start to finish, although the story can have several branching elements. This means that there can be several Main Missions going on at any given moment, but the main story leads to the same conclusion.

Side Mission

Side Missions are usually optional tasks that can be done to enhance the journey. Beyond the obvious fun of completing them, there are often rewards that make it well worth your time to go through each one. These missions can be as quick as a single action or extend throughout the entire adventure. Like the Main Missions, these are given by someone with a blue exclamation mark and are sometimes extra missions given by primary characters, or new missions from general NPCs.

"Hidden" Missions

There are a few missions that are almost hidden because they are not explicitly listed in the mission log. These are not necessarily intended to be "secrets", and they may pop up as a message on screen, but they're easy to overlook or forget about. This includes missions such as the pennant collection in Monsters University and locating very elusive totems in Lone Ranger.

Alert Missions

Many of these missions are repeatable short quests that can appear at various times in an adventure. Generally they are simple tasks, like taking out some enemies or towing a car.

Challenge Missions

Challenges are unlocked as you complete certain tasks or missions in the Play Sets. They give off a yellow beacon, but the beacon will not appear if you are not using the specific character required. If you don't have that character active, the Challenge location is just a flat circle on the ground with that character's picture on it. Most of the missions are meant for all characters of that Play Set, but several are specific to a character. These can be played many times and have three levels of difficulty: easy, medium, and hard. They are a great diversion from the main story or perfect places to hone your skills for multiplayer games.

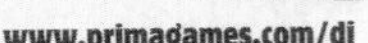

Tools and Packs

Each Play Set has its own unique Tools and Packs, but they are all equipped the same way. Except for vehicles from the Cars Play Set, everyone can equip one Tool and one Pack at a time. The Tools are held in the character's hand (which would be tough for a car!) and the Packs are something the character wears on its back (or, in the case of Cars, somewhere on their chassis). These can be set up with a quick swap on the directional pad to toggle them on and off. While you will generally want to use these awesome upgrades, you have to be aware that it will replace the default functionality of a button press. For example, when one of The Incredibles has the Hover Board active, he or she cannot use a regular attack. Ultimately the extra power of the Tools and Packs will replace your common moves, but being able to toggle back and forth with a quick swap is essential to rounded gameplay.

Decorate/Customize

Inside each Play Set you can change the appearance of buildings and NPCs to customize that world. These are strictly visual changes, but they can alter the way an entire city looks and feels.

Leveling Up

As characters earn Sparks, they will go up in level and be awarded a Spin in the Toy Box Vault. Leveling doesn't effect the character's attributes, and is strictly used to build up Spins to earn more precious toys from the Toy Box.

Collectibles

One of the main functions of the Play Set is to unlock content for the Toy Box. Each Play Set has red and green capsules that can unlock items in the Play Set and Toy Box. There are also Chests and a Vault that can be unlocked by specific characters to unlock exclusive content from that world into the Play Set. Check out the collectibles maps and info at the end of each Play Set to find any customization you are looking for.

Play Set Completion

Disney Infinity does not have a completion meter or percentage for each Play Set. It is meant to be enjoyed to whatever extent the player wants. However for those looking to go the extra distance and complete as much of the game as possible, there are several ways to keep you busy for a long time. The Gold Star missions and achievement/trophies are an obvious goal to shoot for, but to really finish a Play Set means completing all of the following tasks:

- Main and Side Missions
- Challenges completed on all difficulties
- All capsules collected (red and green)
- All Gold Star missions done
- All Toy Store toys unlocked and purchased
- All Chests and Vaults opened

Characters

Pirates of the Caribbean

Game Basics | Characters | Power Discs | Play Sets | Toy Box | Toy Box Collection | Achievements

Got It? ☑ CAPTAIN JACK SPARROW

Join Captain Jack Sparrow in an epic adventure of pirates, treasures, and sea battles. Lead him on his merry and slightly unbalanced way across the Pirates of the Caribbean Play Set. Savvy?

AVAILABLE IN THE DISNEY INFINITY STARTER PACK

Got It? ☑ BARBOSSA

He's a master swordsman and a powerful character to wield. Barbossa is the much-feared, mutinous ex-first-mate of Jack Sparrow and fun to play in the Pirates of the Caribbean Play Set.

CHARACTER SOLD SEPARATELY

Got It? ☑ DAVY JONES

The demon of the deep, Davy Jones is feared by all who sail the seven seas. Beware of the sword-fighting feats and writhing tentacles of the Pirates of the Caribbean villain.

CHARACTER SOLD SEPARATELY

Monsters University

SULLEY

Got It?

The big, loveable future scarer is in training at the Monsters University Play Set. Bust a few cycling moves across campus, set up traps for unsuspecting monsters, and avoid lectures.

AVAILABLE IN THE DISNEY INFINITY STARTER PACK

MIKE

Got It?

Join the campus clown in the Monsters University Play Set. Use a megaphone to scare rival monsters, study being sneaky, or just let Mike perform his signature jig.

CHARACTER SOLD SEPARATELY

RANDY

Got It?

When it comes to creeping into the rival campus for some scare-worthy sabotage, Randy is the sneakiest one in the Monsters University Play Set.

CHARACTER SOLD SEPARATELY

The Incredibles

Game Basics | Characters | Power Discs | Play Sets | Toy Box | Toy Box Collection | Achievements

MR. INCREDIBLE

Got It? ☑

Dedicated to saving the world, Mr. Incredible uses his super strength and super combo attacks to vanquish Syndrome!

AVAILABLE IN THE DISNEY INFINITY STARTER PACK

MRS. INCREDIBLE

Got It? ☑

With her super-stretch skills, Mrs. Incredible can whip across town, yank objects closer, and swing up buildings. Evil-doers beware!

CHARACTER SOLD SEPARATELY

DASH

Got It? ☑

Play The Incredibles Play Set as the fastest kid on the block—Dash. Don't just fight the dreaded the enemy, run circles around them with your superhuman speed.

CHARACTER SOLD SEPARATELY

VIOLET

Got It? ☑

Violet has done her fair share of protecting and her plasma shield is perfect for the job in The Incredibles Play Set. Her power of invisibility also comes in handy for avoiding trouble.

CHARACTER SOLD SEPARATELY

SYNDROME

Got It? 

He's the flame-haired fanboy and self-appointed nemesis in The Incredibles Play Set. Join Syndrome in his campaign to take over the city and put the The Incredibles in danger's way. What happens is up to you!

CHARACTER SOLD SEPARATELY

Cars

MATER

Got It?

Don't judge a book by its cover. Mater might be a bit rusty, but he's also got power under his hood. He's built for towing too, so he's one of the more helpful vehicles in the Cars Play Set.

CHARACTER SOLD SEPARATELY

LIGHTNING MCQUEEN

Got It?

Whatever the task, Lightning McQueen is quick to react. Whether he's jumping a canyon, trailblazing through desert, or towing another character in the Cars Play Set, nothing slows him down.

AVAILABLE IN THE CARS PLAY SET

HOLLEY

Got It?

Holley Shiftwell is as sharp and smart as she looks. Trained for any terrain, take Holley for a spin and she'll make even the hardest corners in the Cars Play Set feel like child's play.

AVAILABLE IN THE CARS PLAY SET

FRANCESCO

Got It?

Top European racer Francesco thinks he's the hottest thing since wheels were invented. With his high-speed racing and gadgetry, the sleek Italian car is Lightning's chief rival. Francesco can zip around the Cars Play Set and still have enough juice for showing off afterwards.

CHARACTER SOLD SEPARATELY

The Lone Ranger

Got It?

THE LONE RANGER

There's never a dull moment playing the smart-shooting, masked man of justice. Even with the odds stacked against you, you can use your climbing, riding, and bullet-ricocheting skills to win in the Lone Ranger Play Set.

AVAILABLE IN THE LONE RANGER PLAY SET

Got It?

TONTO

He's the intelligent, Tomahawk-throwing partner of the Lone Ranger and always fun to play. Tonto is excellent on a horse, a feared adversary, and quite stylish with his crow headgear.

AVAILABLE IN THE LONE RANGER PLAY SET

The Power Discs

Disney Infinity characters and Toy Box Worlds can be modified or customized through the use of Power Discs. Circular Power Discs grant your character special power-ups that can be used in the Play Sets as well as in the Toy Box. Hexagonal Power Discs, on the other hand, unlock special gadgets, vehicles or mounts, and themes to help you personalize the Toy Box even more. By combining different Power Discs, you can get even more different results.

NOTE

There are 20 Power Discs released in Wave 1. These are all covered below. In addition, there will be 20 Power Discs released in Wave 2 and another 15 in Wave 3. Be sure to collect them all. For the circular Power Discs, you can use two of the same disc to get even more power-ups.

Circular Power Discs

Got It?

Bolt's Super Strength

When you have this Power Disc under your character, your character has a 2% chance of inflicting 15 additional damage in both melee and ranged combat. This is cumulative, so if you have two of these discs, you have a 4% chance of inflicting more damage. This is useful in the Play Sets and the Toy Box—especially when you are facing lots of enemies.

Got It?

Fix-It Felix's Repair Power

Put this under your character and you get a 25% chance of receiving 100 more health, which can help keep you in the battle longer. Again, these are cumulative, so you have an even better chance to get health by stacking two of these Power Discs under your character.

Got It?

C.H.R.O.M.E. Armor Shield

While this Power Disc is placed under your character, you have a 3% chance of receiving 4 seconds of invulnerability. Stack two of these so you get a 6% chance for invulnerability.

Got It?

Pieces of Eight

When you are playing in the Play Sets, you need to collect loot or other tokens of the local economy to purchase new tools and toys. Therefore, put one of these Power Discs under your character to get a 2% chance to collect an extra 25 units of loot. If you stack a second one, the greater your chance of getting this bonus.

Combining Circular Power Discs

If you stack two different circular Power Discs under your character, you can sometimes get a bonus special effect.

- Combine C.H.R.O.M.E. Armor Shield and Pieces of Eight to get the Spark Shield. When you get hit, you get Sparks as a result, which help you advance to the next level.
- Combine Bolt's Super Strength and Pieces of Eight to get Overpowering Strength. This gives you additional Sparks when you defeat an enemy.
- Put Fix-It Felix's Repair Power and Pieces of Eight together and you will have Turbo Charge. When you have this and are driving, you have a chance of getting an extra charge of turbo power when you use a turbo boost.

Hexagonal Power Discs

Got It? 

Mickey's Car

While in the Toy Box, put this on the pad and Mickey's Car will appear. Drive it around in the Toy Box and even use it for racing.

Got It? 

Cinderella's Coach

Want to travel and race in style? This Power Disc makes Cinderella's Coach appear in the Toy Box.

Kahn

Kahn carried Mulan into battle. Now this noble steed can take you for a ride.

Stitch's Blaster

Experiment 626 has left behind his blaster. Place this Power Disc on the pad and you can use it to attack your enemies at a distance.

Carl Fredricksen's Cane

Not only does this keep Mr. Fredricksen upright and from falling over, it can also be used to whack enemies. Just pop this Power Disc onto the pad to get this item added to your Tools/Pack collection.

King Candy's Dessert Toppings

While in a Toy Box, place this Power Disc on the pad to change the theme of the ground and themed terrain to that of the Sugar Rush video game in *Wreck-It Ralph*.

Sugar Rush Sky

This Power Disc changes the skydome of your Toy Box World to Sugar Rush, and also includes the music of this theme.

Alice's Wonderland

Theme the land and terrain of your Toy Box World to that of Wonderland.

Tulgey Wood

Change the skydome and music in your Toy Box World to that of *Alice in Wonderland*.

Marlin's Reef

This Power Disc makes the land look like the bottom of the ocean and changes the terrain to an aquatic look.

Nemo's Seascape

The skydome changes to a watery atmosphere when you use this Power Disc.

Rapunzel's Kingdom

The texture and terrain take on a theme from the movie *Tangled* with this Power Disc.

Rapunzel's Birthday Sky

Lanterns fill the night skydome as you listen to music from *Tangled* when you use this Power Disc.

Dumbo the Flying Elephant

Dumbo the Flying Elephant from the Disney theme parks spawns in the Toy Box when you use this Power Disc. Use it to fly around the world.

Astro Blasters Space Cruiser

This vehicle looks like the ride vehicles in the Buzz Lightyear's Astroblasters ride at the Disney theme parks. It stays on the ground, but has a built-in blaster.

Abu the Elephant

Remember when Genie changed Abu the Monkey into an elephant for Prince Ali's entrance into Agrabah? Now he can carry your character around a Toy Box World.

Monsters University

NOTE - For those playing Disney Infinity on the Wii, the Play Sets are a bit different. Access your free eGuide (voucher code on the insert) to access this content.

M.U. Scaring 101

M.U. Campus

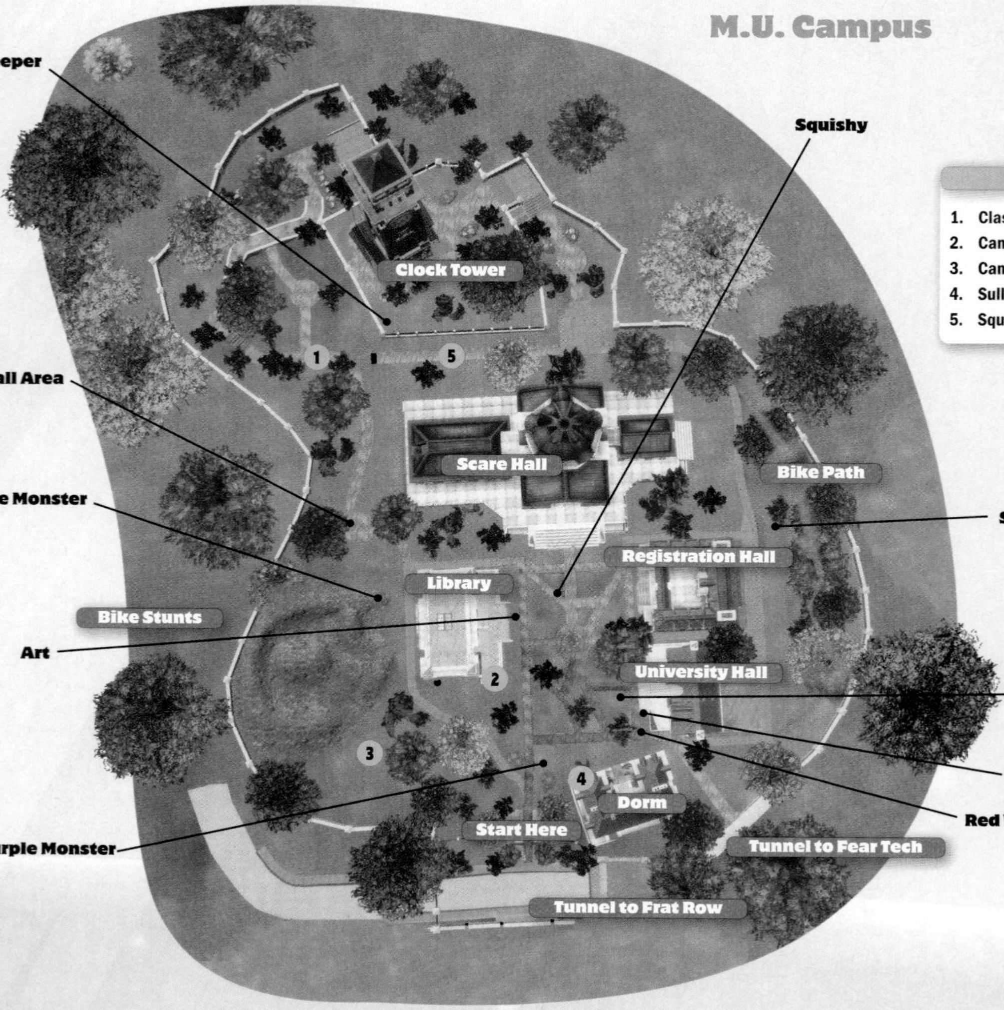

Grounds Keeper
Squishy
Clock Tower
To Paintball Area
Scare Hall
Bike Path
Spikey Blue Monster
Student Union
Registration Hall
Library
Bike Stunts
Art
University Hall
Deliveries
Yellow Monster
Dorm
Red Winged Monster
Start Here
Purple Monster
Tunnel to Fear Tech
Tunnel to Frat Row

Challenges
1. Classroom Run
2. Campus Collector
3. Campus Collector Bike
4. Sulley's Campus Collector
5. Squeal and Steal

Campus Clean Up

Mission Giver: Squishy
Type: Destroy
Rewards: 25 Coins / 20 Sparks

Welcome to M.U.! Unfortunately the rival school, Fear Tech, has really made a mess of the campus. Show off your M.U. spirt and remove the Fear Tech standees littering the school grounds. Follow the compass to locate and shoulder charge each of the five standees. They are all located around the fountain in the center of campus.

New Challenges Available: Sulley's Campus Collector

Scare Simulator

Mission Giver: Squishy
Type: Scare
Rewards: 50 Coins / 25 Sparks

Locate Squishy near the fountain and talk to him to learn about a mission to practice your scaring skills. Several scare simulation dummies are on loan from the School of Scaring to practice surprising the Fear Tech students. Simply walk up to each dummy and press the scare button to frighten all three of them. It is pretty obvious if you're successful as the dummies will let out a loud cry when frightened.

Sneak Peek

Mission Giver: Squishy
Type: Scare
Rewards: 200 Coins / 50 Sparks

Find Squishy again and learn about an advanced scaring skill. The Poloski Sneak and Scream is a great technique to get the drop on Fear Tech students that are more aware of their surroundings than the simulation dummies. The goal of this mission is to learn to slowly sneak up on a target and scare the wits out of them (in this case four of them). The best scares are the ones that nobody sees coming, so you must creep quietly without being seen to scare the really tough students. Next to the first advanced dummy is a blue capsule that will demonstrate the technique. It should be obvious which direction the dummy is facing, but you must note the red field around that dummy that represents its field of awareness. As you get close to this red area you must hold the sneak button to silently approach the target. If the dummy see/hears you, it will sound an alarm and you must get out of its field of view for it to reset. If you get caught, just circle around the back of the dummy and wait for the siren to stop.

Side Missions at M.U.

Doomed Dorm

Mission Giver: Yellow Monster
Type: Platforming
Rewards: 200 Coins / 25 Sparks

Fear Tech totally pranked the dorms and you have to get rid of the large banners before someone sees them. Climb up the front of the dorm using the small light-colored ledges and unhook the edge of the banner.

Drop down a bit to a horizontal ledge and go up to the other side to unhook the other side of the banner. Remove both banners by unhooking all four corners.

Backpack Backtrack

Mission Giver: Purple Monster
Type: Collect
Rewards: 200 Coins / 80 Sparks

The poor purple monster had a bunch of Fear-It-Week tokens, but they fell through a hole in its backpack.

A Land of Hands

Mission Giver: Blue Monster
Type: Collect
Rewards: 100 Coins / 35 Sparks

There are a bunch of Foam Hands all over campus. Fear Tech may think they are number one, but that is probably just how high they can count. Use the compass to find all eight orange hands, located mostly at the front of the buildings.

Clothes Make the Monster

Mission Giver: Art
Type: Customize
Rewards: 100 Coins / 25 Sparks

Fear Tech put their logos on some of the M.U. students and Art is really upset about the mismatched students. Pick them up and toss them into the Student Union building to give them some M.U. blue. Grab the light blue monster right in front of the Student Union and toss it inside to change its hat. You can simply remove its hat or change its hair or horns as long as the Fear Tech item is gone.

Ambush the Bush

Mission Giver: Purple Monster
Type: Scare
Rewards: 200 Coins / 30 Sparks

A student from Fear Tech is attempting to deface your campus by putting up a poster. Creep up on the student behind the bush, using a slow stealthy walk, to get close and scare it back to its school.

Clean Up and Go On the Offensive

Student Aid

Mission Giver: Squishy
Type: Platforming
Rewards: 200 Coins / 30 Sparks

Visit Squishy to hear about one of M.U.'s students getting pranked by Fear Tech. The poor monster was tied up in toilet paper and left on the roof of the library. The library is the red building to the west, and the easiest way to climb the building is with a little boost from a monster in the grass. Scare the blue protruding eyeball to reveal a big monster below that will provide a handy platform.

Leap on top of the platform and climb the drain pipe nearby to get to the roof.

Locate the poor student and scare it to break its paper bonds and free it from its trap.

Remove the Rolls

Mission Giver: Squishy
Type: Scare
Rewards: 100 Coins / 35 Sparks

Squishy has another mission for you and it is a somewhat dirty job. Fear Tech has wrapped several of the statues of the School of Scaring in toilet paper and it is bringing down morale. Use your powerful scare skills to blow the toilet paper off of three statues.

Roll Out

Mission Giver: Squishy
Type: Buy
Rewards: 50 Coins / 25 Sparks

Enough cleaning up after Fear Tech! It's time to take the challenge back to them and put their school on the defensive. Squishy had the M.U. mechanics develop a Toilet Paper Launcher to turn the tables on Fear Tech. Go to the Toy Store menu and buy the awesome toy for 300 coins.

Wait for the monster mail delivery and go to the drop off spot to open the slightly wet box to claim your hot new toy!

New Toy Unlocked: Toilet Paper Launcher

The Road to Fear Tech

Mission Giver: Squishy
Type: Prank
Rewards: N/A

Open the entrance to the scream tunnels that lead to Fear Tech by shooting the three targets above the gate with the Toilet Paper Launcher.

New Toy Unlocked: Beastly Bike

NOTE

Buy and pick up the bike as soon as possible. It is the fastest mode of transportation (until the end) and it makes it a lot more fun going from place to place.

New Challenges Available: Campus Collector, Campus Collector Bike

Find a Friend

Mission Giver: Squishy
Type: Locate
Rewards: 100 Coins / 10 Sparks

Locate the M.U. student at the Fear Teach end of the scream tunnels. Get the new bike you just unlocked as it will make moving through the tunnels go a lot faster. Ride through the tunnel and pick up the walkie-talkie as you locate the student.

Side Mission

Card Counter

Mission Giver: Red Winged Monster
Type: Collect
Rewards: 100 Coins / 30 Sparks

A monster was bullied by one of the guys from Fear Tech and had all of its collectable Scare Cards knocked out of its tentacles. There are seven cards to locate, mostly around Registration Hall.

Prank Fear Tech

Fear Tech

Archie's Pen
Scare School
Sports Statue
Pink Dotted Monster
Botanical
Dorms
Library
Yellow Horned Monster
Science
1
2
3
Door Design School
Tunnel to M.U.
Red Monster
Health & Phys. Ed.
Don
Blue Winged Student
Randy

Challenges

1. Fear Tech Collector
2. Fear Tech Cyclist
3. Randy's Rampage

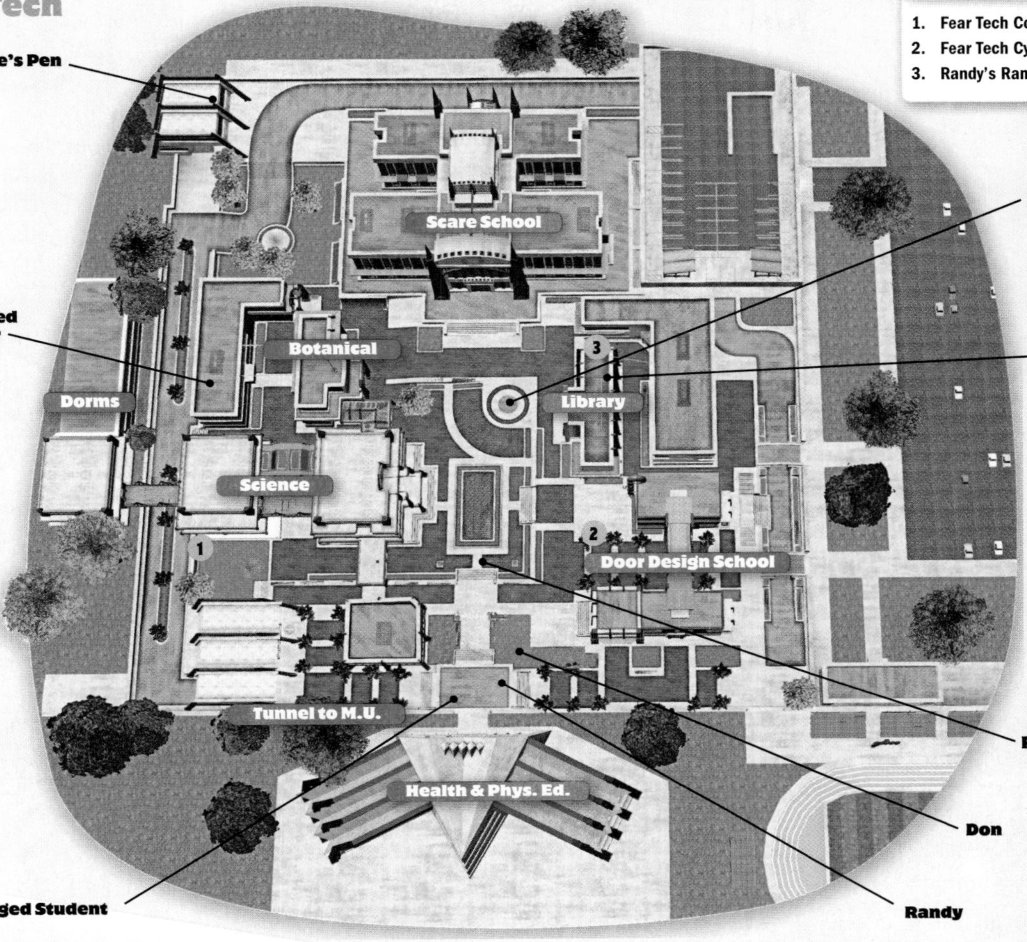

Revenge Grows on Trees

Mission Giver: Green Monster with Purple Hat
Type: Prank
Rewards: 250 Coins / 35 Sparks

Now that you have infiltrated Fear Tech, the first objective is to T.P. four trees in the center of their campus.

New Challenge Available: Randy's Rampage, Fear Tech Cyclist, Fear Tech Collector

New Toy Unlocked: Bat-Winged Pest Bush

Bat-Winged Bush Battle

Mission Giver: Blue Monster
Type: Collect
Rewards: 100 Coins / 30 Sparks

Show some school pride by scaring away the bat-winged pests that keep perching around campus. Follow the compass to a bat-filled bush and let out a roar.

Statue Upgrade

Mission Giver: Don
Type: Prank
Rewards: 250 Coins / 35 Sparks

Don is impressed with your T.P. Launcher and suggests you try it out on two of Fear Tech's statues. Unlike the trees, the statues are guarded by Fear Tech security. If they see you, the screen will turn red around the edges and the guard will pursue you. It is not too difficult to run away when they spot you, so you can let the alarm state cool off. It is possible to try to fight off the guard, but it is really not worth the hassle when you can just get out of the immediate area and let things cool off.

If you like to run and gun, it is possible to shoot the statues while being chased, but if you get hit too many times you get sent into a "locked room". The blue capsule in the room will show you how to escape by jumping over the vent and attacking to slam down and break through it.

Sneak up on the first statue and shoot it twice quickly before the guard can catch you.

The second statue can be tricky because there is not as much cover nearby. Watch the guard's movement and sneak in to fire the first shot. If you get caught, circle around quickly and fire off one more shot to wrap up the mission.

Above and Beyond

Mission Giver: Squishy (radio)
Type: Locate
Rewards: 100 Coins / 25 Sparks

There is a hidden M.U. student at Fear Tech—use the compass to find that student. Climb up the drain pipe on the side of the School of Scaring to get to the roof to locate the student.

A Banner Day

Mission Giver: Yellow Horned Monster
Type: Platforming
Rewards: 100 Coins / 35 Sparks

Climb up the nearby flagpole and unfurl a surprise banner that reads M.U. Rocks!

A View of Blue

Mission Giver: Red Antenna Monster
Type: Platforming
Rewards: 200 Coins / 30 Sparks

Inspired by the first flag you unfurled, this monster wants you to paint the campus blue with two more flags. To get to the first flag, climb up the Science building ledge and scare the guard to knock it out.

Gargoyle Paper Caper

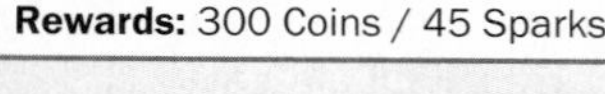

Mission Giver: Pink Dotted Monster
Type: Prank
Rewards: 300 Coins / 45 Sparks

This student really hates the gargoyle statues on the Fear Tech buildings. Do it a favor by wrapping six of them in T.P. and let

Fear Tech know what you think of their architectural style. The first gargoyle statue is on the Science building right behind the student requesting the mission and is an easy shot.

The second one is on the opposite side of the building, so jump across to the adjacent building and walk around the ledge to shoot it.

The third one is just across the other section of the building, which can be accessed by walking on top of a large connecting sky bridge. Jump over to the other section and go up to the third tier to shoot the statue.

Simply follow this ledge around the building to locate number four.

Leap back to the School of Botany rooftop and head toward the Scare School to spot the next gargoyle from the corner of the rooftop.

The last one is on the other side of the front of the Scare School and you will need to scale the Library to get to it. Go to the corner and jump up on the ledge to get a clear shot at it.

Leap up the door behind that monster to get to the second ledge. Follow the narrow ledge around the building and go up to the third tier to finally reach the flag.

Leap off the flagpole to snag the orange pennant and make your way to Door Design School. Scale the building using the dark-colored trim that leads to a narrow ledge you can climb around.

Follow the dark ledge around the building to another set of climbable ledges to make it to the roof. This flagpole is guarded and it is up to you if you want to sneak up and scare the guard or make a run for the flag.

A Lesson in Pride

Mission Giver: Blue Winged Monster
Type: Platforming
Rewards: 200 Coins / 30 Sparks

Know what this campus needs? More M.U. blue! Earn major tokens by putting up four M.U. banners on their Door Design School and Dorms. Climb up to the roof of the Door Design School and grind across the yellow wire to drop the first banner.

Jump across to the rooftop of the Library and grind across another yellow cable to unfurl the second banner.

The last two are both hung across lines on the School of Botany Building, however there are students guarding the rooftops, which makes it really tricky to get to the banners. The goal of course is to scare the guards and casually coast across the yellow wires, but if you get caught, make a run for it and quickly zip to the other side.

Trees a Crowd

Mission Giver: Yellow Horned Monster
Type: Prank
Rewards: 200 Coins / 30 Sparks

The hidden student on the roof that gave you the first flagpole mission wants to really stick it to Fear Tech by T.P.ing five of their trees. It sounds simple but you must avoid the patrolling students to hit the trees. Use the compass to locate three groups of three trees between the School of Botany and Scare School buildings. The other two are just past the trio of trees near the edge of campus. The patrolling student will not make it easy to shoot any of these groups. There are two obvious choices here. The first is to shoot as many trees as possible and run around the School of Botany building to attack the rest from the other side. This is a hit-and-run approach that keeps the guard chasing you while you target the trees.

The other safer option is to sneak up on the guard and scare it to put it out of commission. It can be tough to get the drop on the guard, but once the guard is knocked out you should be able to tag all the trees you need.

Terri and Terry are Missing

Terrifying Techniques

Mission Giver: Randy
Type: Scare
Rewards: 200 Coins / 30 Sparks

Terri and Terry have gone missing, but there is a student nearby who knows where Fear Tech is keeping them. That student is really fast, but if you can sneak up on it and scare it really good it should be knocked off guard long enough to tell you where they have taken Terri and Terry.

Very Scary for Terri and Terry

Mission Giver: Randy
Type: Scare
Rewards: 300 Coins / 40 Sparks

Randy has found the student that knows where Terri and Terry are. Sneak up on the student and scare that monster so it will tell you where they are. This student is very aware of its surroundings and is partially invisible, which makes it hard to locate. Lurk around the back of the School of Botany building and wait for your target to turn and show its back so you can sneak up on it.

Side Missions

Fear Tech Check

Mission Giver: Red Antenna Monster
Type: Scare
Rewards: 300 Coins / 25 Sparks

The Fear Tech student body is getting suspicious and it is up to you to scare two of them so they don't start having funny ideas. Find the first student that is mostly invisible near the Library and give it a good scare.

The second student is not far away from the Library and can be snuck up upon by dropping between the bushes near the Fear Tech statue. Make sure not to get too close to the bushes as your target passes or the student will notice you. Also, you must sneak up on the student slowly or it will hear your footsteps.

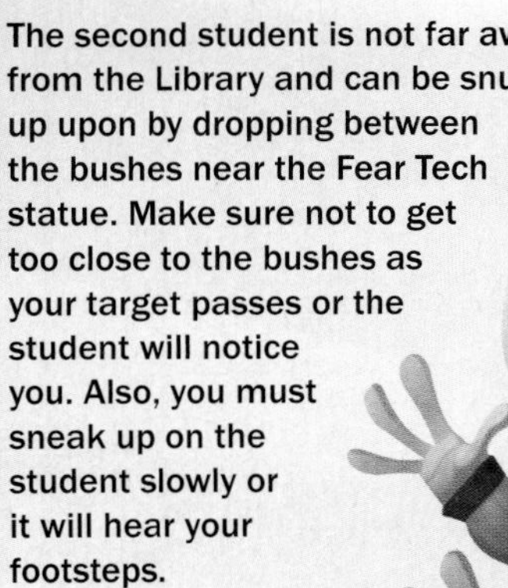

Poster Paints

Mission Giver: Purple Monster
Type: Prank
Rewards: 1,000 Coins / 100 Sparks

A purple monster wants to redecorate the Fear Tech recruitment posters with your handy paintball gun. There are 20 of these and it will not be easy to find them all. It might be tempting to ride around on the bike to scan for them, but you are better off going on foot and using the shoulder charge to dash around. Tackle this chore by searching the perimeter of campus, checking in between buildings, and finally searching the rooftops. Here are shots of all 20 for easy reference!

Alert Mission: Fear Tech Pennant Collection

Mission Giver: Automatic
Type: Platforming
Rewards: 1,000 Coins / 350 Sparks

While completing the previous side mission make sure to collect all the orange Fear Tech pennants. There are 20 of these hidden on their campus. If you can find all of them you will unlock the Sludge Balloon.

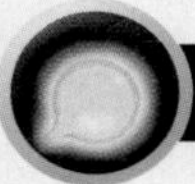

New Toy Unlocked: Fear Tech's Sludge Balloon

Return to M.U. to Hatch a Plan

Talk to Don

Mission Giver: Squishy (radio)
Type: Locate
Rewards: 100 Coins / 20 Sparks

The last monster you scared at Fear Tech gave up the info that Terri and Terry are being held at M.U. in the Clock Tower. Go back through the scream tunnel to look for your friend. However, upon your return it seems that Fear Tech students are running around M.U. like they own the place. Don has some ideas how to catch them so you can question them about your frat brother. Use the compass to find Don and find out what his plan is all about.

New Toy Unlocked: Paintball Gun

NOTE

Once the gun is purchased, a round red-winged monster will mention the Paintball Arena. It is a completely optional area that will be covered at the end of this section.

Practically Joking

Mission Giver: Don
Type: Buy
Rewards: 100 Coins / 30 Sparks

Don was a master prankster in his day and the Toy Store recently got a shipment of new joke items. Buy the sweet Give 'em a Hand Launcher and set it up where Don has indicated.

New Toy Unlocked: Give 'em a Hand Launcher

NOTE

If you have not already received the message, a light blue spiked monster will tell you to go check out Frat Row. This is a completely optional section that will be covered at the end of the story missions.

Alert Mission: Repair the Fountain

Mission Giver: None
Type: Scare/Platforming
Rewards: 100 Coins / 10 Sparks

Use your scare power on the M.U. fountain to clear it of toilet paper.

Several more complicated clean-up missions become available at M.U. These include Repair the Library, University Hall, Registration Hall, and Dorm. These missions involve platforming around each building and removing posters, banners, or toilet paper. They are completely optional but they can be quite challenging and fun.

Alert Mission: Dare to Scare

Mission Giver: None
Type: Scare
Rewards: 250 Coins / 25 Sparks

Get rid of three Fear Tech students roaming around M.U.

Bike Side Missions

Take a Bike

Mission Giver: Light Blue Monster
Type: Riding
Rewards: 100 Coins / 35 Sparks

The spiky-headed light blue monster by the bike stunt area has another challenge for you. Pass through all twenty gates in a leisurely ride around campus.

Reject the Tech

Mission Giver: Light Blue Monster
Type: Customize
Rewards: 200 Coins / 35 Sparks

Some Fear Tech goons force M.U. students to wear their school logo. Use the compass to locate the green monster with the Fear Tech hat and foam hand. Take the monster to the Student Union to remove the accessories or replace them with M.U. gear.

The next student you need to customize is a dark blue monster right in front of the Student Union. Toss this student into the stand and get rid of the pennant and hat it is wearing.

Rescue Terri and Terry at the Clock Tower

Spring Forward

Mission Giver: Squishy
Type: Prank
Rewards: 200 Coins / 30 Sparks

Locate Squishy to find out that the entire section of campus with the Clock Tower is closed for renovation. You must find a way to launch yourself over the gate to get in and look for your friend. Use the newly acquired Joke Launcher and place it near Squishy to catapult yourself over the closed Clock Tower gate. Make sure to rotate it so that the yellow arrow points towards the gate.

New Toy Unlocked: Morning Edition Launcher

Time for a Rescue

Mission Giver: Squishy
Type: Platforming
Rewards: 750 Coins / 50 Sparks

Time to climb the Clock Tower to look for Terri and Terry. Start by scaring an underground monster to make a ledge pop up to allow access to the wooden walkway.

Follow the wooden planks and leap up a series of light grey ledges to get to the corner piece. Travel around this corner section until you reach a wooden platform.

Follow this around the tower again to another section where you can climb up the red bricks to reach a higher ledge of more wooden scaffolding.

Leap up the large corner edges of the tower to a yellow pipe that will take you right next to the face of the clock. Jump up a few more ledges to get to the window at the top.

Once inside the top of the tower climb the black metal ladder to find Terri and Terry!

New Toy Unlocked: School Colors Ender

Secret of the Scare

Mission Giver: Groundskeeper (Dark Grey Monster with Rake)
Type: Scare
Rewards: 100 Coins / 30 Sparks

Talk to the Groundskeeper to learn how to open the gates to the main campus.

Follow the compass to find the monument and roar at its lighted eye target to activate its hidden features that open the gates as well as enable two other switches on University Hall.

New Toy Unlocked: Scream Energy Launcher

New Challenges Available: Classroom Run

Clock Tower Side Missions

Time for a Change

Mission Giver: Art
Type: Platforming
Rewards: 300 Coins / 25 Sparks

After taking care of the Fear Tech banners for Art, he wants you to remove them from the Clock Tower as well. In addition, you need to remove the poster placed by Fear Tech. Start by scaring up a platform to climb up to the wooden plank and bring down the first poster.

Follow the wooden walkway to the next poster and scare it down.

Work your way around the corner ledges to find the third one on a red brick wall.

Climb the red brick ledge from the third one to get to a bit of scaffolding that hides another.

Drop back down and go around the corners to the other red brick wall to climb up to the next tier and find the fifth poster.

The last two targets are the ones holding up the banner. Jump up to the top as you did before and release the banner.

Tech Tock

Mission Giver: Art
Type: Scare
Rewards: 300 Coins / 10 Sparks

Three Fear Tech goons are hanging around on the M.U. campus at the Clock Tower. Sneak up on all of them to send them back to their school with a valuable lesson.

New Toy Unlocked: Breaking News Ender

Alert Mission: Campus Pennant Collection

Mission Giver: Automatic
Type: Platforming
Rewards: 1,000 Coins / 350 Sparks / Glow Urchin

This mission officially begins when you collect the first M.U. pennant, but it can't be completed until the Clock Tower area is unlocked. You must find 20 blue pennants throughout the M.U. campus to earn the Glow Urchin toy. They are scattered all over campus and the trickiest ones are on little ledges on the rooftops of buildings.

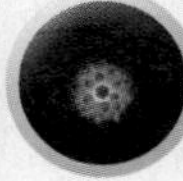

New Toy Unlocked: Glow Urchin

The Ultimate Plan

Secret Meeting

Mission Giver: Squishy
Type: Locate
Rewards: 200 Coins / 20 Sparks

Terry and Terri collected some new info before they were locked up. Go meet Don on the roof of University Hall (a secret place where Fear Tech can't hear you). Locate the glowing eye switch and roar into it to activate a platform.

Leap up the grey ledges and scoot around the top one to get to the roof and meet Don.

New Toy Unlocked: Cracklin' Backpack

Side Missions

This is the Ender

Mission Giver: Yellow Monster
Type: Prank
Rewards: 200 Coins / 35 Sparks

This is a simple request from the yellow monster—it just wants to see a Joke Ender in a specific spot. Locate the area with the compass and place the School Colors Ender you received from saving Terri and Terry. Remember that you can't trigger the joke and must be patient until a student tries it out.

A Peaceful Balance

Mission Giver: Art
Type: Prank
Rewards: 300 Coins / 25 Sparks

Art's meditative state is disrupted by the Fear Tech "decorations" hanging from the School of Scaring. You need to take them down, but getting to the top of the school will not be that obvious. At the side of the school look for the eye switch and roar to make the walls move outward. The two narrow walls allow you to wall jump to the roof.

Walk along the edge of the green roof and step on the two supports holding up the first banner.

On the left side of the building is another eye switch that creates several new ledges. These are the key to getting to the top of the building.

Climb up the lower ledges at the corner and jump across to the left to get a littler higher. Then jump back right to the top corner section that leads around the edge to a green drain pipe leading to the roof.

Jump along the roof and go to the edge to take down all three supports to drop the second banner.

From the corner where you climbed up to the roof, jump to the green section and head to the peak of this vaulted roof to drop the final banner.

New Toy Unlocked: Pile it on Ender

Terri and Terry's Nighttime Capers

Dorm Party!

Mission Giver: Terri and Terry
Type: Prank/Scare
Rewards: 300 Coins / 35 Sparks

It seems that Terri and Terry are up for a little revenge shenanigans involving fireworks blasting into six Fear Tech dorms. They are hanging out at the scream tunnel connecting to M.U. When you accept the mission night will fall and the patrolling guards will break out their flashlights. Quickly make your way to the dorms near the parking lot and sneak up to scare the guard out cold. Equip the backpack and toss fireworks into the windows to get the first two rooms.

Go around the corner to the edge of campus to spot more rooms, but be careful of the guard. Hide in the passage below street level to easily sneak up on the guard and deliver a shocking scare. With the guard sleeping the night away, quickly launch fireworks in the remaining four rooms to finish the mission.

House Party!

Mission Giver: Terri and Terry
Type: Prank
Rewards: 300 Coins / 40 Sparks

Fear Tech students are occupied on Frat Row causing trouble. This is a great time to do some M.U. decorations on the School of Botany. Night falls once again and it's time to sneak up on the guards at the rear of the building. Once the guard is disabled it should be a piece of cake to toss fireworks into several of the rooms. Three are located near the corner of the building.

The other two are a lot tougher to tackle because two guards nearly overlap at your target destination. Scare the somewhat invisible guard that passes right by the two windows and quickly toss the fireworks before the other guard gets close.

New Toy Unlocked: Incoming Call Ender

Decoration Celebration

Mission Giver: Terri and Terry
Type: Prank
Rewards: 500 Coins / 30 Sparks

Fear Tech has had enough fireworks to give them a thrill. Now it's time to add a bit of decorations to their School of Scaring. Make your way to the rooftop and drop down behind a Fear Tech guard to scare them and release the M.U. banner.

The next banner is at the front of the school and must be reached by going to the top of the spiked roof. There is a thin beam you can cross that will connect right where the banner is hanging.

The last banner is on the rooftop to the left (from the front of the school). Wait for the guard to turn around and jump down to sneak up and scare him good. Drop the last banner in the corner next to the gargoyle you T.P.ed earlier.

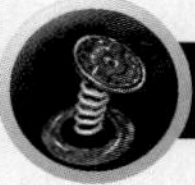

New Toy Unlocked: Scream Tunnel Sludge Ender

Don's Prank Side Missions

NOTE

All jokes must be performed on students, so you must help one start off a combo or just be patient. The best place on Fear Tech to set up combos is in front of the Health and Phys. Ed building.

Double Trouble

Mission Giver: Don
Type: Prank
Rewards: 300 Coins / 30 Sparks

The latest tally on the scoreboard still has Fear Tech in the lead. Don suggests setting up a double Joke Launcher to rack up lots of points. The goal is to chain two Joke Launchers together on Fear Tech's campus, and the location will be important to make it a lot easier to pull off. In front of the Phys. Ed building are several spots to customize jokes. Place two Joke Launchers like the Scream Energy Launcher and aim them at each other for a double combo that is actually an infinite loop.

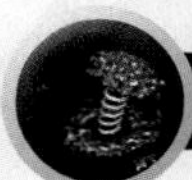

New Toy Unlocked: Leafing So Soon? Launcher

Pranks for Everything

Mission Giver: Don
Type: Prank/Scare
Rewards: 500 Coins / 35 Sparks

The last joke worked so well that Don starting thinking of another combo linking them with an Ender for a great finale. The objective is to use two Joke Launchers with a Joke Ender for a big chained prank combo. The Launchers should already be in place from the previous mission, and all you need to do is add an Ender. Make sure the second Launcher points towards the Ender, and if you test it be sure to replace the Ender if it gets smashed.

New Toy Unlocked: Vender Ender

Triple Trouble

Mission Giver: Don
Type: Prank/Scare
Rewards: 500 Coins / 45 Sparks

To rake in tons of tokens for Fear-It Week, Don wants to pull off a triple Launcher. Return to the same spot as before and replace the Ender with a Launcher to make a quick triple combo.

New Toy Unlocked: Vender Machine Launcher

Capture the Scare Pig

Football Wrapper

Mission Giver: Randy
Type: Prank/Scare
Rewards: 250 Coins / 50 Sparks

Randy needs a diversion to distract the Fear Tech students to find out where they are keeping the Scare Pig. Fear Tech is so proud of their athletics program that the best way to get their attention is to toilet paper their Sports Statue (the football monument). This is another nighttime mission, and it will take three shots to cover the statue. Fear Tech's best sprinters guard that statue on the night shift and it is very likely they will chase you down after a single shot. It is not worth trying to scare all the guards into submission, and if you do get caught the statue keeps the amount of T.P. (number of hits) it already had on it. Sneak in and fire off shots as you circle around it.

New Toy Unlocked: Fly Swatter Launcher

Key to Success

Mission Giver: Randy
Type: Scare
Rewards: 750 Coins / 50 Sparks

Archie the Scare Pig has been located at his pen and he is currently out for feeding time. The guard watching over Archie is tough, but you need to scare him to get the keys to unlock the pen. Wait for the guard to pass by and follow it around the pen, slowly creeping up on it until you are close enough to deliver a good scare.

Race to Victory

Mission Giver: Randy
Type: Riding
Rewards: 1,000 Coins / 100 Sparks

Randy shows up in front of the pen to help out, but the mascot snatching is not going to be that easy because the pen was rigged with an alarm and the guards are coming quick. Your only chance is to hop on the Scare Pig and make a break for the scare tunnel to go back to the M.U. campus.

You need to buy the others some time to open the gates. Hop on Archie and smash through seven mascot statues to keep Fear Tech busy. The first one is right in front of the pen and a quick jump should allow you to get over the ledge and plow right through it.

The next statue is straight ahead, so make the little piggy sprint and crash through it.

As you turn the corner next to the parking lot a guard will probably notice you, but Archie is super fast and you can continue to the next statue without much fear of getting hit.

The fourth statue is right next to the last one and a well-placed jump should take it out easily.

Swerve to the left and make a sharp turn to run directly into statue number five. If the guard in the parking area is giving you a lot of trouble, just circle around the lot a bit and it won't be able to match Archie's pace.

Continue all the way down the edge of the Fear Tech campus and turn right to find statue number six.

The last statue is towards the center of campus by the School of Botany.

After breaking the last mascot statue, the gates will finally be opened and all you have to do is ride Archie through the scream tunnel back to M.U.

New Toy Unlocked: Archie the Scare Pig

New Challenge Available: Archie Challenges

Frat Row Fix Up

Frat Row

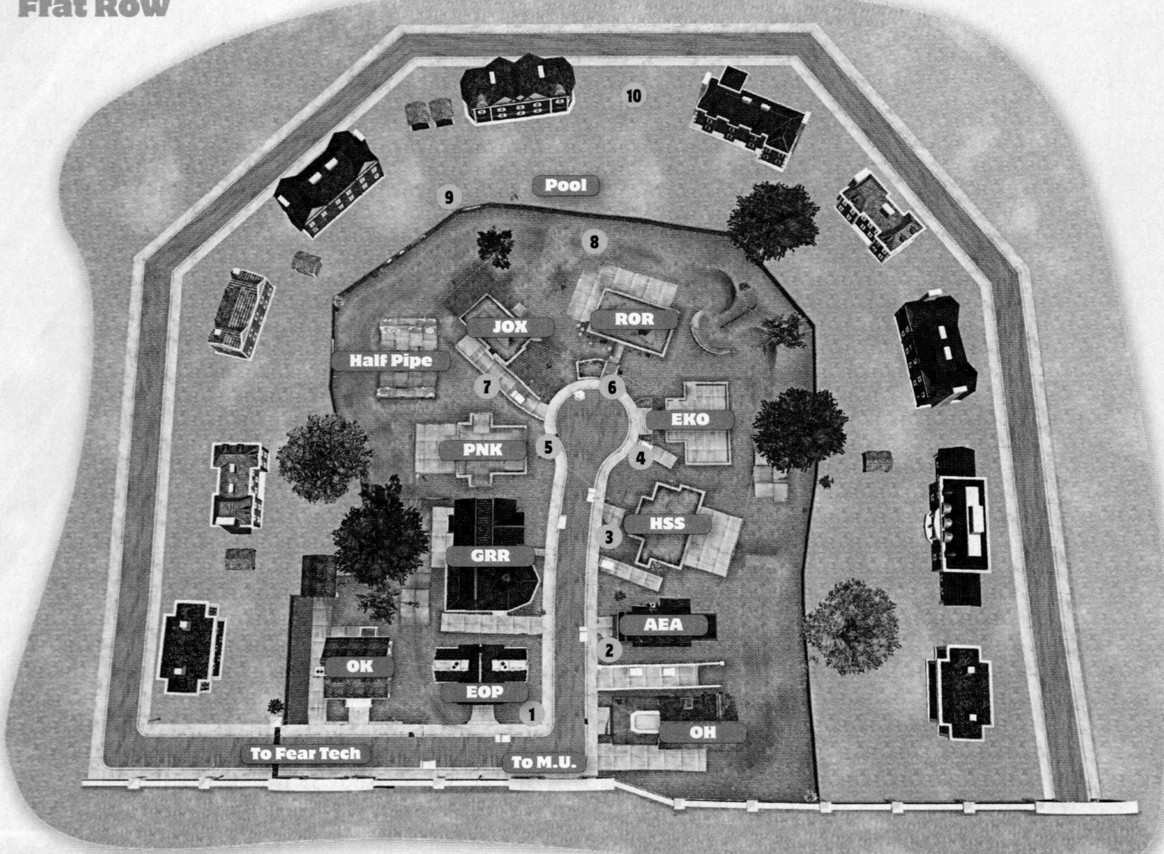

NOTE

All of the events on Frat Row are side missions, but they unlock many items and gold stars.

Challenges

1. Mike's Mayhem
2. Timed Swine
3. Wheels and Thrills
4. Frat Row Round Up
5. Wild Wheels
6. Paint the Frat Collector
7. Paintball Ruckus
8. Round the Row
9. Bike Hop and Pop
10. Crazy Frat Stunts

Alert Mission: OK Pennant Collection

Mission Giver: Automatic
Type: Platforming
Rewards: 1,000 Coins / 350 Sparks

Similar to the previous areas there is a somewhat hidden mission to collect 20 OK pennants at Frat Row. Complete all the Main Missions first to fill out the Row with buildings and ramps that will make it a lot easier to collect the pennants.

New Toy Unlocked: Tiny Terror

Go to the Row

Mission Giver: Light Blue Spiky Monster
Type: Locate
Rewards: 50 Coins / 10 Sparks

Go outside the gates of M.U. to find the tunnel to Frat Row.

Frat Row Fix Up

Trash From the Bash

Mission Giver: Blue Winged Monster
Type: Destroy
Rewards: 250 Coins / 30 Sparks

The frat boys were so excited about Fear-It Week that they threw a party, but left trash all over the place. Use the compass to help clean up by running into five trash piles. The bike will make the task a lot faster, but they are all pretty close and a quick shoulder charge will do the job just as well.

Frat House Makeover

Mission Giver: Brown Four-Armed Monster
Type: Customize
Rewards: 100 Coins / 30 Sparks

They are giving out Fear-It Week tokens for the best of Frat Row. Try to earn some precious coins by decorating the OK House, which is right by the monster.

New Toy Unlocked: Bike Park Table Top

Rebuild the Row

ROR on a Wire

Mission Giver: Light Green Monster
Type: Platforming
Rewards: 250 Coins / 35 Sparks

ROR House had a wild party and put up banners all over the row. You need to slide across the wires to remove the banners and clean up the row. The first part can be accomplished by climbing the nearby light pole and sliding on the wire to remove both banners.

The other two banners can be reached by climbing the OH House and sliding across the power line.

New Toy Unlocked: PNK House

Think PNK

Mission Giver: Yellow Dotted Monster
Type: Buy/Build
Rewards: 100 Coins / 20 Sparks

Go into the Toy Store and buy the PNK House.

New Challenge Available: Wild Wheels

Rooftop Drop

Mission Giver: Yellow Monster
Type: Platforming
Rewards: 100 Coins / 30 Sparks

The GRR guys had a party on their roof and it was off the hook, however one guy is afraid to climb down. Climb up the pole near the GRR House and slide across to the roof to pick up the student. Provide a little encouragement by picking it up and tossing it from the roof.

New Toy Unlocked: Sweet Bike Jump

Bat's a Problem

Mission Giver: Green Monster
Type: Scare
Rewards: 250 Coins / 35 Sparks

Frat Row is overrun with an infestation of bat-winged pests. Use the compass to track them down and scare them away. The first group is on the porch of GRR, another is at OH House, the third is on the roof of EOP, and the last is in the back of AEA.

HSS Story

Mission Giver: Green Monster
Type: Destroy
Rewards: 100 Coins / 20 Sparks

Remove the crates from the HSS area to make room for their house.

New Toy Unlocked: HSS House

HSS House Hunch

Mission Giver: Green Monster
Type: Buy/Build
Rewards: 100 Coins / 20 Sparks

Go into the Toy Store and buy the HSS House.

New Toy Unlocked: Bike Park Berm

New Challenge Available: Wheels and Thrills

JOX Boxes

Mission Giver: Yellow Dotted Monster
Type: Destroy
Rewards: 100 Coins / 20 Sparks

Smash through the JOX crates to make their house look awesome. There are four crates to smash in the open lot at the back of the row.

New Toy Unlocked: JOX House

Where's the JOX House

Mission Giver: Yellow Dotted Monster
Type: Buy/Build
Rewards: 100 Coins / 20 Sparks

Go into the Toy Store and buy the JOX House.

New Toy Unlocked: Bike Park Half Pipe

New Challenge Available: Paintball Ruckus

A Fresh Look

Mission Giver: Purple Monster
Type: Combat
Rewards: 100 Coins / 20 Sparks

Too many freshmen are hanging out at the EKO lot. Find the four youngsters and clear them out by throwing them off the lot.

New Toy Unlocked: EKO House

Is There an EKO?

Mission Giver: Purple Monster
Type: Buy/Build
Rewards: 100 Coins / 20 Sparks

Go into the Toy Store and buy the EKO House.

New Toy Unlocked: Roaring Ramp

New Challenge Available: Frat Row Round-Up

Crate Big ROR

Mission Giver: Aqua Dotted Monster
Type: Destroy
Rewards: 100 Coins / 20 Sparks

Before ROR can move in you need to smash those crates!

Let the ROR Out

New Toy Unlocked: ROR House

Mission Giver: Aqua Dotted Monster
Type: Buy/Build
Rewards: 100 Coins / 20 Sparks

Go into the Toy Store and buy the ROR House.

New Toy Unlocked: Bike Park Dual Pool

New Challenges Available: Round the Row, Paint the Frat Collector, Bike Hop and Pop & Crazy Frat Stunts. (Bike Hop and Pop & Crazy Frat Stunts require the purchase of the "Dual Pool")

NOTE

Buying all the Frat Houses unlocks the Terrifying Two-Wheeler (Sulley's Bike).

New Toy Unlocked: Terrifying Two-Wheeler

Fun at Frat Row

Scale the Walls

Mission Giver: Red Monster
Type: Customize
Rewards: 100 Coins / 25 Sparks

PNK House is looking pretty good, but adding a few touches would really make it shine. Customize the house with any single decoration.

Homework Hero

Mission Giver: Blue Dotted Monster
Type: Riding/Collect
Rewards: 500 Coins / 50 Sparks

The student's scream homework isn't going well. It needs you to collect ten scream cans by performing tricks on the bike. Before you can even hope to collect all the cans, make sure you buy all the bike park items from the Toy Store—the ramps are essential to reach many of the cans. One of the first ones starts from a straight path leading to a large group. A good jump will claim the can.

Continue straight ahead, jump to the balcony, and hit the ramp, pulling to the right to claim another can.

Two more cans can be picked up on the roof of the Frat House by jumping up the dirt ramp and riding along the wooden plank. Continue riding on the balcony and leap off the edge to grab the second one.

To take a break from all the stunts and trick jumps, follow the dirt path to a large mound to easily reach a can.

NOTE

In order to collect all the scream cans and complete the mission, you need to buy all the Bike Ramps.

Grab an easy-to-reach can by JOX House using the dirt mound right underneath it.

The last four are above the halfpipe and will require a good boost of speed to get enough height. It can be really tricky trying to reach without running off the track. Line up under the canisters in a very straight line, back up, and build up some speed while keeping your wheels straight so you can cleanly hit the cans.

Paintball Competition

The Sewers

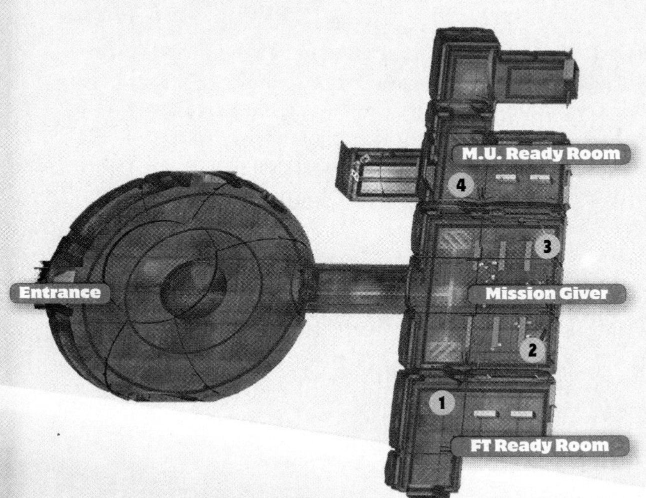

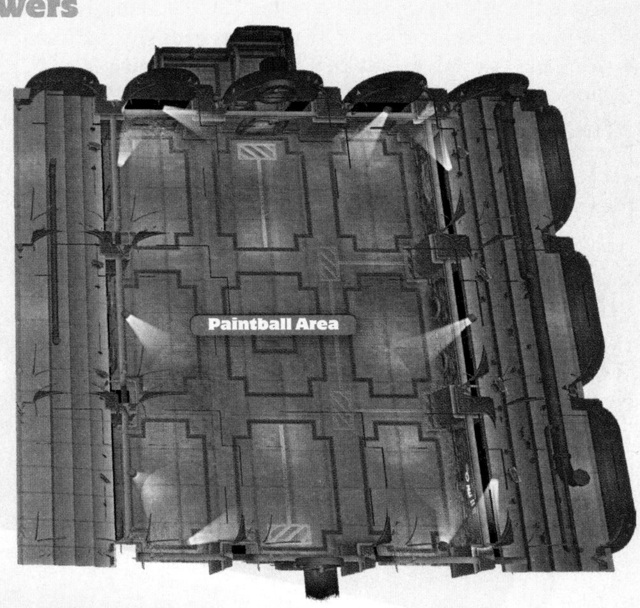

Challenges	
1. Paintball Press	3. Paintball Panic
2. Scream Tunnel Collector	4. Paintball Party

> **NOTE**
>
> **All of the events in the Paintball Arena are optional Side Missions, and they require the purchase of the Paintball Gun.**

Tunnel of Paint

Mission Giver: Red Winged Monster
Type: Locate
Rewards: 100 Coins / 20 Sparks

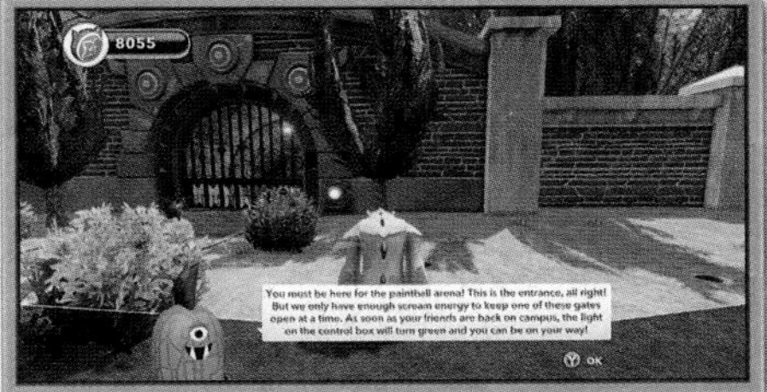

Locate the Paintball Arena.

Have a Paintball!

Mission Giver: Blue Striped Monster
Type: Paintball Match
Rewards: 100 Coins / 25 Sparks

Compete in the first paintball challenge. This is a 1-minute timed event to take down three challengers. Since this is the first event, it will be pretty easy. Just run towards the back of the room and take out the targets. If you have trouble spotting them, look for the red arrow over their heads.

New Challenge Available: Paintball Panic

Paint by Numbers

Mission Giver: Blue Striped Monster
Type: Paintball Match
Rewards: 100 Coins / 30 Sparks

Paintball is a numbers game that earns Fear-It-Week tokens for the school that defeats the opposing students. Get ready for round two in order to win more tokens. Again there is a 1-minute time limit, but you won't have to run around looking for Fear Tech students as they will charge you. Seek cover quickly and pick them off from behind a wall. There are six students to deal with and you have to go to the offensive to quickly track down any monsters hiding behind walls.

New Challenge Available: Paintball Party

Scream Tunnel Tussle

Mission Giver: Blue Striped Monster
Type: Paintball Match
Rewards: 200 Coins / 30 Sparks

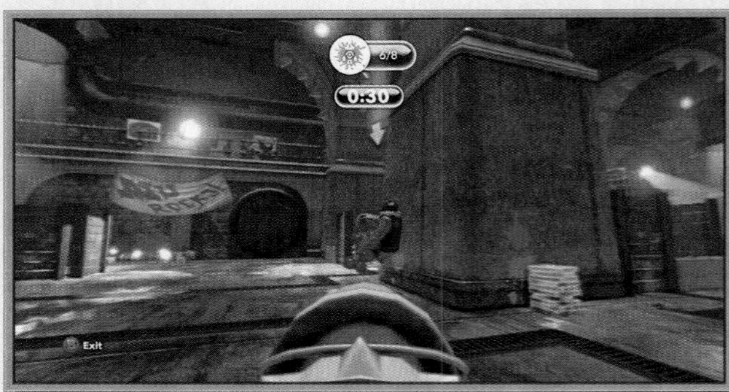

Round 3 starts with 1 minute on the clock and there are now eight students to take down. This round introduces the stationary paintball cannon, which is great to wipe out enemies at a distance. Jump on the big gun right in front of your starting position and blast your targets as they run towards you. Make sure to check the sides to make sure none are hiding out.

New Challenge Available: Paintball Press

The Color of Success

Mission Giver: Blue Striped Monster
Type: Paintball Match
Rewards: 300 Coins / 35 Sparks

This is the final competition and the last chance to really wipe out Fear Tech. There is an extra 15 seconds on the clock and you will probably need it to defeat all ten students. The cannon was a viable option last mission, but it is not going to get you through the entire thing. The enemies are a lot better at hiding behind the small walls and there are too many to stay stationary. Use the shoulder charge to cover ground quickly as well as to bump into the enemy and stun them.

Many of your foes will take cover behind walls and even duck under the low walls making them hard to hit.

Take out targets with a few quick shots and try not to empty your gun tracking them down. Run and gun to get in close and avoid wasting shots chasing them only to leave you empty with a somewhat long load time.

New Challenge Available: Scream Tunnel Collector

New Toy Unlocked: Slithering Cycle

Collectibles

M.U. Campus

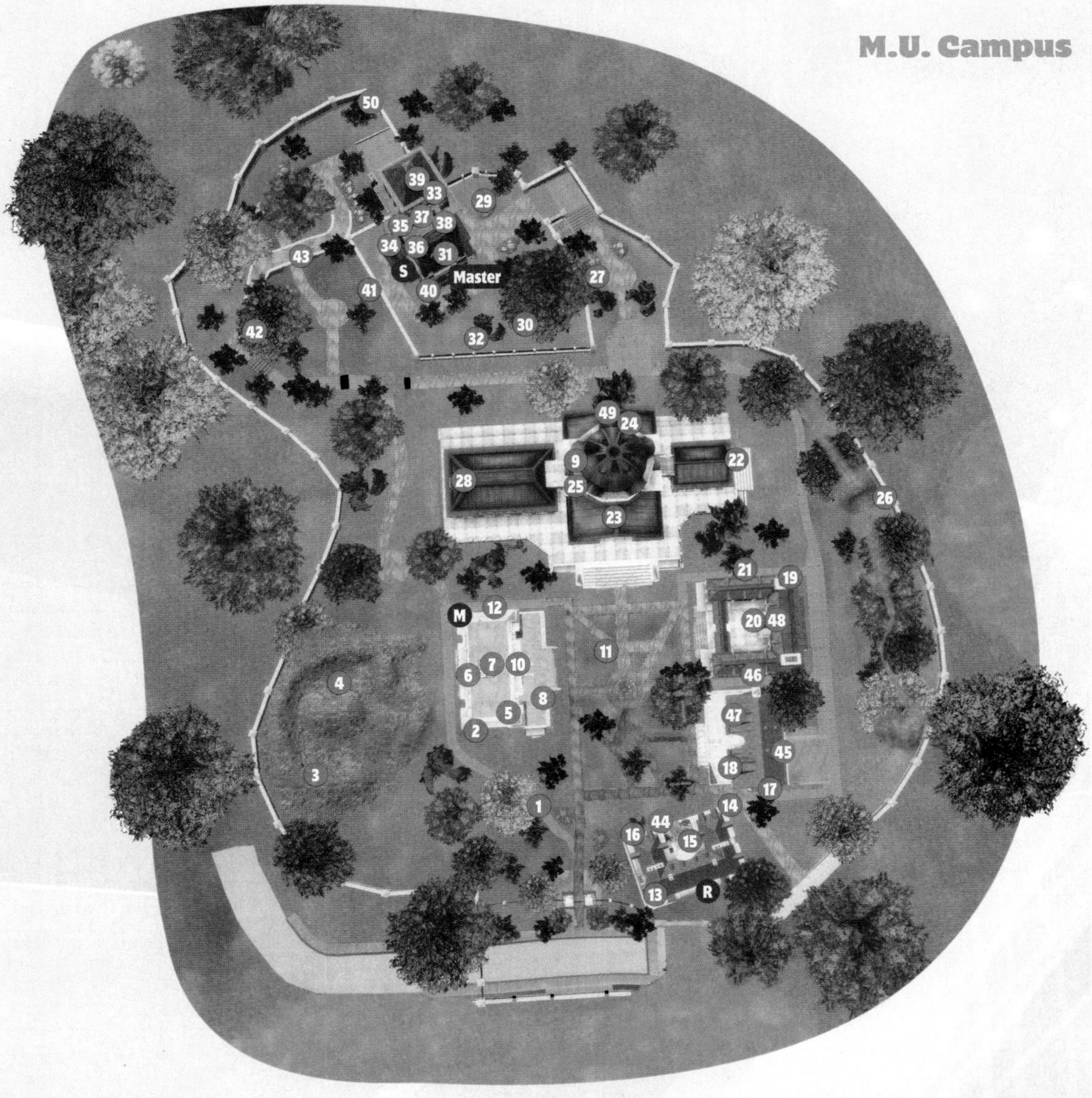

Fear Tech

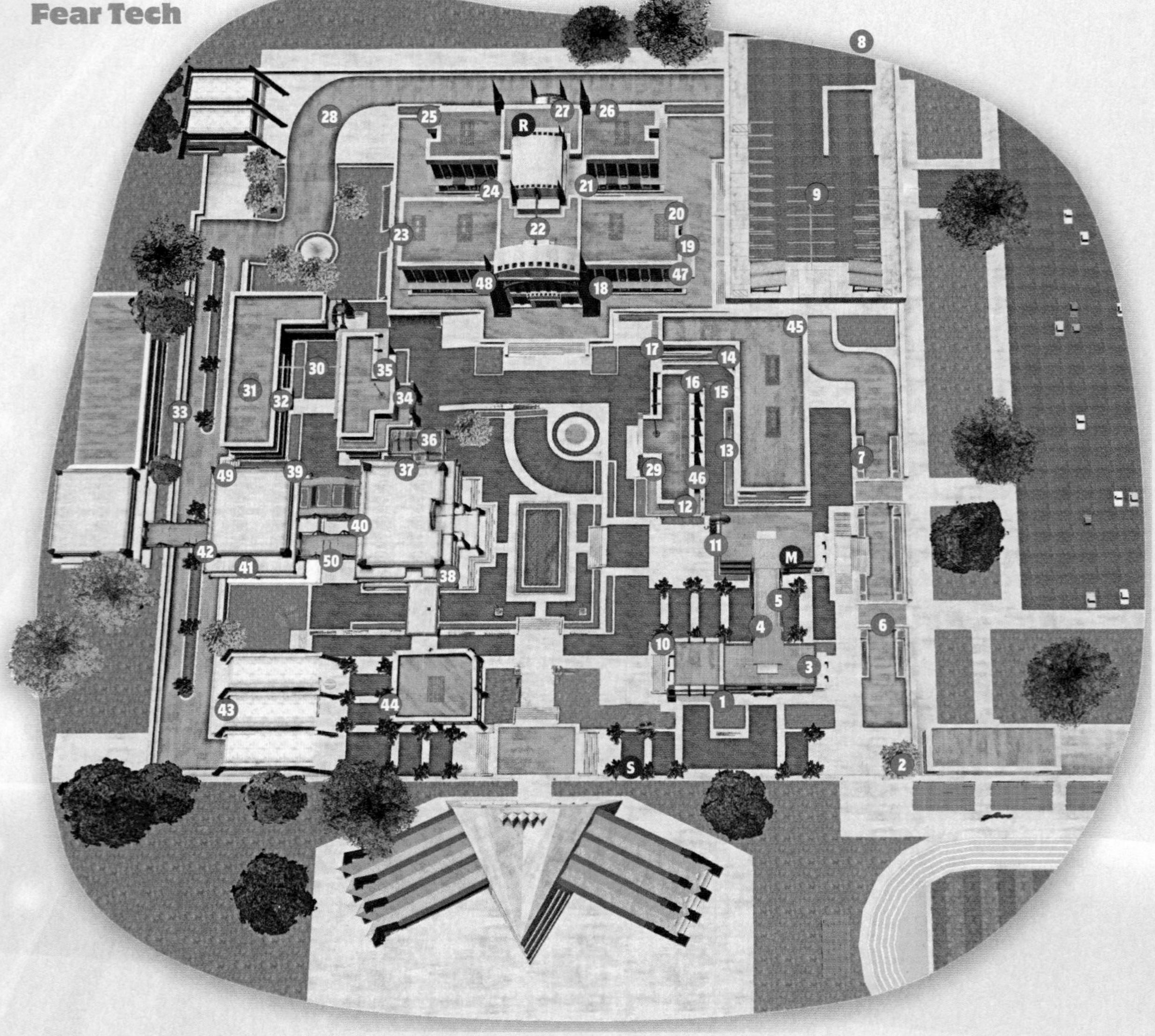

Red Capsules

#	Unlockable Item	Zone	Description
1	Monstrous	M.U. Campus	On the path to the left entering M.U. Campus.
2	Dreamy 'Do	M.U. Campus	On the side of the Library nearest the main entrance to M.U. Campus.
3	Frightening Feathers	M.U. Campus	On the hill at the back of the Bike Stunt area.
4	Warts and Stripes	M.U. Campus	On the far end of the Bike Stunt area.
5	Old Couch	M.U. Campus	On the roof ledge of the Library nearest the entrance to M.U. Campus.
6	Leaf Pile	M.U. Campus	On the roof ledge of the Library nearest the Bike Stunt area.
7	Mike Accent	M.U. Campus	On the roof of the Library.
8	Sneaky Spikes	M.U. Campus	On the upper tentacles that come out of the Library after roaring at the door.
9	Frosty Feathers	M.U. Campus	Inside the secret room in the roof of Scare Hall.
10	The Cooler	M.U. Campus	On the roof ledge of the front of the Library.
11	Glam Gazer	M.U. Campus	In the center of the quad in M.U. Campus.
12	Wee Waggy Wings	M.U. Campus	On the gutter pipe on the far side of the Library near Scare Hall.
13	Scraggly Strands	M.U. Campus	On the corner of the roof of the Dorm nearest the main entrance to M.U. Campus.
14	Loathsome Lights	M.U. Campus	On the corner of the roof of the Dorm nearest the University Hall.
15	Uni-fin	M.U. Campus	Right above the front door to the Dorm.
16	Dungeon Stone	M.U. Campus	On the front corner of the roof of the Dorm nearest the main entrance to M.U. Campus.
17	Longhorns	M.U. Campus	On the chimney of the University Hall.
18	Ghastly Grooves	M.U. Campus	On the front ledge of the University Hall.
19	Plated Tail	M.U. Campus	On the roof of Registration Hall.
20	Freakish Fan	M.U. Campus	On the ledge above the front door of Registration Hall.

Frat Row

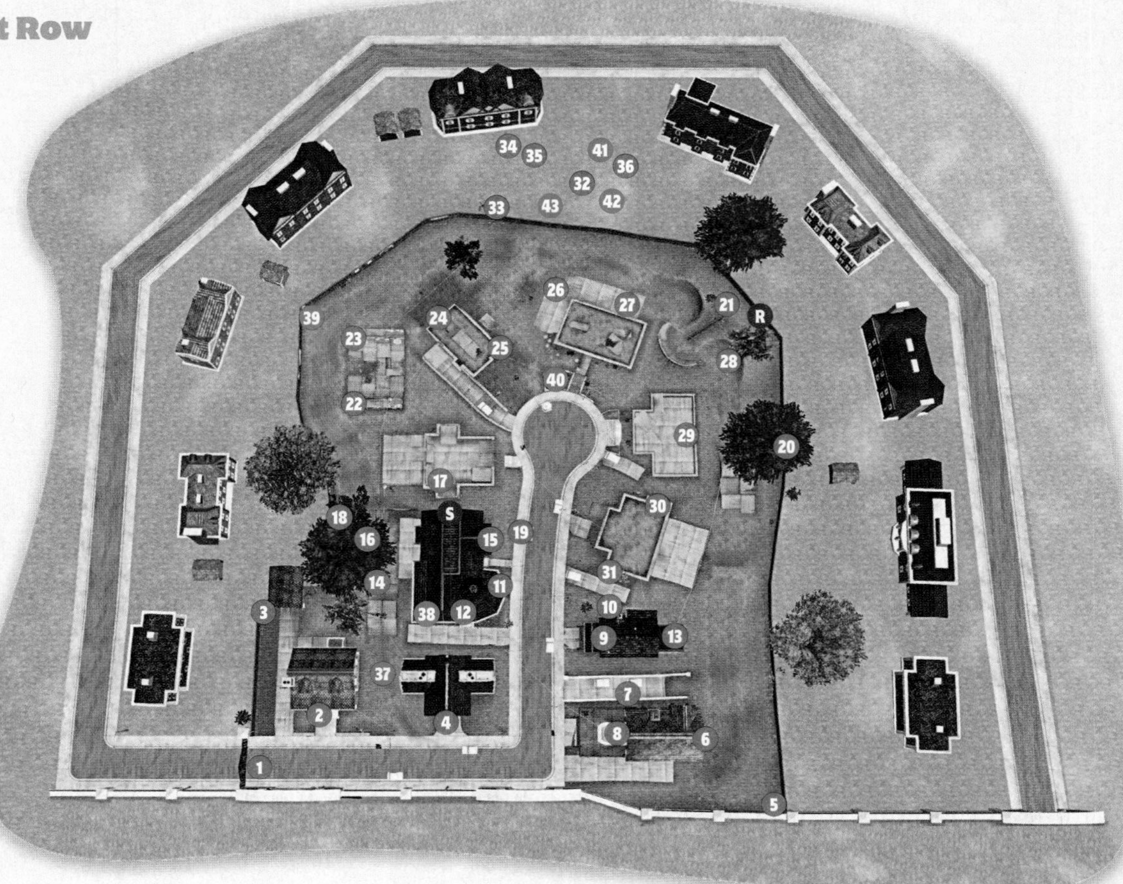

The Sewers

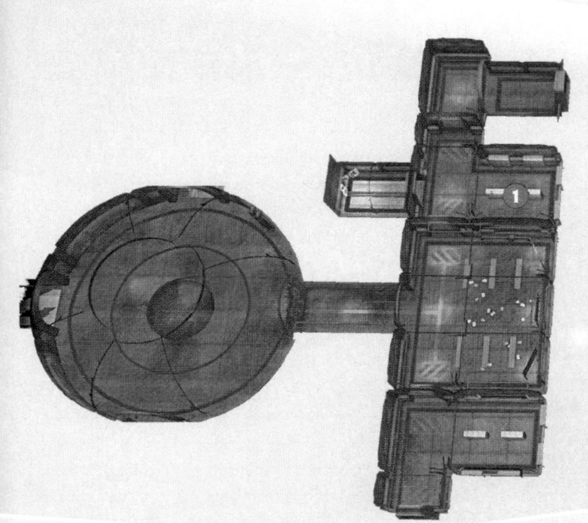

#	Unlockable Item	Zone	Description
21	Sulley Walls	M.U. Campus	On the small ledge at the end of Registration Hall.
22	M.U. Pennant Pride	M.U. Campus	In between the walls on the side of Scare Hall near the Bike Path.
23	Wall Scaler	M.U. Campus	On the roof to the front of Scare Hall.
24	M.U. Hat	M.U. Campus	In the tunnel at the rear of Scare Hall.
25	Newsstand	M.U. Campus	On the ledge on the left wing of Scare Hall.
26	Fishy Accent	M.U. Campus	In the trees along the Bike Path.
27	Terrible Teeth	M.U. Campus	On the little fountain directly behind Scare Hall leading to the Clock Tower.
28	Funny Flappers	M.U. Campus	In between the rooftops on the far left side of Scare Hall near the tunnel to the Paintball Area.
29	Beasty Beanpole	M.U. Campus	In the yard in right side of the Clock Tower.
30	Polka Dot Panic	M.U. Campus	In the yard in front of the Clock Tower.
31	Alarming Arms	M.U. Campus	On the ledge at the front Base of the Clock Tower.
32	Four Fanged	M.U. Campus	In the air near the fence facing Scare Hall.
33	Stripe Accent	M.U. Campus	On the chain-linked scaffolding at the side of the Clock Tower.
34	Randy Scales Wall	M.U. Campus	On the left ledge of the Clock Tower.
35	Curly South-Pointing Horns	M.U. Campus	On the path going up to the Clock Tower.
36	Slippery Slug	M.U. Campus	On the wooden suspended platform on the Clock Tower.
37	Scowling Brown	M.U. Campus	Inside the little room at the top of the Clock Tower.
38	Creepy Comb-Over	M.U. Campus	At the top of the Clock Tower facing M.U. Campus.
39	JOX House Walls	M.U. Campus	At the top of the Clock Tower facing away from M.U. Campus.
40	Three's the Charm	M.U. Campus	On the scaffolding at the back of the Clock Tower.
41	Scary 'Stache	M.U. Campus	On the ledge to the left of the Clock Tower by statue.
42	Shocking Shrimp	M.U. Campus	In the middle of the circular sitting area by the statue.
43	Triclops	M.U. Campus	On the railing of the bridge near the statue.

Green Capsules

#	Unlockable Item	Zone	Description
44	Monstery Metal	M.U. Campus	On the roof of the Dorm facing the quad.
45	Monsters University Student Pack 1	M.U. Campus	On the back of the roof of University Hall.
46	Monsters University Student Pack 4	M.U. Campus	On the gutter pipe between University Hall and Registration Hall.
47	Monsters University Decoration Pack 1	M.U. Campus	On the front of the roof of University Hall.
48	Monsters University Paintball Arena Pack 1	M.U. Campus	On the roof of Registration Hall.
49	Monsters University Decoration Pack 2	M.U. Campus	On the back of the roof of Scare Hall.
50	Creeping Concrete	M.U. Campus	In the very back of the Clock Tower area along the wall.

Infinity Chests/Vault

#	Unlockable Item	Zone	Description
S	Sulley Chest 1	M.U. Campus	On the wooden suspended platform on the Clock Tower.
M	Mike Wazowski Chest 1	M.U. Campus	On the roof of the Library.
R	Randy Chest 1	M.U. Campus	On the roof of the Dorm.
Master	Monsters Avatar Vault - Reward 1	M.U. Campus	At the base of the Clock Tower.

Red Capsules

#	Unlockable Item	Zone	Description
1	Beastly Clothes	Frat Row	By the entrance to Fear Tech.
2	Fancy Scales	Frat Row	On the roof of the OK House.
3	Shrieking Shingles	Frat Row	On top of the EOP House.
4	Freakish Flagstone	Frat Row	In front of the garage to the OK House.
5	Grim Grandma Gauze	Frat Row	In the far back corner past the OH House.
6	Double Fringe Fangs	Frat Row	On the back wall of the OH House.
7	Spooky Spikes	Frat Row	On the driveway of the OH House.
8	Flustered Feathers	Frat Row	On the balcony of the OH House.
9	Terrible Toupee	Frat Row	On top of the AEA House.
10	Beautiful Buck	Frat Row	On the wire next to the AEA House.
11	OK Frat Pennant	Frat Row	On the patio of the GRR House.
12	Pokey Posterior	Frat Row	On the roof of the GRR House.
13	Crabby Accent	Frat Row	On the back balcony of the AEA House.
14	Slick Spike	Frat Row	On the cables that are behind the GRR House.
15	Shiver Shingles	Frat Row	On the roof of the GRR House.
16	Savage Scales	Frat Row	Behind the GRR House by the fence.
17	Roarin' Reptile	Frat Row	On the roof of the PNK House.
18	Hair-Raising Horns	Frat Row	Along the fence behind the PNK House.
19	Bat Trap	Frat Row	On top of the car on the main road.
20	Long Southward Pointers	Frat Row	By the tree along the Bike Trail.
21	Scary Scales	Frat Row	In the back between the ROR House and EKO House.
22	Snake Accent	Frat Row	On top of the Half Pipe.
23	OK Frat Wall	Frat Row	On top of the Half Pipe.

#	Unlockable Item	Zone	Description
24	PNK House Walls	Frat Row	On the back roof of the JOX House.
25	Wild Wood Shingles	Frat Row	On the front roof of the JOX House.
26	Double Trouble Dorsal	Frat Row	On the back of the ROR House.
27	Monster Muscles	Frat Row	On the back of the ROR House.
28	Scaring Manual	Frat Row	On the cable above the Bike Trail.
29	Stubby Buddy	Frat Row	On top of the EKO House.
30	Tenticlegs	Frat Row	On top of the chimney of the HSS House.
31	Janitor's Rake	Frat Row	On top of the HSS House.
32	Morbidly Medium	Frat Row	In the center of the Pool.
33	Scary Cinnamon	Frat Row	Along the fence by the Pool.
34	Goofy Goggles	Frat Row	Along the back part of the fence by the Pool.
35	Fishy Accent	Frat Row	In the back side of the Pool.
36	Diclops	Frat Row	By the trash can by the fence around the Pool.

Green Capsules

#	Unlockable Item	Zone	Description
37	Monsters University Building Pack 2	Frat Row	On the wire to the left of the EOP House.
38	Monsters University Building Pack 3	Frat Row	On the patio of the GRR House.
39	Monsters University Building Pack 1	Frat Row	Along the fence by the Half Pipe.
40	Creepy Concrete Accent	Frat Row	On the wire going from JOX House to EKO House.
41	Monsters University Student Pack 3	Frat Row	In the air at the back of the Pool.
42	Monsters University Paintball Cannon	Frat Row	In the air at the front of the Pool.
43	Monsters University Decoration Pack 4	Frat Row	In the air at the front of the Pool.

Infinity Chests/Vault

#	Unlockable Item	Zone	Description
R	Randy Chest 3	Frat Row	At the end of the Bike Trail.
S	Sulley Chest 3	Frat Row	On top of the GRR House.

Red Capsules

#	Unlockable Item	Zone	Description
1	Mop Top	Fear Tech	On the wall of the Door Design School.
2	Fancy Fangs	Fear Tech	In the corner of the wall past the Door Design School.
3	Fear It Flags	Fear Tech	On the side platform of the Door Design School.
4	Creepy Craters	Fear Tech	On the connecting beam of the Door Design School.
5	Batty Wings	Fear Tech	On the wire above the Door Design School.
6	Vending Machine	Fear Tech	On the ground along the pathway.
7	Horrifying Hide	Fear Tech	On top of the hedge along the pathway.
8	Scream Tunnel Cover	Fear Tech	In the back corner of the wall behind the Library.
9	Creepy Campus Colors	Fear Tech	On top of a car in the parking lot behind the Library.
10	Hulking	Fear Tech	On the front wall of the Door Design School.
11	Polite Pucker	Fear Tech	On the front wall of the Door Design School.
12	HSS House Walls	Fear Tech	On the roof of the Library.
13	Sticker Walls	Fear Tech	In between the Library and the building behind it by the hedges.
14	Petrifying Paths	Fear Tech	In the corner of the wall between the Library and the building behind it.
15	Spikey Seat	Fear Tech	On the wire between the Library and the building behind it.
16	Jumpy Gel	Fear Tech	On the back side of the Library wall.
17	Buggy Antennas	Fear Tech	On the ledge of the dorms closest to Scare School.
18	Daffy Dots	Fear Tech	On the front ledge of Scare School.
19	Night Gliders	Fear Tech	On the side of Scare School up the spider wall.
20	Tentacles Times Two	Fear Tech	On the roof of Scare School by the sunroof.
21	Barbeque Grill	Fear Tech	On the side of Scare School along the inside wall.
22	Curvy Creepers	Fear Tech	At the very top of Scare School on the crossbeam.
23	Roundish Rascal	Fear Tech	On the side of Scare School up the spider wall.
24	Triple Trouble	Fear Tech	On the side of Scare School along the inside wall.
25	Tentacle Wall	Fear Tech	On the back ledge of Scare School.
26	Foot Locker	Fear Tech	On the back ledge of Scare School.
27	Lanky Limbs	Fear Tech	On the pipe at the back of Scare School.
28	Eyeclops	Fear Tech	On the rail right in front of Archie's Pen.
29	Woeful Wagger	Fear Tech	On the wall in the front of the Library.
30	Crazy Kisser	Fear Tech	On the rail to the Botanical Building.
31	Monster Movers	Fear Tech	On the sun roof of the building behind the Botanical Building.
32	Shriveled Sponge	Fear Tech	On the ledge behind the Botanical Building.
33	Scare Squares	Fear Tech	On the walkway by the Dorms.
34	Foam Finger	Fear Tech	Above the main entrance to the Botanical Building.
35	Eerie Earrings	Fear Tech	Up the spider wall in the front of the Botanical Building.

#	Unlockable Item	Zone	Description
36	Dire Spires	Fear Tech	On the glass cover next to the Botanical Building.
37	Gargoyle Wings	Fear Tech	On the ledge of the Science Building.
38	Crazy Coif	Fear Tech	On the ledge of the Science Building.
39	Quadropods	Fear Tech	On the ledge of the Science Building.
40	Pretty Peepers	Fear Tech	On the ledge of the Science Building in between the two connectors.
41	Fur-ocious	Fear Tech	On the ledge of the building on the left from the tunnel to M.U.
42	Teensy Weensy Terror	Fear Tech	On the ledge of the building on the left from the tunnel to M.U.
43	Yucko Stucco	Fear Tech	On the ledge of the building on the left from the tunnel to M.U.
44	Knobby Knobs	Fear Tech	On the ledge of the building on the right from the tunnel to M.U.
45	Curly South-Pointing Horns	Fear Tech	On the roof of the building behind the Library.

Green Capsules

#	Unlockable Item	Zone	Description
46	Monsters University Decoration Pack 3	Fear Tech	On the back wall of the Library.
47	Monsters University Paintball Arena Pack 2	Fear Tech	On the statue at the front of Scare School.
48	Monsters University Critter Pack 1	Fear Tech	On the front ledge of Scare School.
49	Monsters University Student Pack 2	Fear Tech	On the ledge of the Science Building.
50	Monsters University Critter Pack 2	Fear Tech	On the railing of the catwalk on the Science Building.

Infinity Chests/Vault

#	Unlockable Item	Zone	Description
M	Mike Wazowski Chest 2	Fear Tech	On the roof of the Door Design School.
R	Randy Chest 2	Fear Tech	On the very top part of the roof on Scare School.
S	Sulley Chest 2	Fear Tech	Right in front of the Health & Phys. Ed. Building.

Red Capsules

#	Unlockable Item	Zone	Description
1	Lurking Lampshade	Paintball Area	In the locker room.

Monsters University Gold Stars

#	Type	Star Names	Star Description
1	Challenge	Combination Lock	Perform a two-stunt combo on the bike.
2	Easter Egg	Student Switch	Change the appearance of a student.
3	Mission	Buttoned Up	Use a building button to transform a building.
4	Mission	Frat Go	Go to Frat Row.
5	Mission	Remodeller	Customize a Frat Row building.
6	Mission	Just Joking	Place a Prank Object.
7	Mission	Scared Silly	Scare a targeted Fear Tech student.
8	Mission	Save the Twins	Rescue Terri and Terry from their place of captivity.
9	Mission	Exchange Student	Go to Fear Tech.
10	Purchases	Painter	Purchase the Paintball Gun.
11	Mission	Sneaks and Hi-Jinks	Go to Fear Tech at night.
12	Mission	Gold Pedal	Perform 25 stunts on the bike.
13	Mission	Reform School	Repair the School of Scaring.
14	Mission	Get Along, Little Hoggy	Ride Archie through the tunnels to Monsters University.
15	Challenge	The Completist	Complete 15 missions in the Monsters University Play Set.
16	Mission	Paint Master	Complete all Paintball Challenges at any level of difficulty.
17	Easter Egg	The Collector	Find 25 Red Capsules in the Play Set.
18	Mission	Big Monster on Campus	Complete one Activity using the "Hard" difficulty setting.
19	Challenge	Bike Master	Complete all Bike Challenges at any level of difficulty.
20	Challenge	Frat Master	Complete all Frat Row Challenges at any level of difficulty.
21	Mission	Football Wrapper	Cover Fear Tech's sports statue with T.P.
22	Easter Egg	Batty Bush	Scare the bat-winged pests 15 times.
23	Easter Egg	Six Tricks	Create a six Prank Object combo.
24	Easter Egg	Pranks for Nothing	Activate a Prank Object on 25 students.
25	Easter Egg	Monster Modifier	Change the appearance of 10 students.
26	Purchases	Pedal Power	Purchase a bike.
27	Purchases	Jokester	Purchase every Prank Object.
28	Purchases	Leader of the Pack	Purchase the Cracklin' Backpack.
29	Purchases	On a Roll	Purchase the Toilet Paper Launcher.
30	Purchases	Frat Row Pro	Purchase every Frat Row building.

Monsters University Toy List

Toys	Toy Box Export	Toy Type	Commercial
Terrifying Two-Wheeler	Yes	Vehicle/Mount	No
Slithering Cycle	Yes	Vehicle/Mount	No
Tiny Terror	Yes	Vehicle/Mount	No
Beastly Bike	Yes	Vehicle/Mount	Yes
Archie the Scare Pig	Yes	Vehicle/Mount	Yes
Paintball Cannon	Yes	Prop	No
Roarin' Ramp	Yes	Unique	No
Bike Park Dual Pool	Yes	Unique	No
Bike Park Half Pipe	Yes	Unique	No
Bike Park Berm	Yes	Unique	No
Bike Park Table Top	Yes	Unique	No
Sweet Bike Jump	Yes	Unique	No
PNK House	Yes	Building	No
JOX House	Yes	Building	No
HSS House	Yes	Building	No
EKO House	Yes	Building	No
ROR House	Yes	Building	No
Give 'em a Hand Launcher	Yes	Unique	Yes
Scream Energy Launcher	Yes	Unique	No

Toys	Toy Box Export	Toy Type	Commercial
Morning Edition Launcher	Yes	Unique	No
Vending Machine Launcher	Yes	Unique	No
Leafing So Soon? Launcher	Yes	Unique	No
Fly Swatter Launcher	Yes	Unique	No
Vender Ender	Yes	Unique	No
Breaking News Ender	Yes	Unique	No
School Colors Ender	Yes	Unique	Yes
Have a Nice Trip Launcher	Yes	Unique	No
Scream Tunnel Sludge Ender	Yes	Unique	No
Pile It On Ender	Yes	Unique	No
Incoming Call Ender	Yes	Unique	Yes
Paintball Gun	Yes	Held Item	Yes
Toilet Paper Launcher	Yes	Held Item	Yes
Cracklin' Backpack	Yes	Held Item	Yes
Glow Urchin	Yes	Held Item	Yes
Bat-Winged Pest Bush	Yes	Held Item	No
Sludge Balloon	No	Held Item	No

Monsters University Challenges

Name	Location	Description	Character	Requirements		
				Easy	Medium	Hard
Classroom Run	Clock Tower Area	Gather as many collectibles as you can before time runs out.	Any	10 targets in 1:30	20 targets in 1:30	35 targets in 1:30
Fear Tech Collector	Fear Tech below School of Science	Gather as many collectibles as you can before time runs out.	Any	20 targets in 1:00	35 targets in 1:00	48 targets in 1:00
Randy's Rampage	Fear Tech between Library buildings	Break as many collectibles as you can as Randy before the time runs out.	Randy	10 targets in 1:30	20 targets in 1:30	30 targets in 1:30
Fear Tech Cyclist	Fear Tech in front of Health & Phys. Ed. Building	Gather as many collectibles as you can before time runs out.	Any	10 targets in 1:30	10 targets in 1:15	10 targets in 1:00
Paintball Ruckus	Frat Row Alcove	Defeat Fear Tech students in a Paintball competition.	Any	4 targets in 0:50	8 targets in 0:50	12 targets in 0:50
Wheels and Thrills	Frat Row Alcove	Gather as many collectibles as you can before time runs out.	Any	20 targets in 1:30	35 targets in 1:30	50 targets in 1:30
Wild Wheels	Frat Row Alcove	Pass through all the gates before time runs out.	Any	8 checkpoints in 1:00	8 checkpoints in 0:50	8 checkpoints in 0:40
Paint the Frat Collector	Frat Row Alcove	Defeat Fear Tech students in a Paintball competition.	Any	25 targets in 1:20	35 targets in 1:20	45 targets in 1:20
Frat Row Round-Up	Frat Row Alcove	Break as many collectibles as you can before the time runs out.	Any	20 targets in 0:50	30 targets in 0:50	40 targets in 0:50
Round the Row	Frat Row Alcove	Pass through all the gates before time runs out.	Any	10 checkpoints in 1:10	10 checkpoints in 1:00	10 checkpoints in 0:50
Mike's Mayhem	Frat Row Entrance	Gather as many collectibles as you can as Mike before time runs out.	Mike	15 targets in 1:30	30 targets in 1:30	42 targets in 1:30
Timed Swine	Frat Row Entrance	Gather as many collectibles as you can before time runs out.	Any	20 targets in 1:00	40 targets in 1:00	60 targets in 1:00
Crazy Frat Stunts	Frat Row Pool	Do bike tricks to reach the score goal before time runs out.	Any	3000 points in 1:00	6000 points in 1:00	10000 points in 1:00
Bike Hop and Pop	Frat Row Pool	Gather as many collectibles as you can before time runs out.	Any	20 targets in 1:30	35 targets in 1:30	50 targets in 1:30
Campus Collector Bike	M.U. Campus Bike Stunt area	Gather as many collectibles as you can before time runs out.	Any	25 targets in 1:20	35 targets in 1:20	45 targets in 1:20
Campus Collector	M.U. Campus in front of the Library	Gather as many collectibles as you can before time runs out.	Any	12 targets in 2:00	25 targets in 2:00	50 targets in 2:00
Squeal and Steal	M.U. Campus near Clock Tower	Gather as many collectibles as you can before time runs out.	Any	20 targets in 1:00	30 targets in 1:00	40 targets in 1:00
Sulley's Campus Collector	M.U. Campus near University Hall	Gather as many collectibles as you canas Sulley before time runs out.	Sulley	5 targets in 0:40	10 targets in 0:40	15 targets in 0:40
Scream Tunnel Collector	Paintball Arena	Break as many collectibles as you can before the time runs out.	Any	10 targets in 0:45	20 targets in 0:45	30 targets in 0:45
Paintball Press	Paintball Arena	Defeat Fear Tech students in a Paintball competition.	Any	4 enemies in 1:00	8 enemies in 1:00	10 enemies in 1:00
Paintball Panic	Paintball Arena	Defeat Fear Tech students in a Paintball competition.	Any	4 enemies in 1:00	8 enemies in 1:00	10 enemies in 1:00
Paintball Party	Paintball Arena	Defeat Fear Tech students in a Paintball competition.	Any	4 enemies in 1:00	8 enemies in 1:00	10 enemies in 1:00

The Incredibles

NOTE - For those playing Disney Infinity on the Wii, the Play Sets are a bit different. Access your free eGuide (voucher code on the insert) to access this content.

Three notorious criminals apprehended by The Incredibles are about to be sent off to a maximum security prison. However, Syndrome shows up and frees the villains! The arch enemy of The Incredibles sends the heroic family flying off in the distance as he unleashes a horde of robots on the city.

Search and Rescue on the Docks

Where There's Smoke

Mission Giver: Edna
Type: Combat/Platforming
Rewards: N/A

Follow the green compass arrow, jumping up on the demolished building and avoiding the flames. Continue to rush through the flaming wreckage and grab on to the ledge above that is highlighted with a yellow tint.

Attack the water tower on the roof of the building to knock it over and douse the flames.

Follow the path of the toppled tower toward the gas trucks, but that route will become blocked when the trucks explode. Turn to the left towards a tower that has two brown crates that can be jumped over.

Climb the pole to the top of the metal tower and double jump across the moving crates and stack of cargo boxes to get to the tower on the other side.

Run down the metal stairs to confront four attacking robots unleashed by Syndrome. Each of your targets is highlighted by a red arrow. A few simple attacks should take care of each one. However, look out for the rocket-launching robot on the ship that can blast you from a distance. Block its rockets if you can't outrun them, and make that robot your top target.

New Toy Unlocked: Mr. Incredible's Sports Car

Clean Up Syndrome's Mess

Small Island

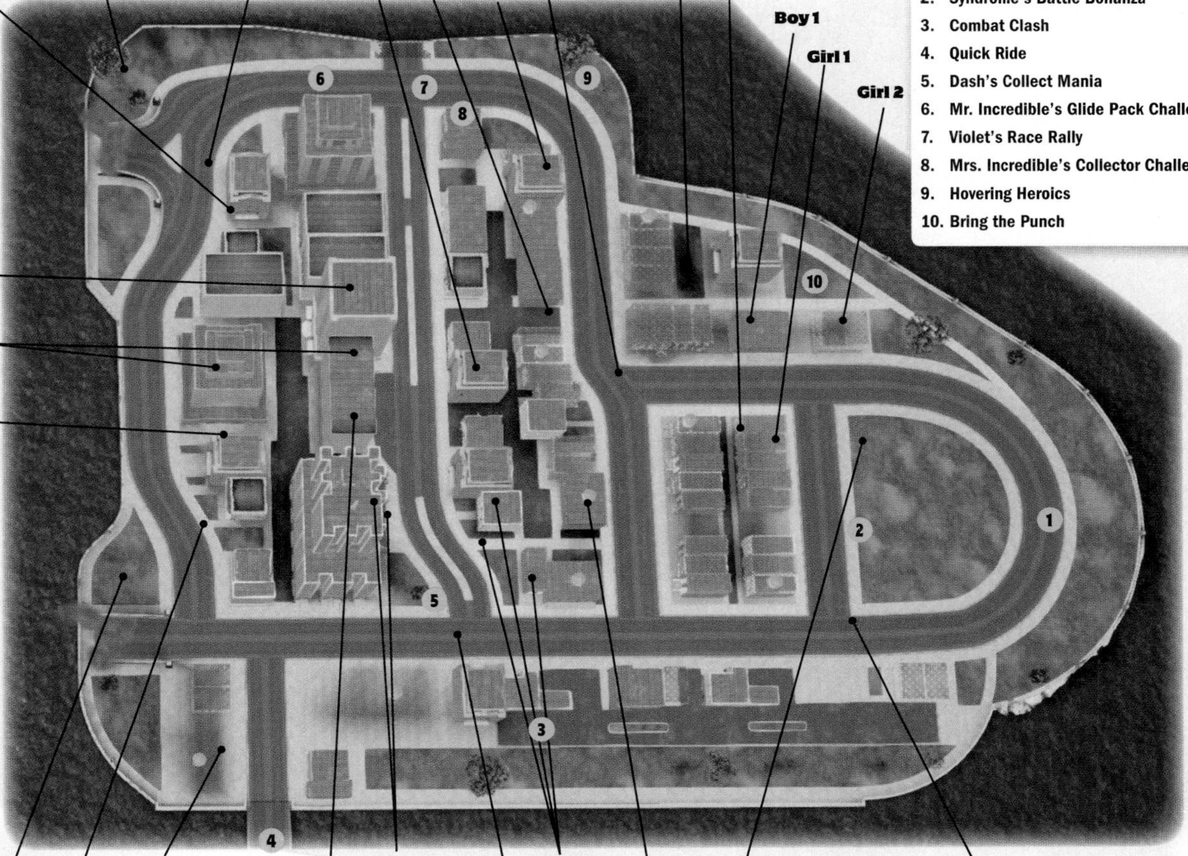

Edna Landing Zone
Hoarder Chest
Poolside 1
Informant
Cop 2 Fire Alarm
Secret Weapon
Hoarder Chest
Cop Lock em Up
Cop 3 Rooftop Rescue
Boy 1
Girl 1
Girl 2
Hoarder Chest
Hoarder Chest
Hoarder Chest
Zoo
Cop 1 Rubble Trouble
Core 2
Core 3
Hoarder Chest
Poolside 2
Hoarder Chest
Building on Fire
Circle
Pod 1

Challenges
1. Race Around Town
2. Syndrome's Battle Bonanza
3. Combat Clash
4. Quick Ride
5. Dash's Collect Mania
6. Mr. Incredible's Glide Pack Challenge
7. Violet's Race Rally
8. Mrs. Incredible's Collector Challenge
9. Hovering Heroics
10. Bring the Punch

Damage Assessment

Mission Giver: Edna
Type: Buy/Locate
Rewards: 300 Coins / 50 Sparks

Edna is on her way, but Syndrome has destroyed all the bridges. Local law enforcement needs your help, but first you need to get the sports car to travel around the city. Go into the Toy Store to buy Mr. Incredible's Sports Car and someone will be nice enough to drop off your car. Jump into the driver's seat and follow the compass to find the first officer trying to deal with the damage from the Omnidroids.

> **NOTE**
>
> This is a three-part mission assisting cops, each with unique tasks to help the city.

New Challenges Available: Violet's Race Rally, Syndrome's Battle Bonanza, Dash's Collect Mania, Collect Crazy, Mrs. Incredible's Collector Challenge, Glide 'n' Grab, Mr. Incredible's Glide Pack Challenge, Hover Board Hustle, Hovering Heroics, Speed Battle, Blast From Above, Eat My Dust.

Bubble Trouble

Mission Giver: Policeman
Type: Fetch
Rewards: 100 Coins / 25 Sparks

The officer mentions that several citizens are trapped under debris. Use the compass to find the six trapped people and smash the debris to set them free.

Fire Alarm!

Mission Giver: Policeman
Type: Platforming
Rewards: 100 Coins / 25 Sparks

A historic building was set on fire by a couple of Syndrome's robots. Use the compass to find the burning building and wipe out the Omnidroids that started the fire. The most obvious path to the top is the yellow highlighted ledges in the front of the building. Use them to quickly climb to the top and smash the water tower to put out the fire.

Rooftop Rescue

Mission Giver: Policeman
Type: Platforming
Rewards: 100 Coins / 25 Sparks

There are three people trapped on rooftops. It's up to you to get up there and take them to safety. The first boy is trapped on the building right in front of the policeman, and the building is easy to climb. The task really isn't to save the boy as much as it is to get him into the circle of yellow blockades. This can be done with one well-aimed toss of the lad—don't worry, this is a superhero city and everyone is very durable. Knock down the big blue billboard on the roof, pick the boy up, and try your best at tossing him into the circle below. If you miss, you will need to jump down and toss him until he is safely in the circle.

Climb to the next building and fling the girl into the safety of the circle below.

Finally, climb back up the red building where you saved the boy, jump across the billboard that was knocked over earlier, and toss the last girl in the ring below.

Reactivate the Headquarters

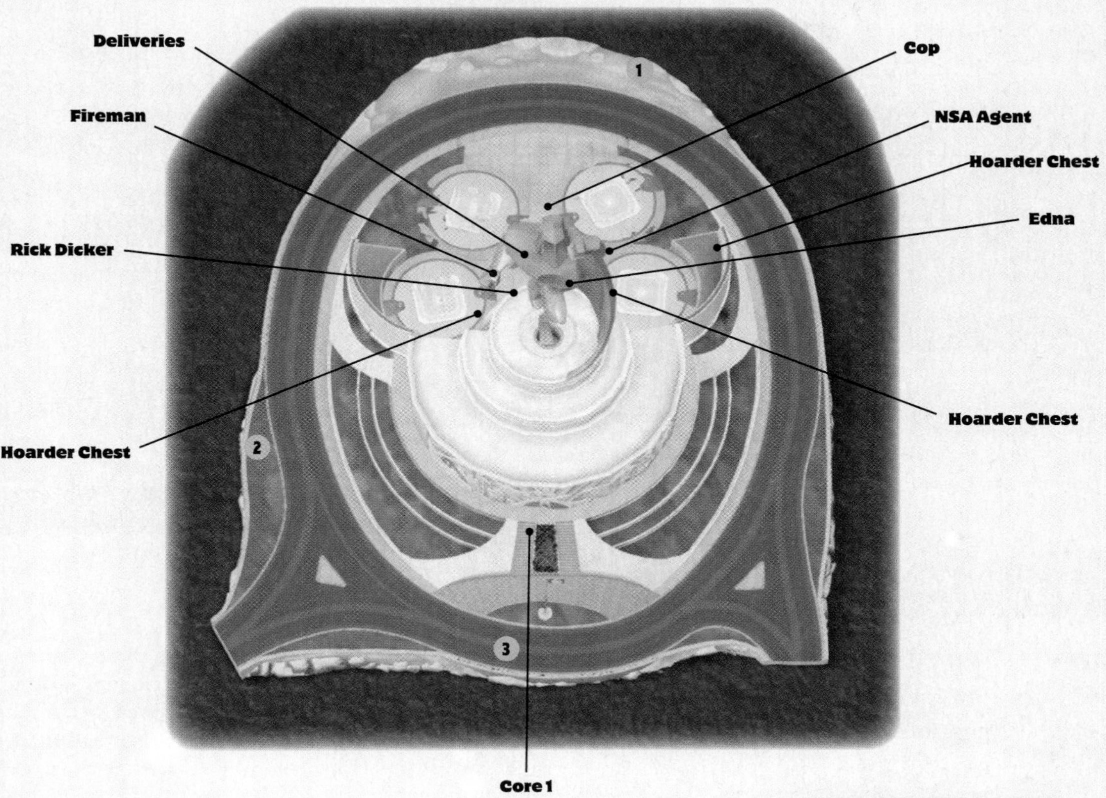

Challenges

1. Collect Crazy (Active Lifestyle Mission)
2. Romp Around Town
3. Blast From Above

Edna Arrives

Mission Giver: Policeman
Type: Combat
Rewards: 500 Coins / 200 Sparks

Edna has almost arrived, but the Omidroids have swarmed the landing zone. Follow the red arrows to Edna's arrival spot and destroy all five robots. One of them is on the roof. To find it you will need to climb up the adjacent building and jump across to take it on.

The Secret of Heroes Island

Mission Giver: Edna
Type: Buy/Build
Rewards: 500 Coins / 100 Sparks

To reactivate the hidden base of operations, the bridge must be repaired. Go in to the Toy Store and buy the bridge for 100 coins.

New Toy Unlocked: Downtown Express Bridge

Make your way across the bridge and run towards the Hall of Heroes. When you arrive, Edna will give you a clue about how to unlock the HQ. Take special note of the triangular buttons that appear when she mentions the mural. Climb the side of the building and work your way around it to the golden buttons. Press both of them to reactivate the HQ.

Climb to the top of the HQ using the ledges that are on the top tier. At the very top, near the statue, step on the platform in the center to reopen the HQ.

New Toy Unlocked: Training Facility

New Toy Unlocked: SuperMax Prison

NOTE

When the HQ is back up and running, three mission paths become available: Training, Prisoner Capture, and Tech Research. The first two are initiated by purchasing the Training Facility and SuperMax Prison respectively, and the last unlocks when those buildings are both bought.

Training Missions

Room to Breathe

Mission Giver: Edna
Type: Buy/Build
Rewards: N/A

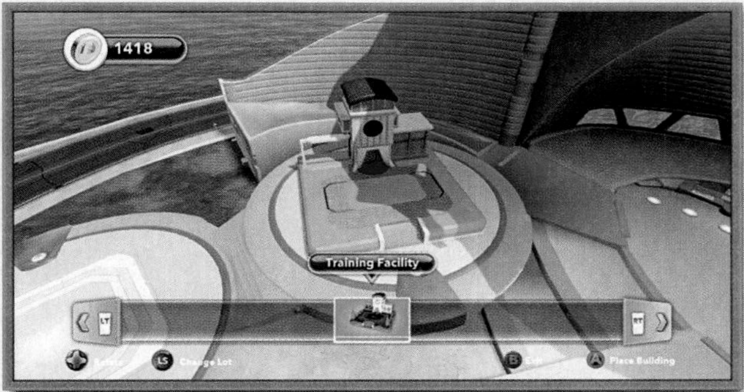

To reach your full potential, you need to buy the National Supers Agency Training Facility from the Toy Store. Enter the Toy Store menu to buy it for 500 coins and place it on one of the four open areas in the HQ.

New Toy Unlocked: Purple Truck

Shape Up!

Mission Giver: Edna
Type: Fetch
Rewards: 100 Coins / 50 Sparks

Edna informs you that your fighting skills are so last season, but the newly built Training Facility can get you up to snuff. Pick up the Sensei in the center of the HQ and take him to the Training Facility to begin your lessons.

NOTE

The first training mission illustrates how to use the super attack. This is a unique attack for each of The Incredibles and Syndrome, so there are five gold star missions available if you have all of the characters for this Play Set.

Sensei Missions

NOTE

These are unique missions for each character to teach them their super move. Only the current character has to complete his or her mission to proceed, but if you want to use the super move for another character in this Play Set, return to the Sensei to learn it.

The Power Within

Mission Giver: Sensei
Type: Training
Rewards: 100 Coins / 100 Sparks

The first lesson for Mr. Incredible to defeat Omidroids is to call upon your strength. Learn to use the Super Ground Pound by pressing the super attack button. This is a great attack for crowd control as it damages all enemies in its path.

Fantastic Elastic

Mission Giver: Sensei
Type: Training
Rewards: 100 Coins / 100 Sparks

Mrs. Incredible can use her Elasti-Hand move to pull herself to an Omnidroid and get past its blocking defenses. This is a very important part of her attacking arsenal to break through an Omnidroid's block state.

Vanishing Act

Mission Giver: Sensei
Type: Training
Rewards: 100 Coins / 100 Sparks

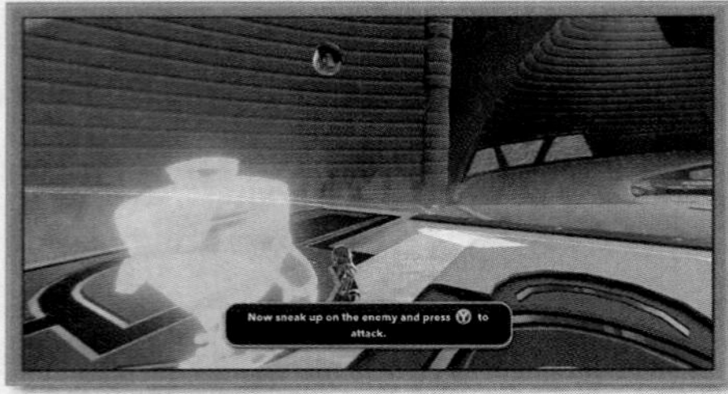

Using invisibility, Violet can avoid detection from enemies or make enemies that are aware of her lose sight of her. Use her power of invisibility to drop out of sight from the Omnidroid and sneak up to attack it.

A Burst of Speed

Mission Giver: Sensei
Type: Training
Rewards: 100 Coins / 100 Sparks

Dash's super speed can deal high damage to a single Omnidroid, breaking through its block state. Use his fast attack to become a mobile weapon as well as a method to travel around the city quickly.

Zero Point Power Surge

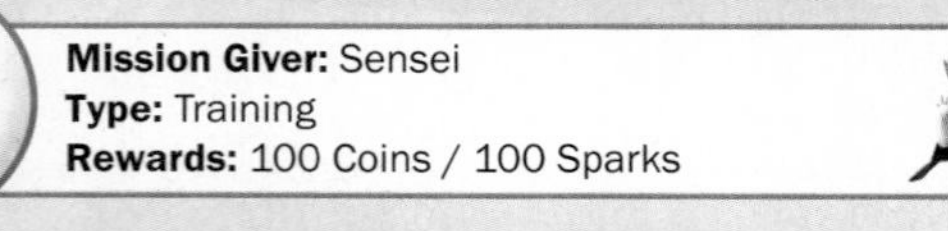

Mission Giver: Sensei
Type: Training
Rewards: 100 Coins / 100 Sparks

The Zero Point Energy tool can freeze Omnidroids and lift them overhead so they can be tossed around like toys. Throwing the Omnidroids deals high damage to them or others that they smash into.

New Toy Unlocked: Glide Pack

> **NOTE**
>
> After buying the Glide Pack, go through the tutorial on how to equip Packs and Tools.

Learning to Glide

Mission Giver: Edna
Type: Training
Rewards: 100 Coins / 100 Sparks

Take the elevator to the top of the HQ and open the blue capsule to learn how to glide. Fly through all the green rings and dive bomb down to the circle of yellow gates below.

Training Side Missions

Uppercut Aficionado

Mission Giver: Sensei
Type: Training
Rewards: 100 Coins / 50 Sparks

After the initial lesson, which is different for each character, continue to speak to the Sensei to learn all of the other combat techniques. The next move to master is the uppercut combo. The first part can be done by pressing and holding the attack button to launch the enemy and yourself into the air. While airborne press attack again to perform the second part of the combo. Do the combo three times to prove you have mastered the move.

Handling a Crowd

Mission Giver: Sensei
Type: Training
Rewards: 100 Coins / 50 Sparks

This is a simple but effective lesson about quickly switching between targets. Simply flick the movement stick in the direction of an enemy to target and attack it. This is a very useful technique when fighting groups of enemies that surround you.

Dodge

Mission Giver: Sensei
Type: Training
Rewards: 100 Coins / 50 Sparks

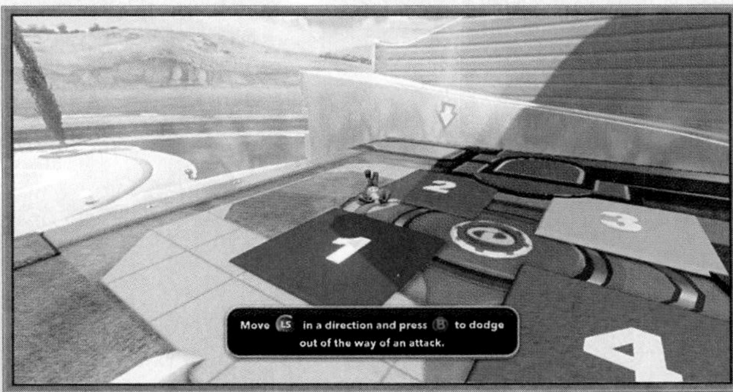

Combat is not simply about fighting and blocking. Sometimes the best maneuver is to dodge an attack entirely. Move the directional stick while pressing the same button to block in order to dive out of the way. This can be done while running or blocking.

New Challenge Available: Collect Crazy

Active Lifestyle

Mission Giver: Sensei
Type: Collect
Rewards: N/A

Complete the Collect Crazy activity located around the back side of the HQ.

Collector Challenge

Mission Giver: Sensei
Type: Collect
Rewards: 25 Coins

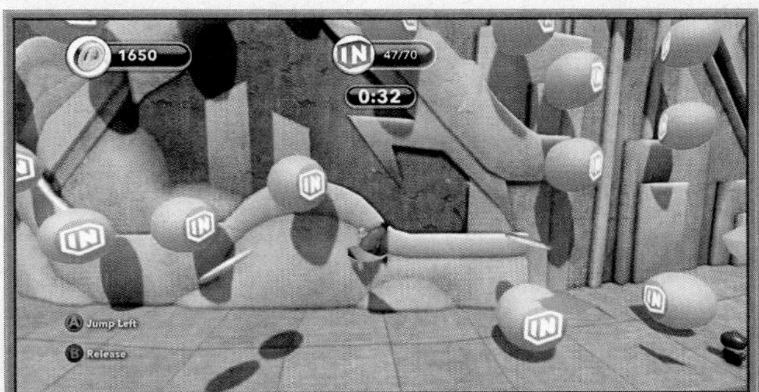

Collecting enough balls shouldn't be too hard if you start in a big cluster and keep moving in one direction to clear out all of them at that level. Jump up to the next climbable ledge and pick up the balls, following them to the next set.

Game Basics | Characters | Power Discs | Play Sets | Toy Box | Toy Box Collection | Achievements

Prisoner Capture Missions

No Escape

Mission Giver: Rick Dicker
Type: Buy/Build
Rewards: 100 Coins / 25 Sparks

Buy the Super-Max Prison in the Toy Store to house criminals and open several missions to apprehend the villains that Syndrome set free.

New Toy Unlocked: Ice Cream Truck

New Toy Unlocked: Newspaper Stand

Animal Pandemonium!

Mission Giver: Fireman at HQ
Type: Fetch
Rewards: 100 Coins / 200 Sparks

A devious droid has released the animals from the local zoo. You need to help round them up and toss them back into the zoo. Head towards the zoo and use the compass to locate all six animals including a panda, giraffe, lion, elephant, monkey, and penguin.

Lock 'em Up

Mission Giver: Cop
Type: Locate
Rewards: 100 Coins / 100 Sparks

A local policeman wants to see every crook and criminal locked up behind bars. Look for the criminals that are dressed in black-and-white-striped clothes. Luckily the first one is right next to the officer.

Grab the crook and follow the compass to a police van to toss the villain inside. Track down all five crooks to clean up the streets of Metroville.

The Hoarder Pursuit and Capture

Hide and Seek

Mission Giver: Rick Dicker
Type: Locate
Rewards: 100 Coins

Now that the prison is built, it is time to bring in the villains Syndrome unleashed on the city. The first target is The Hoarder, who has been sighted at the docks. Use the compass to make your way there to check it out. It is a long walk back to the city, so look for a blue sign with a car on it to summon a vehicle.

When you arrive at the designated spot at the docks, The Hoarder shows up and traps a cop with the mysterious UFO device he is riding. This machine fails to work on your character and The Hoarder is apprehended by the police.

Find All

Mission Giver: Rick Dicker
Type: Locate
Rewards: N/A

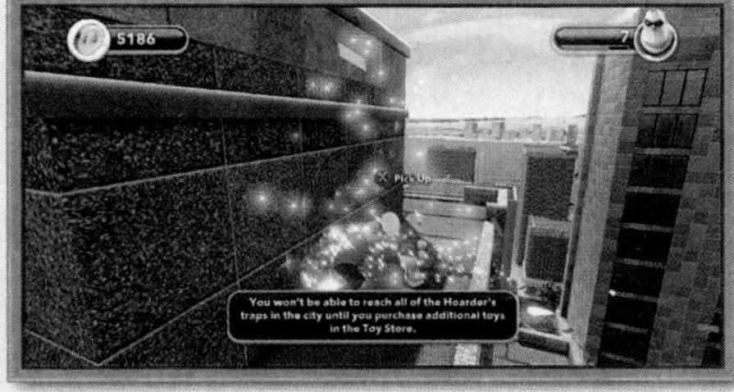

Find and destroy all of The Hoarder's traps around the city. This is a very tough mission to complete. Smash the traps as you find them, but wait for the helicopter before you really scour the city. Releasing the hostages will uncover several new superheroes that can be recruited at the HQ to join you in combat.

Tight Spaces

Mission Giver: Rick Dicker (radio)
Type: Platforming
Rewards: 250 Coins / 50 Sparks

Before The Hoarder can be prosecuted, you must smash his traps to release all the hostages. Use the compass to locate and rescue five citizens scattered around the pier. The last person you save will join your cause and go to the HQ, ready to fight with you when he is recruited.

New Toy Unlocked: Forklift

Prisoner Delivery

Mission Giver: Rick Dicker (radio)
Type: Escort
Rewards: 500 Coins / 200 Sparks

With The Hoarder in custody, it's time to transport the villain to the SuperMax Prison at HQ. Escort the paddy wagon to headquarters as you defend against Syndrome's attacks.

Keep an eye on the paddy wagon's yellow bar to see how much damage it is taking—if it is completely depleted your mission will fail.

The goal is to keep the Omnidroids from damaging the paddy wagon. But keep your guard up—Syndrome's forces will do everything they can to prevent the truck from reaching HQ. Enlist the aid of the local police by smashing the yellow barricades. This will not only open a clear route for the truck, but the cops will attack the robots and distract them.

Remember that the paddy wagon can't move if there is anything blocking it. That includes robots, barricades, and even chucks of road debris. Try to stay a little ahead of the truck to keep the path clear and eliminate any robots in front of it.

Once the truck finally makes it to HQ, grab The Hoarder and toss him into the prison to lock him up once and for all.

New Toy Unlocked: Pink Family Car

New Challenges Available: Quick Ride, Romp Around Town

NOTE

Completion of this mission lowers the bridges to allow access to the Big island, however there is a lot more to do on the Small island. At this point it is probably best to follow the Tech Missions until you get the Hover Board.

Snoring Gloria's Pods

Find Snoring Gloria

Mission Giver: Rick Dicker
Type: Locate
Rewards: N/A

The next villain has been spotted in the city. Use the compass to track down Snoring Gloria. She unleashes a mutated version of her plants that puts citizens to sleep. The only way to destroy the large pod is to take out the smaller ones first.

Rise and Shine

Mission Giver: Rick Dicker
Type: Destroy
Rewards: 500 Coins / 100 Sparks

You must destroy two groups of pods (six smaller and two larger ones), and luckily the first group of pods appears right in front of you. Follow the red arrow to one of the smaller pods on the grass and destroy it. Each time one of the smaller pods is eliminated, the vine leading to the large pod will disappear and the larger pod will lose some of its leafy defenses.

The other two smaller pods are on the rooftops. Use the red arrow to find them, but if you have trouble locating their exact position, follow the green vines coming out of the large pod for a clue. Go after pod number two by climbing a light-colored building with plenty of ledges to help you climb up.

The last little pod of this group can easily been seen from the roof where you took on the second one. Jump down to the street and climb up the blue front of the building to reach the last one.

Finally, jump down to the street and take out the defenseless large pod amongst the outcropping of little blue sleep-inducing pods.

Track the next group using the red arrows to locate the second group of pods just down the street. Tackle the first smaller pod by climbing a dark stone facade next to a light blue one. Smash the pod on the roof and jump across to the air conditioners and pipe leading to the roof of the next one.

The last smaller pod is across the street on a roof near a water tower. Glide across to the building or jump down to the street to climb up the front of it.

NOTE

This building can catch fire but it is easily put out by knocking over the water tower on the roof.

New Toy Unlocked: Edna's Costume Shop

NOTE

Side Missions: Sprawling Sleep Pods is open at this point, but it takes place on the Big island. It might be worthwhile to wait for the Tech Mission path to catch up.

Sprawling Sleep Pods

Mission Giver: Rick Dicker
Type: Destroy
Rewards: 100 Coins / 200 Sparks

Snoring Gloria has placed her sleep-inducing plants all over the city. Track them down and destroy them all! The larger pods only have two smaller support pods this time, but you must destroy five large pods to complete the mission.

Pods Set 1

The first set of pods is just across the bridge and is not very challenging. The smaller pods are not very high up, so it will be quick work to wipe them all out.

Pods Set 2

You can find the next set of pods by using the red arrow to go across the docks. The first small pod is right on the street and can be taken out by slamming into it with the Hover Board.

The second small pod is on a rooftop of a dark-colored building with green widows. This place may light on fire, but there is a handy water tower on the roof to handle the blaze.

The last smaller pod is on the roof of the brown building next door, but it is not possible to climb that structure to get to the roof. Go to the roof where you met Mirage and glide over to the dark building to wall jump to the ledge. From here, glide down to the pod, smash it, and leap to the street below to wipe out the large pod.

Pods Set 3

Follow the red arrow to the next set of pods and climb a light tan building using a pipe to get to the first small pod.

Leap down to the street and smash the smaller pod out in the open.

The last little pod of this group is on top of a dark grey building. Climb the building next to it with the blue windows. Jump around and to the side of the dark building to catch on to a yellow ledge and climb up. Leap to a pipe to the right to get to the roof and smash the last little pod. Finish off the big pod below and head just up the street to the next group.

Pods Set 4

Take out the first smaller pod on the ground level next to the large one.

Follow the vine leading up a light-colored building and climb the building next to it to get to the roof. Knock over a blue-backed billboard and destroy the second pod on the adjacent roof.

The third pod with the long vine going up the side of the light-colored building has to be climbed from the opposite side of that vine. Leap up to the rooftops and jump across to the scaffolding under the sunny billboard. Use the pipe on the left to make it to the roof and remove that third little pod.

Pods Set 5

The last group is by the bridge leading to HQ. Wipe out the pod on the street.

Climb the building with the light blue windows and the vine on it to get to the roof and smash the pod.

The last one is a bit tricky as the red arrow can point down from this roof when the pod is really high above on the next rooftop.

Jump across to a platform with a horizontal pipe and grind on it to the front under a billboard. Continue to go around the building, grinding on another pipe and finally climbing to the roof to destroy the last pod.

Edna's Shop Missions

A Shop of Her Own

Mission Giver: Edna
Type: Buy/Build
Rewards: 100 Coins / 25 Sparks

In order for Edna to create her new masterpieces, she needs her workshop that is unlocked after completing the Rise and Shine mission. Simply go into the Toy Box to buy and place the building once you have completed that mission.

New Toy Unlocked: Orange Car

NOTE

The completion of Edna's Costume Shop will prevent Syndrome's Zero Point Energy weapon from working on you. That is some impressive fabric she is using!

Witness Protection

Mission Giver: Edna
Type: Customize
Rewards: 100 Coins / 50 Sparks

Someone hanging around HQ thinks that Syndrome is after him. Pick the man up and throw him into Edna's Costume Shop to change his appearance.

Which Witness?

Mission Giver: Edna
Type: Customize
Rewards: 100 Coins / 50 Sparks

Syndrome has targeted one of your agency's undercover operatives. Use the compass to find the man, dressed as a construction worker, and bring him to Edna's Costume Shop for a makeover.

Tech Research Missions

It's a Secret

Mission Giver: NSA Agent (suit and glasses guy at HQ)
Type: Locate
Rewards: 100 Coins / 50 Sparks

There is an informant in the city that you need to meet. She knows a contact inside Syndrome's organization who is willing to defect to the side of the good guys. Use the compass to find the female informant, but it is not safe to talk in the open. Follow her up to the roof and grind across two power lines to a safe area.

The defector is waiting on a nearby rooftop on a very tall building. Using the compass, locate the tall building and climb up to the rooftop of the light tan building next to it. Leap onto the air conditioner and double jump up to the next air conditioner to gain access to a pipe leading to the roof of the building next door.

The mysterious defector can't speak in the city. She will meet you back at HQ.

New Toy Unlocked: HQ Research Station

NOTE

The Glide Pack and Learning to Glide missions will be unlocked if the Sensei missions were not completed.

NOTE

Three new Mayor Side Missions are now unlocked.

Mayor Side Missions

Yacht Party

Mission Giver: Cop
Type: Platforming
Rewards: 100 Coins / 50 Sparks

A cop across from the docks will inform you that the Mayor is late for a fund-raising event and needs you to get him there fast. The mission will automatically warp you to a rooftop at the dock with the Mayor nearby. The goal is to pick up the Mayor and get him to the boat in 30 seconds. There is a blue capsule nearby that will demonstrate how to dive bomb and swoop to gain more distance and height from gliding.

The concept behind swooping is to use the speed of diving down to ricochet you back up, allowing you to go further than simply slowly gliding downward.

Mayor Menace

Mission Giver: Mayor
Type: Platforming
Rewards: 100 Coins / 50 Sparks

The Mayor is roaming the streets in dire straits. He has to get home before his wife or he will be in big trouble. Without asking any questions, you need to use the Glide Pack to quickly get him to his house in 45 seconds. The actual mission begins on a ledge with the Mayor's house off in the distance. The only way to get to the Mayor's house first is by gliding and swooping twice. Double jump off the ledge to get some height and swoop as you approach the two light-colored vent shafts.

After that swoop, continue gliding for a bit until you are close to his house. Do one last swoop just as you go over the street and zip up to safely land on the roof.

Mayor of the Skies

Mission Giver: Mayor
Type: Platforming
Rewards: 100 Coins / 50 Sparks

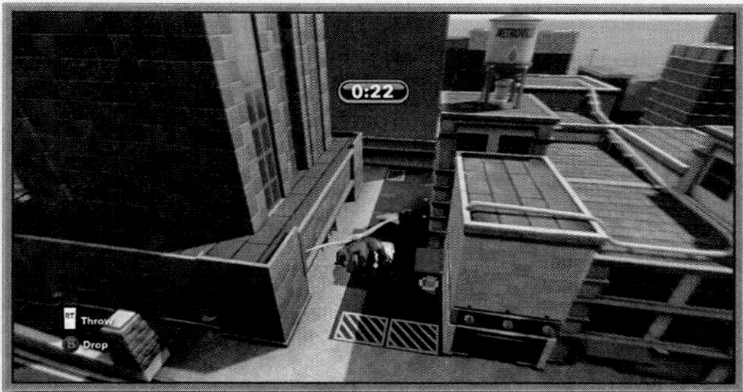

For the last time, the Mayor needs your help to meet someone for lunch because he is running late... again. How this guy ever got elected is a mystery. Still, as a hero it is your job to help all of the citizens of Metroville. You have 30 seconds to complete this mission, but it is a lot easier than the previous one. The same method of double swooping should be used, but it is a lot harder to find the target.

There is a lot more room for error on this mission and you can land on the roof or even in the alley and still have enough time to run to the target circle.

Gadgets Galore

Mission Giver: Mirage
Type: Buy/Build
Rewards: 100 Coins

NOTE

Requires completion of Tight Spaces mission.

Mirage managed to smuggle out some data on Syndrome's newest tech he is using, but she needs a Research Station to access it. Go into the Toy Store menu to buy it and then place the station.

Super Recruits

Mission Giver: Cop
Type: Locate
Rewards: 100 Coins / 25 Sparks

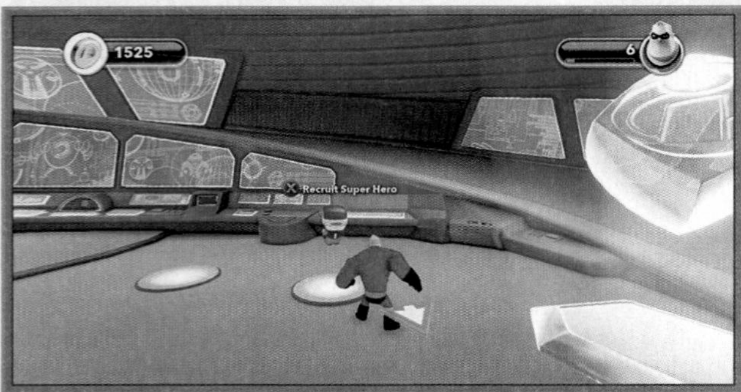

A policeman at the HQ mentions that there is a Super at the HQ waiting to help in combat. After freeing the last hostage from The Hoarder's trap in mission Tight Spaces, the little hero will appear at the HQ near the elevator to the top. Speak to the little blue hero and recruit him to help you battle the bad guys.

> **NOTE**
>
> **You must be close to the HQ to activate this mission.**

Emergency at Headquarters

Mission Giver: Edna (radio)
Type: Combat
Rewards: 300 Coins / 100 Sparks

The Omnidroids are invading the new headquarters. Follow the red arrows to their location and destroy them all! Keep your cool when fighting the big attack wave and jump from foe to foe as you learned from your Sensei. Whenever possible, pound on the robots and then pick them up to right before they explode to toss them at others and damage multiple Omnidroids in a single shot. This is going to be a long and difficult battle, so take your time and try to eliminate them one at a time.

New Toy Unlocked: Ambulance

> **NOTE**
>
> **Completing this mission unlocks the second round of the Sensei's missions.**

Sensei Side Missions

Throwing Things

Mission Giver: Sensei
Type: Training
Rewards: 100 Coins / 50 Sparks

Pick up the green car and hurl it at the Omnidroid. Throwing things at enemies is a great way to take out groups of robots rapidly.

> **NOTE**
>
> **This mission is for Mr. Incredible only.**

Muscle Memory

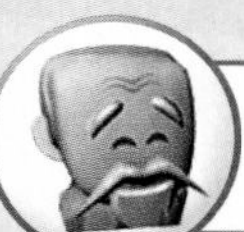

Mission Giver: Sensei
Type: Training
Rewards: 100 Coins / 50 Sparks

Mr. Incredible's super power is his super strength. This allows him to lift heavy objects and throw them—including Omidroids. Lift the holographic Omnidroid and toss it at the group of robots.

Science to the Rescue

Mission Giver: Mirage
Type: Fetch/Combat
Rewards: N/A

A Science Agent has a powerful weapon secretly placed in the city. Take him there and protect the weapon to buy him enough time to activate the device. Pick up the green-haired agent and hop into a car to hightail it to the weapon.

Throw the scientist into the machine to get him to work activating the device, which will trigger several waves of Omnidroids. The goal is to wipe out the robots quickly before they can damage the weapon. Stay close to the weapon to keep an eye on it and try to wipe out the opposition as quickly as possible by attacking and tossing the Omnidroids into each other.

The first wave has three Omnidroids that will be easy to handle but the next has six: three on each side of the weapon. The third wave has five foes, but it features the upgraded robots with rocket launchers and flamethrowers. Grab one of the two deadly robots and toss it at the trio of basic Omnidroids.

After that last wave the secret weapon will activate, but it needs some time to prepare to launch. Continue to protect the device and keep an eye on its yellow energy bar to make sure it doesn't get destroyed.

New Toy Unlocked: Hover Board

The Sky has Fallen

Mission Giver: Mirage (radio)
Type: Fetch
Rewards: 350 Coins / 100 Sparks

The weapon worked and now Mirage wants the data core from one of the fallen Omnidroid's spawners to analyze it. Follow the compass just up the street to confront several robots around the core. Pick up the core and quickly make your way back to the HQ to place it on the scanner in front of the Research Station.

New Toy Unlocked: Grey Utility Truck

New Challenge Available: Defeat Omnidroids 2

Tech Research Part 2

Big Island

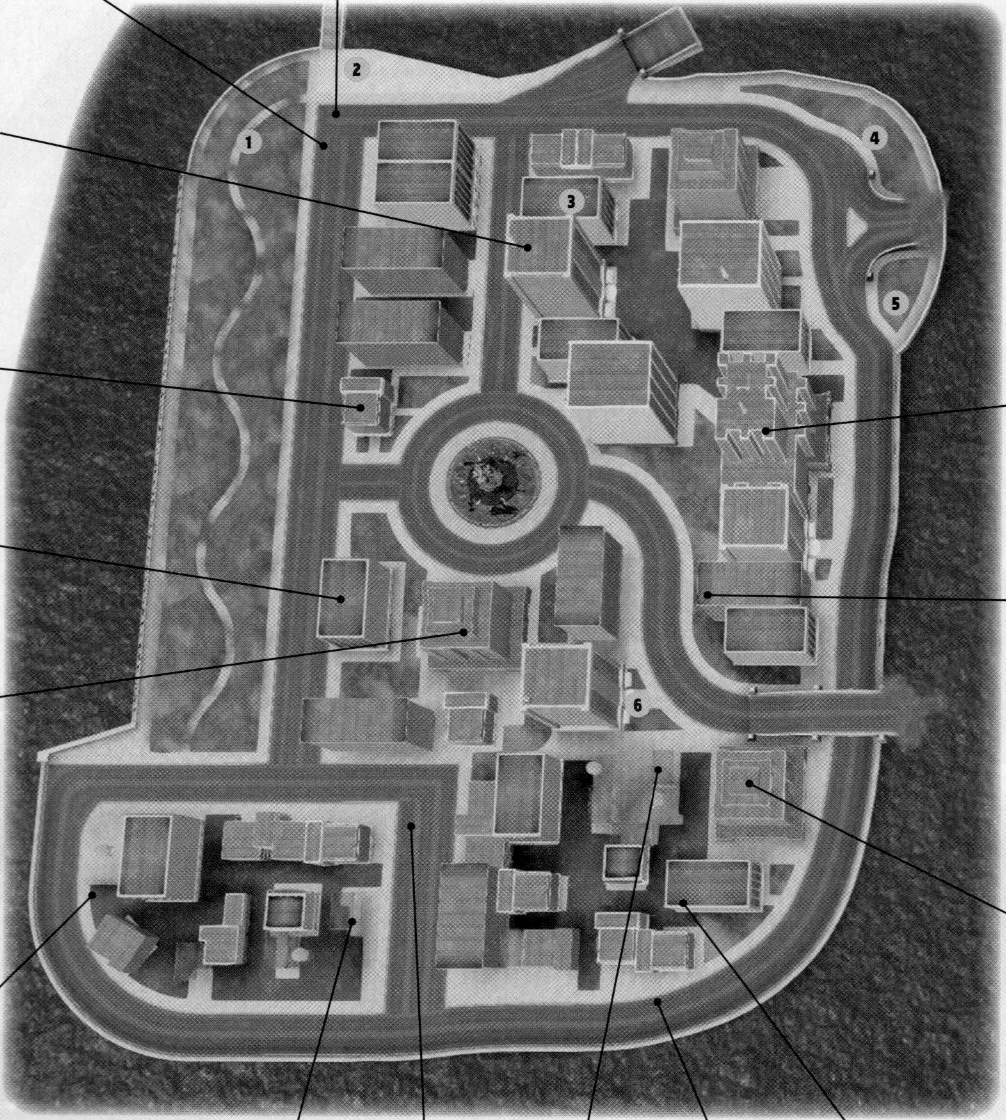

Pool Side 5

Core 4

Hoarder Chest

Hoarder Chest

Hoarder Chest

Hoarder Chest

Hoarder Chest

Hoarder Chest

Hoarder Chest

Pool Side 4

Hoarder Chest

Pool Side 3

Hoarder Chest

Core 5

Hoarder Chest

NOTE

Once the Big island is unlocked, several of the current mission paths can be completed. Missions such as Sprawling Sleep Pods and Technical Deliveries span both the Small and Big islands.

Challenges

1. Hover Board Hustle
2. Speed Battle
3. Eat My Dust
4. Go, Fight, Win
5. Power Punch
6. Glide 'n' Grab

Technical Deliveries

NOTE

This mission requires the Glide Pack or Hover Board to get to some objectives.

Mission Giver: Mirage (radio)
Type: Fetch
Rewards: 350 Coins / 100 Sparks

Thanks to the new weapon there are deactivated Omnidroid sky spawners all over the city. Track down five of them, smash them open, and return the cores to be scanned at the Research Station. The first one can be found right by the HQ. Take the elevator to the top and use the compass to drop down two levels to find it.

The next core is on the roof of a building near the water across from the docks.

Return to the rooftop where you met Mirage. Knock over the large blue-backed billboard to create a launching pad. From this spot, the goal is to hover or glide across the street below to the building to the left.

When you land, use the wall jump ability to bounce between two narrow sections of the building and gain access to the upper ledge.

Glide or hover from the ledge to reach the adjacent building with a scaffolding and collect the tricky core.

NOTE

The next two cores require access to the Big Island.

The fourth core is easy to find but the area is usually swarming with Omnidroids. Smash open the sky spawner and return the core to the Research Station.

The final core is located on the Big Island on the roof of a building adorned with blue glass windows; it is near the water's edge and close to a bridge. Expect to deal with lots of Omnidroids to obtain this core.

Hovering Heroes

Mission Giver: Mirage
Type: Buy
Rewards: 100 Coins / 25 Sparks

This mission is a reminder to get the Hover Board. If it is already purchased the mission will instantly be completed.

Mayor Side Mission

NOTE

Requires purchase of the Hover Board.

Island Getaway

Mission Giver: Cop
Type: Escort
Rewards: 100 Coins / 100 Sparks

Speak to the cop near the small pier to help escort the Mayor to the luau on his private island. This is a one-minute timed mission, so you need to act quickly. The situation can get complicated very quickly as one of Baron Von Ruthless's bombs conveniently arrives at that moment, turning the Mayor and other citizens into monsters. Look for the green arrow over the Mayor monster, attack him to change him back, and pick him up to get out of there fast.

Activate the Hover Board and drive off the pier, making sure to go over the red buoys. The Hover Board can't go over water for long, but going over the red floating objects resets the amount of time it can hover.

Crash Landing

Mission Giver: Edna (radio)
Type: Training
Rewards: 500 Coins / 100 Sparks

Something crash landed on the Big Island. Follow the compass to check it out. That "something" turns out to be a Tank Omnidroid that is bigger, tougher, and more powerful than its robot cousins. Its large metal claws will crush you if you are too close and not active enough to avoid them. But its main weapon is a long, powerful red laser. Circle around the large robot and dodge whenever necessary. The goal is to become a moving target to avoid its laser while providing a chance to attack from the side or back. Throwing objects at it can be effective, but the range of its laser can make that a bit of a challenge. There will be plenty more of these from now on, so take your time and learn how to hit and run.

New Toy Unlocked: School Bus

Side Mission

Protective Measures

Mission Giver: Edna
Type: Escort/Combat
Rewards: 100 Coins / 200 Sparks

Toss all ten of the criminals into the paddy wagon and protect it as it drives towards the HQ. Pick up the first criminal in the black-and-white stripes to get the wagon moving.

Make sure to smash the barricades to get some much needed help from the cops. Not only do you have to protect the wagon from the Omnidroids, but you have to collect the roaming criminals at the same time. The police can be a great distraction to keep the Omnidroids busy while you collect the men in stripes.

Don't spend too much time trying to clear out every robot because they keep on coming. Get the criminals into the paddy wagon and clear its path, including rasing the barrier on the bridge by pushing the large IN button.

Sensei Side Mission — Final Lesson

Straight Ahead

Mission Giver: Sensei
Type: Training
Rewards: 100 Coins / 100 Sparks

Your training has come along nicely and it's time to learn an advanced technique from the Sensei. This maneuver is a two-hit combo performed by pressing and briefly holding the attack button to launch the enemy in the air, and then pressing attack again to dash in and hit them as they land.

NOTE

This final training mission uses the same button commands for each character in the Play Set, but how they perform the move is unique to each character's personality.

Stranded Witness

Mission Giver: Edna
Type: Fetch/Customize
Rewards: 100 Coins / 50 Sparks

An informant is hiding out on a deserted island, but it's time to bring him to the costume shop and give him a new disguise. Use the compass to find the area, but it will not be that easy to get there, unless you wait until you have the helicopter. It is possible to get to the island using the Hover Board from the small nearby pier. If you time it just right and leap at the end you can make it to the island before you sink. The truly tough part is trying to get back to that small nearby pier with the informant. This will require a very well-timed jump to land on the pier before you run out of hover power.

The other route is actually part of a challenge and uses the red buoys to keep you hovering along. This can be a little tough at first, since you need to navigate several of them in a wide arch, but it is good option if the other path is too frustrating. Once the informant is back at HQ, give him a makeover to complete the mission.

Baron Von Ruthless Pursuit

Ruthless Discovery

Mission Giver: Rick Dicker
Type: Locate
Rewards: 100 Coins / 100 Sparks

Baron Von Ruthless has been spotted in the city. Track him down using the compass, but don't expect him to stand still. The Baron will quickly move to several key locations and you must follow him. The first spot to track him is on a building with brown brick bands and light-colored squares. Climb the pipe to make it to the rooftops.

From here, climb up the side of the billboard to make your way to the very top of the roof.

The hunt continues on a rooftop in the distance. This is a great spot to use the Hover Board to quickly travel from roof to roof.

Next, climb up a few vent shafts on that roof and slide across the black wire to another building. Make your way up to the top of the roof to finally find the Baron.

Bomb Scare

Mission Giver: Rick Dicker (radio)
Type: Locate
Rewards: 100 Coins / 50 Sparks

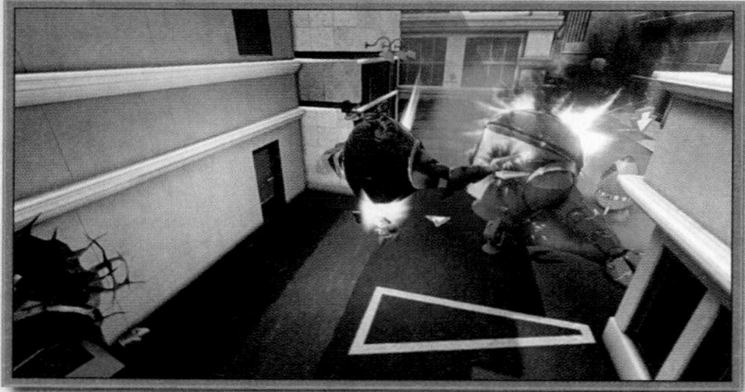

Baron Von Ruthless is living up to his namesake by placing a bomb that transforms citizens into monsters. If you just finished Ruthless Discovery, you can simply jump from the rooftop and land right next to the bomb. Take out any Omnidroids in the area and pick up the bomb to carry it near the water's edge. The only way to destroy the Baron's bombs are to immerse them in water. This fact will be very important in later missions.

Bombs Galore

Mission Giver: Rick Dicker (radio)
Type: Locate
Rewards: 500 Coins / 100 Sparks

You didn't think with a name like Baron Von Ruthless that he would settle for placing a single bomb, did you? He has upped the ante and placed four of them around the fountain on the Big Island. Use the compass to track them down and toss them into the fountain to destroy them.

The bombs will infect any citizen that gets close to the toxic fumes, turning them into green hulking monsters. To make matters worse, Omnidroids will swarm the scene, making it tough to carry the bombs to the fountain.

If you start to get overwhelmed, toss the bomb in the direction of the fountain and clear out any nearby threats to make it easier to get the bomb under water without getting harassed.

New Toy Unlocked: The Incredicar

Prisoner Capture Missions Part 2 Snoring Gloria Capture

Fountain of Trouble

Mission Giver: Rick Dicker
Type: Locate
Rewards: 100 Coins

Snoring Gloria has been spotted in the city near the fountain located on the larger island. Track her down with the compass and capture her.

New Toy Unlocked: Green Sports Car

Path to Justice

Mission Giver: Rick Dicker (radio)
Type: Locate
Rewards: 2,000 Coins / 200 Sparks

Snoring Gloria is in custody but needs to be transported to the prison. This is a simple mission, because you only need to locate the paddy wagon to complete it.

Escorting Gloria

Mission Giver: Cop
Type: Locate
Rewards: N/A

Gloria is securely in the wagon, and it's time to escort it and her to the HQ to throw her in the clink. However, this trip has an added complication—Baron Von Ruthless has placed bombs along the way. Follow the wagon and pick up the first bomb to chuck it into the fountain. The bombs must be disposed of in water to destroy them.

The paddy wagon won't move while there are bombs around it, and worse yet the bombs will transform the citizens of Metroville into green monsters. A few quick attacks will return the citizens to normal, but try to ignore them when bombs are present and focus on getting rid of the bombs causing all the problems.

Battle a group of Omidroids on the bridge and follow the wagon around HQ. There are still plenty of bombs to dispose of as well as tough Omnidroids to deal with. Try to stay a little ahead of the wagon to quickly grab the bombs and toss them in the water. Even this close to the HQ there are lots of citizens that can get affected, making it difficult to protect the wagon.

Once the wagon finally makes it to the HQ, pick up Gloria and toss her into the SuperMax Prison.

New Toy Unlocked: The Incredicopter

Baron Von Ruthless Capture

Hideout Discovery

Mission Giver: Rick Dicker
Type: Combat
Rewards: 100 Coins / 100 Sparks

Baron Von Ruthless has transformed himself into a monster and it will require heavy airborne firepower to change him back. Buy The Incredicopter to blast him and change him and his hulking monsters back to normal. Get in the copter and get familiar with the controls before following the red arrows. Look for the five green monsters with a red arrow above them. You may have to fly pretty low to locate some of these targets.

After the fourth target has been hit, Baron Von Ruthless will transform into a monster near the fountain. Blast him to turn him back to normal and destroy the Omnidroids in the area before landing The Incredicopter.

Baron Von Ruthless Transformed

Mission Giver: Cop
Type: Combat
Rewards: 2,000 Coins / 200 Sparks

You know the drill: escort the paddy wagon back to HQ, keeping it safe from Syndrome's attacks. The twist to this mission is that you can and should use The Incredicopter to provide support from above. Keep the wagon in sight at all times and destroy the Omnidroids in the surrounding area. Also, make sure to take out the barricades and enlist the help of the local police.

Throw the final villain in prison to put an end to Syndrome's evil distraction.

New Toy Unlocked: Zero Point Energy Gauntlet

All Out Attack

Mission Giver: NSA Agent
Type: Combat
Rewards: 100 Coins / 200 Sparks

Omnidroids are attacking all over the city. It's time to put that new helicopter to use! This is a timed mission that requires you to destroy 32 Omnidroids in seven minutes. While the Omnidroids are in groups, they are generally small groups and they are strewn through the Big and Small Islands as well as the HQ towards the end of the mission.

What makes the mission difficult is the distance they cover as well as the different altitudes. Some are way up on the rooftops while others are hiding amongst the streets and alleyways. Changing altitude is a slow process, so avoiding going too high or low in search of your targets.

Defeat Syndrome

Zero Point Power Up

Mission Giver: Mirage
Type: Buy/Combat
Rewards: 100 Coins / 50 Sparks

Thanks to all your valiant efforts, the secrets to Syndrome's Zero Point Energy weapon have been unlocked. Buy it at the Toy Store and get ready to put it to the test. Syndrome drops off several Omnidroids for target practice for your new toy. Get out of the middle of the group, quickly target one of the robots, and hurl it into the group of other droids. You can expect a lot of laser fire from these massive Omnidroids. The best thing you can do is get in back of them and toss them around to split them up. Don't bother trying to attack them. Just pick them up and toss them around as fast as you can.

The Final Showdown

Mission Giver: Cop
Type: Combat
Rewards: 2,500 Coins / 300 Sparks

The cop at the HQ thinks it's about time to take on Syndrome directly. Use the compass to track him down for a final confrontation. He is on top of a building that can be tricky to climb. Climb up to the rooftop near the building he is on and jump across to the scaffolding with the sunny billboard.

Slide across the black wire to the other scaffolding and climb the brown stone ledges on the light-colored building.

On the rooftop use the Hover Board to make it to the other side to find Syndrome.

Round 1

The first round against Syndrome starts out slow. He tosses purple energy balls that explode with a sizeable area of effect. To deal with this attack, continue running back and forth on the rooftop so he can't get a bead on you.

He will also drop two robots on the roof, but this is actually a good thing. Pick one up with your Zero Point Energy Gauntlet and hurl it at him!

Round 2

Syndrome will still toss the exploding spheres and drop a pair of droids on your side of the roof, but he has a trio of rocket-launching Omnidroids on his side that make it impossible to hit him until they are gone. Between Syndrome's attacks and the rocket barrage, it is very tough to have a chance to pick up one of the robots to throw at Syndrome. Remember that both of these attacks can be blocked as well as dodged.

Timing is everything during this battle and it takes practice and experience to know when you have a clean opportunity to toss one of the droids. The good news is that as you destroy the rocket-shooting robots on his side it becomes easier to launch your robots.

Round 3

For the final round, Syndrome calls in two laser-shooting Omnidroid Tanks. Luckily they are not as fast at firing their beams as the rocket Omnidroid Tanks were at shooting you. However, what they lose in speed they more than make up for in durability as it takes several hits from your robots to take out those laser-shooting tanks. Dodge the beams by racing back and forth, but make sure to have plenty of room to roll in either direction.

The most threatening attacks are the lasers, but there is a slight pause between when one Omnidroid finishes and the other fires. Use this delay as the prime time to toss one of your robots at them. Of course, Syndrome may throw one of his energy balls at that moment, but there is a good chance the robot you are holding would block it. It is important to note that you can use the robots on your side as a shield to some extent, but you are better off tossing them as soon as you get a chance.

When all of Syndrome's Omnidroid Tanks are gone, toss one last robot at him to finish him off.

Collectibles

Small Island

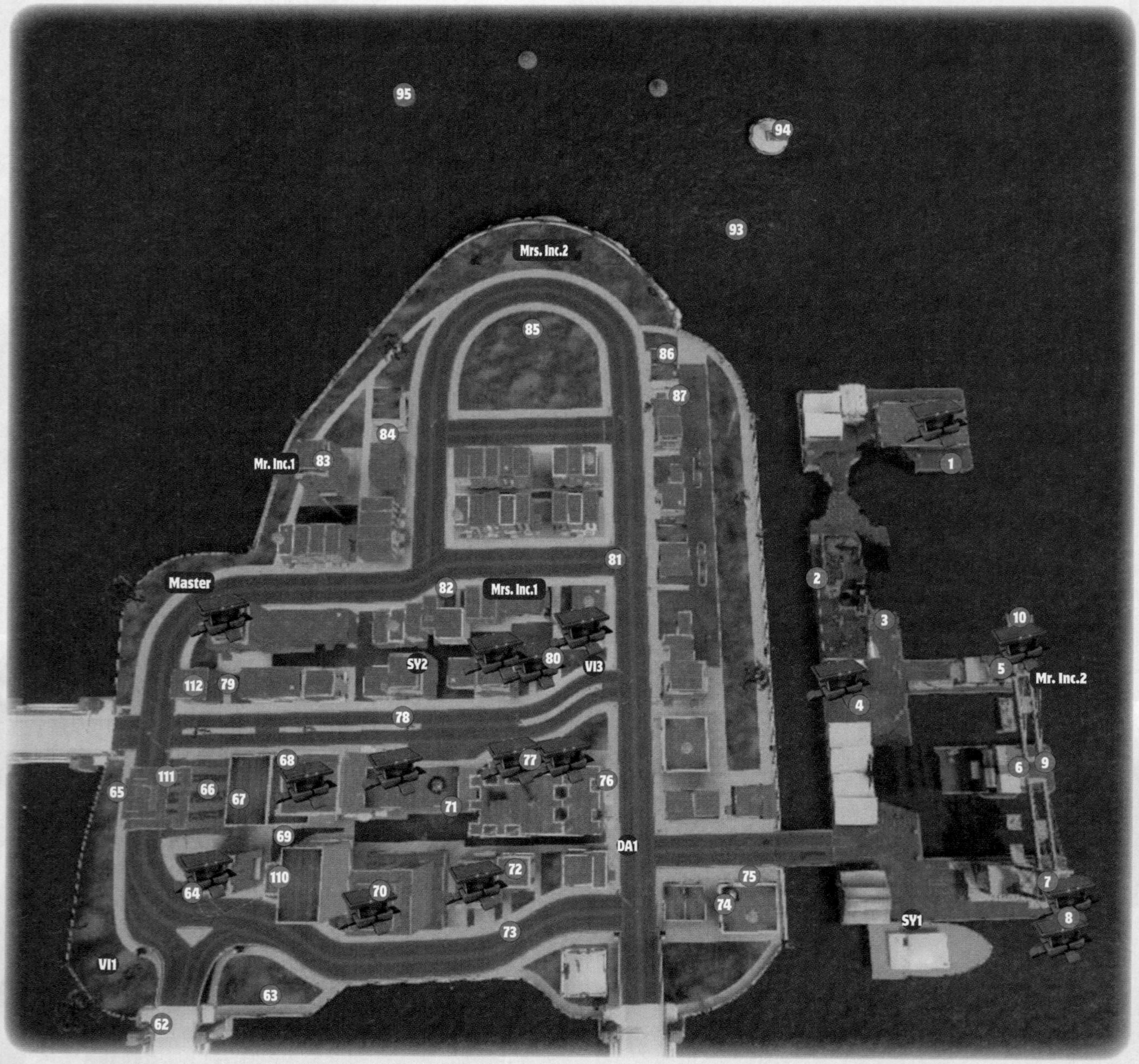

Red Capsules

#	Unlockable Item	Zone	Description
1	Fancy Suit	Metroville Docks	On the building directly to the left at the start.
2	Ice Cream Cone	Metroville Docks	Around the right side of the building in front of the start.
3	Boy Hero Body	Metroville Docks	Around the left side of the first building on fire.
4	Surgeon Hair	Metroville Docks	Hiding behind the crates in the main area of the Big Docks.
5	Surgeon Body (Surgeon Suit)	Metroville Docks	At the end of the dock under the first crane to the left.
6	Mad Scientist Hair	Metroville Docks	On the back side of the stack of cargo crates.
7	Chauffeur Head (Chauffeur Face)	Metroville Docks	At the end of the dock under the second crane to the left.
8	Construction Foreman Body	Metroville Docks	On the top of the crane that is nearest the boat.
9	Police Chief Body (Policeman Uniform)	Metroville Docks	In the air in between the two cranes.
10	Dark Dress	Metroville Docks	On the top of the crane that is nearest the starting position.

HQ

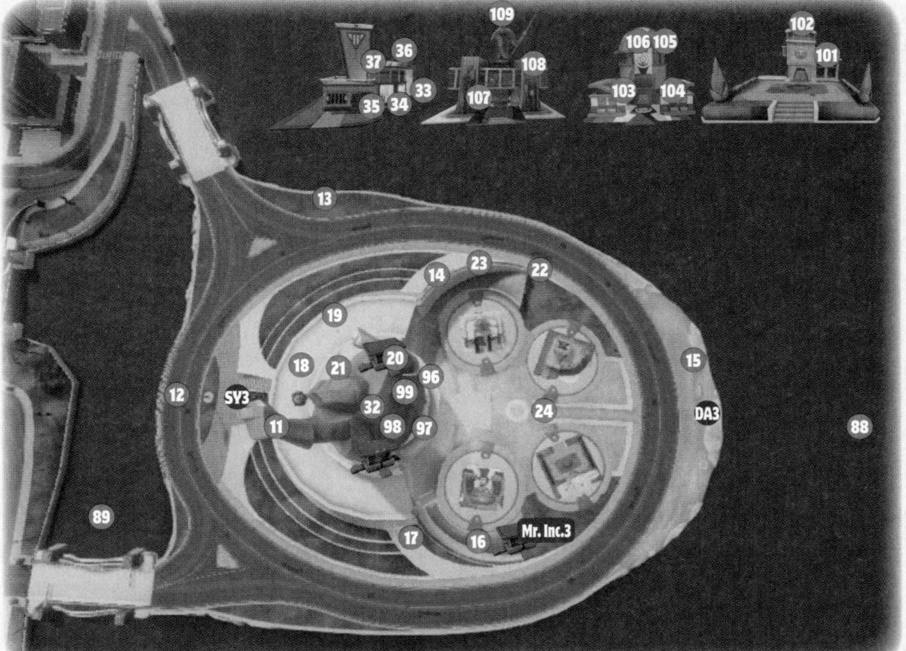

109
102
106 105
36
37
108
101
33
103
104
35
34
107
13
23
22
14
19
20
15
18
21
96
12
SY3
99
24
DA3
88
32
11
98
97
89
17
16
Mr. Inc.3

Big Island

92
91
115
90
42
30
41
DA2
40
29
31
117
43
44
28
116
46
38
25
47
39
VI1
26
49
50
27
51
48
45
114
57
52
58
60
56
59
53
54
113
55
Mrs. Inc.3
61

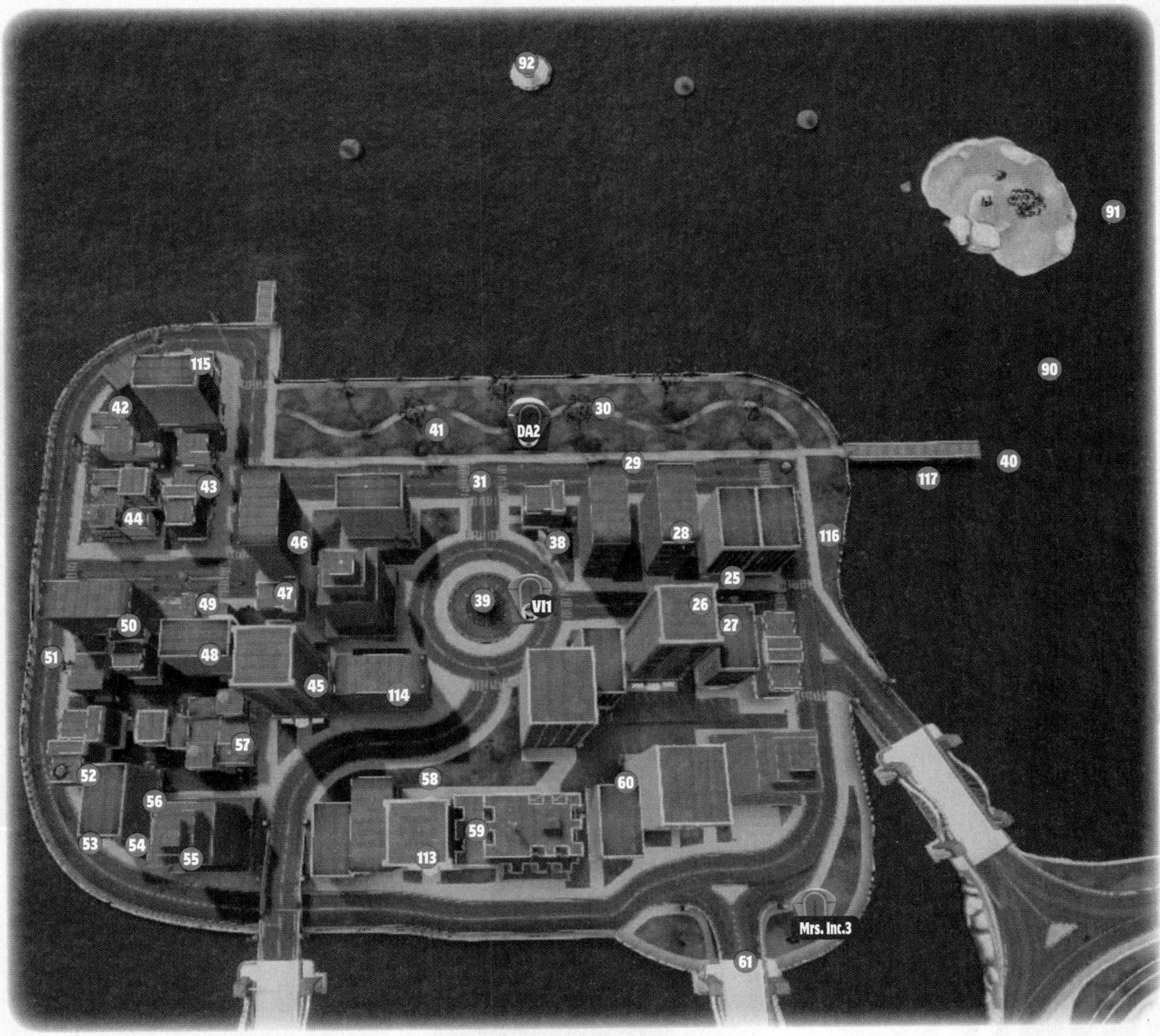

#	Unlockable Item	Zone	Description
11	Cute Dress	Metroville NSA HQ	On the right side of the wall at the base of the statue.
12	Medical Bag	Metroville NSA HQ	At the very top of the flagpole by the HQ.
13	Boy Outfit	Metroville NSA HQ	On the grass near the bridge leading to the Big Island.
14	Vest Outfit	Metroville NSA HQ	On the thin strip of grass to the left side of the HQ building.
15	Grey Hair	Metroville NSA HQ	Behind the HQ building on the dirt.
16	Old Lady Head (Old Lady Face)	Metroville NSA HQ	Behind the HQ building to the right.
17	Coffee Mug	Metroville NSA HQ	On the thin strip of grass to the right side of the HQ building.
18	Bald	Metroville NSA HQ	On the first tier of the HQ building in front of the statue.
19	Suit and Pocket Watch	Metroville NSA HQ	On the second tier of the HQ building in front of the statue.
20	Jackhammer	Metroville NSA HQ	On the third tier of the HQ building at the feet of the statue.
21	Syndrome Walls	Metroville NSA HQ	In the air by the fist of the statue.
22	Mad Scientist	Metroville NSA HQ	On the right side of the wall after opening the HQ.
23	Businessman Hair	Metroville NSA HQ	On the right side of the wall after opening the HQ.
24	Cute Face	Metroville NSA HQ	In the air above the HQ.
25	Fireman Head (Fireman Helmet)	Metroville Big Island	On the side of the building on the ledge facing HQ Island.
26	Female Happy Face	Metroville Big Island	On the ledge in front of the billboard.
27	Pink Nurse Hair	Metroville Big Island	On the building with the air vents jutting out facing HQ Island.
28	Construction Foreman Head (Face)	Metroville Big Island	On the knocked down railing that over looks the fountain.
29	Special Ops Body	Metroville Big Island	On the center billboard ledge by the fountain.
30	Underminer Walls	Metroville Big Island	In the grass along the pathway that goes along the waterline.
31	Construction Helmet	Metroville Big Island	On the power line near the fountain.
32	Policeman Face	Metroville NSA HQ	Behind the elevator in the HQ.
33	Mr. Incredible Captures The Hoarder (Captured The Hoarder)	Metroville NSA HQ	In front of the Super Max Prison.
34	Snoring Gloria	Metroville NSA HQ	In front of the Super Max Prison.
35	Baron Von Ruthless	Metroville NSA HQ	In front of the Super Max Prison.
36	Syndrome	Metroville NSA HQ	On top of the Super Max Prison.
37	The Hoarder	Metroville NSA HQ	On top of the Super Max Prison.
38	Nurse Outfit	Metroville Big Island	On the ledge near the billboard facing the fountain.
39	Superhero Walls	Metroville Big Island	At the top of the fountain in the Big Island.
40	Tiled Walls	Metroville Big Island	On the dock that is on the same side as HQ Island.
41	Superhero Accent	Metroville Big Island	In the grass along the pathway that goes along the waterline.
42	Boy Hero Hair	Metroville Big Island	On the window washing ledge facing away from the fountain.
43	Underminer Trim	Metroville Big Island	At the top of the building that views the entire length of the curved pathway.
44	Boy Hero Head	Metroville Big Island	On the roof of the building next to the road.
45	Masked Criminal Face	Metroville Big Island	On the ledge in front of the billboard facing away from the Big Docks.
46	Businesswoman Head (Business Woman Face)	Metroville Big Island	In the air atop of the skyscraper with elevators that is near the fountain.
47	Happy Guy Face	Metroville Big Island	On the knocked down railing that is by the skyscraper near the fountain.
48	Lavender Dress	Metroville Big Island	On the roof of the building at the bend of the road that leads to the Small Island.
49	Villain Hair	Metroville Big Island	On the roof ledge of the building at the bend of the road that leads to the Small Island.
50	Aviator Hair	Metroville Big Island	On the side of the building near the end of the Island on the same side as the Big Docks.
51	Underminer Accent	Metroville Big Island	Off the side of the tall building near the end of the Island on the same side as the Big Docks.
52	Executive Head	Metroville Big Island	On the billboard ledge that is facing the water.
53	Fireman Uniform	Metroville Big Island	On the edge of the building at the bend near the bridge to the Small Island.
54	Power Suit	Metroville Big Island	On a power line connecting two buildings facing the Big Docks.
55	Mayor Head (Mayor Face)	Metroville Big Island	On the edge of the building with elevators at the bend near the bridge to the Small Island.
56	Business Dress	Metroville Big Island	At the very top of the skyscraper nearest the bridge to the Small Island.
57	Hair and Glasses	Metroville Big Island	In the air off the pipe jump that is right next to the bridge leading to the Small Island.
58	Stubbly Head	Metroville Big Island	On a ledge of the building at the bend of the road facing the fountain.
59	Surfer Dude Hair (Surfer Hair)	Metroville Big Island	On the roof of the building in between both bridges leading to the Small Island.
60	Syndrome Accent	Metroville Big Island	On the knocked down railing that is at the top of the skyscraper near the bridge to Small Island.
61	Mayor Hair	Metroville Big Island	Under the bridge leading to the Small Island.
62	Surfboard	Metroville Small Island	Under the bridge leading to the Big Island.
63	Business Casual	Metroville Small Island	To the left of the bridge leading to the Big Island.
64	Face with Makeup	Metroville Small Island	On the roof of the building closest to the bridge leading to the Big Island.
65	Grey Suit	Metroville Small Island	On the roof of the building closest to the bridge leading to HQ Island.
66	Brushed Metal Trim	Metroville Small Island	In between two buildings along the road that leads directly to HQ Island
67	Monocle and Mustache	Metroville Small Island	High up in the air next to the skyscraper near the bridge leading to HQ Island.
68	Combat Trainer Head (Combat Helmet)	Metroville Small Island	On the roof of the highest building along the road to HQ Island.
69	Fireman Axe	Metroville Small Island	In the air off of the roof ramp between the buildings that are nested inside the two streets.
70	Happy Gentleman Face	Metroville Small Island	On the upper ledge of the skyscraper that is along the road to the Big Island.
71	Executive Hair	Metroville Small Island	On the window washing ledge facing the Big Island.
72	Mad Scientist Body (Mad Scientist Suit)	Metroville Small Island	On the roof of the building right across from the zoo.
73	Happy Lady Face	Metroville Small Island	In the air in between the zoo and the building across it.
74	Chauffeur Body (Chauffeur Suit)	Metroville Small Island	On the building with the water tower that is nearest the Big Docks.

#	Unlockable Item	Zone	Description
75	Fancy Handbag	Metroville Small Island	On the wall of the building with the water tower that is nearest the Big Docks.
76	Combat Trainer Sword	Metroville Small Island	High up the spider wall running up the skyscraper facing the Big Docks.
77	Spiked Hair and Glasses	Metroville Small Island	High up the spider wall running up the skyscraper facing the Park.
78	Combat Trainer Body (Combat Trainer Outfit)	Metroville Small Island	Off the antenna that is over the road that goes straight to HQ Island.
79	Chauffeur Hat	Metroville Small Island	On the building closest to the bridge leading to HQ Island.
80	Scientist Suit	Metroville Small Island	Near the air vent coming from the building.
81	Villain Face	Metroville Small Island	Floating on the power line that is parallel to the main street headed to the Park.
82	Villain Costume	Metroville Small Island	On the power line directly across from the other power line.
83	Fireman Face	Metroville Small Island	On the roof of the building by the Park that is facing HQ Island.
84	Businessman Face	Metroville Small Island	On the roof of the building nearest the Park.
85	Summer Outfit	Metroville Small Island	On the ground in the middle of the Park.
86	Combat Trainer Hair	Metroville Small Island	On the roof of the building to the right of the Park.
87	Pig Tails	Metroville Small Island	On the ground in between two buildings to the right of the Park.
88	Dark Hair and Round Glasses	Metroville NSA HQ	Out on the water behind HQ Island.
89	Policeman Hair	Metroville NSA HQ	Out on the water by the bridge to the Small Island.
90	Hair and Pearls	Metroville Big Island	On the water past the dock that is on the same side as HQ Island.
91	Frozone Wall	Metroville Big Island	On the water past the tiny island that is near the Big Island.
92	Combed Hair	Metroville Big Island	On the tiny island past the Big Island at the top of the radio tower.
93	Brown Hairdo	Metroville Big Island	On the water in between the Park and the tiny island.
94	Mayor Outfit	Metroville Big Island	On the tiny island behind the radio tower.
95	Briefcase	Metroville Small Island	On the far left red dinghy past the Park.
96	Syndrome	Metroville NSA HQ	At the base of the HQ building.
97	Mr. and Mrs. Incredible	Metroville NSA HQ	At the base of the HQ building.
98	Violet	Metroville NSA HQ	At the base of the HQ building.
99	Dash	Metroville NSA HQ	At the base of the HQ building.

Green Capsules

#	Unlockable Item	Zone	Description
100	Metroville Townsperson Toy Pack 1	Metroville NSA HQ	At the very top of the Super Max Prison.
101	Metroville Building Toy Pack 2	Metroville NSA HQ	On top of the Training Facility.
102	Metroville Building Toy Pack 3	Metroville NSA HQ	On top of the Training Facility.
103	Metroville Zoo Toy Pack	Metroville NSA HQ	On the Research Facility.
104	Metroville Building Toy Pack 1	Metroville NSA HQ	On the Research Facility.
105	Villain Toy Pack	Metroville NSA HQ	On the Research Facility.
106	Hero Toy Pack	Metroville NSA HQ	On the Research Facility.
107	Townsperson Toy Pack 1	Metroville NSA HQ	On Edna's Costume Shop.
108	Townsperson Toy Pack 2	Metroville NSA HQ	On Edna's Costume Shop.
109	Townsperson Toy Pack 3	Metroville NSA HQ	On Edna's Costume Shop.
110	Metroville Decorations Toy Pack 5	Metroville Small Island	On a ledge of the building facing HQ Island near the bridge to the Big Island.
111	Metroville Decorations Toy Pack 3	Metroville Small Island	On a ledge of the building near the bridge to HQ Island.
112	Metroville Decorations Toy Pack 4	Metroville Small Island	On a ledge of the building near the bridge to HQ Island.
113	Metroville Decorations Toy Pack 2	Metroville Big Island	On the roof of the skyscraper in between the two bridges to the Small Island.
114	Metroville Decorations Toy Pack 1	Metroville Big Island	On the roof top of the building across from the billboard near the fountain.
115	Metroville Plants Toy Pack	Metroville Big Island	On the building directly at the end of the curved walkway near the water.
116	Metroville Decorations Toy Pack 6	Metroville Big Island	On the ledge in front of the billboard near the bridge to HQ Island.
117	Metroville Building Toy Pack 4	Metroville Big Island	On the dock that is on the same side as HQ Island.

Infinity Chests/Vault

#	Unlockable Item	Zone	Description
Da-1	Dash Chest 1	Metroville Small Island	At the base of the building directly in front of the street to the Big Docks.
Da-2	Dash Chest 2	Metroville Big Island	On the grass near the curved walkway by the fountain.
Da-3	Dash Chest 3	Metroville NSA HQ	At the back of the HQ building past the road.
Master	Incredibles Avatar Vault - Reward 1	Metroville Small Island	On the roof of the building near the bend in the road headed to HQ Island.
Mr. Inc-1	Mr. Incredible Chest 1	Metroville Small Island	At the base of the building near the pathway to the bridge heading to HQ Island.
Mr. Inc-2	Mr. Incredible Chest 2	Metroville Docks	On the second level of the first crane.
Mr. Inc-3	Mr. Incredible Chest 3	Metroville NSA HQ	On the left side of the HQ base.
Mrs. Inc-1	Mrs. Incredible Chest 1	Metroville Small Island	On top of the building on the street headed to HQ Island with the water tower.
Mrs. Inc-2	Mrs. Incredible Chest 2	Metroville Small Island	In the grass area by the Park.
Mrs. Inc-3	Mrs. Incredible Chest 3	Metroville Big Island	By the bridge nearest HQ Island going to the Small Island.
Sy-1	Syndrome Chest 1	Metroville Docks	On top of the boat in the Big Docks.
Sy-2	Syndrome Chest 2	Metroville Small Island	On the top of the building with the white antenna.
Sy-3	Syndrome Chest 3	Metroville NSA HQ	At the base of the stairs to the front of the statue.
Vi-1	Violet Chest 1	Metroville Big Island	In front of the fountain.
Vi-2	Violet Chest 2	Metroville Small Island	In the grass near the bridge headed to HQ Island.
Vi-3	Violet Chest 3	Metroville Small Island	On the ground near the intersection.

The Incredibles Gold Stars

#	Type	Star Names	Star Description
1	Mission	Where There's Smoke...	Complete this mission.
2	Mission	The Secret of Heroes Island	Complete this mission.
3	Mission	Prisoner Delivery	Complete this mission.
4	Mission	No More Traps	Complete this mission.
5	Mission	Active Lifestyle	Complete this mission.
6	Mission	Animal Pandemonium!	Complete this mission.
7	Mission	Sprawling Sleep Pods	Complete this mission.
8	Mission	Science to the Rescue	Complete this mission.
9	Mission	The Power Within – Mr. Incredible	Complete this mission with Mr. Incredilble.
10	Mission	Fantastic Elastic – Mrs. Incredible	Complete this mission with Mrs. Incredilble.
11	Mission	A Burst of Speed – Dash	Complete this mission with Dash.
12	Mission	Vanishing Act – Violet	Complete this mission with Violet.
13	Mission	Zero Point Power Surge – Syndrome	Complete this mission with Syndrome.
14	Mission	Crash Landing	Complete this mission.
15	Mission	Escorting Gloria	Complete this mission.
16	Mission	Baron Von Ruthless Transformed	Complete this mission.
17	Mission	Technical Support	Complete this mission.
18	Mission	The Final Showdown	Complete this mission.
19	Collectibles	A Headache for the Hoarder	Find and break open 10 The Hoarder chests.
20	Collectibles	Trap Springer	Find and break open 20 The Hoarder chests.
21	Collectibles	Deliver 3 Tech Pieces	Find and deliver three tech objects to the Tech building.
22	Collectibles	Find 50 red capsules	Find 50 red capsules.
23	Challenge	Up for the Challenge	Complete ten Challenges on any difficulty.
24	Challenge	Super Challenge	Complete every Challenge on any difficulty.
25	Combat	Your Own Worst Enemy	Defeat an Omnidroid using another Omnidroid.
26	Combat	Zero Point Hero.	Defeat an Omnidroid using Zero Point Energy.
27	Combat	Heavy Landing	Damage multiple Omnidroids with a single Glide Pack Dive Bomb.
28	Combat	Chopper Dropper	Defeat multiple Omnidroids using a single Helicopter Bomb.
29	Combat	Pulse Power	Hit multiple Omnidroids with a single EMP shot from The Incredicar.
30	Combat	Omnidriod Destroyer	Destroy 50 Omnidroids.

The Incredibles Toy List

Toys	Toy Box Export	Toy Type	Commercial
Bridge 1	Yes	Unique	Yes
Super Max Prison	Yes	Building	Yes
Glide Pack	Yes	Prop	Yes
Tech Building	Yes	Building	Yes
Training Facility	Yes	Building	Yes
Hover Board	Yes	Prop	Yes
Edna's Costume Shop	Yes	Building	Yes
Bridge 2	Yes	Unique	No
Bridge 3	Yes	Unique	No
Bridge 4	Yes	Unique	No
Incredicar	Yes	Vehicle/Mount	Yes
Townspeople Newspaper Stand	Yes	Unique	Yes
Hot Dog Stand	Yes	Unique	Yes
Orange Car	Yes	Unique	No

Toys	Toy Box Export	Toy Type	Commercial
Bus	Yes	Unique	No
Green Sports Car	Yes	Unique	No
Grey Diesel	Yes	Unique	No
Pink Car	Yes	Unique	No
Ambulance	Yes	Unique	No
Health Upgrade 1	No	Unique	Yes
Health Upgrade 2	No	Unique	Yes
Incredicopter	Yes	Vehicle/Mount	Yes
Mr. Incredible's Sports Car	Yes	Vehicle/Mount	Yes
Zero Point Energy Toy	Yes	Held Item	Yes
Townspeople #1	Yes	Townsperson	Yes
Townspeople #2	Yes	Townsperson	No
Townspeople #3	Yes	Townsperson	No
Townspeople #4	Yes	Townsperson	No

Toys	Toy Box Export	Toy Type	Commercial
Townspeople #5	Yes	Townsperson	No
SH Townspeople 1	Yes	Unique	No
SH Townspeople 2	Yes	Unique	No
SH Townspeople 3	Yes	Unique	No
SH Townspeople 4	Yes	Unique	No
Mirage	No	Mission Giver	No
Sensei Townspeople	Yes	Mission Giver	No
SH Townspeople 5	Yes	Unique	No
Super Strength Gloves	No	Held Item	Yes
Sticky Hand	No	Held Item	Yes

Toys	Toy Box Export	Toy Type	Commercial
Dash Speed Boots	No	Held Item	Yes
Violet Invisibility Toy	No	Held Item	Yes
Townspeople Forklift	No	Unique	No
Purple Truck	No	Unique	No
Ice Cream truck	No	Unique	No
Super Ground Pound	Yes	Unique	No
Sticky Hand Ability	Yes	Unique	No
Super Speed Ability	Yes	Unique	No
Invisibility Ability	Yes	Unique	No
Zero-Point Energy Ability	Yes	Unique	No

The Incredibles Challenges

Name	Location	Description	Character	Requirements		
				Easy	Medium	Hard
Quick Ride	Next to the toy store	Pass through all the Challenge Gates before the time runs out.	Any	12 checkpoints in 1:00	12 checkpoints in 0:50	12 checkpoints in 0:45
Violet's Race Rally	Near the bridge leading to the HQ	Pass through all the Challenge Gates as Violet before the time runs out.	Violet	11 checkpoints in 1:00	11 checkpoints in 0:50	11 checkpoints in 0:40
Hovering Heroics	Near the bridge leading to the HQ	Using the Hover Board, pass through all the Challenge Gates before the time runs out.	Any-Hover Board	14 checkpoints in 0:55	14 checkpoints in 0:50	14 checkpoints in 0:45
Mrs. Incredible's Collector Challenge	Near the bridge leading to the HQ	Collect as many orbs as possible as Mrs. Incredible before the time runs out.	Mrs. Incred-ible	20 targets in 1:10	30 targets in 1:10	40 targets in 1:10
Bring the Punch	Just outside of the park going towards HQ	Defeat all the enemies before the time runs out.	Any	5 enemies in 2:00	10 enemies in 2:00	15 enemies in 2:00
Syndrome's Battle Bonanza	Park	Defeat all the enemies as Syndrome before the time runs out.	Syndrome	5 enemies in 1:30	10 enemies in 2:00	10 enemies in 2:00
Race Around Town	Park	Pass through all the Challenge Gates before the time runs out.	Any	8 checkpoints in 0:50	8 checkpoints in 0:35	8 checkpoints in 0:30
Combat Clash	By the Park clos-er to the docks	Defeat all the enemies before the time runs out.	Any	2 enemies in 2:30	4 enemies in 2:30	6 enemies in 2:30
Dash's Collect Mania	Main Street	Gather as many collectibles as you can as Dash before the time runs out.	Dash	20 targets in 0:50	30 targets in 0:50	40 targets in 0:50
Mr. Incredible's Glide Pack Challenge	Near the bridge leading to the HQ	Gather as many collectibles as you can as Mr. Incredible and using the Glide Pack before the time runs out.	Mr. Incred-ible-Glide Pack	70 targets in 1:15	80 targets in 1:15	90 targets in 1:15
Collect Crazy	In back of the HQ	Collect as many orbs as possible before the time runs out.	Any	70 targets in 1:15	80 targets in 1:15	90 targets in 1:15
Romp Around Town	In the back of the HQ	Pass through all the Challenge Gates before the time runs out.	Any	70 targets in 1:15	80 targets in 1:15	90 targets in 1:15
Blast From Above	On the other side of the road in front of the HQ	Use The Incredicopter to defeat all the enemies before time runs out.	Any-The In-credicopter	70 targets in 1:15	80 targets in 1:15	90 targets in 1:15
Power Punch	Near the bridge to the Small Island	Use the Glide Pack or Hover Board to defeat all of the enemies before time runs out.	Any-Glide Pack or Hov-er Board	10 enemies in 3:00	14 enemies in 3:00	16 enemies in 3:00
Go, Fight, Win	Near the bridge to the Small Island	Defeat the enemies before time runs out.	Any	5 enemies in 1:50	10 enemies in 1:50	15 enemies in 1:50
Eat My Dust	On a rooftop	Use The Incredicopter to go through all the Challenge Gates before the time runs out.	Any-Incredi-copter	16 checkpoints in 1:40	16 checkpoints in 1:30	16 checkpoints in 1:10
Hover Board Hustle	Near the path extending to the water	Pass through all the Challenge Gates using the Hover Board before the time runs out.	Any-Hover Board	18 checkpoints in 1:25	18 checkpoints in 1:15	18 checkpoints in 1:10
Speed Battle	Near the path extending to the water	Use The Incredicar to defeat all the enemies before time runs out.	Any-Incredi-car	12 enemies in 1:00	24 enemies in 1:00	34 enemies in 1:00
Glide 'n' Grab	Near the bridge leading to the Small Island near the docks	Gather as many collectibles as you can using the Glide Pack before your time runs out.	Any-Glide Pack	30 targets in 0:50	45 targets in 0:50	70 targets in 0:50

Pirates of the Caribbean

NOTE - For those playing Disney Infinity on the Wii, the Play Sets are a bit different. Access your free eGuide (voucher code on the insert) to access this content.

Rescue Gibbs and the Map

Treasure
Map
Clock Tower Lady
Navigator
Treasure
Mr. Gibbs
Deliveries
Dock

Challenges

1. Buccaneer Break
2. Brawl at the Bay
3. Buccaneer Bay Ballyhoo

Dock and Cover

Mission Giver: Automatic
Type: Sailing
Rewards: 50 Coins / 100 Sparks

Row the dinghy through town and find a safe place to dock. Simply follow the green compass arrow and you can't miss it.

We Know Where Gibbs Be!

Mission Giver: Pintel and Ragetti
Type: Combat
Rewards: 50 Coins / 100 Sparks

Smash through the crates with your sword and speak to Pintel and Ragetti. They know where Mr. Gibbs is (in jail), and he is critical if you ever hope to sail on a boat larger than that dinghy. Follow the men and take aim with your Flintlock Pistol to shoot open the gate.

Keeping following the men until you run into an ambush. There are three enemies to deal with, but some quick swordplay will wipe them all out while Pintel and Ragetti work on unlocking the next gate.

Rescue Master Gibbs!

Mission Giver: Pintel and Ragetti (automatic)
Type: Platforming
Rewards: 50 Coins / 100 Sparks

Mr. Gibbs is being held in the fort's prison tower. Run through the open gate and follow the compass up several staircases.

Wait for the convenient cannonball that blows away the debris blocking your path, and shoot the lock to open a gate.

Keeping climbing the stairs while wiping out small waves of enemies until you finally get to the tower that Mr. Gibbs is being held in.

Climb up the metal ledges near the blue tutorial capsule and work your way up and to the left around the trestle.

Finally, drop down over the doorway and shoot open the lock on the door to set Mr. Gibbs free. Make sure to run inside the cell to grab the Vengeance Mid Hull capsule that is needed for a side mission.

The Map's Hiding Place

Mission Giver: Mr. Gibbs (automatic)
Type: Platforming
Rewards: 50 Coins / 100 Sparks

Davy Jones is looking for the map, but luckily only Mr. Gibbs knows where it is at. Follow Mr. Gibbs and the green compass arrows to slide down a long rail.

The map is hidden in a cave above Mr. Gibbs' location. To get there, grab on to the thin edges in the mountain-side and leap up to the cave.

Unfortunately, you are a bit slow retrieving the map and Maccus, a hammerhead-looking beast, grabs the map for Davy Jones. Grab the red capsule that holds the Vengeance Front Hull next to the mapless chest.

Slew of Side Missions

I Wants to be a Navigator

Mission Giver: Educated Townsperson
Type: Customize
Rewards: 50 Coins / 50 Sparks

A well-educated man has studied the stars and maps and is ready to join a crew as a navigator. The only problem is he doesn't look the part. Not far from the man is a shop, next to a blue tutorial capsule, that can change people's appearance. However, before he can truly look like a navigator you need the proper customizations. The navigator's hats and body pieces are located near the Challenge beacon. One is under an awning near a lamppost and the other is next to the staircase. The last piece of this puzzle is just around the corner of the customizing shop. Pick the man up and throw him into the shop to change is body, head, and hat into a navigator.

Treasure Outside of Town

Mission Giver: Pintel and Ragetti
Type: Locate
Rewards: 200 Coins / 50 Sparks

There's a treasure hidden just outside of town and a quick pan of the camera gives you a clue. Use the compass to track the treasure near an archway on the beach.

Heavy Sleeper

Mission Giver: Pirate Townsperson (Man 1)
Type: Delivery/Fetch
Rewards: 50 Coins / 50 Sparks

A lazy pirate complains about not wanting to do anything, but at least he is kind enough to offer the cure to his dilemma. He says the only way to motive him is to toss him in the water. Oblige the man by picking him up and throwing him into the water.

Rid Us O' Them Crates!

Mission Giver: Pirate Townsperson (Man 1)
Type: Destroy
Rewards: 50 Coins / 50 Sparks

The lazy townsperson was true to his word and a quick dunk brought him back with another mission. The man is upset about the East India Trading Company trying to set up port in his town. He wants you to destroy all five EITC crates. The closest one is right next to a red capsule with the Vengeance Rear Hull.

The next one is on a balcony in back of the building where you just smashed the first crate.

Slide across a rail to the top of a building with a red capsule that has the Vengeance Sails. Leap down to the thatched roof and jump to the balcony to find the third crate.

Go over the nearby bridge with the red smoldering wreckage and leap down the side to find the fourth one.

This final one is a short distance away at the edge of a water wheel.

Ye Own Quest

Mission Giver: Pirate Townsperson (Man 2)
Type: Locate
Rewards: 50 Coins / 50 Sparks

If the last treasure wasn't exciting enough, now there is a special treasure with your very face on it. This treasure is actually a Vault/Chest but you don't have to open it, just get close. It by the blue tutorial capsule.

Treasure on the Trusses

Mission Giver: Pirate Townsperson (Man 2)
Type: Locate
Rewards: 50 Coins / 50 Sparks

One of the men rebuilding the fort mentioned that he saw treasure in the scaffolding. The chest you are looking for is near your ship and is not too far off. Jump down from your location and leap around the blockade on the stairs. Climb up the wooden scaffolding to locate the pirate chest.

Time Has Stopped

Mission Giver: Pirate Townsperson (Woman)
Type: Locate
Rewards: 50 Coins / 50 Sparks

Davy Jones destroyed the clock tower, and for some reason this woman wants to see it but can't get there. Pick her up like a human taxi and carry her there.

Time For Vengeance

Mission Giver: Pirate Townsperson (Woman)
Type: Locate
Rewards: 50 Coins / 50 Sparks

After seeing the clock tower, the woman mentions that if you collect all five parts of the ship *Vengeance* from red capsules, you can customize your own ship to look just like it. At this point you should have four parts, and the last one is by your ship. Climb up a pole to reach a high platform and rail slide across to find the Vengeance Theme on the other side.

Get a Ship and Set Sail

NOTE

If you are having trouble getting your bearings on the open sea, climb all the way to the top of the crow's nest and you can locate islands and land masses.

A Captain Needs a Ship!

Mission Giver: Mr. Gibbs (automatic)
Type: Buy
Rewards: 50 Coins / 100 Sparks

The only way to go after the treasure without the map is to speak to Tia Dalma who knows the route. Of course to visit her will require a ship and the money to pay for it. Go into the Toy Store and buy the ship as long as you have 600 coins to spare.

To actually get the ship in the water, you must pick it up from the delivery platform that can be found using the compass. Shoot open the locked gate and go pick up your pirate package.

New Challenges Available: Brawl at the Bay (Barbossa), Buccaneer Bay Ballyhoo

New Toy Unlocked: Player's Pirate Ship

Blast Ye Out O' the Cove!

Mission Giver: Mr. Gibbs (automatic)
Type: Ship Combat
Reward: 50 Coins

This is your first time on a big ship and you need to pay attention to all the tutorials to really master controlling the vessel and using its many views. Once you get the hang of it, get to the task at hand. There is a bunch of debris blocking your ship from leaving the cove. Open fire with the cannons to clear a way out.

What's our Heading?

Mission Giver: Mr. Gibbs (automatic)
Type: Sailing
Reward: 200 Coins

Set a course to visit Tia Dalma. She is the only person who can help you get your hands on the treasure before Davy Jones. She lives on an island called Pantano Bayou, which is right across from Buccaneer Bay, and the compass will guide you there. However, you can't dock until the attacking pirates have been sunk.

Ship Upgrade Side Missions

NOTE

Upgrades to your ship will happen automatically after you pick up the pirate package. However, new cannons must be swapped out with current ones at each station to take advantage of their unique abilities. Also, cannons can fire a single shot by pressing the attack button but if you hold that button you can charge up the attack and the cannons will fire several shots at once.

New Cannons

Long Range Cannons, a Must!

Mission Giver: Crew (Headband)
Type: Buy
Reward: 50 Sparks

One of the crew points out that far away ships would be a lot easier to hit if you bought the Long Range Cannon. The man is right; the increased range is very helpful for firing on ships that are normally too far away and can't fire back. This is a great upgrade and is well worth the coins. Go into the Toy Store and buy it as soon as you can afford to. After buying the cannon, you have to open the package and actually have to swap the cannon by going close to it and pressing the button to flip it to the next cannon.

New Toy Unlocked: Long Range Cannon

Get Ye a Flamethrowing Cannon

Mission Giver: Crew (Headband)
Type: Buy
Reward: 50 Sparks

Buy the Flamethrower Cannon and shoot flaming fury at anyone unwise enough to get within range.

New Toy Unlocked: Flamethrower Cannon

They Says Yer a Rat, Sir!

Mission Giver: Crew (Headband)
Type: Buy
Rewards: 1,000 Coins / 50 Sparks

Some braggart pirates told your crew that they could easily shoot your vessel out of the sea. Follow the compass to locate the braggart pirates and prepare to take on three waves of assault ships. This is a very rough battle and the only good news is that your ship will recover in between battles. The first wave has five ships.

Ain't No Cannon Like the Triple Shot!

Mission Giver: Crew (Headband)
Type: Buy
Reward: 50 Sparks

Triple Shot Cannons are not just three cannons shooting at once, the cannons alternate shots, essentially giving you rapid-fire machine-gun-like firepower.

New Toy Unlocked: Triple Shot Cannon

Upgrade Your Firepower

Hit Them With Another Broadside!

Mission Giver: Crew (Bald with eye patch)
Type: Buy
Reward: 50 Sparks

The bigger ships will be easier to take on with more Broadside Cannons. Essentially this can double your fire and is a must for any real pirate that expects to survive on the high seas.

New Toy Unlocked: Extra Broadside Cannons

More Gunpower!

Mission Giver: Crew (Bald with eye patch)
Type: Buy
Reward: 50 Sparks

The Blunderbuss is an upgraded gun that packs a big wallop. A single shot from this weapon can send enemies flying into the air.

New Toy Unlocked: Blunderbuss

Upgrade Your Ship

A Better Rudder, Cap'n

Mission Giver: Crew (Hat and beard)
Type: Buy
Reward: 50 Sparks

A new rudder will allow the ship to turn faster in battle and the increased maneuverability will help position your ship to maximize your firepower.

New Toy Unlocked: Rudder

A New Helm, Sir!

Mission Giver: Crew (Hat and beard)
Type: Buy
Reward: 50 Sparks

Get a new helm to move fast and stay quick while turning the ship.

New Toy Unlocked: Helm

We Need Us Some Fish!

Mission Giver: Crew (Hat and beard)
Type: Buy
Reward: 50 Sparks

A member of the crew intelligently points out that the sea is full of fish and it makes sense to get a fisherman onboard to catch them for the crew. Go into the Toy Store to buy the Fisherman.

New Toy Unlocked: Fisherman

Ship Combat Side Mission

Ship Off the Port Bow!

Mission Giver: Mr. Gibbs (automatic)
Type: Ship Combat
Rewards: 200 Coins / 50 Sparks

Upon entering the open seas you will almost immediately be drawn into your first naval battle. Hopefully you had enough coins to upgrade your cannons or buy the long-range version. Even without any upgrades this won't be a tough battle if you can circle around the ships and blast them in the front while you unload with your Broadside Cannons. There is one wave of three ships and you will know the battle is won when you hear Mr. Gibbs bellow, "Patch her up lads".

Masts at the Ready

Mission Giver: Mr. Gibbs (automatic)
Type: Buy
Reward: 50 Sparks

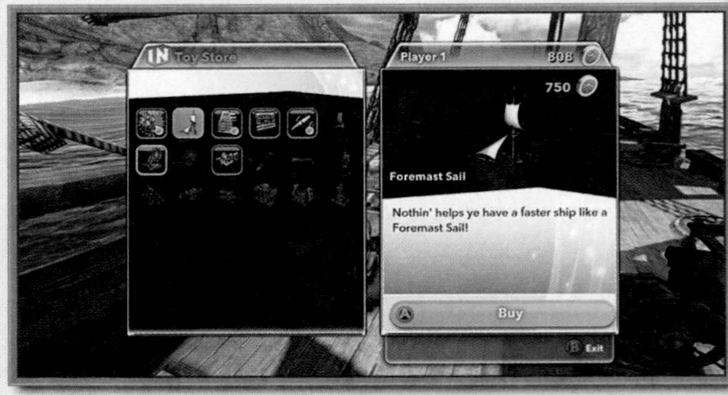

Purchase the Foremast Sail from the Toy Store to increase the speed of your ship.

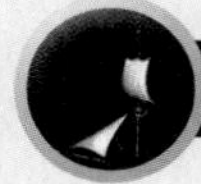

New Toy Unlocked: Foremast Sail

Ship Customizing Missions

A Facelift for the Ship!

Mission Giver: Crew (Big hair)
Type: Buy
Rewards: 500 Coins / 50 Sparks

A member of the crew is itching to get the ship a new look. He suggests that as you travel, pick up new pieces to make the boat look ship-shape. Change the appearance of the ship by going to the delivery area on the boat and selecting Customize. As you gain more pieces from capsules, you will be able to make additional alterations to your ship. You should have several themes available at this point. Change to any one of them to complete the mission.

One Ship, Many Faces

Mission Giver: Crew (Big hair)
Type: Buy
Rewards: 1,000 Coins / 50 Sparks

This guy must have been an interior decorator before becoming a pirate. He wants you to collect more pieces to develop more looks for the ship. To meet the requirements of this mission you need to collect five different complete themes, which will require you to visit many of the small islands. Check out the collectibles map and data at the end of the chapter to find all of the pieces.

Darken the Sails

Mission Giver: Crew (Big hair)
Type: Buy
Rewards: 1,000 Coins / 50 Sparks

This final makeover for the ship is to collect all the black ship pieces to turn it dark. Check out the collectibles map and data at the end of the chapter to find all of the pieces.

Pantano Bayou

Statue Piece 3
Dock
Pads
Statue Puzzle
Kraken's Bane
Dock
1
2
Dinghy
Dock
Statue Piece 2
Dock
Statue Piece 1
Stinky Man
Tia Dalma
Button
Cave

Challenges

1. Shootin' Up the Swamp
2. Pantano Bayou Dash

Find Tia Dalma

Mission Giver: Mr. Gibbs
Type: Locate
Rewards: 50 Coins / 100 Sparks

Use the dinghy to sail up the river of the bayou to find Tia Dalma's home. Use the onboard cannon to shoot any of the nasty bomb-tossing turtles and floating debris.

Dock the ship and take out a tougher pair of enemies that can block. Rather than get into a battle of attrition, block their attack and counter with a combo.

Continue to follow the compass and climb up the wooden ladder to find Tia Dalma.

Help Me an' I Help You

Mission Giver: Tia Dalma
Type: Platforming
Rewards: 200 Coins / 100 Sparks

Tia tells you the importance of the map and finding the five pieces of the Kraken's Bane. However, before she tells you where to look for them she has a statue that needs fixing and you're just the pirate for the job. Jump down from her treetop dwelling and leap across a small gap.

Leap up to a thin edge on a rock wall and follow it all the way around to the left. Jump down to encounter the Stinky Man and follow the path up several plateaus.

Eventually you will find the wooden ladder that leads to the first piece of the statue—the head. Wipe out the turtle guard and grab the head, which will teleport to its proper place next to the ladder leading up to Tia Dalma.

Slide down the nearby yellow rope that places you right where the statue will reside. From here, the second piece is in the same direction as the docks, but up a narrow ramp instead.

Follow the compass to cross two small bridges and leap up a series of ledges to find the second piece of the statue—a skull-like hunk of stone.

Run around the corner of the tree to find a rope that you can slide down to reach a stone structure in the middle of the swamp. Climb up the stony ruins and use the rail slide technique once more to reach the final piece. Take note of the nearby gate with a bomb symbol on it. You can't open these types of doors yet, but on your return trip you will have the ability to do so.

The statue will re-form near the base of the ladder to Tia Dalma. Go back to her now that it has been restored and learn about the five pieces of the Kraken's Bane.

Side Mission

He Smells of Fetid Chum

Mission Giver: Stinky Man (Man in hat)
Type: Fetch
Rewards: 50 Coins / 50 Sparks

A man has been fishing for days on end and smells like low tide on a hot day. Pick him up and toss him in the swamp to clean him off.

The First Piece of the Kraken's Bane

De First Piece O' De Bane

Mission Giver: Tia Dalma
Type: Platforming
Reward: None

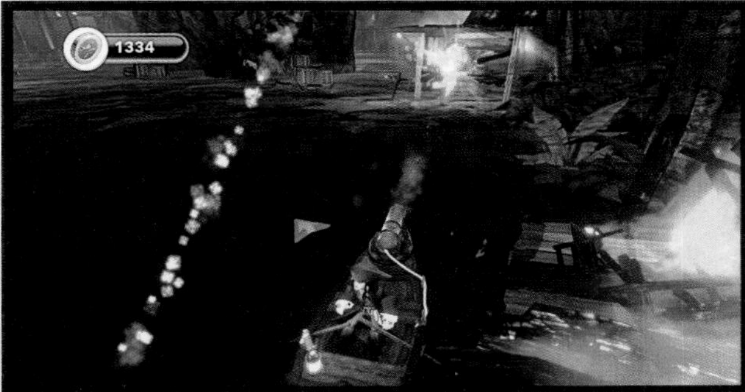

The five pieces of the Kraken's Bane is your only hope to defeat Davy Jones. Now that Tia Dalma is satisfied with your efforts, she tells you that the first piece is located in the ruins and the compass will guide you there. Jump down from her tree house and hop back in the dinghy. Tia has raised a water gate that grants access to the ruins and it's time to row, row, row your boat to check them out.

As you sail through the bayou, shoot the floating debris and blow up the bomb-chucking turtles as you go.

Dock the boat and go up the ramp or the nearby ladder to the ridge above. There is a lady here offering the Missin' Me Sister side mission as well as a gate that requires pressing a hidden button to gain access.

Drop the lady off by her sister and climb the snake rope near the gate right next to the blue tutorial capsule. At the top of that ridge is an IN button that opens the gate below. There is a bunch of booty in the little cave you just unlocked as well as the El Caleuche Rear Hull.

Back on the trail of the first Bane piece, go into the temple ruins and wipe out several swordsmen and a bomb-throwing turtle. You are safe from the bombs as long as you stay under the roof of the ruins and that is a great spot to wipe out the swordsmen. When they are gone, block any incoming explosives until you wall jump up to the turtle and take it down.

Run down a long ramp and break out the Flintlock Pistol to shoot a few enemies in the distance. The gun is a great weapon at long range, but you have to be pretty quick on the draw or the swordsman will charge you and cut you down. There is another bombable lock you can't open in this area, but continue your journey under the ruins.

Welcome to your first puzzle! There is a large statue in the center of this area that must be rotated into the proper position to get to the piece of the Bane at the top. Standing on the pads placed around this statue will rotate its sections. To solve the puzzle, you have to notice which sections move as you step on each pad.

The pad in front of the statue rotates the top two segments counter-clockwise 90 degrees.

Jump up a few ledges and slide across a line to get to the second pad that spins the entire statue counterclock-wise.

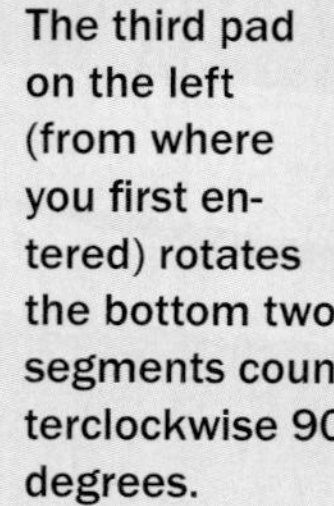

The third pad on the left (from where you first entered) rotates the bottom two segments counterclockwise 90 degrees.

Now that you know how the pads move the statue, the first objective is to line up the statue so all the faces are aligned. This can be done by getting two pieces correct and then spinning those two in order to line up with the third. Start by trying to line up the bottom and middle pieces by repeatedly stepping on the center pad.

With the bottom two pieces aligned, go to the pad on the left and turn both of these pieces until they line up with the top.

After all pieces are lined up, go to the pad on the right across the wire and keep turning it until the entire statue is in the correct position.

The spherical top of the statue will blow apart, revealing the first piece of the Kraken's Bane. The faces of the statue will act as ledges you can climb to reach it.

New Toy Unlocked: Atlas Blade

New Challenge Available: Pantano Bayou Dash

Side Mission

Missin' Me Sister

Mission Giver: Female Townsperson (Woman with hair net)
Type: Fetch
Rewards: 50 Coins / 50 Sparks

The woman is in dire straits because her sister needs her and apparently she has lost the ability to walk. She needs you to pick her up and carry her to her sister near the docks. It's a short trip and all you need to do is hoist her overhead and drop off the edge near the ladder to find her sister.

Dere Are More Pieces!

Mission Giver: Tia Dalma (automatic)
Type: Locate
Reward: 100 Sparks

Ride the wires all the way down to the dock area where Tia Dalma awaits you. The next piece of the Bane is at Fort St. Grande on the other side of Demon's Cape. The rocks blocking the entrance to the Demon's Cape will crumble into the sea to allow passage into the mysterious area.

A metal gate will open allowing you to leave.

NOTE

This opens two mission paths that send you in search of the rest of the pieces of the Kraken's Bane. One path takes you to Fort St. Grande (It's At Fort St. Grande!) and the other leads through Demon's Cape (Demon's Cape Sounds Invitin'), which has two more missions.

Tia Dalma Side Missions

Lost Me Some Light

Mission Giver: Tia Dalma
Type: Fetch
Rewards: 200 Coins / 50 Sparks

The Ore of Light is a powerful metal that glows. Tia Dalma wants your help collecting five pieces that are located around her hut. Jump up on the top of her house to collect the first and leap down for the second.

The third one is on the tip of a branch and the fourth is near the right side of the house.

The final one is on a little platform on a branch above the tree house.

Dis' Swamp is a Mess!

Mission Giver: Tia Dalma
Type: Destroy
Rewards: 200 Coins / 50 Sparks

Clean up all the wreckage littering the island and Tia Dalma will give you a reward. Go back to the dinghy and follow the compass to navigate the swamps and shoot six piles of debris.

New Challenge Available: Shootin' Up the Swamp

You Wan' Magic? So Do I

Mission Giver: Tia Dalma
Type: Locate
Rewards: 500 Coins / 50 Sparks

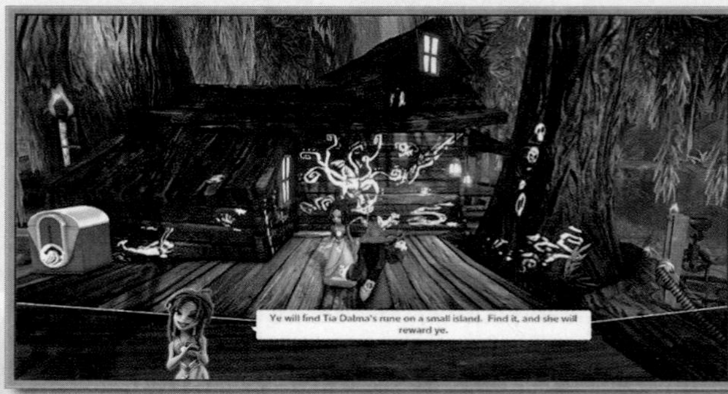

Tia Dalma's Magic Rune is on a small island, but you can't get there yet.

This mission leads to Port Talon Island. Tia Dalma will greet you at the entrance to a cave, and when you blow up the fiery mess in the middle and open the chest, the gates will slam closed. There are three pirates to take down if you want to leave this cave with the Magic Rune.

NOTE

This next mission unlocks when you return to Pantano Bayou and speak to Tia Dalma after collecting the rune she requested.

Rid Me O' Dem Pirates!

Mission Giver: Tia Dalma
Type: Ship Combat
Rewards: 1,000 Coins / 50 Sparks

After completing that rune fetching mission, return to Tia Dalma for one last side mission. Several pirate ships have swarmed Pantano Bayou and she needs you to get rid of them. There are three waves of ships to deal with and it is a good idea to move out a bit further to create some distance and let the range of your cannons keep them at bay. Also, don't forget to use your power-up items you earned from other missions. They can easily wipe out one ship while you focus your guns on another.

Fort St. Grande

1
2

Crate Side Missions

2nd Piece of Kraken's Bane

Fort

Challenges

1. Gatherin' Grande
2. Rally on the Fort

It's at Fort St. Grande!

Mission Giver: Tia Dalma
Type: Locate
Rewards: 200 Coins / 100 Sparks

This mission will be completed when you get close to Fort St. Grande.

Send Them to the Depths!

Mission Giver: Mr. Gibbs
Type: Combat
Reward: 500 Coins

Other ships are already circling Fort St. Grande and they happen to be Navy ships. If you can destroy them you can salvage the pieces to make your boat look like one from the Royal Navy. There are two waves of ships to destroy and it's best to keep moving to avoid taking too much damage in each wave. Wipe out the first wave of three ships and prepare for the next battle.

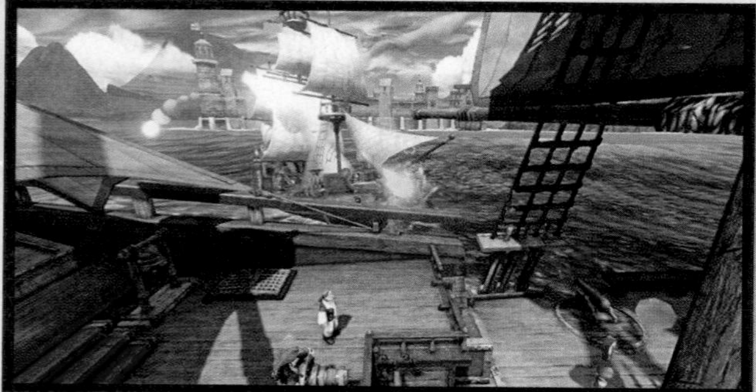

Wave two has only one ship to deal with, but it has a lot of Broadside Cannons.

Goin' in Under Cover

Mission Giver: Crew (Big hair)
Type: Customize
Rewards: 200 Coins / 100 Sparks

To sneak into Fort St. Grande and infiltrate it, make your boat look like a Royal Navy vessel by customizing it from the ship menu and selecting the Royal Naval Theme Pack. Dock at the fort under cover and disembark to complete the mission.

We Be in the Navy Now

Mission Giver: Pirates (automatic)
Type: Locate/Combat
Rewards: 200 Coins / 100 Sparks

When you set foot on land, a mission will automatically appear to get to the top of the fort. Even though your ship is camouflaged, your character is not. It is probably a good idea to avoid the naval townspeople and go around the ledges to the left.

Take the long way around to the fort by following the outside perimeter close to the city wall and climbing up a rickety-looking ladder.

Continue the journey to the top of the fort, climbing another ladder. Davy Jones' crew will assault the city. Jump up on some crates and climb a ladder up the side of a small tower to reach a ledge at the top of the fort.

Defend the Fort!

Mission Giver: Pirates (automatic)
Type: Combat
Reward: 100 Sparks

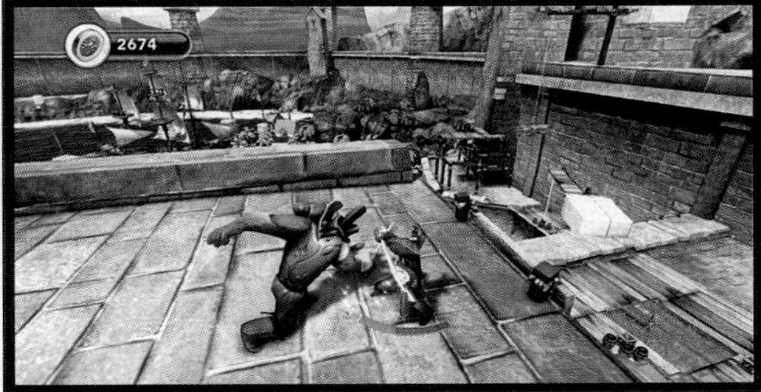

At the top of the Fort, Davy Jones' men will greet you with swords. There is a new enemy with extra armor along with a pair of swordsmen. Try to knock the swordsmen off the ledge you are on or wipe them out quickly to deal with the new enemy that is the real threat. This new oyster-looking foe has a very long sword that adds to its range when using its leaping attack. Don't take any chances with this tough enemy—simply block and wait for it to attack, then counterattack with a three-hit combo.

Go inside the fort tower and leap up the wooden support beams and binding rope to make it to the top next to an IN button.

Hit the button to open the gate and continue your ascension, climbing a wooden structure to reach the very top of the Fort.

Waiting for you on the top of the fort is Maccus, the one who stole the map back in Buccaneer Bay. Block and wait for Maccus to stop attacking—Maccus can strike three times in a row—before you counterstrike with a two-hit combo of your own.

Maccus' other attack is a rolling move that ends with the hammerhead leaping out at the end. If you can dodge this move, Maccus is very vulnerable to strikes on his back while he is stunned.

Second Piece O' the Kraken's Bane

Mission Giver: Tia Dalma (automatic)
Type: Combat
Rewards: 2,000 Coins / 250 Sparks

Make your way back down using the rail slide technique several times and confront Maccus once again. He won't do the rolling attack here, but he has a new trick that consists of shooting you at close range. Block this attack as well as his sword swipes and resort to countering.

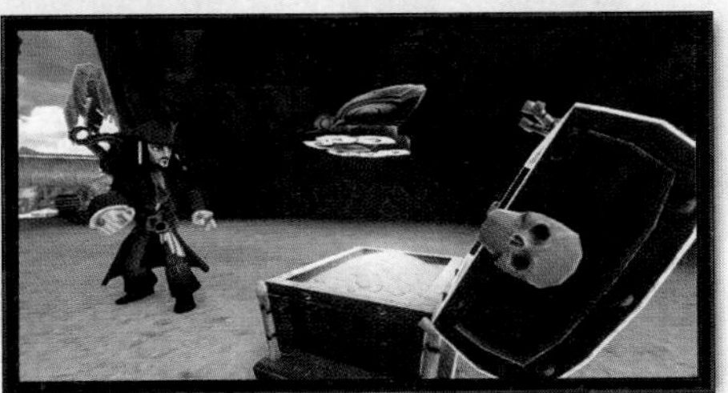

After taking enough damage, you can make a break for the ladder nearby and finally find the chest with the second piece of the Kraken's Bane. At the end of the mission is another ship upgrade that is a great buy for making travel quicker on the open seas.

New Toy Unlocked: Speed Burst

As soon as you set sail from Fort St. Grande, expect the Royal Navy to engage you in ship-to-ship combat. There are only a few ships to deal with, and if you'd rather not fight use the Speed Burst to run away.

New Challenges Available: Gatherin' Grande and Rally on the Fort

Side Mission

Fightin' Fish for the Fort

Mission Giver: Generic Pirate man and woman - Automatic after returning to the fort after getting the Kraken pieces from Dead Man's Cove and Shipwreck Shoals
Type: Combat
Reward: 500 Coins / 50 Sparks

Head up to the top tier of the fort to battle Davy Jones's crew. There are a lot of fishmen to deal with and it is a good idea to block to prevent being overwhelmed. Wipe them out one at a time to even the odds.

Journey to Demon's Cape

Demon's Cape Sounds Invitin'

Mission Giver: Tia Dalma
Type: Locate
Rewards: 500 Coins / 100 Sparks

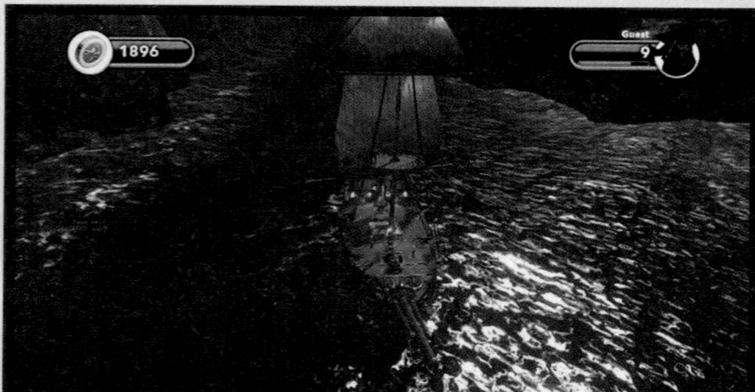

Set sail through the dark and mysterious passage on Demon's Cape. After sailing through the entrance it will automatically put you on the other side of the sea.

New Toy Unlocked: Mizzen Mast Sail

As soon as you emerge from the Demon's Cape, a bunch of pirates will attack. Circle around the ship and try to avoid lining up side by side. Hit the enemy at the front of their ship where they have fewer cannons.

NOTE

There are two paths to take after going through the Demon's Cape and each one holds a piece of the Kraken's Bane. Head out to Dead Man's Cove (Off to Dead Man's Cove!) or the Shipwreck Shoals (Da Next Piece Awaits Ye).

Find the Shipwreck Shoals

Da Next Piece Awaits Ye

Mission Giver: Tia Dalma
Type: Buy
Rewards: 500 Coins / 100 Sparks

After sailing through the Demon's Cape, make your way to the Shipwreck Shoals to find the next piece of the Kraken's Bane.

Who Needs Voodoo? You Do

Mission Giver: Tia Dalma
Type: Buy
Rewards: 100 Sparks

Set sail through the dark and mysterious passage on Demon's Cape. After sailing through the entrance, it will automatically put you on the other side of the sea. Tia Dalma will chime in about a very special type of cannon that can be purchased. This is not an optional upgrade, and is required in order to protect Tia Dalma as she pulls the wreckage from the sea.

Buy the cannon, open the package, and make sure those cannons are active for the next mission. The only way to take down the ghostly sunken ships is with the Voodoo Cannon.

New Toy Unlocked: Voodoo Cannon

Keep the Sea Witch Safe

Mission Giver: Tia Dalma
Type: Buy
Rewards: 1,000 Coins / 100 Sparks

Blast the attacking sunken ships so Tia Dalma can get the piece of the Kraken's Bane. There are nine ships to sink, so don't expect a quick battle to get the next piece. For a real thrill, man one of the Voodoo Cannons yourself and shoot ghostly skulls at the enemy ships.

> **NOTE**
>
> **Tia Dalma will raise a sunken shipwrecked island right out of the sea, but it won't stay for long. Search the island for the next piece of the Kraken's Bane quickly.**

Find the Next Piece on Shipwreck Shoals

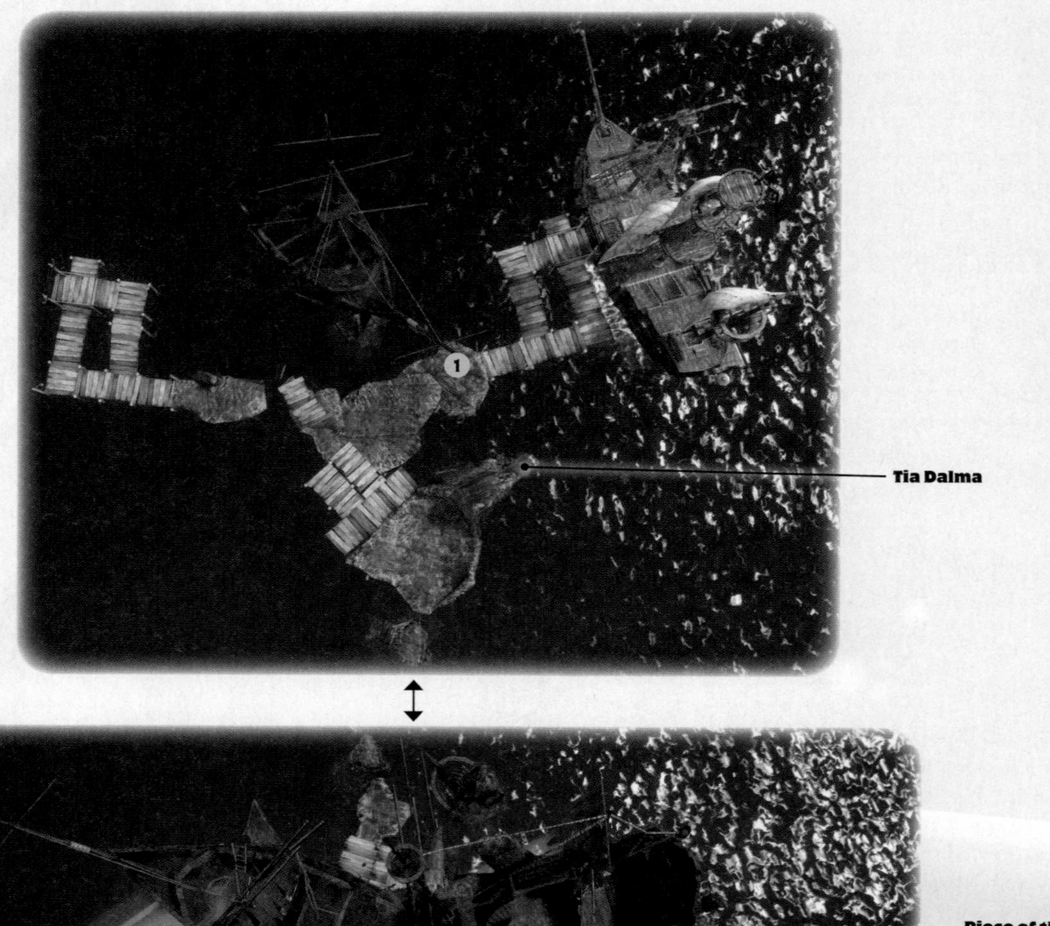

Piece of the Kraken's Bane

NOTE

The pieces for the Sunken Ship Theme are located on this island, and you need to make sure you collect them all before you leave.

Challenges

1. Scurry on the Shipwreck

On the Ship O' the Dead

Mission Giver: Mr. Gibbs
Type: Locate
Rewards: 200 Coins / 100 Sparks

The sunken ship island will only last for a short time. Disembark your ship and search the outlining area of the island for capsules before you make your way to the main path.

Bane From Beneath

Mission Giver: Mr. Gibbs
Type: Platforming
Rewards: 2,000 Coins / 250 Sparks

Leap up a few ledges and climb up the ropes to the top tier. At the top, make sure to grab the Sunken Ship Theme in a capsule to the left.

Go up a few more ledges and use the Blunderbuss to blow away some pirates. Look out for the bomb-tossing turtle that has as much range with its bombs as you have with your gun.

Leap up another web of ropes and climb hand over hand to collect the Sunken Shipwreck Rear Hull from a red capsule. Leap up the ledge to find the chest with the next piece of the Kraken's Bane.

Opening the chest allows you to collect Calypso's Rage, which is one of several power-ups that can be placed on the ship to provide a new feature. This one allows you to create a storm that turns the sea against your enemy.

New Toy Unlocked: Calypso's Rage

Back to Me Ship!

Mission Giver: Mr. Gibbs
Type: Platforming
Rewards: 200 Coins / 100 Sparks

Grabbing the Kraken's Bane will trigger the island to slowly start to sink, and it's time to get out of there fast. Slide down a few wooden poles to get off the sinking island, but only after you have all five pieces of the Sunken Ship Theme.

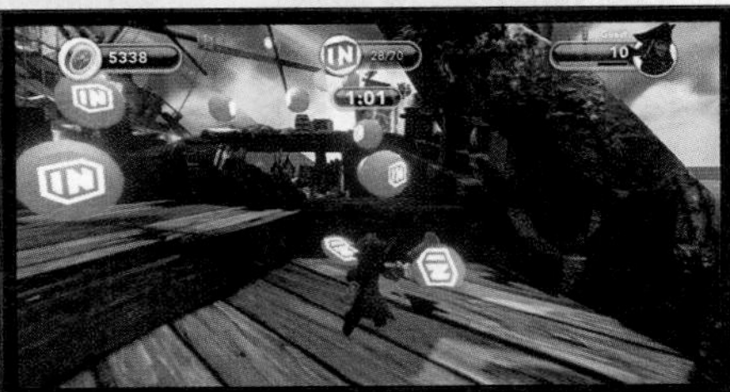

Even though most of the island will sink, the challenge Scurry on the Shipwreck will still be available.

Dead Man's Cove

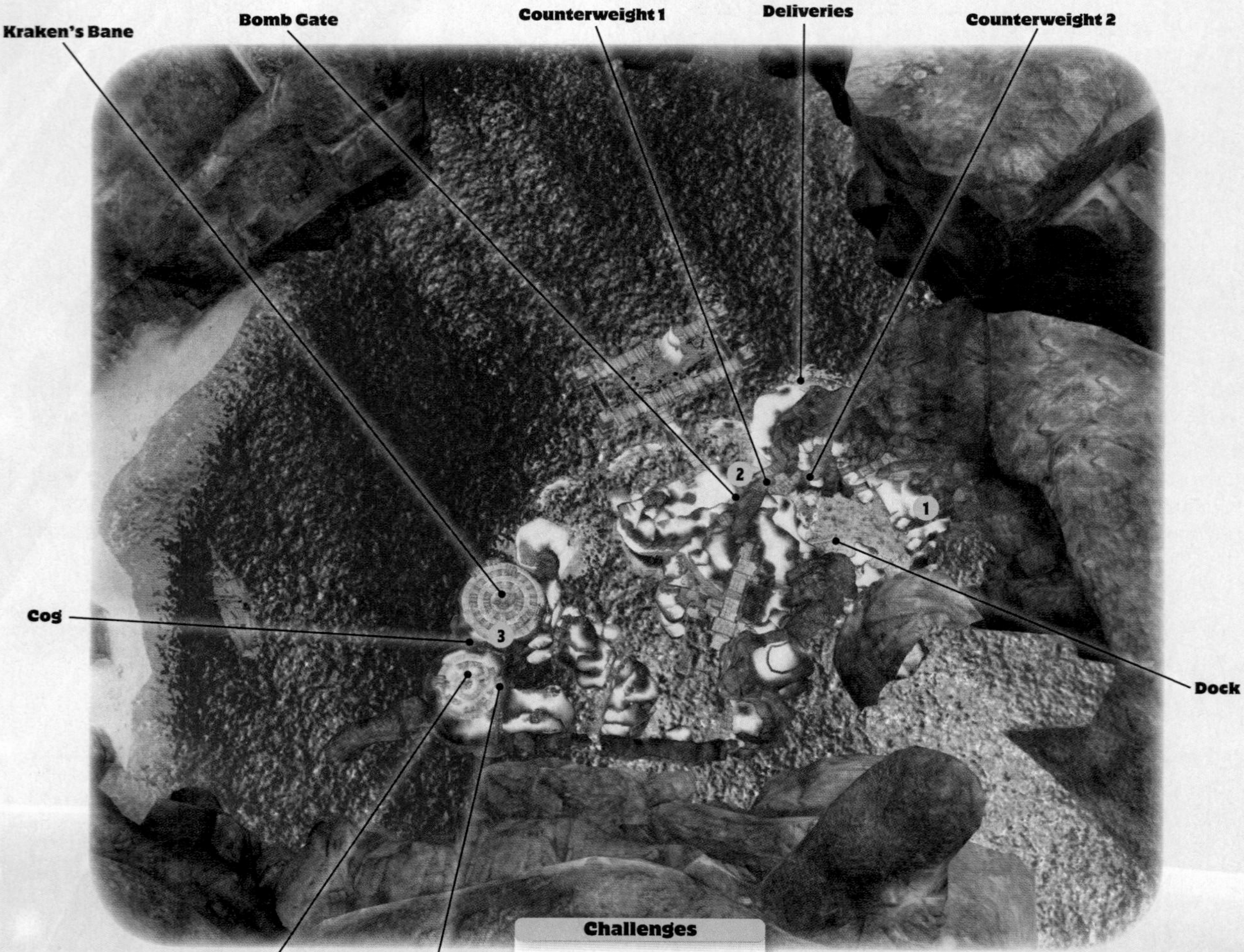
Kraken's Bane
Bomb Gate
Counterweight 1
Deliveries
Counterweight 2
Cog
Dock
Jones' Crew
Cog
1
2
3

Challenges

1. Pitching With Power
2. Clear Out Dead Man's Cove
3. Cove Collect

Off to Dead Man's Cove!

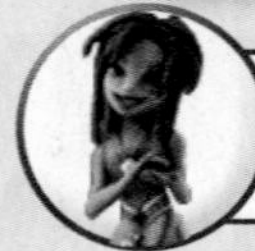

Mission Giver: Tia Dalma (automatic)
Type: Locate
Rewards: 500 Coins / 100 Sparks

5230
Guest
10

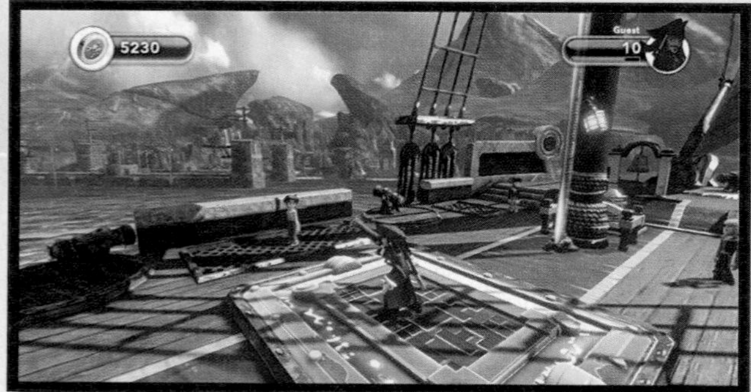

Another piece of the Kraken's Bane is at Dead Man's Cove. You must pass through the Demon's Cape to get there and sail deep inside the cover to find this island.

Blasting Is the Only Way!

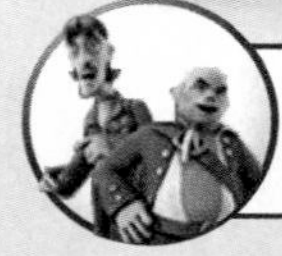

Mission Giver: Pintel and Ragetti
Type: Buy
Reward: 200 Coins

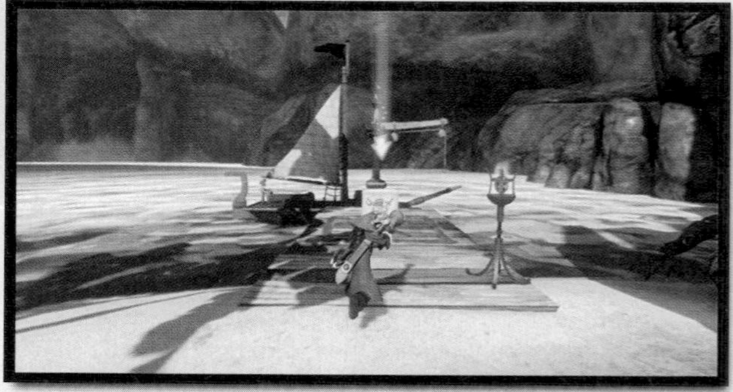

Remember those locks with the bomb symbol on them? Well you can finally open them once you purchase and pick up the Pirate Bomb.

Equip your new tool and teach that locked gate a lesson for trying to keep you out. Blow it up with a bomb, and remember to go back to the other places you might have been shut out from.

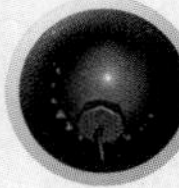

New Toy Unlocked: Pirate Bomb

New Challenges Available: Clear Out Dead Man's Cove

Knock Really Hard. Savvy?

Mission Giver: Pintel and Ragetti
Type: Buy
Rewards: 200 Coins / 100 Sparks

First Counterweight

To get around at the cove, and the other side of the island, you need a boat. But there isn't one waiting for you as there was back at the Bayou. Follow the compass to the docks, but you need to remove the counterweights to allow passage. The first step is to go through a long tunnel until you emerge back out in the sunlight.

The only way to get past these junk-filled areas is to use the Pirate Bomb to blow up the mess. The red color in the junk heap is dead giveaway that it can be blown up.

The Pirate Bombs can also be used on the red somewhat-rusted-looking bars to destroy them and reveal a thin ledge in the rock.

Leap up the ledge when it is clear and jump up to the upper walkway. Follow the wooden road to the right and blow up the pile of junk, then blow up the gate with the bomb symbol around the corner.

Several of Jones' men will rush you, but this is a great chance to use the Pirate Bombs to blow them to smithereens before they even get close. The bombs are very powerful, but they follow a large arc that only makes them useful at a distance.

Continue through the gates the pirates came out of and toss a bomb to knock out the first counterweight.

Second Counterweight

Starting from the docks, run behind Pintel and Ragetti to go up a series of plateaus. Leap across a split in the path and slide down near the docks on the opposite side you started from.

A bunch of pirates will greet you, but if you stay on the higher ledge and drop bombs on them, they will never get a chance to touch you.

Run through the gate they came out of and leap up a ledge to a spot where you can blow up some cluttered junk on the right side. When it is gone, go down that path and blast open a pair of bombable gates.

The gate to the left leads to the second counter-weight that can be blown up to finally drop the blockade.

Return to the dock and get into the dinghy to row it through the newly opened passage.

Follow the compass and blast any enemies you see until you can park the boat at the next dock, which of course is full of enemies.

Up to the Ruins

Mission Giver: Pintel and Ragetti
Type: Platform
Reward: 200 Coins

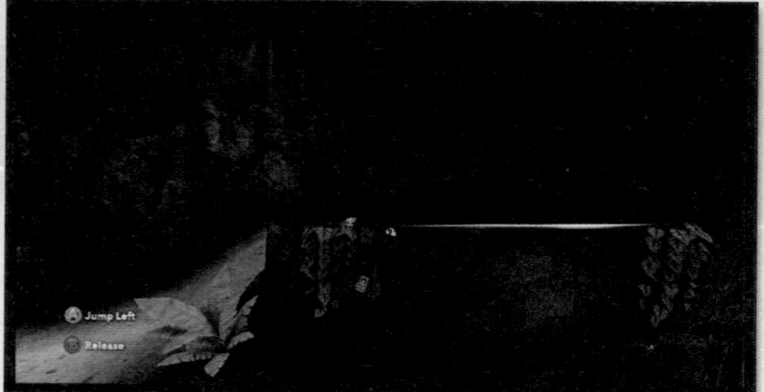

To get to the fort, blow up some rubble and use the ledge to the right to find the Cursed Theme Pack. Continue up the ramp where the debris once was.

Leap up a series of ledges and destroy the clutter on the side of the rocky pillar. Jump to this pillar once it is clear and move along a ledge to the right.

Blow up a few piles of burning junk to clear a path. Remove the clutter on a rocky wall to allow you to climb along the ledge to the right.

Wipe out the infestation of pirates and perform a wall jump on the narrow passage to reach the top level near the fort.

Fightin' the Fish Faces

Mission Giver: Pintel and Ragetti
Type: Combat
Reward: 200 Coins

Davy Jones' crew is looking for the piece of the Kraken's Bane too. You have to fight them in the old ruined fort to beat them to it. However, before you get into the fort, you have to open the door. This is a simple task considering the cog you need is right by you and a green arrow will hover over it. Pick up the old cog and place it near the others on the wall next to the IN button.

When the cog is in place, press the IN button and enter the circular arena for a big battle with Jones' men. Start out the fight by tossing some bombs at the enemies before the swordsmen charge you.

Continue to run and use bombs at long range for as long as you can, but the oyster-looking pirate will track you soon enough. Block its incoming attacks and counter, but only when you are safe from the bombing turtle nearby.

Bombs and Booby Traps

Mission Giver: Pintel and Ragetti
Type: Combat
Rewards: 500 Coins / 100 Sparks

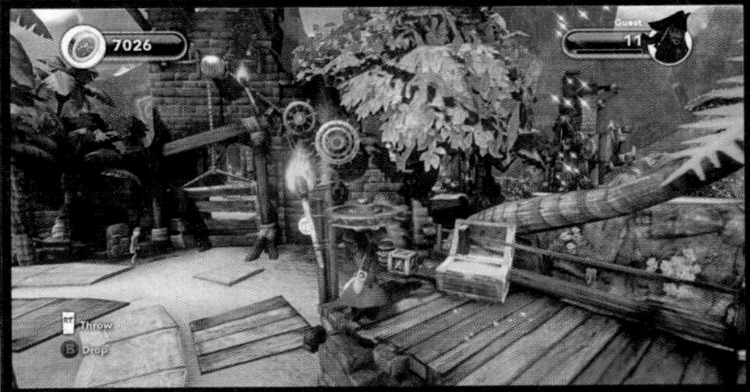

Find the cog to solve the gate puzzle and get to the piece of the Kraken's Bane. The cog is on a small platform. Pick it up and put it with the others on the wall. Push the IN button and open the gate.

New Challenges Available: Pitching With Power

Schools of Fish to Fight

Mission Giver: Pintel and Ragetti
Type: Combat
Rewards: 500 Coins / 100 Sparks

It's time to take down Maccus and several more of Jones' crew. When the gate is open, don't charge into the next area—instead let them come to you. Run away to get some distance and open fire with the Blunderbuss or Pirate Bombs. Try to do as much damage as possible from a distance so that you don't get overwhelmed by their superior numbers.

Maccus will be the last foe standing. Battle him the same way you have before by blocking and countering when he is done with his assault.

Another Piece Be Here

Mission Giver: Pintel and Ragetti
Type: Combat
Rewards: 2,000 Coins / 250 Sparks

The goal is to get to the top of the moving platforms, but first you need to find another cog to get things moving—literally. Smash a bunch of crates by a red capsule to find the cog.

Getting to the top of the center pillar is not that difficult if you take your time and let the moving platforms line up. Jump on the lowest moving platform and wait for the next taller platform to get close enough to jump to.

Near the top of the ascension you will get a break by jumping to a stationary ledge. Wait for the tallest moving platform and hop on board to get to the center and another piece of the Kraken's Bane.

New Toy Unlocked: Phase Shift

New Challenges Available: Cove Collect

Side Mission

Find Some Shine!

Mission Giver: Tia Dalma (automatic)
Type: Locate
Rewards: 1,000 Coins / 50 Sparks

One of the crew heard rumors that someone stashed treasure on Dead Man's Cove. There is only one chest to search for and it is in a circular area where you went to take care of one of the counterweights.

As soon as you open the chest, the gates will lock and you must wipe out the trio of pirates to get out alive.

Alert Mission: Helpin' Other Pirates

Type: Locate
Rewards: 1,000 Coins / 100 Sparks

While sailing the open seas, you may come across other pirates under attack by the Royal Navy. This is a very long battle with several waves and it is best to have your favorite power-up in the set up before you get surrounded. Remember that the ship will repair over time. If you need to, get away from the heat of combat to take a break.

The Final Piece at Buccaneer Bay

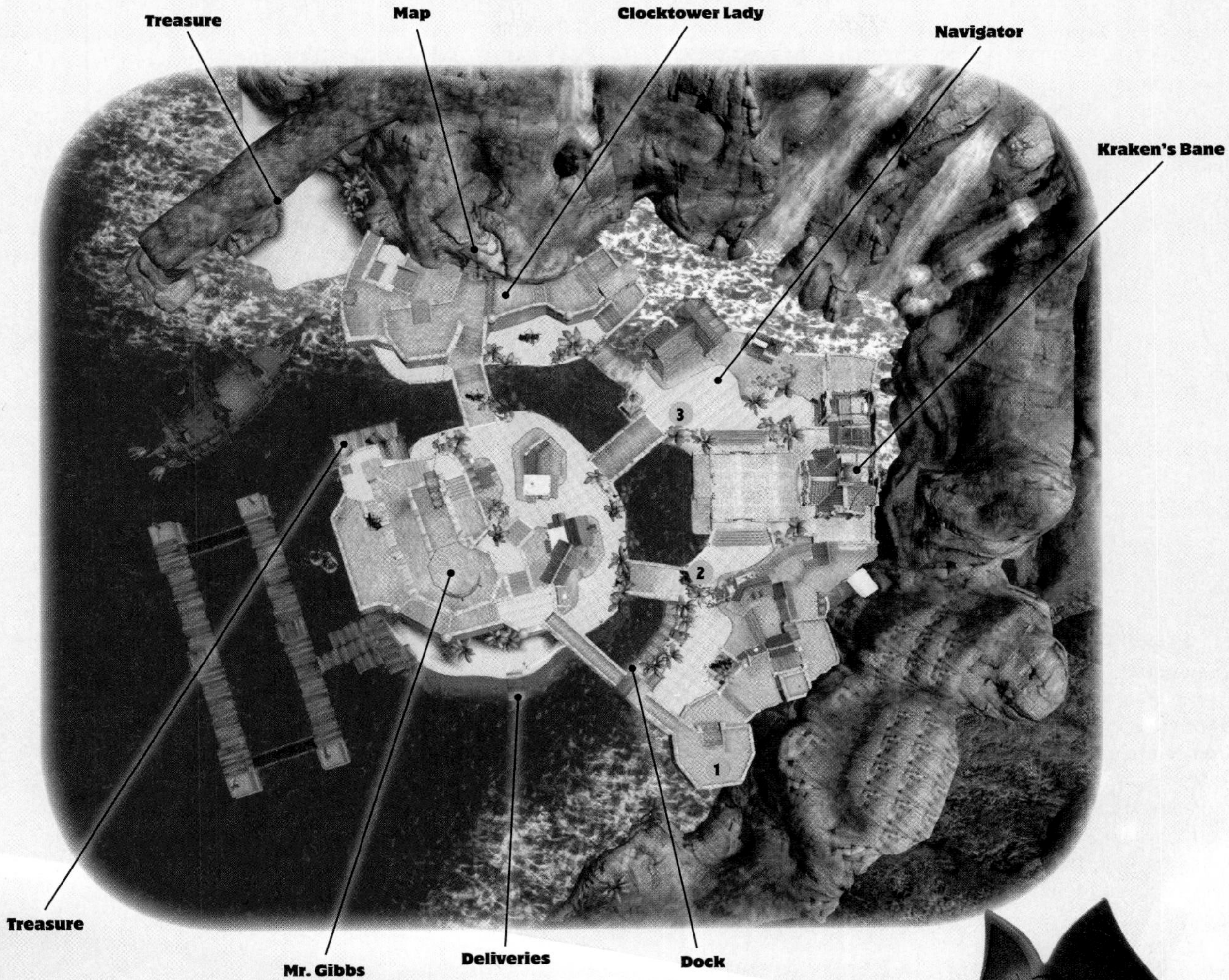

Treasure
Map
Clocktower Lady
Navigator
Kraken's Bane
Treasure
Mr. Gibbs
Deliveries
Dock

Challenges

1. Buccaneer Break
2. Brawl at the Bay
3. Buccaneer Bay Ballyhoo

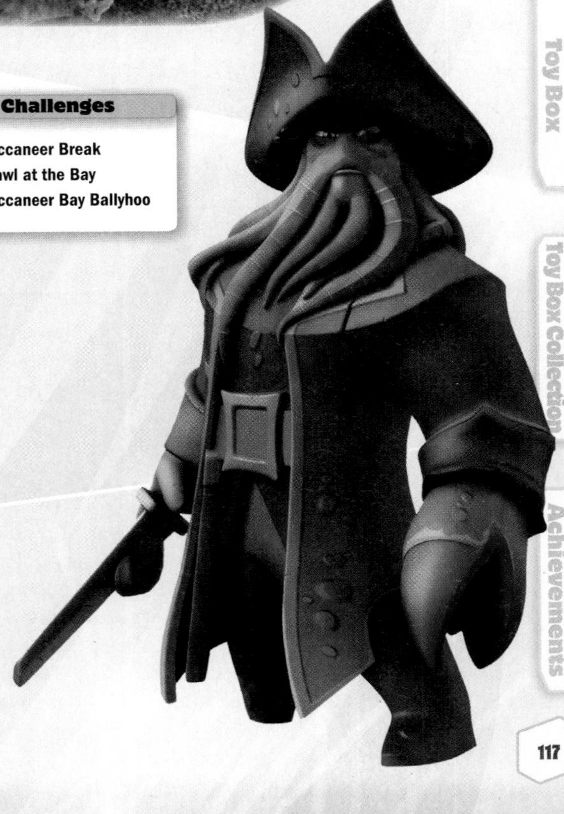

To Buccaneer Bay wit' You!

Mission Giver: Tia Dalma (automatic)
Type: Locate
Rewards: 500 Coins / 100 Sparks

Sail back to where it all started at Buccaneer Bay and speak to Tia Dalma when you land.

Last Piece, Matey

Mission Giver: Tia Dalma
Type: Combat
Rewards: 1,000 Coins / 250 Sparks

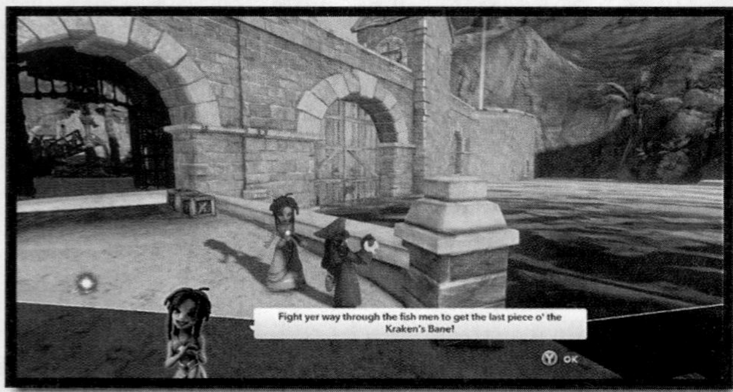

It's time to take the last piece of the Kraken's Bane, but you have to fight through all the fish men from Davy Jones to get it.

Wipe out the first batch of fish men with bombs or the Atlas blade. The turtles and oyster-looking fish men carry shields and the enemies are now better at blocking. Speaking of blocking, if you get surrounded, be patient and block, waiting for your chance to strike. Trying to attack and overpower superior numbers will not work and will become frustrating. Take out one enemy at a time, and when they are gone, blow up the debris on the bridge to clear a path.

The next big battle will take place where you had your first fight. There are more of Jones' crew to deal with, but Maccus joins them this time. Bombs do a lot of damage and are a great choice at a distance, but only if you can avoid the incoming fire from the turtles. Either block their bombs or dodge them and return with one of your own. It can be tough to fight fire with fire in this scenario and is only worth the effort if you can hit several enemies with a bomb. Otherwise, resort to your Blunderbuss for range attacks and keep Maccus at bay for as long as possible.

All Together!

Mission Giver: Tia Dalma (automatic)
Type: Locate
Rewards: 5,000 Coins / 1,000 Sparks

After the battle, the bell in the tower will crash to the ground and reveal the last hidden piece of the Kraken's Bane. Grab the final piece and get back to your ship.

Defeat Davy Jones

Back to Your Locker, Jones!

Mission Giver: Mr. Gibbs
Type: Ship Combat
Rewards: 2,000 Coins / 250 Sparks

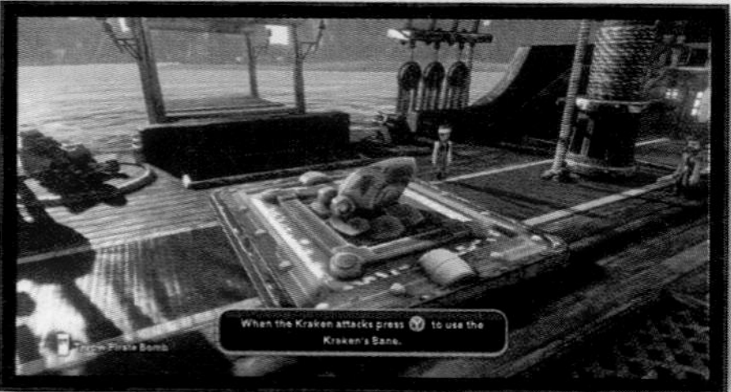

Now that you finally have the Kraken's Bane, it is time to take on Davy Jones. Make sure the Kraken's Bane is equipped on the ship as it will be essential to repel the monster while fighting Jones. This is a five-wave fight that will really test your sea savviness. Not only are there a lot of ships to deal with, but the Kraken can creep up at any time. The only thing in your favor is that the ship will recover in between waves.

Head out to sea in search of the *Flying Dutchman*. Try to maneuver away from its sides that have the most cannons, but make sure to keep firing as you circle around it.

The Kraken will attack throughout the sea battle, and this would normally send other pirates to the bottom of the ocean. However, with the Kraken's Bane equipped, you can zap the Kraken and send it back into the sea.

The *Flying Dutchman* can be sunk, but unlike normal ships it will pop right back out of the water. In fact, it has to be sunk several times to proceed to the next phase of the battle.

After taking enough damage, Jones will call in some reinforcements. There are four ships to sink in this wave, but they are relatively small. Keep firing on the enemies' ships while aiming for the front or back of their ships.

Mr. Gibbs will usually announce that the Kraken is coming by saying something like "Cap'n, it's the Kraken!" or "Sea Monster!" and at the end of this wave, it will launch a quick surprise attack.

NOTE

Most of the time Mr. Gibbs will alert you to a Kraken attack, but it can launch a sneak attack that is very hard to notice. Keep your eyes peeled and the Kraken's Bane charged. Failing to use the Bane in time is instant defeat!

Wave three is a fight with the *Flying Dutchman* again. Blast it at a distance if at all possible, and always move away from its Broadside Cannons.

The fourth attack wave has six ships to deal with and the goal is to avoid getting sandwiched between two enemy ships. Try to keep foes on one side (within range) and blast away.

The final wave is your last battle with the *Flying Dutchman*! The ship has a lot of health, but if you can get it out of position and expose the front of it to the full might of your cannons, it will go down without too much of a problem.

Defeating Jones will unlock the Kraken Hammer, allowing you to now summon the Kraken and sick it on enemies!

New Toy Unlocked: Kraken Hammer

Buccaneer Bay

Dead Man's Cove

Devil's Bow Island

Citadel Coast

Fort St. Grande

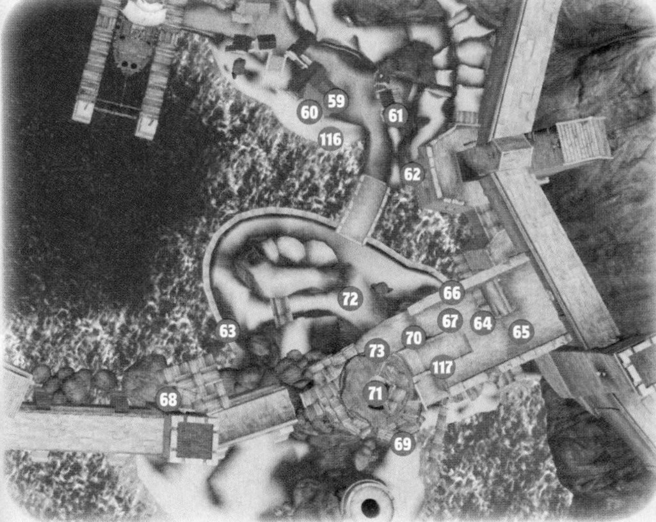

Isla Enoja

Port Talon

Light Haven

34
112
33

Pantano Bayou

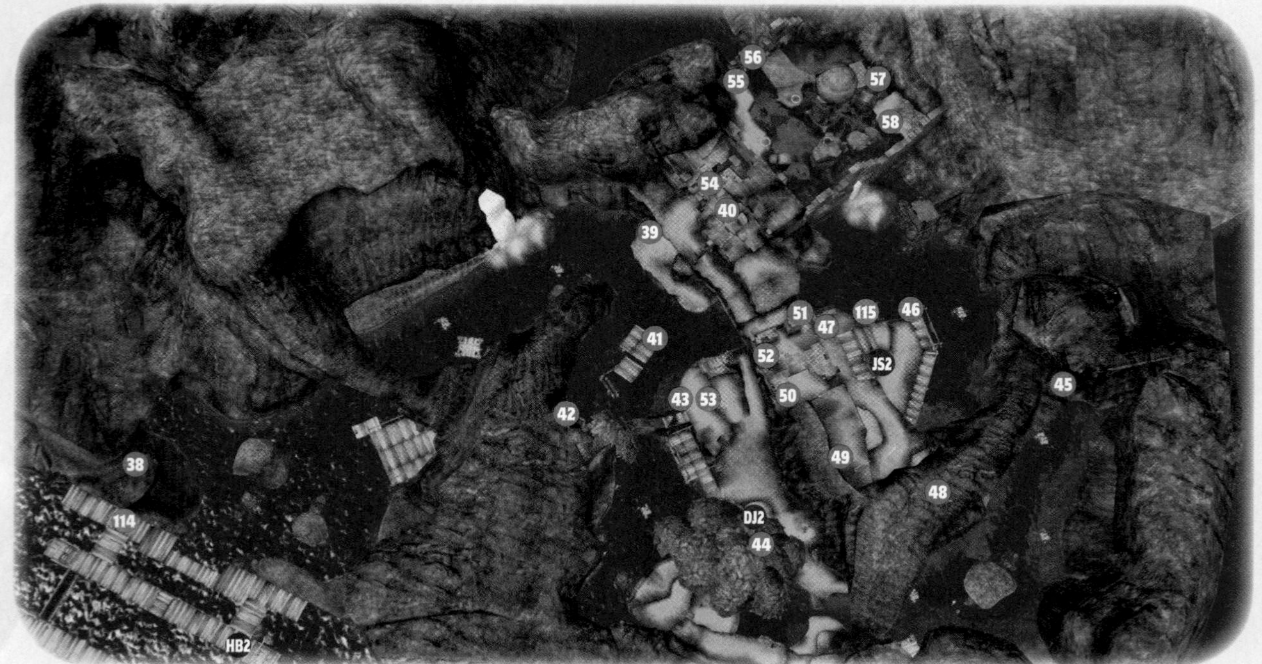

Shipwreck Shoals 1

Shipwreck Shoals 2

Port Talon

Red Capsules

#	Unlockable Item	Zone	Description
1	Bayou Beauty's Hat	Buccaneer Bay	On the left side of the pathway at the start.
2	Pirate Carpenter's Head	Buccaneer Bay	On the wall to the right after docking the dinghy.
3	Bayou Beauty's Head	Buccaneer Bay	Near the third set of stairs leading up to the outer walls.
4	Privateer's Head	Buccaneer Bay	Near the first set of stairs leading up to the outer walls.
5	Pirate Carpenter's Hair	Buccaneer Bay	On the roof of the building near the gate requiring bombs.
6	Black Hull Front	Buccaneer Bay	On the rope above the locked gate.
7	Privateer's Hair	Buccaneer Bay	On the ground near the waterfalls.
8	Navigator's Body	Buccaneer Bay	At the base of the stairs near the chapel.
9	Navigator's Head	Buccaneer Bay	Behind the building near the waterfalls.
10	Navigator's Hat	Buccaneer Bay	In front of the building with the water wheel.
11	Vengeance Front Hull	Buccaneer Bay	At the back of the tunnel where the map was.
12	Pirate Carpenter's Body	Buccaneer Bay	On the arch where the sand meets the stairs.
13	Vengeance Rear Hull	Buccaneer Bay	In front of the building at the base of the stairs leading to the tower.
14	Vengeance Sails	Buccaneer Bay	On top of the building at the base of the stairs leading to the tower.
15	Bayou Beauty's Body	Buccaneer Bay	At the top of the front stairs leading to the tower.
16	Dragon Woman's Body	Buccaneer Bay	In the building at the base of the stairs leading to the tower.
17	Dragon Woman's Hat	Buccaneer Bay	On the back pathway up the tower facing the dock.
18	Vengeance Theme Pack	Buccaneer Bay	On the wooden platform above the dock.
19	Privateer's Body	Buccaneer Bay	On the back pathway up the tower.
20	Dragon Woman's Head	Buccaneer Bay	On the front ledge halfway up the tower.
21	Vengeance Mid Hull	Buccaneer Bay	Inside the cell at the top of the tower.
22	Shen Zhou Mid Hull	Devil's Bow	Past the wooden gate near all the treasure chests.
23	Shen Zhou Front Hull	Devil's Bow	On the ledge across from the steps.
24	Gunner's Bandana	Citadel Coast	On top of the tower under the cage.
25	Gunner's Head	Citadel Coast	On top of the tower under the cage.
26	Shen Zhou Theme Pack	Citadel Coast	On the ledge under the tower.
27	Shen Zhou Sails	Siren Song	Inside the cell in the wall by the docks.
28	Gunner's Body	Siren Song	On the upper level of the rock formation on a platform near the dock.
29	Shen Zhou Rear Hull	Siren Song	At the very top of the rock formation.
30	Musician's Head	Port Talon	In front of the gate in the cave.
31	Shivaji Theme Pack	Port Talon	Inside the cave near the treasure chests.
32	Musician's Hat	Port Talon	On the wooden platform near the mouth of the cave.
33	Shivaji Sails	Light Haven	Tucked along the wall near the cliff wall.
34	Shivaji Rear Hull	Light Haven	On the side of the tower.
35	Shivaji Mid Hull	Isla Enoja	On the platforms near the cannon.
36	Shivaji Front Hull	Isla Enoja	On the wooden platform inside the cave.
37	Musician's Body	Isla Enoja	Along the ridge near the waterfall inside the cave.
38	El Caleuche Front Hull	Pantano Bayou	On the rock plateau near the dock.
39	Fisherman's Body	Pantano Bayou	In front of the locked gate requiring bombs.
40	Black Hull Rear	Pantano Bayou	Inside the cave past the locked gate requiring bombs.
41	Bounty Hunter's Head	Pantano Bayou	On top of the wooden platform before the big bridge.
42	Fisherman's Head	Pantano Bayou	On the cliff with the rope coming from the wooden platform.
43	Bounty Hunter's Hair	Pantano Bayou	Right near the big bridge made of stone past the wooden platform.
44	Bayou Raftman Head	Pantano Bayou	On the ladder leading up to the painted house.
45	El Caleuche Sails	Pantano Bayou	Inside the little water cave with the cages.
46	Bounty Hunter's Body	Pantano Bayou	On the rope above the second dock in the bayou.
47	Bayou Raftman Body	Pantano Bayou	Up the ramp from the second dock and by the wall.

#	Unlockable Item	Zone	Description
48	El Caleuche Rear Hull	Pantano Bayou	Behind the gate that requires a button to open.
49	Quartermaster's Head	Pantano Bayou	Up on the ledge near the button.
50	Quartermaster's Body	Pantano Bayou	By the pillar holding up the stone platform.
51	Bayou Rascal Head	Pantano Bayou	Tucked in the wall past the stone platform.
52	El Caleuche Theme Pack	Pantano Bayou	In the air by the stacked stone blocks on top of the stone platform.
53	Quartermaster's Eye Patch	Pantano Bayou	Tucked in the wall past the small wooden bridge.
54	El Caleuche Mid Hull	Pantano Bayou	In the cell behind the gate requiring bombs.
55	Bayou Raftman Hair	Pantano Bayou	By the left wall entering the big statue area.
56	Fisherman's Hair	Pantano Bayou	On the left wall entering the big statue area.
57	Bayou Rascal Body	Pantano Bayou	On the top of the platform in the big statue area.
58	Bayou Rascal Hair	Pantano Bayou	On the rope leading from top of the platform in the big statue area.
59	Royal Marine's Body	Fort St. Grande	Behind the building nearest the bridge but along the beach.
60	Captain's Head	Fort St. Grande	On the roof of the building nearest the bridge but along the beach.
61	Skeletal Theme Pack	Fort St. Grande	On the roof of the building nearest the bridge.
62	Skeletal Rear Hull	Fort St. Grande	On the ledge with the tree nearest the bridge.
63	Skeletal Front Hull	Fort St. Grande	Across the bridge at the end of the paved beachfront.
64	Captain's Body	Fort St. Grande	On the ledge under the archway leading outside of the Fort walls.
65	Skeletal Mid Hull	Fort St. Grande	On the wooden beam under the archway leading outside of the Fort walls.
66	Black Sails	Fort St. Grande	In the room inside the wall that is locked by a bomb gate.
67	Captain's Hair	Fort St. Grande	In the window of the room inside the wall that is locked by a bomb gate.
68	Lieutenant's Body	Fort St. Grande	On the wooden platform on the far side of the Fort wall.
69	Royal Marine's Hat	Fort St. Grande	On the rope from the tower past the Fort wall.
70	Lieutenant's Hair	Fort St. Grande	On the wooden platform near the gates on top of the wall.
71	Royal Marine's Head	Fort St. Grande	Inside the tower at the top of the Fort wall.
72	Skeletal Sails	Fort St. Grande	On the rope leading away from the Fort wall.
73	Lieutenant's Head	Fort St. Grande	On the rope wrapping around the top of the tower.
74	Sunken Shipwreck Mid Hull	Shipwreck Shoals	On the rock pathway in front of the dock.
75	Sunken Shipwreck Theme Pack	Shipwreck Shoals	At the top of the wooden platform with the rope ladder.
76	Sunken Shipwreck Front Hull	Shipwreck Shoals	On the platform surrounded by waterfalls.
77	Sunken Shipwreck Sails	Shipwreck Shoals	On the broken mast connecting two waterfalls
78	Sunken Shipwreck Rear Hull	Shipwreck Shoals	On the ledge at the top near the treasure.
79	Swabbie's Bandanna	Dead Man's Cove	On the bridge by the dock.
80	Lady Buccaneer's Bandana	Dead Man's Cove	Behind the two fences that require bombs.
81	Lady Buccaneer's Body	Dead Man's Cove	On the rope connected to the dinghy dock directly past the bomb gate.
82	Admiral's Daughter's Hair	Dead Man's Cove	Under the bridge directly in front of the ship dock.
83	Pirate Lord's Body	Dead Man's Cove	On the water between all of the rock islands to the right of the ship dock.
84	Cursed Sails	Dead Man's Cove	On the very top of the tallest rock islands to the right of the ship dock.
85	Pirate Smithy's Head	Dead Man's Cove	On the fallen mast near the Skull Cave.
86	Cursed Mid Hull	Dead Man's Cove	On the ledge inside Skull Cave.
87	Pirate Smithy's Body	Dead Man's Cove	In the very back of Dead Man's Cove inside the gated cave.
88	Pirate Smithy's Bandana	Dead Man's Cove	On the end of the elevated wooden platform on the near the Fort.
89	Admiral's Daughter's Head	Dead Man's Cove	Right on the beach in front of the dinghy dock.
90	Cursed Theme Pack	Dead Man's Cove	On the wooden platform past the beach and wall climb.
91	Swabbie's Body	Dead Man's Cove	At the edge of the pathway from the beach.
92	Cursed Fore Hull	Dead Man's Cove	On the rope connecting the two big islands in Dead Man's Cove.
93	Lady Buccaneer's Head	Dead Man's Cove	On the little island platform under the long rope connecting the two main islands.

#	Unlockable Item	Zone	Description
94	Pirate Lord's Hat	Dead Man's Cove	On the ledge near the back of the island by the two waterfalls.
95	Cursed Rear Hull	Dead Man's Cove	On the dinghy dock near the back of the island by the two waterfalls.
96	Black Theme Pack	Dead Man's Cove	Behind the rock near the back of the island by the two waterfalls.
97	Swabbie's Head	Dead Man's Cove	Behind the bomb gate on the ledge near the entrance to the Fort.
98	Pirate Lord's Head	Dead Man's Cove	On a couple crates straight past the gate at the Fort.
99	Admiral's Daughter's Body	Dead Man's Cove	Past the second gate in the Fort and to the left.
100	Black Hull Mid	Dead Man's Cove	On the upper ledge of the moving platforms.
101	Flying Dutchman Theme Pack	Buccaneer Bay (Return)	On the roof of the building at the base of the stairs leading to the tower.
102	Flying Dutchman Mid Hull	Buccaneer Bay (Return)	On the back of the tower near the dock.
103	Flying Dutchman Front Hull	Buccaneer Bay (Return)	By the stairs leading down to the beach.
104	Flying Dutchman Sails	Buccaneer Bay (Return)	At the top of the stairs behind the water wheel near the waterfalls.
105	Flying Dutchman Rear Hull	Buccaneer Bay (Return)	On the rope above the locked gate.

Green Capsules

#	Unlockable Item	Zone	Description
106	Pirates Decorations Toy Pack 2	Buccaneer Bay	Inside the chapel after returning.
107	Pirates Crewman Toy Pack 2	Buccaneer Bay	On the rope above the dock.
108	Pirates Town Set Toy Pack 1	Devil's Bow	On the ledge under the tower.
109	Pirates Town Set Toy Pack 3	Citadel Coast	On the top of the steps by the dock.
110	Pirates Town Set Toy Pack 4	Siren Song	On the uppermost part of the rock formation.
111	Pirates Town Set Toy Pack 2	Port Talon	Behind the trees near the dock.
112	Pirates Plants Toy Pack 1	Light Haven	At the base of the tower.
113	Pirates Plants Toy Pack 2	Isla Enoja	In front of the entrance to the cave.
114	Pirates Crewman Toy Pack 1	Pantano Bayou	On the far side of the docks.
115	Pirates Townsperson Toy Pack 3	Pantano Bayou	To the right of the ramp by the second dock.
116	Pirates Townsperson Toy Pack 2	Fort St. Grande	Behind the building nearest the bridge but along the beach.
117	Pirates Townsperson Toy Pack 4	Fort St. Grande	Behind the crate leading to the tower at the top of the Fort wall.
118	Pirates Decorations Toy Pack 1	Shipwreck Shoals	On the rock pathway in front of the dock.
119	Pirates Townsperson Toy Pack 1	Dead Man's Cove	On the far side of the bridge by the dock.

Infinity Chests/Vault

#	Unlockable Item	Zone	Description
DJ-1	Davy Jones Chest 1	Buccaneer Bay	Near the docks on the same side as the delivery platform.
DJ-2	Davy Jones Chest 2	Pantano Bayou	On the ground right by the wooden house with paintings in it.
DJ-3	Davy Jones Chest 3	Dead Man's Cove	Next to the bridge.
HB-1	Hector Barbossa Chest 1	Buccaneer Bay	At the top of the stairs behind the water wheel near the waterfalls.
HB-2	Hector Barbossa Chest 2	Pantano Bayou	On the dock.
HB-3	Hector Barbossa Chest 3	Dead Man's Cove	On the ledge near the back of the island by the two waterfalls.
JS-1	Jack Sparrow Chest 1	Buccaneer Bay	Near the buildings in front of the tower.
JS-2	Jack Sparrow Chest 2	Pantano Bayou	Right by the second dock in the bayou.
JS-3	Jack Sparrow Chest 3	Dead Man's Cove	On the elevated wooden platform on the near the Fort.
Master	Pirates Avatar Vault - Reward 1	Buccaneer Bay	In the entryway near the Chapel.

Pirates of the Caribbean Gold Stars

#	Type	Star Names	Star Description
1	Mission	Rescue Master Gibbs!	Complete "Rescue Master Gibbs!" mission.
2	Mission	Buy Yerself a Ship!	Complete "A Captain Needs a Ship!" mission.
3	Mission	That Be Demon's Cape	Complete "Demon's Cape Sounds Invitin'" mission.
4	Mission	Find Tia Dalma	Complete "Find Tia Dalma" mission.
5	Mission	Keep the Sea Witch Safe	Complete "Keep the Sea Witch Safe" mission.
6	Mission	Darken the Sails!	Complete "Darken the Sails!" mission.
7	Mission	De First Piece O' De Bane	Complete "De First Piece O' De Bane" mission.
8	Mission	Second Piece o' the Kraken's Bane	Complete "Second Piece O' the Kraken's Bane" mission.
9	Mission	Another Piece Be Here	Complete "Another Piece Be Here" mission.
10	Mission	Bane From Beneath	Complete "Bane From Beneath" mission.
11	Mission	Last Piece, Matey	Complete "All Together" mission.
12	Mission	Ship Off the Port Bow!	Complete "Ship Off the Port Bow!" mission.
13	Mission	Sink the Scurvy Rats.	Complete "Rid Me O' Dem Pirates!" mission.
14	Mission	Man the Cannon!	Purchase all cannon abilities.
15	Mission	Back To Your Locker, Jones!	Complete "Back to Your Locker, Jones!" mission.
16	Challenge	Accomplished Pirate	Complete all Challenges.
17	Easter Egg	Big Impact	Throw 100 Pirate Bombs.
18	Easter Egg	Down to the Depths	Sink 30 ships.
19	Easter Egg	Island Explorer	Visited all small islands.
20	Easter Egg	Creatin' a Crew	Customize ten townspeople.
21	Easter Egg	One Ship, Many Faces	Customize the ship five times.
22	Easter Egg	Crow's Nest Climb	Climb to the crow's nest on your ship.
23	Easter Egg	Pillage and Plunder	Break 100 crates or barrels.
24	Easter Egg	There Be Gold, Mate	Find 10 treasure chests.
25	Easter Egg	Salty Old Sailor	Sail for two hours total in your ship.
26	Easter Egg	Small but Powerful	Defeat seven enemies in your dinghy.
27	Easter Egg	Down Ye Goes!	Sink a ship using the deck cannon turret.
28	Easter Egg	All Hands On Deck	Sail out of an island with your friend on the ship.
29	Easter Egg	Own the Hammer	Buy Kraken Hammer.
30	Purchases	Monarch of the Sea	Purchase all ship abilities.

Pirates of the Caribbean Toy List

Toys	Toy Box Export	Toy Type	Commercial
Fisherman	Yes	Crewman	No
Blunderbuss	Yes	Held Item	Yes
Atlas Sword	Yes	Prop	No
Pirate Bomb	Yes	Held Item	Yes
Calypso's Rage	No	Ship Ability	Yes
Kraken Hammer	No	Ship Ability	Yes
Phase Shift	No	Ship Ability	No
Speed Burst	No	Ship Ability	No
Extra Broadside Cannons	No	Ship Upgrade	No
Flamethrower Cannon	Yes	Ship Upgrade	Yes

Toys	Toy Box Export	Toy Type	Commercial
Foremast Sail	No	Ship Upgrade	No
Helm	No	Ship Upgrade	No
Long Range Cannon	Yes	Ship Upgrade	Yes
Mizzen Mast Sail	No	Ship Upgrade	Yes
Rudder	No	Ship Upgrade	No
Triple Shot Cannon	Yes	Ship Upgrade	Yes
Voodoo Cannon	Yes	Ship Upgrade	Yes
Player Pirate Ship	No	Vehicle/ Mount	Yes

Pirates of the Caribbean Challenges

Name	Location	Description	Character	Requirements		
				Easy	Medium	Hard
Brawl at the Bay	Buccaneer Bay near bell tower	Defeat enemies as Barbossa before time runs out.	Barbossa	3 enemies in 3:00	6 enemies in 3:00	10 enemies in 3:00
Buccaneer Bay Ballyhoo	Buccaneer Bay near customize shop	Gather as many collectibles as you can before time runs out.	Any	30 targets in 1:30	45 targets in 1:30	60 targets in 1:30
Buccaneer Break	Buccaneer Bay upper embank-ment	Gather as many collectibles as you can before time runs out.	Any	20 targets in 1:30	35 targets in 1:30	50 targets in 1:30
Gatherin' Grande	Fort. St. Grande beach plateau	Gather as many collectibles as you can as Davy Jones before time runs out.	Davy Jones	25 targets in 2:00	40 targets in 2:00	55 targets in 2:00
Rally on the Fort	Fort. St. Grande near upper fort	Gather as many collectibles as you can before time runs out.	Any	30 targets in 2:15	50 targets in 2:15	70 targets in 2:15
Pantano Bayou Dash	Pantano Bayou near temple ruins	Gather as many collectibles as you can before time runs out.	Any	40 targets in 1:30	50 targets in 1:30	60 targets in 1:30
Shootin' up the Swamp	Pantano Bayou near dock by Tia Dalma	Gather as many collectibles as you can before time runs out.	Any	10 targets in 2:00	15 targets in 2:00	21 targets in 2:00
Clear out Dead Man's Cove	Dead Man's Cove near your ship	Defeat enemies before time runs out.	Any	3 enemies in 3:00	6 enemies in 3:00	10 enemies in 3:00
Cove Collect	Dead Man's Cove near moving platform puzzle	Gather as many collectibles as you can as Captain Jack Sparrow before time runs out.	Captain Jack Sparrow	10 targets in 3:00	15 targets in 3:00	20 targets in 3:00
Pitching with Power!	Dead Man's Cove near counter-weight	Gather as many collectibles as you can before time runs out.	Any	10 targets in 2:30	15 targets in 2:30	20 targets in 2:30
Scurry on the Ship-wreck	Shipwreck Shoals	Gather as many collectibles as you can before time runs out.	Any	25 targets in 2:00	50 targets in 2:00	70 targets in 2:30

Cars
Luigis
CASA DELLA TIRES
LIGHTYEAR

NOTE - For those playing Disney Infinity on the Wii, the Play Sets are a bit different. Access your free eGuide (voucher code on the insert) to access this content.

Welcome To Radiator Springs

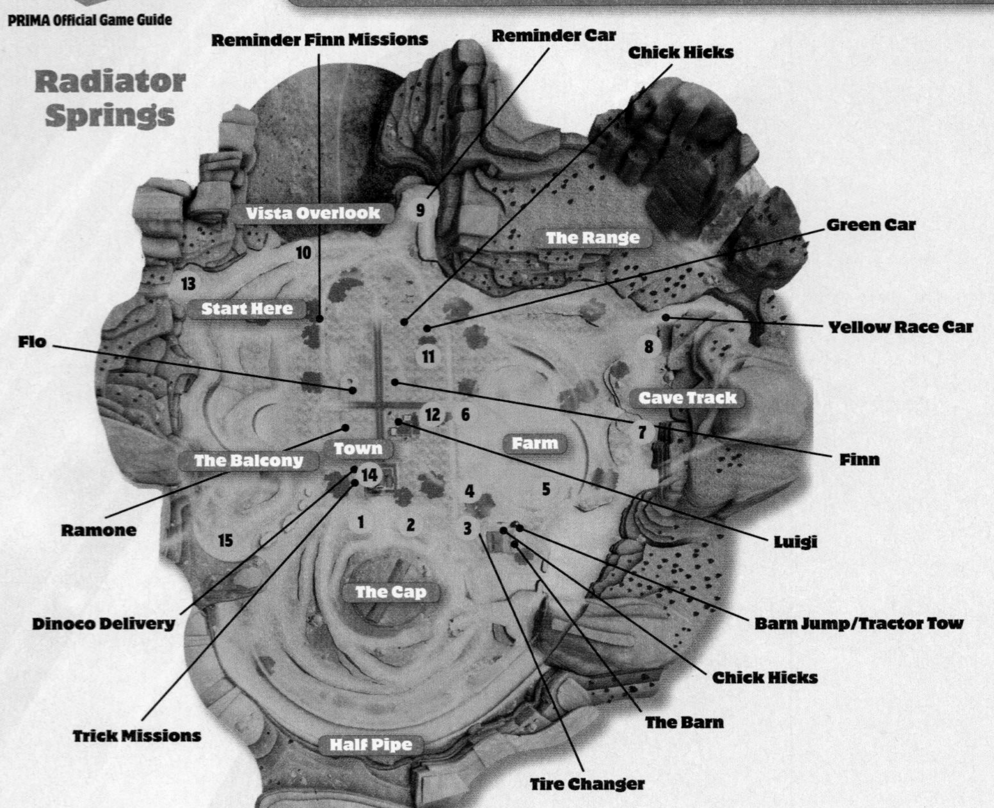

Challenges

1. Radiator C.H.R.O.M.E. Race
2. Radiator Race
3. Farm C.H.R.O.M.E. Race
4. Farm Race
5. Radiator Biathlon
6. Grab 'n' Go
7. Cave Race
8. Cave C.H.R.O.M.E. Race
9. Monster Match
10. Shoot for Loot
11. Town Race
12. Flash of Lightning
13. Throw and Go
14. Score More
15. Monster Mash

Find Luigi

Mission Giver: Luigi
Type: Locate
Rewards: 50 Coins / 25 Sparks

This mission is designed to teach the basics of controlling the car by using the accelerator, working the brake/reverse, and learning to jump. Try out all of the basic driving abilities and follow the green compass arrow to find Luigi's shop.

Calibrate GPS

Mission Giver: Luigi
Type: Collect
Rewards: 50 Coins / 25 Sparks

Use the built-in GPS system (green compass arrow) to collect all the green balls with a white arrow pointing up.

NOTE

What's Next?

At this point a lot of options become available. There are two main mission paths to choose from as well as numerous side quests. Each initial choice has a chain of events that will follow, but you can jump from one chain to another if you want. The most straightforward method to cover them all is to pick one path and continue until you unlock the new toys, such as the Turbo Level 1 or Tow Chain Level 2, and then switch to another branch.

Main Missions: Jump at Flo's and Meet Chick at the Barn

Side Quests: Clear the Race Track, Smash and Bash, Jump into the Barn

Flo's Missions

Jump at Flo's

Mission Giver: Flo
Type: Trick/Stunt
Rewards: N/A

Flo needs something flashy to draw attention to her Café. There is nothing like a fantastic jump to get folks to notice the place. In order to perform a leap of that level, Flo's place needs some big ramps. Each place at Radiator Springs can be adjusted into a more stunt-friendly area by pushing the large green buttons in their locations. Press the green button near the fuel stalls and get some distance to zoom up the canopies and perform an amazing jump.

Challenge Available: Radiator Cap Race

Bales of Fire

Mission Giver: Flo
Type: Destroy/Combat
Rewards: 200 Coins / 100 Sparks

A tractor with a bad case of backfire caught several hay bales on fire. They have to be smashed before the town burns to the ground. There are seven bales that need to be bashed to bits and they are all located in a rough circle around The Barn at The Farm.

Challenge Available: Grab n' Go

Rescue Ramone

Mission Giver: Flo
Type: Delivery (tow)
Rewards: 50 Coins / 50 Sparks

Putting out the fires was pretty exciting, but Flo's pal Ramone missed all the action. She is worried about him and it is up to you to locate him. Follow the compass to find him stuck on a rocky ledge.

NOTE

At this point the most obvious choice is to complete the Tow Ramone mission, but you can leave him stranded and go back to Flo's to continue her other missions.

Alert Mission:Out of Gas

Mission Giver: Little Grey Car (blue picture in mission list)
Type: Delivery (tow)
Rewards: 50 Coins / 25 Sparks

This is a repeatable mission that will be unlocked at this point. A small car just outside of town has run out of gas. Activate your tow cable and drag the car back to Flo's to quickly get it back on the road.

Catch a Speeder

Mission Giver: Flo
Type: Delivery (tow)
Rewards: 200 Coins / 100 Sparks

Hot rods are tearing up the streets and scaring away Flo's customers. Somebody has to catch the reckless drivers and lock them up in Mater's Impound until they cool off. The hot heads are easy to spot by the red flashing light around them. Also, they are driving very fast and dangerously. It won't be that easy to stop the speeders. Follow behind one and stick with it until you can gain enough ground to get close enough to use the tow cable.

Once the speeder is apprehended, take it to the Impound to get it off the streets.

New Toy Unlocked: Sarge's Surplus Hut

New Toy Unlocked: Turbo Level 1

NOTE

When the Turbo is unlocked, Luigi will remind you to buy it. Once you acquire it, a new path of missions will unlock, starting with Drift Tutorial.

Buy Sarge's Hut

Mission Giver: Flo
Type: Buy/Build
Rewards: 50 Coins / 25 Sparks

The Sheriff is out of town as well as Sarge, the military vehicle that helps keep the town in line. Radiator Springs needs some law and order and the best way to solve that is to buy Sarge's Surplus Hut from the Toy Store. It costs 500 coins and you might not have that much to spend so early on. If you want it buy the building now, go smash some hay bales or complete a few more missions to save up. Once the building is placed, a new path of missions will become available at Sarge's place.

Postal Problem

Mission Giver: Flo
Type: Unique
Rewards: 250 Coins / 50 Sparks

Flo's mailbox was knocked over by the speeders zipping around town. Help her find a new one by locating a red capsule with the object and place it on the spot indicated near the Café. Follow the compass around The Cap and find the red capsule on a small ledge. Return to Flo's V8 Café and drive around to the back to locate the small grey nub where a Decorate message will appear. Go into the Decorate menu and select Flo's Mailbox to place it and complete the mission.

In a Jam

Mission Giver: Flo
Type: Combat
Rewards: 200 Coins / 50 Sparks

Flo's mail problems aren't over after her mailbox has been replaced. There is a big traffic jam in town and the mail can't get through. Smash through the cluster of cars to clear out the traffic jam at the four-way intersection.

New Toy Unlocked: Radiator Springs Curios

Side Missions

Collector Plates

Mission Giver: Flo
Type: Collect
Rewards: 250 Coins / 50 Sparks

Some of the hot rods speeding around town stole 15 license plates from Radiator Springs Curios. With the help of the compass, track down all 15 plates that are spread around the outskirts of town and even hidden on ledges and behind hay bales.

Clear the Race Track

Mission Giver: Little Dark Grey Car (green picture by tree near Mater in mission list)
Type: Destroy
Rewards: 100 Coins / 50 Sparks

A little car northeast of town drove three hours to watch his friend race, but the roadway is all jammed up with debris. Follow the compass to the race track at the range and caves and drive along the track smashing ten piles of debris.

Find a Friend to Race

Mission Giver: Little Dark Grey Car (green picture in mission list)
Type: Locate
Rewards: 100 Coins / 25 Sparks

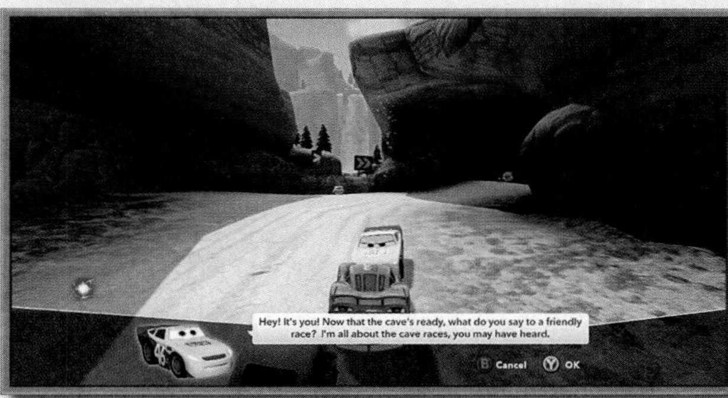

Return to the little car after clearing out the debris and he will mention that his friend is eager to race you. Use the compass to find his friend at the entrance to the caves.

Cave Race

Mission Giver: Yellow Race Car
Type: Race
Rewards: 50 Sparks

Now that the caves are clear to race, a sporty yellow car is waiting to meet you at the entrance to the caves. The car is very excited to race, but you must come in first place to complete the mission. This is a relatively short race requiring only two laps, but it's not easy. At the start of the race, rapidly press the accelerator to build up the turbo meter and launch from the start at full speed.

There is an alternate route through the caves that can give you an edge, but the real key to victory is drifting into the turns.

Make sure to drift into each large turn and fill that turbo meter as much as possible. As soon as you find a straight section of track, or an area you can navigate really well, hit the turbo for a much-needed speed boost.

Challenges Available: Cave Race and Cave Battle (when Machine Gun Challenge is purchased)

New Toy Unlocked: Turbo Level 1

Main Street Maker

Mission Giver: Little Dark Grey Car (green picture in mission list)
Type: Decorate
Rewards: 100 Coins / 25 Sparks

The town would attract a lot more tourists with a makeover. Go to any building in town and decorate it with at least one alteration to complete the mission.

Luigi's Missions

Purchase Turbo

Mission Giver: Luigi (at The Farm)
Type: Buy
Rewards: 25 Coins / 25 Sparks

This is pretty obvious—just go into the Toy Store to buy the Turbo. However, you still need to pick up the package that arrives on the Dinoco drop point. Make your way to the drop point and open the box to acquire the ability to use a turbo boost.

Drifting Drill

Mission Giver: Luigi
Type: Tutorial
Rewards: 50 Coins / 25 Sparks

Luigi can be found at The Farm in the center of one of the fenced areas amongst the hay bales. Speak to him to learn about drifting. All the famous race cars are doing it, and Fillmore's special fuel will build up your turbo power each time you do. A drift is performed by pressing the accelerator and brake at the same time while steering in the direction you want to go. A drift can be held as long as you like, but it is mainly used in turns. To complete the mission, perform a drift while following the arrows in a circle around Luigi. When the turbo meter is filled, the mission will be over.

Challenge Available: Radiator Cap Race

Find Guido!

Mission Giver: Luigi
Type: Locate
Rewards: 50 Coins / 25 Sparks

Guido likes playing tricks on Luigi, but now is not a great time. Luigi is preparing a new racetrack and needs Guido back ASAP. Follow the compass to find Guido at the Base of The Cap and bounce into the little blue jokester.

Find Luigi's Crates

Mission Giver: Luigi
Type: Collect
Rewards: 200 Coins / 50 Sparks

Luigi has a big surprise for the town, but all the supplies have fallen off the helicopter that was supposed to deliver them. Use the compass to locate all three of the Dinoco crates around Radiator Springs and tow them back to Luigi.

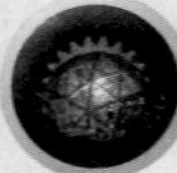

New Toy Unlocked: Fillmore's Organic Fuels

NOTE

Purchasing this toy unlocks Fillmore's Missions. See his mission path for his first mission.

Follow Guido's Balloons

Mission Giver: Luigi
Type: Destroy
Rewards: 100 Coins / 25 Sparks

With the crates returned to Luigi, he can reveal the big surprise—a racing hub. Follow the compass to pass through the 13 red balloons.

NOTE

After completing this mission, Willy's Butte will be open. However, there is still a lot to do in Radiator Springs before you jump into the racing and stunt tracks.

Side Missions

Smash and Bash

Mission Giver: Yellow car near The Barn (blue picture in mission list)
Type: Destroy
Rewards: 100 Coins / 50 Sparks

Smash through one of the fenced areas at The Farm and drive into 15 hay bales to help clear the air for this poor highly allergic vehicle.

TIP

Hay bales aren't worth a lot of coins, but they regenerate pretty quickly and there are enough of them that they can be "farmed" for some extra coins if you run low.

Challenge Available: Grab 'n' Go

Stunt Practice

Mission Giver: Little Tan Car (blue picture in mission list)
Type: Stunt/Trick
Rewards: 100 Coins / 50 Sparks

Next to the Fire Station is a small car that is looking for someone to do air tricks. Simply follow the request from the little car to learn how to jump and perform a flat spin, barrel roll, front flip, and back flip. They are all simple moves that require a jump and a press of the control stick in one of four directions. This must be completed in 1 minute and 30 seconds.

Perform Tricks

Mission Giver: Little Tan Car (blue picture in mission list)
Type: Stunt/Trick
Rewards: 250 Coins / 50 Sparks

Now that you know how to perform several tricks, the same car that gave you the quick tutorial wants to see three cool stunts done from a high place. This event has a 1 minute and 30 seconds time limit, but that shouldn't present any problems. Luckily the Fire Station right next to the little car has a ramp that is a great spot to do all three of these tricks.

Drive up the hill opposite the Fire Station and hit the ramp with as much speed as possible. The first trick the little car wants to see is a double front flip, so hit the ramp and hold forward to flip twice in a row before landing. Next up is the barrel roll. That can be done by holding right on the stick. Finally, do a double back flip by holding back on the control stick.

Challenge Available: Town Race

Jump into The Barn

Mission Giver: Little Grey Car (blue picture in mission list)
Type: Trick/Stunt
Rewards: 100 Coins / 50 Sparks

A little car in front of The Barn heard that it was impossible to jump all the way through The Barn. To prove it wrong, press the button on the silo to drop the ramp and build up the turbo meter.

The jump will be easy if you can get enough speed when you hit the ramp, and a turbo boost will take care of that issue. Note that you don't need to jump through the entire barn, but merely get up to the top section and then you can drive through.

Little Bo Beep

Mission Giver: Little Grey Car (blue picture in mission list)
Type: Delivery (tow)
Rewards: 200 Coins / 50 Sparks

Speak to the car out front of The Barn again to find out about the missing tractors. Use the compass to locate three tractors and tow them back inside The Barn.

Challenge Available: Town Race

NOTE

This is one of two requirements to unlock the challenge Timed Tractor Tipping. The storm clean up must also be completed to fully unlock this mission.

Finn's Missions

NOTE

A small grey (blue picture in mission list) car in the northwest part of town will remind you to purchase the toys that Finn mentions. These missions don't have to be completed to purchase the toys, and if you buy them before speaking to the car, they will be automatically be completed when you talk to it.

Spy Training

Mission Giver: Finn
Type: Tutorial
Rewards: 50 Coins / 50 Sparks

Finn is on holiday and stopped by Radiator Springs to unwind. Sarge was nice enough to let him stay at his Surplus Hut while he is out. The news about the big race at Radiator Springs is attracting a lot of attention and C.H.R.O.M.E. has decided to activate you as an agent. There is a catch of course. You must prove you can handle their training regimen—the C.H.R.O.M.E-athalon. The regimen turns out to be some basic ability tests including a jump, quick turn, and side bash (used to smash into cars when racing).

New Toy Unlocked: Missiles Challenge

NOTE

Buying the Missiles Challenge unlocks the following challenges.

Challenge Available: Battle Race in Radiator Springs and C.H.R.O.M.E.-athalon

Alert Mission: Speeder

Mission Giver: Little Grey Car (blue picture in mission list)
Type: Delivery (tow)
Rewards: 50 Coins / 25 Sparks

This is a repeatable mission that will be unlocked at this point. Chase down the speeding car with a red flashing light and tow it to Mater's Impound.

Tractor Tipping

Mission Giver: Finn
Type: Combat
Rewards: 100 Coins / 25 Sparks

There is some suspicious activity around town and Finn suggests that you brush up on your stealth skills by surprising five tractors. Go to the fenced farm area and sneak up on the tractors. Get in close and honk the horn to scare the hapless tractors and cause them to tip over.

New Toy Unlocked: Machine Gun Challenge

NOTE

Buying the Machine Gun Challenge unlocks the following challenges.

Challenge Available: Shoot for Loot and Throw and Go (when Impact Mine Challenge is purchased)

Chick Hicks' Missions

Meet Chick at The Barn

Mission Giver: Chick (near Mater's Impound)
Type: Locate
Rewards: 25 Coins / 25 Sparks

Chick wants to race you to The Barn, but it's not really a race. Take your time to get there and follow the green arrow to find him out front.

Take a Practice Lap

Mission Giver: Chick (near The Barn)
Type: Race
Rewards: 50 Coins / 25 Sparks

Chick is all about racing and he wants to challenge you to a spin around town. However, out of the pure generosity of his motor he will let you take a practice lap first, so you don't hurt yourself. There is no pressure on the practice lap around Radiator Springs, so take it easy and learn the course.

Chick's Challenge

Mission Giver: Chick (near The Barn)
Type: Race
Rewards: 250 Coins / 100 Sparks

Talk to Chick and get ready to race for real this time! Rev your engine to max out the turbo meter and take first

place from the start of the race. However don't expect to hold that spot for the entire race. Chick is very aggressive and he may overtake the number one spot. Don't give up even if your car goes off the track or falls into second place. The race is meant to be close and with three laps there is a lot of opportunity to retake the lead. One good spot to use is the springing platform in front of Sarge's Surplus Hut. This tricky spot will hurl your vehicle into the air, allowing your car to cut across a bit of the track and gain an advantage.

Drift into every corner to fill the turbo meter and blaze across the field to cut off sections of track to gain a bit of an edge. Keep in mind that in general cars will always go faster on the track versus cutting corners in the grass or dirt. This race is very forgiving in terms of straying off course and there are a few alternative routes that can be taken as long as your car is close to the track.

Challenge Available: Radiator Farm Race and Farm Battle (if Missile Challenge has been purchased)

New Toy Unlocked: Turbo Level 1

Ramone's Missions

NOTE

There is a small grey car in the far north, near a ramp leading up the rocky hills. This little vehicle will remind you to purchase the tow chain upgrades unlocked from Ramone's missions. These missions don't have to be completed to purchase the toys, and if you buy them before speaking to the car, they will be automatically be completed when you talk to it.

Tow Ramone

Mission Giver: Flo
Type: Delivery (tow)
Rewards: 100 Coins / 50 Sparks

Ramone is in a pretty embarrassing spot for a car—he ran out of gas! He was cruising around and completely lost track of his fuel level. Tow Mater may not be around, but any of the Cars Characters can tow cars almost as well as the famous brown truck. Get near Ramone and activate the tow cable. Once he is hooked up, drive him back to Flo's for a fill-up.

New Toy Unlocked: Tow Chain Level 2

Misplaced Paint

Mission Giver: Ramone (near Flo's)
Type: Collect
Rewards: 200 Coins / 100 Sparks

Ramone is trying out for a new reality show called Detail My Dents, but he is missing his premium paint cans. Use the compass to collect ten hidden paint cans. Collecting the cans is pretty obvious and won't require a lot of tricky leaps, but a few are on higher ledges.

New Toy Unlocked: Tow Chain Level 3

NOTE

Buy and collect Tow Chain Level 3 to unlock the following.

New Toy Unlocked: Tow Chain Level 4

New Toy Unlocked: Turbo Level 1

New Toy Unlocked: Ramone's House of Body Art

New Paint Job

Mission Giver: Ramone (near Flo's)
Type: Decorate
Rewards: 200 Coins / 100 Sparks

Detail My Dents features lots of tricked-out sedans. If Ramone wants to get on the show he has to give one of his customers a new custom color. Buy Ramone's House of Body Art and tow a car to the shop to decorate it with a new color.

Fillmore's Missions

Corny Concoction

Mission Giver: Fillmore
Type: Collect
Rewards: 50 Sparks

Fillmore's organic fuels are awesome, but he is working on making the ultimate fuel that only requires one tank. The groovy van needs some new materials and asks your help to collect three corn for his new recipe. Follow the compass and use the tow cable to collect the corn.

When the corn is attached to your car, tow it back to Fillmore's and go to the back near several colorful barrels to drop it off in the mixer.

New Toy Unlocked: Turbo Level 2

Stunts and Racing Tracks

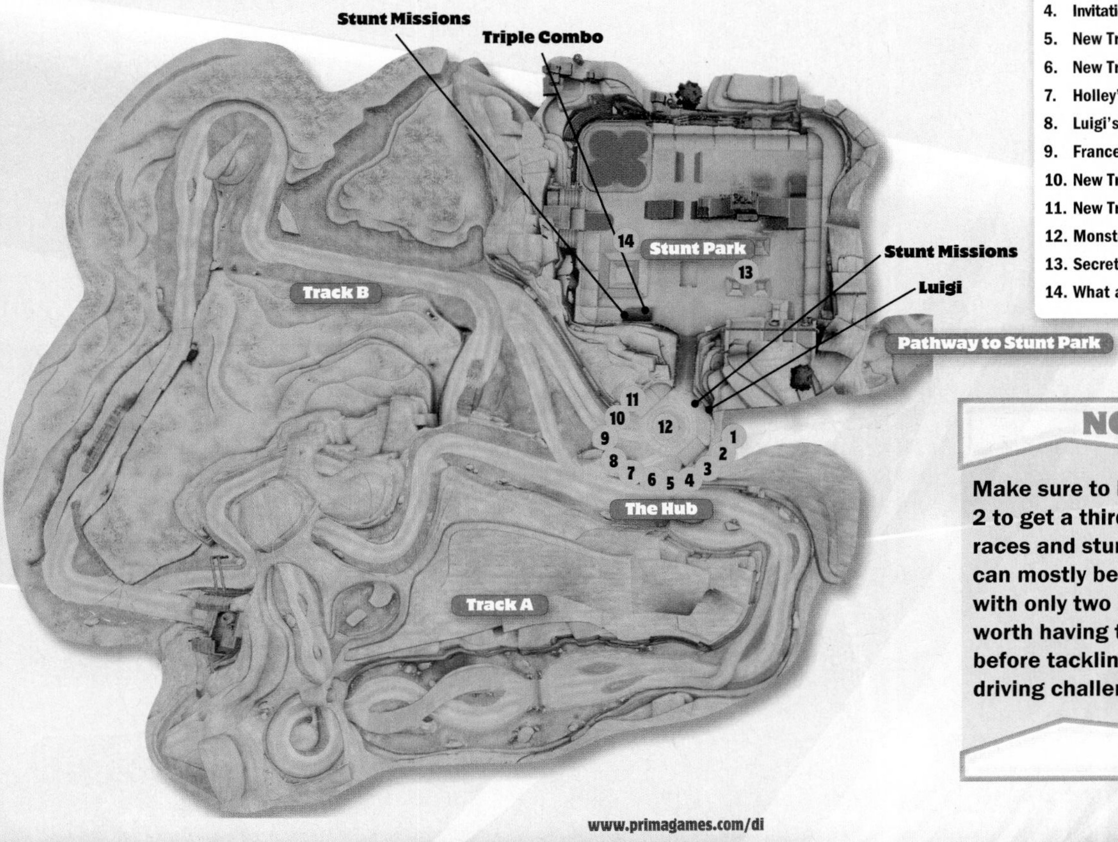

Challenges

1. Invitational Race
2. Invitational Battle Race
3. Invitational Reverse Race
4. Invitational Reverse Battle Race
5. New Track Race
6. New Track Battle
7. Holley's Awesome Challenge
8. Luigi's Track Race
9. Francesco's Battle Race
10. New Track Battle Reverse
11. New Track Race Reverse
12. Monster Truck Race
13. Secret Agent Mater
14. What a Stunt

Willy's Butte

Stunt Missions
Triple Combo
Stunt Park
Stunt Missions
Luigi
Track B
Pathway to Stunt Park
The Hub
Track A

NOTE

Make sure to buy Turbo Level 2 to get a third turbo bar. The races and stunts in this area can mostly be completed with only two bars, but it is worth having the upgrade before tackling any of these driving challenges.

The Hub (Racing Missions)

Track Trash Takedown

Mission Giver: Luigi (at The Hub)
Type: Destroy
Rewards: 100 Coins / 25 Sparks

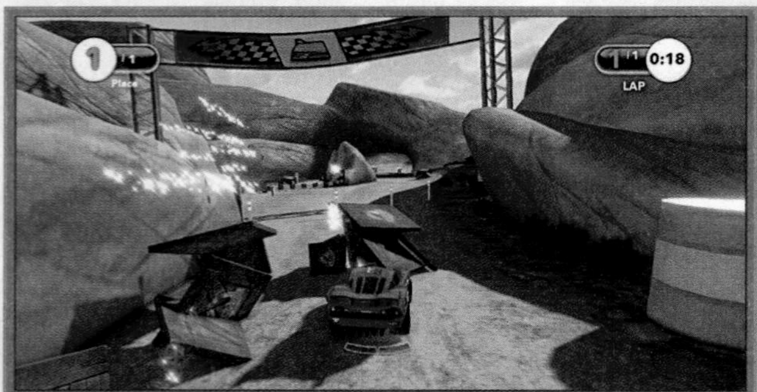

Luigi's new track is ready to go... well except for all the shipping crates littering the course. Take a practice lap on the new track and smash through all the trash.

Race The King

Mission Giver: Dark Grey Car (green picture in mission list)
Type: Race
Rewards: 300 Coins / 75 Sparks

It seems that The King helped Luigi with the supplies for the track and now that it is finished he is looking for someone to race. Take up the challenge and try out the first real race on the new track. Start out with a full turbo boost and make sure to drift into each corner. This track is a lot more complex than previous ones and there are a lot more alternate routes as well as obstacles. While the obstacles are not that hard to avoid, hitting them will cost precious time. Avoid the orange-and-yellow barrels or they will explode and set you back a bit. Also, make sure to avoid or simply jump over the blue-and-white-striped rails.

Drifting and possibly doing tricks in the air can fill your turbo meter, but make sure to grab the fuel cans that can help top off your turbo quickly.

There are lots of options to take advantage of on this course, but don't expect them to simply be short cuts. Following the main track is faster than going through the dirt, but with a good boost you can cut off sections of the track and save time. Also, there are lots of traffic blockages with white-and-orange-striped planks. These can be smashed through to open a new route. However, taking an alternate path is not a guarantee that it is quicker than following the track.

What makes the optional paths attractive is when it has turbo cans! The tricky path to the left has a lot of turbo refilling cans, but if your turbo meter is already full it would be better off to use the boost on the long straightaway and cover more ground quickly and safely.

New Toy Unlocked: Cozy Cone Motel

Challenge Available: Race Track A Forward

Side Mission

Cozy Cone Launch

Mission Giver: Yellow Car (blue picture in mission list)
Type: Delivery (tow)
Rewards: 200 Coins / 50 Sparks

This car on the outskirts of town wants to go to the Cozy Cone. Simply tow the vehicle to the Cozy Cone and toss it in.

Balloon Poppin'

Mission Giver: Luigi
Type: Collect/Destroy
Rewards: 100 Coins / 25 Sparks

Guido was up to his old tricks or he did a terrible job of placing the red balloons. Luigi wants you to pop all three. This won't require any special tricks—just line up beneath them on the ramps, turn around and get some distance, flip back around once more, and gun it to reach the balloons.

NOTE

Completing this mission opens the Stunt Park side missions.

New Toy Unlocked: Impact Mine Challenge

Challenge Available: Throw and Go (after purchasing Impact Mine Challenge)

Race Reversal

Mission Giver: Luigi
Type: Race
Rewards: 300 Coins / 75 Sparks

Poor Luigi. It seems nobody is impressed with his track. He wants his track to be numero uno, not just "fine". Luigi has an idea rumbling under his hood to reverse the track to create The Backwards Track Race. This is the same track you raced The King, but driving on it backwards opens up some new options. It's important to note that you don't have to win the race; coming in second will still complete the mission.

There are several paths to take, but don't always be swayed by a bunch of turbo cans. The path might be tempting, but only if you can navigate it well. Otherwise it is best to stick to the track and drift to build up the turbo meter.

Dirt path shortcuts are great only if you have the speed (turbo boost) to make up for the rough surface that slows you down. Going through these areas without a boost can actually slow you down.

Challenge Available: Race Track A Reverse and Battle Race Track A (if Machine Gun Challenge was purchased)

NOTE

Carlos Veloso Arrives

Race Track B

Luigi's New Track B

Mission Giver: Luigi
Type: Race
Rewards: 300 Coins / 75 Sparks

How does Luigi manage to get so many race tracks made in such a short time? There is a brand new track and it is attracting all the international racers. This is only a two-lap race, and even though you start out in first it is possible to re-take the lead from almost any position. Collect the turbo fuel cans, but don't drive recklessly to get them. There are often several options, so pick the one that is most comfortable to navigate.

If you hit the ramp with enough speed, it will propel you to the top level. There are two large holes to drive around, but there are also several turbo boosting cans. Going to the top level is a gamble that only pays off if you can get the cans without crashing.

New Toy Unlocked: Monster Truck Tires

Challenge Available: Race Track B Forward, Battle Race Track B, and Monster Truck Race in Radiator Springs (if Monster Truck Tires were purchased)

NOTE

After completing the initial racing path and stunt missions it is time to return to Radiator Springs for a new event.

Stunt Side Mission

NOTE

All of the tricky stunt missions are completely optional and do not tie in directly to the story. However, there is one gold star to earn on this path, and performing tricks is a really fun part of the game that you simply do not want to miss!

Stunted Growth

Mission Giver: Dark Grey Car (green picture in mission list)
Type: Trick/Stunt
Rewards: 50 Sparks

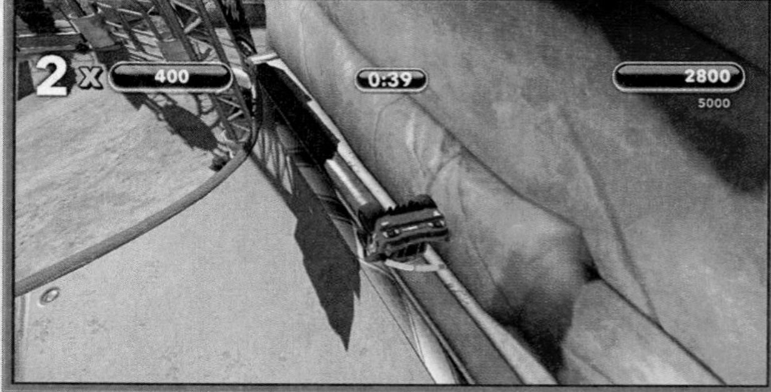

Perform enough tricks in the hub to earn at least 5,000 points before the 2 minute time limit expires. Drift in a circle and completely fill your turbo power, then hit one of the grey halfpipes at full speed to perform a double or triple trick. The method to rack up points fast is to quickly perform a trick and immediately after perform a different trick in another direction.

NOTE

Completing this mission opens the Stunt Park side missions.

Stunt Park

Ring Round Up

Mission Giver: Dark Grey Car (green picture in mission list)
Type: Trick/Stunt
Rewards: 100 Coins / 25 Sparks

To prove you are a master trickster, do a trick through 15 rings around the Stunt Park in 3 minutes. In reality, you don't need to do a fancy trick through the rings as a simple jump will do the job. There should be plenty of time to go through all the rings as long as you don't chase them around the course. Each corner has several in close proximity and the best approach is to complete the rings in groups that are very close. There are more than 15 rings on the track, so don't spend too much time trying to go through one if it's giving you trouble.

New Toy Unlocked: Super Pipe

Challenge Available: Monster Truck Race Track B (after purchasing Monster Tires)

Learn Grind

Mission Giver: Dark Grey Car (green picture in mission list)
Type: Tutorial
Rewards: 100 Coins / 25 Sparks

The little car in the Stunt Park will teach you to grind on special rails after purchasing the Super Pipe. Drifting on the rails will allow the car to grind and build the turbo meter as well. Drive up the ramp to the right of the car and grind through the red balloons over the car.

Double Combos

Mission Giver: Dark Grey Car (green picture in mission list)
Type: Trick/Stunt
Rewards: 500 Coins / 100 Sparks

This car wants to see some cool double combos. A double trick is performing the same trick twice while a double combo is doing two different tricks in a row. You have 2 minutes to perform 3 combos that consist of a front flip and spin, spin and roll, and back and front flip combos.

New Toy Unlocked: Super Ramp

Challenge Available: Monster Truck Race Track B (after purchasing Monster Tires)

Triple Combos

Mission Giver: Tan Car (green picture in mission list)
Type: Trick/Stunt
Rewards: 750 Coins / 100 Sparks

The other car in the Stunt Park wants to see if you can pull off three triple combos in 2 minutes. However, it gets to choose the tricks, and they are not simply doing the same trick three times. The first combo trick is a front flip, back flip, and front flip. The second combo is a barrel roll, front flip, and spin. The final combo series is a spin, barrel roll, and spin. To do the triple tricks make sure to drift until your turbo power is maximized.

New Toy Unlocked: Stunt Clover Pool

Challenge Available: Extended Time Stunt (after purchasing Stunt Clover Pool, Super Pipe, and Full Pipe)

NOTE

After completing the racing path and stunt missions, it is time to return to Radiator Springs for a new event.

Fillmore's Missions

Tricky, Tricky

Mission Giver: Fillmore
Type: Trick/Stunt
Rewards: 500 Coins / 100 Sparks

Stop in to check on your pal Fillmore to get an update on his new fuel formula. Apparently a famous stunt car wants to use the newly opened Stunt Park and it is up to you to do some tricks around town to get that stunt car's attention. The goal of this mission is to perform enough stunts to earn 3,000 points in 1 minute and 30 seconds. There are lots places to pull off stunts in the town, but if you put Ramone's Body Art shop in the default spot it will have a ramp right next to Fillmore. With a decent amount of speed, it should be fairly easy to use that ramp to pull of double combos like a spin and barrel roll for 2 x 600 points.

New Toy Unlocked: Full Pipe

Challenge Available: Radiator Stunt Score and Stunt Park Stunt Score + Extended Time Stunt [Mater Only] (after purchasing Full Pipe)

Gourd Gatherer

Mission Giver: Fillmore
Type: Collect
Rewards: 100 Sparks

The last batch of fuel Fillmore was cooking up didn't quite meet his expectations. To get more zing he wants to try a new ingredient and is enlisting your help to collect three pumpkins. Follow the compass to tow back the pumpkin to the barrel mixer for his new brew.

NOTE

Incoming Storm - Tornado Alert

Tractor Rescue

Mission Giver: Fillmore
Type: Delivery (tow)
Rewards: 300 Coins / 100 Sparks

The tractors are scared of the storm and need to be towed back to The Barn. Drive by The Farm and use the tow cable to haul five of them safely in The Barn. This is a great time to use the multiple tow cables you bought to drag in several tractors at a time. When all five of them are safe the storm will subside.

Side Mission

Monster Mess

Mission Giver: Dark Grey Car (blue picture in mission list)
Type: Destroy
Rewards: 300 Coins / 100 Sparks

Everyone loves a good monster truck smash-up! This car wants to see a bunch of broken trailers crushed with the Monster Tires. Equip the Monster Tires at the Tire Change Pad and hunt down the trailers with the compass.

Challenge Available: Monster Mash (after purchasing Monster Tires)

Storm Damage

Mission Giver: Ramone
Type: Decorate
Rewards: 300 Coins / 100 Sparks

While you were taking care of the tractors, the storm caused a lot of damage to the town. Check in with Ramone to help repair and repaint four storm-damaged buildings: Flo's, the Fire Station, Luigi's Casa Della Tires, and Mater's Impound.

Stanley's Travels

Mission Giver: Finn
Type: Delivery (tow)
Rewards: 300 Coins / 100 Sparks

The famous statue of Stanley in front of the Fire Station blew away in the storm. Use the compass to find the statue and tow it back to its rightful place in front of the Fire Station. When it is returned it will give the town a much needed morale boost after the storm's devastation.

Wrong Turn

Mission Giver: Finn
Type: Locate
Rewards: 500 Coins / 100 Sparks

The C.H.R.O.M.E. satellite is showing that five tourist cars are stuck in precarious spots around town, thanks to the storm. Use the compass to track down the cars to perform some search and rescue operations. Many of the cars are indeed stuck in tough spots that will require some tricky jumps. Make sure to build up enough speed when hitting the ramps and activate the tow cable as soon as you get close so you don't sail past the cars. Ultimately, the cars don't need to be towed anywhere and simply need to be touched.

Side Mission

Timed Tractor Tip

NOTE

Requires completion of the Little Bo Beep mission.

Mission Giver: Little Grey Car (Blue picture)
Type: Combat
Rewards: 300 Coins / 50 Sparks

The little car in front of The Barn doesn't seem to have a lot of sympathy for the trauma the tractors went through after the storm. It wants you to try to tip five tractors in 1 minute. An easy way to meet this goal is simply to find one tractor and keep tipping it, by honking, as soon as it gets back on its wheels.

NOTE

Storm Clean Up Completed

Paint the Town

Mission Giver: Flo
Type: Decorate
Rewards: 500 Coins / 100 Sparks

Now that the storm has subsided and the town has been repaired, it's time to add a bit of "ka-chow" to show off to the other racers who they support. Customize three buildings using the Ka-chow! texture found in a red capsule.

Ready to Race at Willy's Butte

With the new Race Track B ready to go and the storm under control, the focus of the town shifts to racing. Many famous international racers are heading to Radiator Springs. One of the first famous cars to arrive is Shu Todoroki from Japan.

Double Back Dash

Mission Giver: Luigi
Type: Race
Rewards: 500 Coins / 100 Sparks

A new reverse race track (Track B) is now open to celebrate the re-beautification of Radiator Springs. Compete in the new reverse race going up against Shu Todoroki and take the number one spot! This is a relatively short race with only two laps, so there is not a lot of time to get comfortable on the track. On your first attempt, just get familiar with the course and don't feel pressured to win. Once you have a good understanding of its alternate paths and turbo boosting areas it will be a lot easier to win.

The ramps are fun for a thrill, but they don't always provide an edge in racing. Soaring through the air is slower than using a turbo in a straightaway and landing might not put you in a good position to collect turbo cans.

Look for any spot to cut corners where you can avoid a decent amount of the track. However, make sure to drift into corners and use the speed of turbo on rough terrains.

A fully upgraded turbo will provide four bars of speed-boosting power. There is no reason to hold on to that race-winning speed for too long, but it is a good idea to save one meter towards the end. Often a last lap turbo boost at the end can be used to steal a victory in a come-from-behind photo finish.

Challenge Available: Race Track B Reverse and Battle Race B Reverse (after purchasing Missile Challenge)

Side Mission

Francesco's Challenge

NOTE

This side mission requires completion of the Double Combos mission.

Mission Giver: Dark Grey Car Hub (blue picture in mission list)
Type: Race
Rewards: 750 Coins / 150 Sparks

Francesco Bernoulli has arrived on the scene and he's set up a race with trick barrels scattered around the track. This race is between you and the Italian sports car. It is the same reverse course you just beat Shu Todoroki on, so it should be very familiar. This race is only two laps, but it is a lot more treacherous due to all the explosive red-and-yellow-striped barrels.

Avoid the main central path, as that is usually a prime spot for barrels. Also, be careful of ramps that can land you in a bad spot right in front of a group of explosive problems. Stick to the outside areas to collect turbo boosts and avoid the road hazards Francesco has left for you.

Radiator Springs Wrap Up

Fillmore's Ultimate Fuel

Mission Giver: Fillmore
Type: Collect
Rewards: 300 Coins / 100 Sparks

Fillmore thinks he finally figured out the ingredient he needs for the ultimate fuel. To make a hot organic fuel, he needs a hot organic vegetable like a spicy red pepper. Use the compass to round up three peppers. These are a lot harder to get a hold of than the corn and pumpkins. Some will require daring jumps and require you to activate the tow cable in mid-air to grab the hot veggies.

Impound Go-Round

Mission Giver: Finn
Type: Delivery (tow)
Rewards: 300 Coins / 100 Sparks

The vandals that were captured earlier have escaped from Mater's Impound. Bring them all back before they can do any damage to the town. Track down the hot rods and tow the five mischievous cars back to the Impound. If the hot rods are tough to capture, build up the turbo meter and use a boost on a straight stretch of road to overtake them.

The Final Race — International Race Invitational

Radiator Springs Invitational

Mission Giver: Luigi
Type: Race
Rewards: 1,000 Coins / 100 Sparks

When six of the best racing cars in the world are competing in a five-lap race, you know it will be tough to win. The good and bad thing about this race is that any car can catch up to first place. There are enough variations from car crashes, vehicle bashing, and great drifting or turbo usage that almost any car can win from any position. This means don't give up hope if you fall several spots back. Simply try to always improve your position. The best thing about holding first place is that there are not a lot of distractions. When the track is open, there are lots of options to grab turbo boosting cans.

If the other racers start to pack together, look for alternate routes—not simply to lower your track time, but to break away from the bunch. The other racers are pretty adept at smashing into you, and that could easily cause a loss of one or two places. There are several sections like this plateau that can shave off a bit of time, but more importantly it can allow you a way to avoid the crowd.

Experience on the track is invaluable because it teaches when to use a turbo to maximize speed and when to coast a bit to slow down enough to grab turbo boosting cans. For example, it can be a good idea to boost when there is a long stretch of track, but hitting the top of the hill at top speed will send your car too high in the air, preventing you from being able to grab all the turbo cans as you land.

Of course drifting is important in this race and you use it whenever you can, but that doesn't mean holding it so that you slow down or crash. There are a few very tight turns such as this that requires heavy drifting to keep top speed in the turns. Right before this, spot another sharp turn and several turbo tanks. While it is good to max out the turbo meter, it is a waste to not use it whenever possible.

Challenges Available: Race Track C Forward and Race Track C Reverse, Battle Race Track C Forward (after purchasing Machine Gun Challenge), Battle Race Track C Reverse (after purchasing Mine Challenge)

Collectibles

Radiator Springs

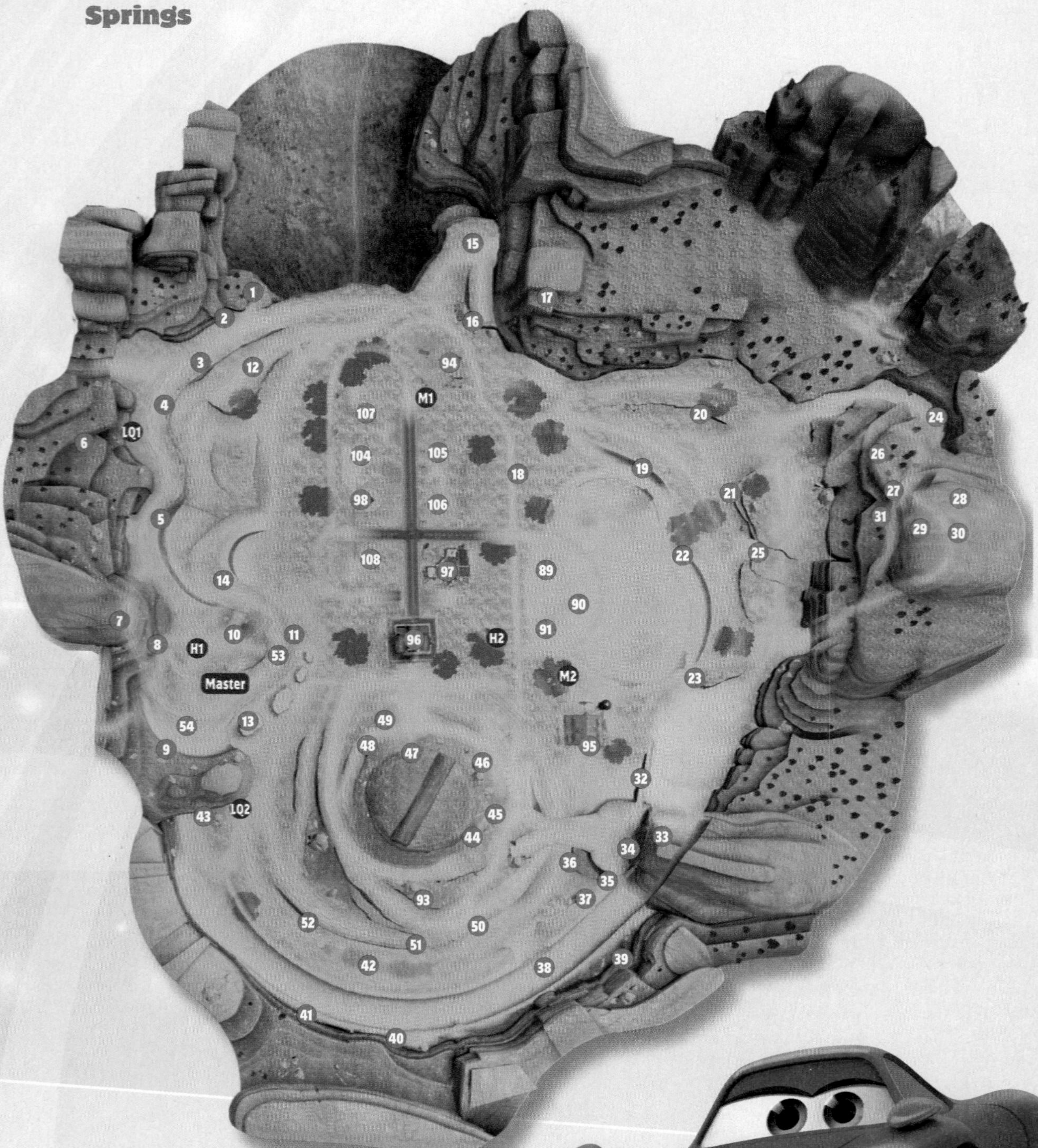

Willy's Butte

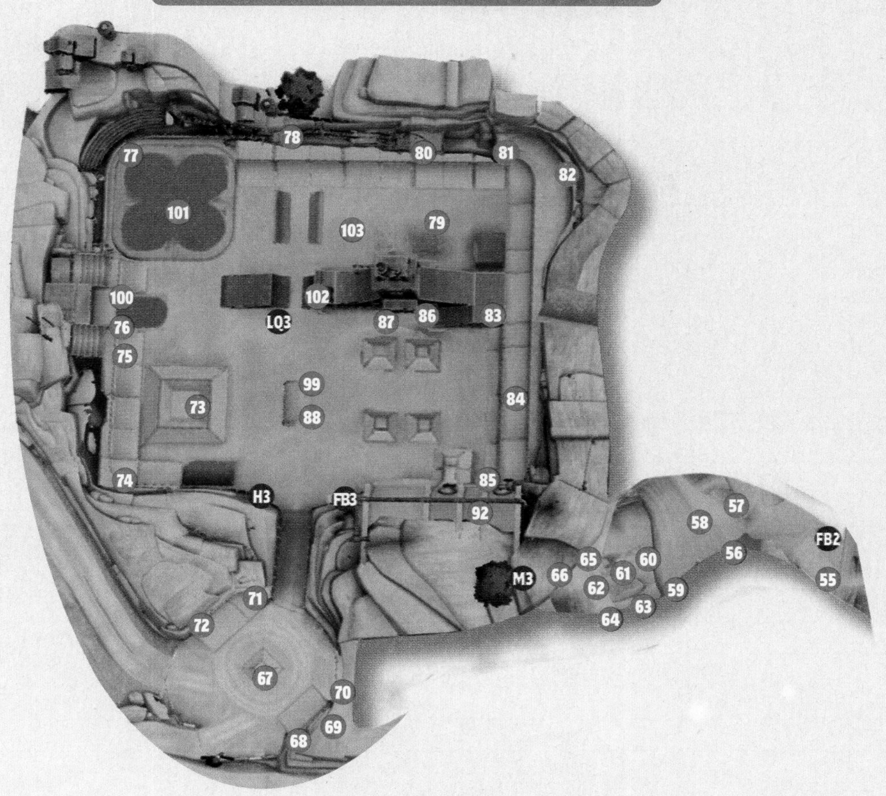

Red Capsules

#	Unlockable Item	Zone	Description
1	Fillmore Wall	Vista Overlook	On the Vista Overlook nearest the Old Road.
2	Sheet Metal Trim	Old Road	Driving up the Old Road from the Vista Overlook on the right.
3	Holley Purple Trim	Old Road	At the end of the rail nearest the Vista Overlook.
4	Carbon Fiber Trim	Old Road	On the middle of the railing on the Old Road.
5	Aqua Stucco	Old Road	At the end of the rail nearest the Balcony.
6	Shingle Accent	Old Road	In the middle of the tunnel in the Old Road.
7	Camouflage	Balcony	In the middle of the tunnel in the Balcony.
8	Camera	Balcony	Floating at the peak of the ramp jump in the Balcony.
9	Wood Accent	Balcony	At the top of the banked wall on the Balcony.
10	Camo Accent	Balcony	In between the two ramps facing out on the Balcony.
11	Gold Piston Cup	Balcony	On the lower part of the Balcony at the end of the railing.
12	Top Hat	Old Road	At the edge of the Old Road facing the Town.
13	Spare Parts Windmill	Balcony	On the island ramp jumps that lead to the Balcony.
14	Crown	Balcony	On the top of the ramp that leads to the Balcony from the Town.
15	Spiked Wheels	Range	At the Range nearest the Vista Overlook.
16	Small Wheels	Range	On the ramp at the Range.
17	Wind Chime	Range	Inside the tunnel at the Range.
18	Colored Tires	Town	In between the Mater's Impound Lot and the Farm.
19	Rusteze Baseball Hat	Cave Track	In between the Farm and the Cave Track main entrance.
20	Guido at Work Sign	Cave Track	Along the ledge leading to the Cave Track from the Range.
21	Tire Tree	Cave Track	On the ledge near the main front entrance of the Cave Track.
22	Tiara	Cave Track	On the little ledge right by the Farm.
23	Flower Quilt Accent	Cave Track	On the top of the rock near the Farm.
24	Sheet Metal Accent	Cave Track	Near the turning sign at the back of the main entrance of the Cave Track.
25	Italian Afro	Cave Track	Near the bottom entrance to the Cave Track nearest the Farm.
26	Bow	Cave Track	On the right part of the main entrance to the Cave Track.
27	Blue Flags	Cave Track	Off the ledge on the upper level of the Cave Track.
28	Tank Treads	Cave Track	On the raised platform in the side of the wall on the upper level of the Cave Track.
29	Stop Sign	Cave Track	On the larger island jump platform on the upper level of the Cave Track.

#	Unlockable Item	Zone	Description
30	Stickers	Cave Track	On the ledge across from the island jumps on the upper level of the Cave Track.
31	Interstate Sign	Cave Track	Along the wall on the lower level of the Cave Track.
32	Pizza Planet Rocket	Farm	In the air on the ramp jump behind the Farm.
33	Holley Accent	Half Pipe Gulch	In the tunnel at Half Pipe.
34	Tractor Wheels	Half Pipe Gulch	Up on the side of the wall at Half Pipe.
35	Surfboard	Half Pipe Gulch	In the air on the ramp jump next to the tunnel in Half Pipe.
36	Tractor Crossing Sign	Half Pipe Gulch	On the ledge near the tunnel in Half Pipe.
37	Sports Car Topiary	Half Pipe Gulch	Under the ramp jump next to the tunnel in Half Pipe.
38	Pink Camo	Half Pipe Gulch	On top of some barrels in Half Pipe.
39	Shiny Wood Accent	Half Pipe Gulch	On top of the Half Pipe ledge near the tunnel.
40	Tin	Half Pipe Gulch	On top of the Half Pipe ledge near the bend.
41	Sandbag Barricade	Half Pipe Gulch	On top of the Half Pipe ledge near the bend.
42	Pink Flamingo 1	Half Pipe Gulch	In the air on the ramp jump at the bend of Half Pipe.
43	Red Mailbox	Half Pipe Gulch	Next to a rock near the opposite side of the tunnel in Half Pipe.
44	Gas Hat	Cap	On the rail that is sticking out of the trail on the Cap.
45	Cars Crossing Sign	Cap	On top of a rock at the front Base of the Cap.
46	Holley's Wall	Cap	On the trail, nearest the Farm, leading up to the top of the Cap.
47	Tree Camo	Cap	On the Cap under the "RS" letters.
48	Mater Trim	Cap	On the trail, nearest the Balcony, leading up to the top of the Cap.
49	Red Brick	Cap	On a lip nearest the Balcony of the Cap.
50	Parking Meter	Cap	On the end of the rail at the very back side of the Cap.
51	Sarge's Antique Cannon	Cap	On the middle of the rail at the very back side of the Cap.
52	Holley's Hubcap Pinwheel	Cap	On the end of the rail at the very back side of the Cap.
53	Basic Brick	Balcony	Underneath the Balcony nearest the Town.
54	Mater Wall	Balcony	Underneath the Balcony nearest the island jumps.
55	Beige Stucco	Pathway to Stunt Park	At the entrance to the Pathway to Stunt Park.
56	Pink Flamingo 2	Pathway to Stunt Park	On the ramp to the left near the entrance to the Pathway to Stunt Park.
57	Rusty Trim	Pathway to Stunt Park	On the ground to the right near the entrance to the Pathway to Stunt Park.
58	Hangin' Tire	Pathway to Stunt Park	On the wall to the right near the entrance to the Pathway to Stunt Park.
59	Baseball Hat	Pathway to Stunt Park	On the upper ledge on the left side of the Pathway to Stunt Park.
60	Tire Tracks	Pathway to Stunt Park	Under the ramp jump in the Pathway to Stunt Park.
61	Motorin' Topiary	Pathway to Stunt Park	In the air on the ramp jump in the Pathway to Stunt Park.
62	Monster Wheels	Pathway to Stunt Park	On the wall past the jump in the Pathway to Stunt Park.
63	Orange Cone	Pathway to Stunt Park	On the ledge to the left past the jump in the Pathway to Stunt Park.
64	Mohawk	Pathway to Stunt Park	On the far side of the jump in the Pathway to Stunt Park.
65	Grass Accent	Pathway to Stunt Park	Tucked in the bottom of the wall on landing part of the ramp.
66	Gold Parking Meter	Pathway to Stunt Park	At the exit of the Pathway to Stunt Park.
67	Wood Plank	Hub	In the middle of the Hub on the platform.
68	Dinoco Feather Hat	Hub	On the right side of the ramp near the Pathway to Stunt Park.
69	Blue Burnout	Hub	On the center of the ramp near the Pathway to Stunt Park.
70	Wood Trim	Hub	On the left side of the ramp near the Pathway to Stunt Park.
71	Highway Walls	Hub	On the ramp to the right near Stunt Park.
72	Corrugated Wall	Hub	On the ramp to the left near Stunt Park.
73	Mattress	Stunt Park	Inside the Square Pool to the left as you enter.
74	Starting Gate Lights	Stunt Park	Above the 1/4 Pipe Turn.
75	Concrete Accent	Stunt Park	On the rail leading to the top of the Cradle Pool.
76	Yellow Flags	Stunt Park	Above the Cradle Pool.
77	Wood Planks Accent	Stunt Park	At the back of the Clover Pool.
78	Low Profile Wheels	Stunt Park	On the Mine Car Track.
79	Rusty Wall	Stunt Park	On top of the four-way ramp in the back of Stunt Park.
80	Dinoco Baseball Hat	Stunt Park	On the far side of the Mine Car Track.
81	Tire Shrub	Stunt Park	On the upper part of the Bank Jump.

#	Unlockable Item	Zone	Description
82	White Stucco	Stunt Park	In the corner on the upper part of the Bank Jump.
83	Tire Accent	Stunt Park	On the ramp leading to the Big Jump in Stunt Park.
84	Announcer Speakers	Stunt Park	On the ledge for the 1/4 Pipe Edge.
85	Winner's Circle	Stunt Park	In the corner of the 1/4 Pipe Edge.
86	Checkered Flags	Stunt Park	In the circular tunnel inside the Big Jump Tower.
87	Blue Mailbox	Stunt Park	In the square tunnel inside the Big Jump Tower.
88	Checkerboard Trim	Stunt Park	Inside the Full Pipe.
89	Thin Wheels	Farm	In a hay bale in the Farm.
90	Traffic Cone	Farm	In a hay bale in the Farm.
91	Red Firestone	Farm	In a hay bale in the Farm.
92	Bronze Piston Cup	Stunt Park	Inside the wall tunnel to the right entering Stunt Park.
93	Flo's Mailbox	Cap	On the back ledge of the Cap; appears only after Flo's Mission.

Green Capsules

#	Unlockable Item	Zone	Description
94	Radiator Springs Plants Toy Pack 1	Town	On the roof of Mater's Building.
95	Flo's V8 Café	Town	In the barn on the second level at the Farm.
96	Radiator Springs Vehicle Toy Pack	Town	Inside the Court House in the Town.
97	Tow Mater Impound Lot	Town	On top of Luigi's Building.
98	Radiator Springs Plants Toy Pack 3	Town	Inside of Flo's Café.
99	Radiator Springs Decoration Toy Pack 3	Stunt Park	On top of the Full Pipe at Stunt Park.
100	Radiator Springs Decoration Toy Pack 4	Stunt Park	In the Cradle Pool at Stunt Park.
101	Radiator Springs Courthouse	Stunt Park	In the Clover Pool at Stunt Park.
102	Luigi's Casa Della Tires	Stunt Park	Off the Big Jump at Stunt Park.
103	Radiator Springs Farmhouse	Stunt Park	In the air past the Quarter Pipe.
104	Radiator Springs Decoration Toy Pack 2	Town	On top of Sarge's Building.
105	Radiator Springs Plants Toy Pack 4	Town	On top of the Curios Building.
106	Radiator Springs Decoration Toy Pack 1	Town	Inside the Body Art Building.
107	Radiator Springs Plants Toy Pack 2	Town	Inside Fillmore's Building.
108	Radiator Springs Critter Toy Pack	Town	On the roof of Cozy Cone.

Infinity Chests/Vault

#	Unlockable Item	Zone	Description
FB-1	Francesco Bernoulli Chest 1	Town	By the tree behind Flo's building.
FB-2	Francesco Bernoulli Chest 2	Connector Tunnel	At the entrance to the Pathway to Stunt Park.
FB-3	Francesco Bernoulli Chest 3	Stunt Park	Directly to the right exiting the Pathway to Stunt Park.
Holley-1	Holley Shiftwell Chest 1	Balcony	On the Balcony near the jumps.
Holley-2	Holley Shiftwell Chest 2	Stunt Park	Directly to the left exiting the Pathway to Stunt Park.
Holley-3	Holley Shiftwell Chest 3	Town	Near the road in front of the Farm.
LQ-1	Lightning McQueen Chest 1	Old Road	On the top part of the Old Road near the middle of railing.
LQ-2	Lightning McQueen Chest 2	Town	On the ground near the Balcony and Half Pipe.
LQ-3	Lightning McQueen Chest 3	Stunt Park	At the Base of the Big Jump.
Master	Cars Avatar Vault - Reward 1	Balcony	Under the Balcony.
Mater-1	Mater Chest 1	Town	Right out front of Mater's Building.
Mater-2	Mater Chest 2	Farm	Right in front of the Farm.
Mater-3	Mater Chest 3	Pathway to Stunt Park	Near the exit to the Pathway to Stunt Park.

Cars Gold Stars

#	Type	Star Names	Star Description
1	Mission	Blazin' Bales!	Bash through all the flaming hay bales.
2	Mission	Finn's In	Purchase and place Sarge's Surplus Hut.
3	Mission	Chick 'n' Farm	Win a race against Chick at the Farm.
4	Mission	Tidyin' Town	Restore the town after the tornado.
5	Mission	Race the King	Complete a race with "The King".
6	Mission	Backtrack	Win a race on the backward version of Luigi's first track.
7	Mission	Speedway Special	Win a race on Luigi's second track.
8	Mission	Drivin' in Reverse	Win a race on the backward version of Luigi's second track.
9	Mission	Higher Tires	Complete a Monster Truck race.
10	Mission	Showstopper	Complete the "Jump at Flo's" mission.
11	Mission	What a Stunt!	Complete the "Tricky, Tricky" mission.
12	Mission	Trickster	Complete the "Triple Combos" mission.
13	Mission	Ring-a-Ding	Complete the "Ring Round Up" mission.
14	Mission	Our Town	Customize buildings in Radiator Springs.
15	Mission	International Race Pro	Finish the Radiator Springs Invitational in First Place.
16	Challenge	Monster Master	Complete two Monster Tire Events.
17	Challenge	Best Battler	Win all Battle Race Challenges at any skill level.
18	Challenge	Race Master	Win all Race Challenges at any skill level.
19	Challenge	Lizzie's License Plates	Collect every license plate.
20	Challenge	Kachow! Customizer	Collect 80 red capsules.
21	Easter Egg	Trick Master	Perform 100 Air Tricks of any kind.
22	Easter Egg	Paint Job Pro	Perform 50 customizations on tourist cars.
23	Easter Egg	Decorator	Place ten decorations.
24	Easter Egg	Never Miss a Trick	Complete every trick mission.
25	Easter Egg	Speed Trap	Catch five speeders.
26	Purchases	Builder	Place every building in the Play Set.
27	Purchases	Tow Master	Purchase every tow chain upgrade.
28	Purchases	Turbo Master	Purchase every turbo upgrade.
29	Purchases	Stunt Master	Purchase every Stunt Park upgrade.
30	Purchases	C.H.R.O.M.E. Agent	Purchase every Weapon Challenge.

Cars Toy List

Toys	Toy Box Export	Toy Type	Commercial
Traffic Truck	Yes	Townsperson	No
Traffic Van	Yes	Townsperson	No
Towable Wrecking Ball	Yes	Unique	No
Towable Ramp	Yes	Unique	No
Turbo Level 1	No	Unique	Yes
Turbo Level 2	No	Unique	No
Full Turbo	No	Unique	No
Sarge's Surplus Hut	Yes	Building	Yes
Fillmore's Organic Fuels	Yes	Building	Yes
Ramone's House of Body Art	Yes	Building	Yes
Radiator Springs Curios	Yes	Building	Yes
Cozy Cone Motel	Yes	Building	Yes

Toys	Toy Box Export	Toy Type	Commercial
Tow Chain Level 2	No	Unique	Yes
Tow Chain Level 3	No	Unique	No
Tow Chain Level 4	No	Unique	No
Machine Gun Challenge	Yes	Unique	Yes
Missiles Challenge	Yes	Unique	Yes
Impact Mine Challenge	Yes	Unique	Yes
Monster Truck Tires	No	Unique	Yes
Super Pipe	No	Building	Yes
Super Ramp	No	Building	No
Full Pipe	Yes	Building	No
Stunt Clover Pool	Yes	Building	No

Cars Challenges

Name	Location	Description	Character	Requirements		
				Easy	Medium	Hard
Holley's Awesome Challenge	Willy's Butte Hub	Take first place as Holley.	Holley	1st place in 3 laps	1st place in 3 laps	1st place in 3 laps
Francesco's Battle Race	Willy's Butte Hub	Win first place in this Battle Race as Francesco Bernoulli.	Francesco	1st place in 3 laps	1st place in 3 laps	1st place in 3 laps
Secret Agent Mater	Stunt Park	Perform tricks as Mater to achieve the point minimum before time runs out.	Mater	10,000 points in 4:20	15,000 points in 4:20	25,000 points in 4:20
Monster Truck Race	Willy's Butte Hub	Compete in a Monster Truck Race with Monster Tires.	Any-Monster Tires	1st place in 3 laps	1st place in 3 laps	1st place in 3 laps
Invitational Reverse Battle Race	Willy's Butte Hub	Use C.H.R.O.M.E. gadgets to defeat the other racers.	Any	1st place in 3 laps	1st place in 3 laps	1st place in 3 laps
Invitational Reverse Race	Willy's Butte Hub	Finish the race in first place.	Any	1st place in 3 laps	1st place in 3 laps	1st place in 3 laps
Invitational Race	Willy's Butte Hub	Finish the race in first place.	Any	1st place in 3 laps	1st place in 3 laps	1st place in 3 laps
Luigi's Track Race	Willy's Butte Hub	Finish the race in first place.	Any	1st place in 3 laps	1st place in 3 laps	1st place in 3 laps
New Track Battle Reverse	Willy's Butte Hub	Use C.H.R.O.M.E. gadgets to defeat the other racers.	Any	1st place in 3 laps	1st place in 3 laps	1st place in 3 laps
New Track Race Reverse	Willy's Butte Hub	Finish the race in first place	Any	1st place in 3 laps	1st place in 3 laps	1st place in 3 laps
New Track Battle	Willy's Butte Hub	Use C.H.R.O.M.E. gadgets to defeat the other racers.	Any	1st place in 3 laps	1st place in 3 laps	1st place in 3 laps
New Track Race	Willy's Butte Hub	Finish the race in first place.	Any	1st place in 3 laps	1st place in 3 laps	1st place in 3 laps
Invitational Battle Race	Willy's Butte Hub	Use C.H.R.O.M.E. gadgets to defeat the other racers.	Any	1st place in 3 laps	1st place in 3 laps	1st place in 3 laps
What a Stunt!	Stunt Park	Earn the minimum required points by performing tricks.	Any	7,500 points in 3:00	12,500 points in 3:00	16,500 points in 3:00
Cave Race	On rock near the Range and Caves	Finish the race in first place to win.	Any	1st place in 3 laps	1st place in 3 laps	1st place in 3 laps
Monster Match	Near the spawn point by the Toy Store	Pass through all checkpoints in time allowed using Monster Tires.	Any-Monster Tires	20 checkpoints in 2:00	20 checkpoints in 1:45	20 checkpoints in 1:30
Shoot for Loot	Vista Overlook	Break as many collectibles as you can before the time runs out.	Any	10 targets in 1:30	15 targets in 1:30	21 targets in 1:30
Farm Race	Near the Barn	Finish the race in first place to win.	Any	1st place in 3 laps	1st place in 3 laps	1st place in 3 laps
Score More	In back of Flo's near the Balcony	Earn the minimum required points by performing tricks.	Any	5,000 points in 3:00	10,000 points in 3:00	15,000 points in 3:00
Farm C.H.R.O.M.E. Race	Near the Barn	Use C.H.R.O.M.E. gadgets to defeat the other racers.	Any	1st place in 3 laps	1st place in 3 laps	1st place in 3 laps
Grab 'n' Go	South section of the Farm	Gather as many collectibles as you can before time runs out.	Any	15 targets in 0:45	20 targets in 0:45	25 targets in 0:45
Flash of Lightning	Between the Farm and Town	Lightning McQueen must win a battle race.	Lightning McQueen	1st place in 3 laps	1st place in 3 laps	1st place in 3 laps
Radiator Race	In back of the Firehouse	Finish the race in first place.	Any	1st place in 3 laps	1st place in 3 laps	1st place in 3 laps
Radiator C.H.R.O.M.E. Race	In back of the Firehouse	Use C.H.R.O.M.E. gadgets to defeat the other racers.	Any	1st place in 3 laps	1st place in 3 laps	1st place in 3 laps
Radiator Biathlon	At the Farm	Break as many collectibles as you can before the time runs out.	Any	7 targets in 1:30	14 targets in 1:30	21 targets in 1:30
Cave C.H.R.O.M.E. Race	On rock near the Range and Caves	Use C.H.R.O.M.E. gadgets to defeat the other racers.	Any	1st place in 3 laps	1st place in 3 laps	1st place in 3 laps
Monster Smash	At the Balcony	Break as many collectibles as you can before the time runs out using Monster Tires.	Any-Monster Tires	15 targets in 0:45	20 targets in 0:45	24 targets in 0:45
Town Race	Between the Farm and Town	Finish the race in first place to win.	Any	1st place in 3 laps	1st place in 3 laps	1st place in 3 laps
Throw and Go	Near the Old Road	Break as many collectibles as you can before the time runs out.	Any	15 targets in 0:30	17 targets in 0:30	18 targets in 0:30

The Lone Ranger
COLBY ROOMING HOUSE

NOTE - For those playing Disney Infinity on the Wii, the Play Sets are a bit different. Access your free eGuide (voucher code on the insert) to access this content.

Cavendish Chaos in Colby

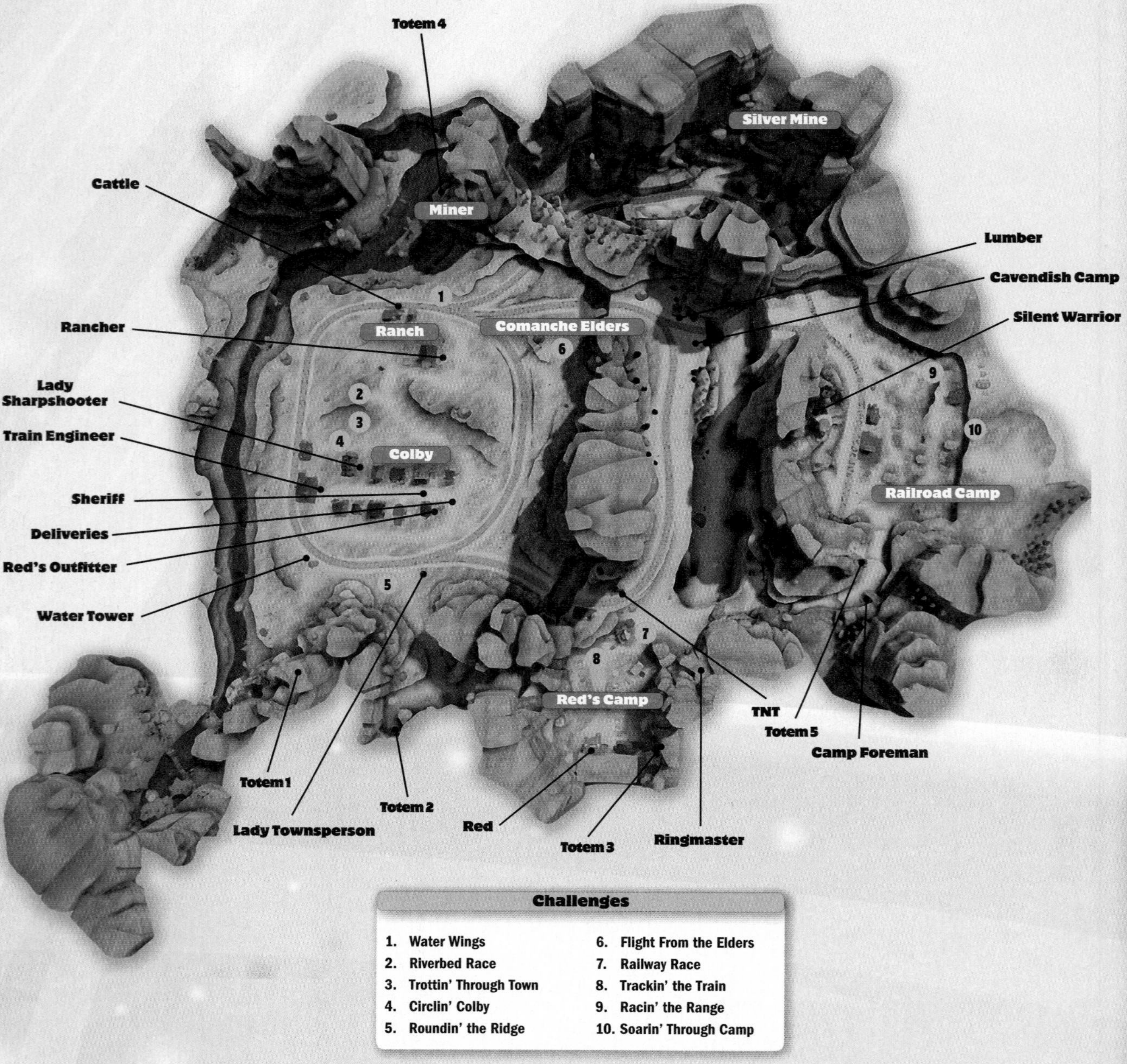

Totem 4
Silver Mine
Miner
Cattle
Lumber
Cavendish Camp
Silent Warrior
Rancher
Ranch
Comanche Elders
Lady Sharpshooter
Train Engineer
Colby
Railroad Camp
Sheriff
Deliveries
Red's Outfitter
Water Tower
Red's Camp
TNT
Totem 5
Camp Foreman
Totem 1
Totem 2
Lady Townsperson
Red
Totem 3
Ringmaster

Challenges

1. Water Wings
2. Riverbed Race
3. Trottin' Through Town
4. Circlin' Colby
5. Roundin' the Ridge
6. Flight From the Elders
7. Railway Race
8. Trackin' the Train
9. Racin' the Range
10. Soarin' Through Camp

Savin' Colby

Mission Giver: Automatic
Type: Combat
Rewards: 500 Coins

Things move fast in the wild west. As soon as the mission starts you are under fire. Take down five members of the Cavendish Gang.

Soakin' the Saloon

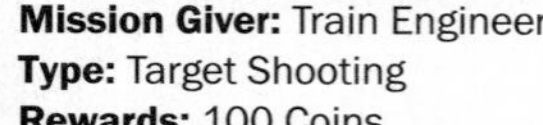

Mission Giver: Train Engineer
Type: Target Shooting
Rewards: 100 Coins

The Saloon is on fire! Put it out by releasing a flood of water from the tower on the roof. Enter first-person-shooting mode to aim for the target on the water tower and put out the fire.

ACCESS YOUR FREE eGUIDE:

Go to
www.primagames.com/DI
and enter the code below

UNLOCK THIS GUIDE
Enter your code:

5su2-2yxa-82wf-q2mj

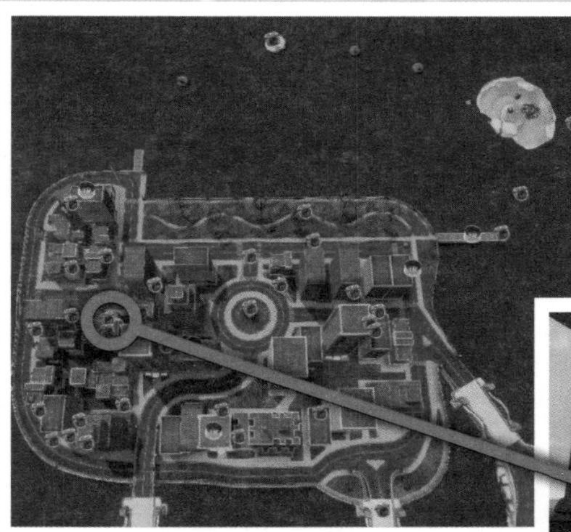

Get a closer look at the PLAY SETS and ZOOM in on MAPS!

Quickly find what you are looking for like ITEMS and COLLECTIBLES with SEARCHABLE and SORTABLE TABLES!

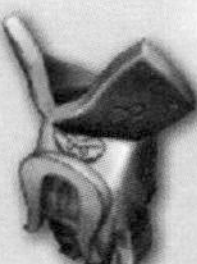

Access your guide from anywhere with an internet connection!

Buildin' Relationships

Mission Giver: Sheriff
Type: Build
Rewards: 250 Coins / 50 Sparks

The Cavendish Gang made a mess of Colby and you need to help repair the city. Run up to the destroyed structures and select Repair Building to fix and repair three of the buildings.

Side Mission

Target Practice

Mission Giver: Lady Sharpshooter
Type: Target Shooting
Rewards: 100 Coins / 20 Sparks

There is a lady in town that is obsessed with shooting skills. She will provide lots of sharpshooting side missions and the first is to literally hit the side of a barn. Take aim at the target on the side of the stable and open fire.

Roundin' Em Up

Mission Giver: Train Engineer
Type: Fetch
Rewards: 250 Coins / 50 Sparks

Looks like some mules broke out of the corral during the initial chaos. Help the town out by searching for four stray mules and riding them back to the stable. Follow the compass to find two on each side of the town and round them up by jumping into the stable.

New Toy Unlocked: Silver

New Toy Unlocked: Scout

Mount Up

Mission Giver: Sheriff
Type: Buy
Rewards: 100 Coins / 20 Sparks

The Sheriff gives some good advice: buy a horse. Traveling around the west is tiring work and the only way to get around is on horseback. Go into the Toy Store and buy your first horse.

NOTE

Each race challenge must be completed once to unlock the next one in order.

New Challenges Available: Starts with Circling Colby and then unlocks in order as follows: Trottin' Through Town, Riverbed Race, Railway Race, Racin' the Range

Townsperson Side Missions

Missing Her Man

Mission Giver: Lady Townsperson
Type: Destroy
Rewards: 250 Coins / 50 Sparks

A young woman is worried about her husband who went hunting in the hills near the telegraph lines. Get on your horse, which seems to be on the roof of the bank, and use the compass to track the husband.

Jump up the ledges and climb around a large rock structure to find the husband in a cave.

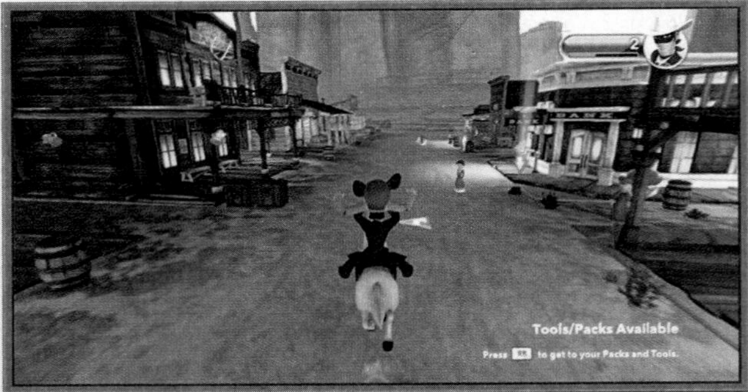

Pick up the man and get back on your horse to take him back to Colby to drop him off in front of his wife.

New Toy Unlocked: Black Horse

Damsel in This Dress

Mission Giver: Lady Townsperson
Type: Customize
Rewards: 100 Coins / 20 Sparks

The poor lady's dress is ruined and she can't afford a new one. Pick her up and toss her into one of Red's traveling outfitters to change her dress.

Get the Train Running

Clearin' the Rails

Mission Giver: Train Engineer
Type: Destroy/Combat
Rewards: 250 Coins / 50 Sparks

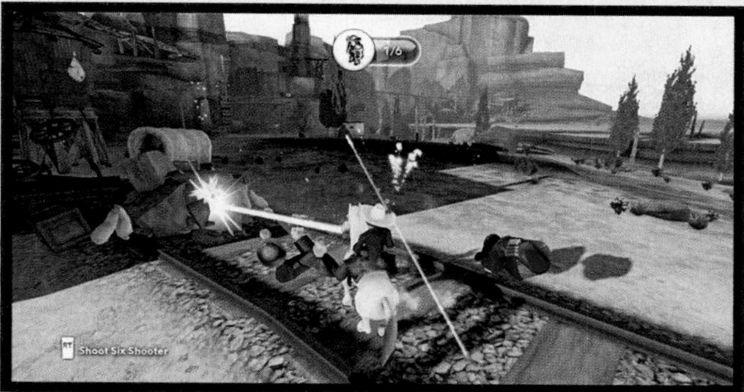

The Cavendish Gang built blockades on the tracks to keep the trains from running. Use the compass to find the blockade and shoot the TNT by them to clear the tracks. You also have to deal with members of the gang that are patrolling the blockades. Take out the first blockade next to the water tower.

Follow the tracks to locate the second group on the right of the train station and try to focus on hitting the TNT so the explosion wipes out a few of the Cavendish Gang.

The last blockade is on the left side of the train station and should be an easy shot after clearing out most of the guards.

Trainin' Day

Mission Giver: Train Engineer
Type: Buy
Rewards: 100 Coins / 20 Sparks

Now that the tracks are clear it's time to get a train. Go into the Toy Store and buy the Constitution Engine.

New Toy Unlocked: Constitution Engine

New Toy Unlocked: Target Package 1

Alert Mission: Keepin' the Peace

Mission Giver: Automatic
Type: Combat
Rewards: 100 Coins / 50 Sparks

Three thugs from the Cavendish Gang will return to Colby. Run them out of town with some fancy shooting.

Alert Mission: Save the Train

Mission Giver: Automatic
Type: Combat
Rewards: 100 Coins / 50 Sparks

A trio of the Cavendish Gang likes to lurk around the tracks and ambush the train. Waste them whenever they show their ugly mugs and teach them not to mess with public transportation.

NOTE

There are two additional Alert Missions that can pop up as you go through this adventure. Save the Bank and Save the Camp are similar to the other alert missions in rewards and objective. Like the others, they involve ridding the world of several members of the Cavendish Gang.

Rancher Missions

Ranch Hand

Mission Giver: Sheriff
Type: Combat
Rewards: 500 Coins / 50 Sparks

There is trouble out at the ranch and you need to deal with those Cavendish boys to the keep the rancher safe. Follow the red arrows to ride out to the ranch and clear out the four punks.

New Toy Unlocked: Box Car

Liberatin' the Tower

Mission Giver: Rancher
Type: Combat
Rewards: 250 Coins / 175 Sparks

The drought is taking its toll on the town and it seems the train hasn't been delivering any water. Check out the water tower and defeat the gang members that have surrounded the tower.

New Toy Unlocked: TNT Pack

Side Mission

Runnin' the Mill

Mission Giver: Rancher
Type: Target Shooting
Rewards: 100 Coins / 20 Sparks

The windmill at the ranch is jammed, so go check it out! This is an easy one to take care of—just go to the windmill and shoot the target to get it moving again.

Comanche Elders Side Missions

Thundering Stallion

Mission Giver: Comanche Elders
Type: Locate
Rewards: 250 Coins / 20 Sparks

Speak to the Comanche Elders to find the Thundering Stallion and make contact. This mission can only be done at night, so make sure to try it whenever the sun goes down.

If you spot the ghostly spirit, sprint towards it and touch it before it runs away.

New Toy Unlocked: Palomino

Chasing Thunder

Mission Giver: Comanche Elders
Type: Locate
Rewards: 250 Coins / 20 Sparks

The spirit horse still runs wild. Wait until nightfall and make contact with the Thundering Stallion around Colby.

New Toy Unlocked: Chestnut Horse

The Thundering Horse

Mission Giver: Comanche Elders
Type: Locate
Rewards: 250 Coins / 50 Sparks

Return to the Comanche Elders after meeting Red for the final trial of the Thundering Horse. For the last time, wait until night and make contact with the spirit horse around Colby or the temporary Cavendish Camp.

Catching the spirit horse for the third time pays off with a special pack that gives you additional "horsepower" by allowing you to call upon the Thundering Stallion to stampede right through enemies.

New Toy Unlocked: Thundering Hooves Pack

Way of the Warrior

Mission Giver: Comanche Elders
Type: Locate
Rewards: 250 Coins / 50 Sparks

After buying the Bridge to the Railroad Camp, the Comanche Elders tell you about a mysterious Silent Warrior that can fight by your side if he finds you worthy. Follow the compass past Red's Traveling Entertainments through a tunnel to reach the Railroad Camp.

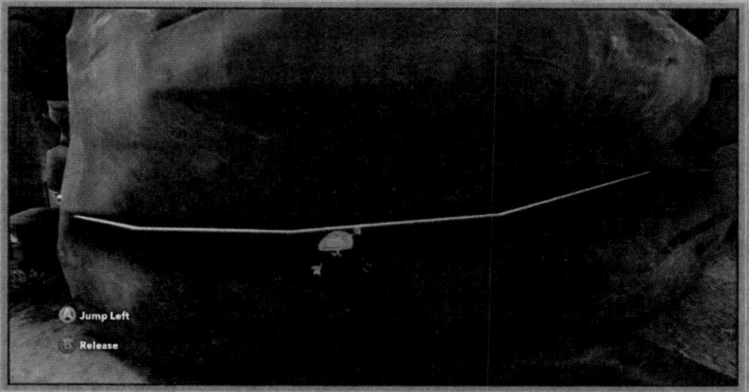

Ride toward the hills on the left and work your way up the rocky plateaus by jumping up a ledge and grabbing on to a thin edge of a boulder.

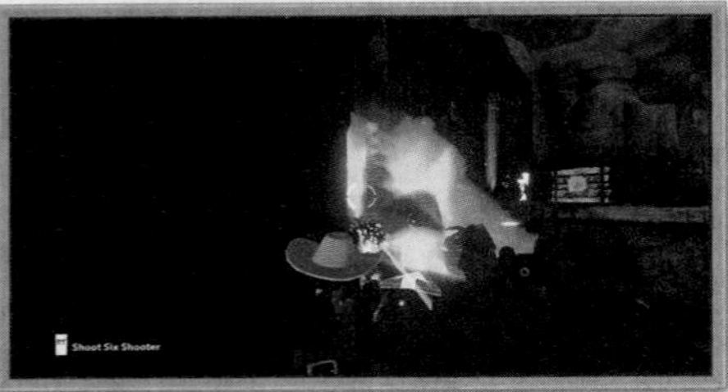

To get up to the higher level you need to remove the rubble by the wooden planks by shooting the dynamite buried in the debris. Climb up the first wooden ladder and shoot the next set of dynamite in the rock.

Leap across the long gap to land on the ledge with the Silent Warrior. It is well worth the trip to seek out the warrior, because he will grant you an extra set of fists to fight off enemies.

New Toy Unlocked: Silent Warrior Pack

Sharpshooting Side Missions

Runnin' and Gunnin'

Mission Giver: Lady Sharpshooter
Type: Target Shooting
Rewards: 100 Coins / 50 Sparks

The little lady wants to see how fast you can knock out a bunch of targets in town. You only have 30 seconds to complete the task, but there are also only five targets on the main streets of Colby. On foot you might have to hustle, but on horseback you can trot along and take them out with well-placed zoomed-in shots.

Aimin' to Ride

Mission Giver: Lady Sharpshooter
Type: Target Shooting
Rewards: 250 Coins / 50 Sparks

She wasn't that impressed with your previous performance and wants to witness how well you can shoot on horseback. Ride towards the five targets at a slow pace and keep firing as you move around the ranch.

New Toy Unlocked: Black Pinto

Train Time

Rarin' to Go

Mission Giver: Train Engineer
Type: Buy
Rewards: 100 Coins / 20 Sparks

The train engineer knows the rancher needs water but to make that kind of delivery you will need a way to transport water. Go into the Toy Store and buy the newly unlocked Water Car.

New Toy Unlocked: Water Car

Railroad Switch

Mission Giver: Train Engineer
Type: Customize
Rewards: 250 Coins / 50 Sparks

To customize the train you need to signal the train to stop at the station by shooting the switch target. The switch will change the green-tipped bars to red ones and cause the train to stop at that station.

When the train has stopped, step into the circle next to the station to select Place Train Cars or Customize Train Cars. Add the Water Car you just bought to one of the empty slots called Flatbed Cars.

NOTE

There are several Flatbed Cars that can be replaced by pressing the directional stick to switch cars.

Endin' the Drought

Mission Giver: Train Engineer
Type: Train Delivery
Rewards: 250 Coins / 175 Sparks

The train is ready to go, but the Water Car has to be filled before you can transport water from the water tower in Colby to the ranch. Shoot the switch to turn the gates back to green and quickly ride out to the water tower. Shoot the target to activate the tower and it will fill the Water Car. The train doesn't need to be babysat while it makes the delivery. Look for the message to pop up on screen to let you know it has done its job.

Any of the delivery towers (water, livestock, lumber, and TNT) will only produce one set of cargo each time the target is hit. That means you must shoot the target again after the train has picked up the load and dropped it off.

New Toy Unlocked: Cattle Car

Townsperson Side Mission

Skirting the Issue

Mission Giver: Lady Townsperson
Type: Customize
Rewards: 100 Coins / 20 Sparks

This woman is really concerned about her wardrobe and now her dress doesn't fit quite right. Pick her up and throw her into Red's traveling outfitters to give her a new dress.

Getting TNT

Patrollin' the Canyon

Mission Giver: Sheriff
Type: Combat
Rewards: 250 Coins / 50 Sparks

Some of Cavendish's men have been spotted fleeing into the canyon. Follow the red arrows to hunt them down and wipe them out.

New Toy Unlocked: Dining Car

Minin' His Business

Mission Giver: Sheriff
Type: Combat
Rewards: 100 Coins / 20 Sparks

The Cavendish Gang is hiding out in a cave or cavern, but the problem is there is no way to get to them without a generous use of TNT. The old miner is know for stocking TNT and maybe he will give you some. Use the compass to find the miner on a ledge near a deep ravine.

New Toy Unlocked: Golden Horse

Seein' Red

Mission Giver: Miner
Type: Combat
Rewards: 100 Coins / 50 Sparks

The miner would be happy to give you some TNT but the Cavendish Gang took all of it. Red Harrington might have some. She tends to have stuff that nobody else does. The bridge to get to Red's encampment costs 1,500 coins and if you don't have the money you might need to shoot around town or complete a few other missions. Follow the compass out to the encampment and head to the back to find Red.

New Toy Unlocked: Bridge to Red's

New Toy Unlocked: Target Package 2

Cattle Drivin'

Mission Giver: Red
Type: Combat
Rewards: 250 Coins / 175 Sparks

If you want Red's TNT you'll have to do her a favor first. She is interested in cattle but is not about to do a cattle drive to bring them in. The only way to get cattle to Red is to bring them by train from the ranch. Ride out to the ranch and shoot the target to the cattle supply station.

Buy the Cattle Car if you haven't already and place it on the train, then just wait for it to pick up the cattle and deliver them to Red's camp.

New Toy Unlocked: TNT Car

Cavendish Clear Out

Back for More

Mission Giver: Rancher
Type: Locate
Rewards: 100 Coins / 20 Sparks

The rancher hears a ruckus going on in Colby. Ride into town and check it out!

A Heap O' Trouble

Mission Giver: Sheriff
Type: Combat
Rewards: 250 Coins / 50 Sparks

The Cavendish Gang blew up the jail and busted their men out. Take down all four bandits to clean up Colby.

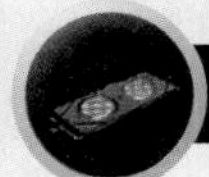

New Toy Unlocked: Gatling Gun Car

Repair and Reform

Mission Giver: Sheriff
Type: Build
Rewards: 100 Coins / 20 Sparks

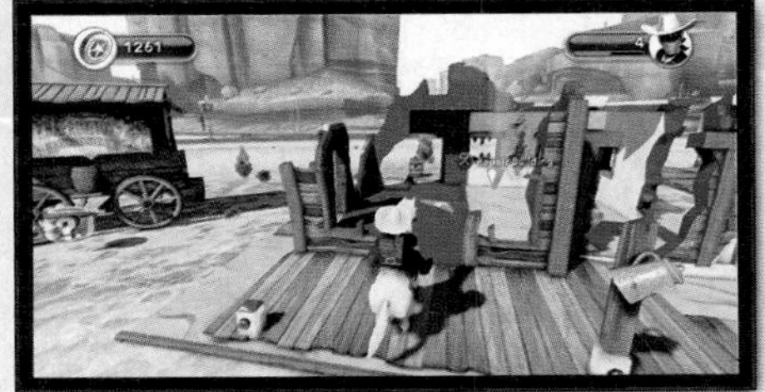

When the Cavendish boys broke their buddies out of jail they really wrecked the place. Go to the building that usually has the Sheriff sign on it and repair it.

New Toy Unlocked: Cannon Car

Gatling/Cannon Side Missions

NOTE

Requires purchase of Cannon and Gatling Car or Combo Car.

Trainin' Your Sights

Mission Giver: Lady Sharpshooter
Type: Target Shooting
Rewards: 250 Coins / 50 Sparks

It's time to up the ante on shooting and break out the big guns. Go to the train station and stop the train to equip it with the Gatling Gun Car. Shoot the switch to start the train again and hop on board to use one of the guns.

It takes a little while to get used to the big weapon, but keep your eyes on the green arrows and try to line up your shots before you get too close. Don't try to get all 20 targets in one trip by swinging from the left to the right. Concentrate on your accuracy and successfully hitting the targets instead of chasing where each one is located. Also, remember that the gun has great range and can be used to hit targets at significant distances.

New Toy Unlocked: Gatling Gun Targets

Shootin' Down the Track

Mission Giver: Lady Sharpshooter
Type: Target Shooting
Rewards: 250 Coins / 50 Sparks

Load a cannon on the train (or use the Combo Gun Car) and practice your making cannon fodder out of the green targets placed around the train tracks.

New Toy Unlocked: Cannon Targets

Aimin' High

Mission Giver: Lady Sharpshooter
Type: Target Shooting
Rewards: 100 Coins / 50 Sparks

There is only one target to hit in this mission, but the trick is getting a clean shot at it. You need to get to the top of the hills and the journey begins by leaping up a few plateaus on the rocky mountainside.

Jump up to a thin yellow-highlighted ledge and run around the rock to the right.

Go through a small tunnel and climb the wooden planks to a ledge. Make your way up another set of planks and the target will be in plain sight next to the totem.

Side Mission

Fetchin' Water

Mission Giver: Train Engineer
Type: Train Delivery
Rewards: 100 Coins / 50 Sparks

If you removed the Water Car, stop it at the station and replace it. Shoot the target at the water tower to reset it and let the train fill up and make the delivery.

Sheriff Missions

Clearin' the Lines

Mission Giver: Sheriff
Type: Platforming
Rewards: 250 Coins / 175 Sparks

The telegraph is down and the town is cut off from communications. The Sheriff asks you to check the wire to find out what is causing all the trouble. Follow the compass to find the problem on the lines—bird's nests are disrupting the signal. Shoot the first nest to clear the line and continue to follow it to find the next obstruction.

The second nest can be targeted from the ground and it is the last one that will be so easy to spot. Go to the edge of a stream and look way up into the sky to find the nest near the tracks.

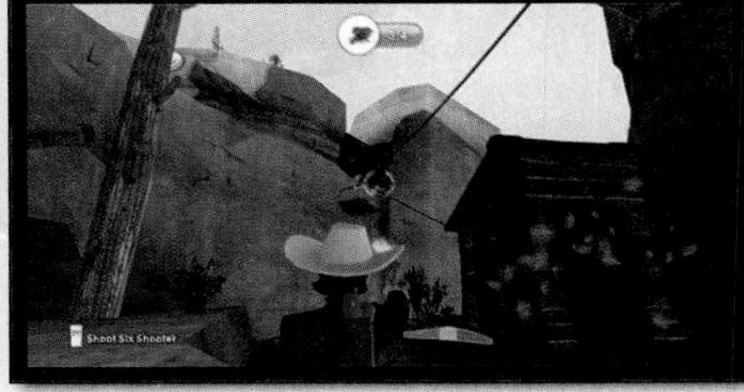

The lines continue high up over the rocky mountains and it is time to get off the horse for some old-school platforming. Jump up the wooden planks and follow a ledge to the right to find another set of planks to climb to the top of a plateau. Search for the nest from this vantage point and shoot it down.

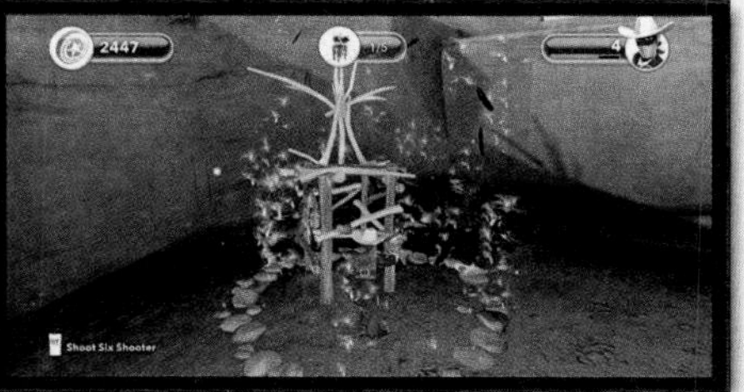

Turn to the left and leap up several more wooden planks to reach a totem.

Drop down to a plateau next to where you shot the nest and take aim at the target on the wooden bridge to bring down the nest. Double jump across it to find that last nest.

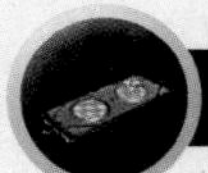

New Toy Unlocked: Combo Gun Car

Disruptin' the Blast

Mission Giver: Sheriff
Type: Platforming
Rewards: 250 Coins / 50 Sparks

Security must not be a top priority in Colby because there is dynamite all over town. In under 2 minutes you have to find all five bundles of dynamite before they blow. Run up the ramp in back of the Colby Rooming House and leap to the ledge to get to the roof and defuse the first one.

From the roof of the hotel, double jump across to the bank and continue up the street by leaping to the next rooftop with another stack of dynamite. It is a long jump but if you get on the ledge and double jump as you fly towards the building (for length not height), it is possible to grab the ledge and get to the roof of the jail.

Jump up to the awning of the General Merchandise store and take care of the dynamite.

The next bundle is across the way near the water tower. Leap off the roof of the General Merchandise store to land on a balcony of the saloon. Climb up to the roof and make one more leap to the next building to find another stash of dynamite.

The last batch is at the stable and doesn't require any fancy roof jumping—well the other's didn't either but it makes the mission a lot faster to complete. Jump up to the small roof in back near a pile of lumber and blow out the fuse on the dynamite dilemma.

New Toy Unlocked: The Jupiter

Pursuin' the Posse

Mission Giver: Sheriff
Type: Combat
Rewards: 250 Coins / 50 Sparks

A bunch of thieves stole loads of silver from the town and are making a getaway on horseback. Run all three down right in town and shoot them quickly to avoid having to chase them around on horseback.

New Toy Unlocked: Brown Pinto

Rancher and Necklace Side Missions

Checkin' In

Mission Giver: Rancher
Type: Combat
Rewards: 100 Coins / 50 Sparks

The rancher heard an explosion coming from the hills beyond the train tracks. The spot he is referring to is where the miner hangs out. Make your way out to the hill and wipe out the three members of the Cavendish Gang that are laying siege to the miner's hideout.

Stolen Goods

Mission Giver: Rancher
Type: Fetch
Rewards: 100 Coins / 50 Sparks

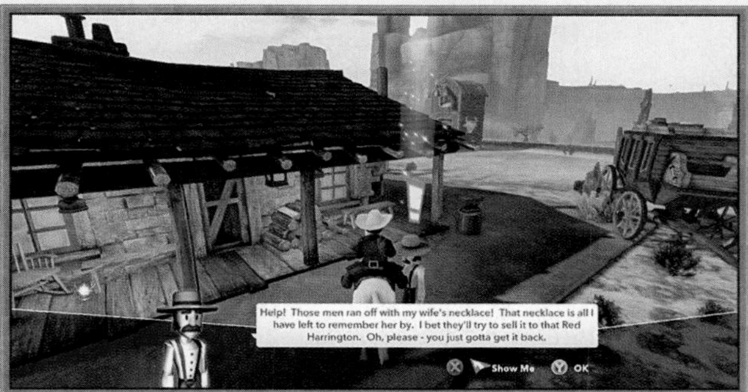

Some men ran off with the rancher's wife's necklace. The jewelry is very sentimental because it's all the man has left to remember his wife. The only place they can pawn something like that is at Red's. It is time to pay her a visit.

An Honest Trade

Mission Giver: Red
Type: Fetch
Rewards: 100 Coins / 50 Sparks

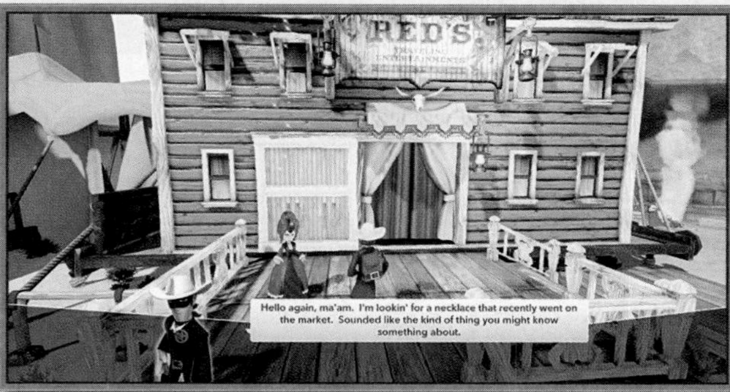

Red recalls a gentleman bringing her a trinket but she paid dearly for it. All you have to do is bring her something of significantly higher value and the necklace is yours. That doesn't sounds like a great deal, but you have to help the rancher! The only thing that will satisfy Red is some silver ore.

Red's Traveling Entertainment Missions Ringmaster Side Missions

The Golden Skunk

Mission Giver: Ringmaster
Type: Fetch
Rewards: 100 Coins / 20 Sparks

The Ringmaster in Red's camp is looking for a golden skunk for his collection. Use the compass to find one outside of Colby and bring it back to him.

Seein' Elephants

Mission Giver: Ringmaster
Type: Buy
Rewards: 100 Coins / 20 Sparks

Most folks haven't seen an elephant and the Ringmaster thinks he can make a ton of money charging people to see it. This mission will unlock the elephant in the Toy Store and you simply need to buy it for the Ringmaster.

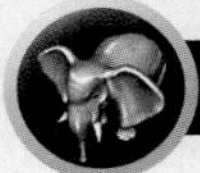

New Toy Unlocked: Elephant

Armadillo Round-Up

Mission Giver: Ringmaster
Type: Fetch
Rewards: 100 Coins / 50 Sparks

How about a performing armadillo? Maybe that will get people's attention. Ride out next to the ranch to find another animal performer for the Ringmaster and bring it to him.

Dealing with Bandits

Cavendish Returns

Mission Giver: Fortune Teller
Type: Combat
Rewards: 250 Coins / 50 Sparks

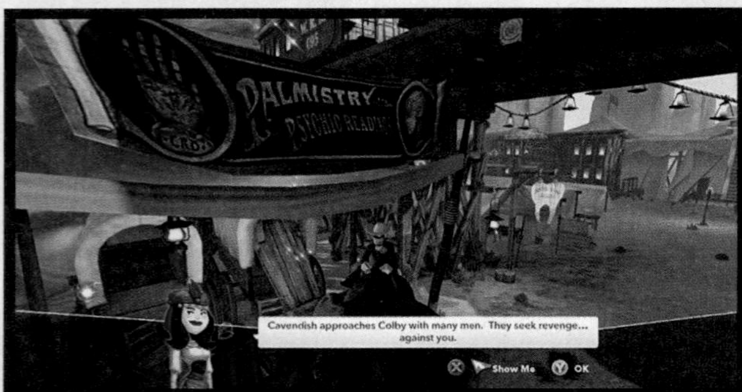

When visiting Red's camp stop by to speak with the fortune teller. She has an ominous message about Cavendish approaching Colby to seek revenge.

Ride back to Colby to confront Butch Cavendish and his gang. Open fire and light up the red arrow targets to wipe all five out.

Elephant-Back Ridin'

Mission Giver: Red
Type: Combat
Rewards: 250 Coins / 50 Sparks

Cavendish's men snuck into the camp at night and made off with the elephant you gave the Ringmaster. Ride out near the temporary Cavendish Camp to locate the stolen elephant and wipe out the gang that took it.

Hop on the elephant and ride the slow-moving pachyderm all the way back to the corral at Red's Traveling Entertainments.

Tramplin' the Camp

Mission Giver: Red
Type: Combat
Rewards: 250 Coins / 50 Sparks

The Cavendish Gang set up camp right near the railroad track so they can stop the trains and take all their supplies. To get back at them, take the elephant for a stroll through the Cavendish camp. You must return the elephant to the Ringmaster to complete the mission.

Railroad Camp

Trompin' Around

Mission Giver: Ringmaster
Type: Platforming
Rewards: 250 Coins / 20 Sparks

The Ringmaster's elephant has become restless and needs some exercise. He has set up a course of checkpoints (green arrows) that he wants you to run through with his cooped up pachyderm. They lead all the way to the Railroad Camp.

Chasin' Elephants

Mission Giver: Red
Type: Combat/Fetch
Rewards: 250 Coins / 50 Sparks

That gang of bandits is really fixated on the elephant. They took him again and stole some of Red's money as well. You have 3 minutes and 20 seconds to track down the Cavendish Gang to get back Red's silver and reclaim the elephant. The red arrows will point you to the first bandit close to Red's.

Continue to the lumber station next to the temporary camp to wipe out the other two bandits. Hop on the elephant and take it back to the Ringmaster once again.

Ringmaster Side Missions, Part 2

Runnin' Robbers

Mission Giver: Ringmaster
Type: Combat
Rewards: 250 Coins / 50 Sparks

A bunch of thieves took the Ringmaster's money. Luckily they didn't get too far as they are lurking around just outside of the encampment. Hop on your horse and chase down the three thieves before they can get away. Make sure to return to the Ringmaster to return his stolen goods.

Wild Horse Round-Up

Mission Giver: Ringmaster
Type: Fetch
Rewards: 100 Coins / 20 Sparks

It seems the rabbit you brought is a stubborn thing and this time the Ringmaster is looking for something he knows he can train—a wild horse. You have 1 minute and 20 seconds to follow the compass and retrieve a wild horse. Sprint out to the canyon and quickly change steeds to the black horse, then run all the way back to the Ringmaster.

Rejected Skunk

Mission Giver: Ringmaster
Type: Fetch
Rewards: 100 Coins / 50 Sparks

A golden skunk isn't drawing the crowds the Ringmaster hoped for—in fact it might be driving them away. Pick up the golden stinker and take it back to the desert where you found it.

Rabbit Round-Up

Mission Giver: Ringmaster
Type: Fetch
Rewards: 100 Coins / 50 Sparks

Surprisingly or not, the armadillo you brought is untrainable. Now the Ringmaster wants a performing rabbit that is hanging out near the railroad tracks. Follow the compass to capture the bunny and see if the Ringmaster has better luck with this critter.

Bridge to Railroad Camp

Bridgin' the Gap

Mission Giver: Train Engineer
Type: Buy
Rewards: 100 Coins / 50 Sparks

Go into the Toy Store and buy the Bridge to Railroad Camp to open up access to that area by train.

New Toy Unlocked: Bridge to Railroad Camp

Retakin' the Camp

Mission Giver: Camp Foreman
Type: Combat
Rewards: 500 Coins / 175 Sparks

While you are out strolling with the elephant in the previous mission stop to talk to the Camp Foreman. The Cavendish Gang is attempting to stop the trains by shutting down the Railroad Camp. Fight them off before they destroy the whole encampment.

New Toy Unlocked: Lumber Car

Lumberin' Along

Mission Giver: Camp Foreman
Type: Buy
Rewards: 100 Coins / 50 Sparks

The Railroad Camp is low on supplies and could really use some lumber. Go to any train station and buy the Lumber Car if you haven't purchased it already. Shoot the switch to stop the train and load the Lumber Car on the train. Ride along the track to find the lumber station and shoot the target to restock it for delivery to the camp.

New Toy Unlocked: Target Package 3

Thirstin' for More

Mission Giver: Red
Type: Train Delivery
Rewards: 100 Coins / 50 Sparks

The water supply in Red's encampment is running low. Load the Water Car on the train and hit the target on the water tower to quench their thirst.

Lumberin' Away

Mission Giver: Red
Type: Train Delivery
Rewards: 100 Coins / 50 Sparks

Deliver lumber by train from the lumber station to Red's.

Train Delivery Side Missions

Moovin' 'Em In

Mission Giver: Train Engineer
Type: Train Delivery
Rewards: 100 Coins / 50 Sparks

The Sheriff wants to deliver some livestock to Colby. Stop and load the train with the Cattle Car and make sure to shoot the target at the cattle supply station for the train to pick up and make the delivery.

Barrelin' Through

Mission Giver: Train Engineer
Type: Train Delivery
Rewards: 100 Coins / 50 Sparks

Buy and load the TNT Car onto the train. Ride out towards Red's and shoot the target on the TNT station. Wait for the train to pick up its load and deliver the TNT to the ranch.

Wood if You Could

Mission Giver: Train Engineer
Type: Train Delivery
Rewards: 100 Coins / 50 Sparks

The rancher is doing some repairs on his property and needs some lumber. Make sure to load the Lumber Car on the train and shoot the target at the lumber station to reset and prepare a fresh bundle of lumber.

Dynamite Delivery

Mission Giver: Train Engineer
Type: Train Delivery
Rewards: 100 Coins / 50 Sparks

Deliver TNT by train from Red's to Colby.

Timber Trail

Mission Giver: Train Engineer
Type: Train Delivery
Rewards: 100 Coins / 50 Sparks

Some of the old buildings in Colby need fixing up. Transport some lumber to the town by placing the Lumber Car on the train and shooting the lumber station to refill its supply.

Supply Errands

Campin' Out

Mission Giver: Camp Foreman
Type: Train Delivery
Rewards: 100 Coins / 50 Sparks

Climb up into the hills using the same path you traversed to find the Silent Warrior. Shoot the target on the bridge to lower it and double jump across to the ledge with the Gatling gun.

Strikin' Camp

Mission Giver: Camp Foreman
Type: Combat
Rewards: 250 Coins / 50 Sparks

You didn't think you were going to climb all the way up by the Gatling gun just to drop off some supplies, did you? Put that ammunition to use and jump on the big gun to wipe out Cavendish's Gang below. It takes several shots to take down these tough bandits but the gun has infinite ammo so take your time.

NOTE

At this point the first flying mission can be completed if you buy the Crow Wing Pack. See the end of the chapter for how to unlock this awesome ability to fly.

Side Missions

Night Watch

Mission Giver: Fortune Teller
Type: Combat
Rewards: 100 Coins / 50 Sparks

After clearing out the Railroad Camp, the fortune teller will have a premonition that it's in danger. This is a shoot 'em up at the camp and there are five bandits that need to be cleared out.

Helping the Herd

Mission Giver: Red
Type: Train Delivery
Rewards: 100 Coins / 50 Sparks

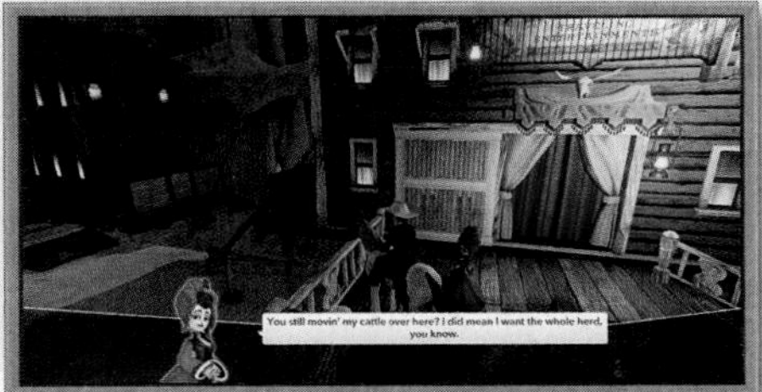

Deliver cattle by train from the ranch to Red's.

Drinkin' It In

Mission Giver: Camp Foreman
Type: Train Delivery
Rewards: 100 Coins / 50 Sparks

Transport water by train from the water tower in Colby to the Railroad Camp.

A Bang Up Job

Mission Giver: Camp Foreman
Type: Train Delivery
Rewards: 100 Coins / 50 Sparks

Deliver TNT by train from Red's to the Railroad Camp.

Confront Butch Cavendish

Mine Blast

Mission Giver: Sheriff
Type: Train Delivery
Rewards: 1,000 Coins / 175 Sparks

Butch Cavendish and his men are holed up at the silver mine and it is time to take care of them once and for all. To do that you need to load up the TNT Car with plenty of explosive power and blow up the entrance to the silver mine. Make sure the TNT Car is placed on the train and the TNT station is ready to fill the car.

Then, make sure the track switch near the silver mine entrance is pointing towards the boarded-up entrance. It should switch when the TNT is loaded and the train is heading down that track.

Nowhere to Hide

Mission Giver: Sheriff (automatic)
Type: Combat
Rewards: 1,000 Coins / 175 Sparks

Follow the train into the silver mine and climb up the hills to turn the Gatling guns and cannons on the Cavendish Gang.

The full description of the mission is very important to pay attention to. It clearly states to use the guns to destroy their hideout at the silver mine, not the bandits. In fact, the bandits will just keep regenerating no matter how many times you shoot them. It can take a while to figure that out if you jump early on the big guns and open fire. The real objective is to use the Gatling gun to take out the red targets around the small buildings and then switch to the cannon to hit the green target and finish it off. However, this doesn't mean you can ignore the bandits because they can still hit you and even wreck your Gatling gun, causing it to smoke or light on fire.

The first building to fall is the one on the bottom level in the center. After that is gone, wipe out a bunch of the bandits to trigger the next targets.

The other three buildings will sprout Gatling targets and can be taken out in any order. Try to hit the Gatling targets as quickly as possible to reveal the green cannon target and move on to the next.

Finally, when all four buildings are gone, take out any straggling bandits. To finish the job, there is one more cannon target to shoot in order to close the book on Butch Cavendish.

New Toy Unlocked: Thundering Stallion

Side Mission Wrap Up

Helpin' a Stranger

Mission Giver: Rancher
Type: Locate
Rewards: 100 Coins / 50 Sparks

A friend of the rancher went out to the silver mine and hasn't returned. The rancher wants you to check the mine to see what happened to his friend. Ride out to the silver mine and look behind one of the small buildings on the ground level to find a whole group of people hiding out.

Cattle Call

Mission Giver: Camp Foreman
Type: Train Delivery
Rewards: 100 Coins / 50 Sparks

Deliver cattle by train from the cattle station near Colby to the Railroad Camp.

Lumberin' About

Mission Giver: Camp Foreman
Type: Train Delivery
Rewards: 100 Coins / 50 Sparks

Deliver lumber by train from the lumber station to the Railroad Camp.

Minin' for Silver

Mission Giver: Camp Foreman
Type: Platforming
Rewards: 100 Coins / 50 Sparks

The foreman came across a secret cave high in the hills that is full with silver. He is happy to share the silver up there if you can get to it. Getting to the four spots where the silver is hidden will be easy if you can get the Crow Wing Pack, but it IS possible to get to all of them without it—it's just a lot harder!

Go to the silver mine area and enter the cave where you destroyed Cavendish's men and buildings. Follow the tracks until you emerge back outside and immediately look to your right to find the first batch of silver.

One of the stashes of silver is pretty easy to get to. This one is hidden in the far end of the mine and simply requires a few double jumps onto some ledges.

The third one can be found with some basic platforming. Jump up the narrow passage in the hills and shoot the dynamite to clear a thin ridge you can climb around.

Leap to another ledge in the giant rock and run onto the wooden platforms. Jump up to the ledge and get up to the top tier to find the third stash of silver.

This final stash is where flying would be really useful, yet it can be found on foot if you are careful. Start out by jumping on the slanted part of this building, jump down to the balcony, and run around the building.

This is where it gets tricky. Run around to the corner of the building near a large rock. Walk up to the corner of the very edge of this area (not on the boulder) and jump to the rock next to the roof.

Jump onto the chute and slowly walk all the way to the end of the line. It is very easy to fall off, so take your time!

Leap down to the roof below and slide down the long roof panel to a smaller section of roof right next to the tracks. Perform a long double jump to land on the track and follow it towards the green arrow.

When the track breaks up, carefully step along the remaining wooden beam to the left. Take it nice and slow until you can double jump to the other side of the track.

Finally, use one more long double jump to get to the last stash and clear the mission without the ability to fly.

Dry Spell

Mission Giver: Fortune Teller
Type: Train Delivery
Rewards: 100 Coins / 175 Sparks

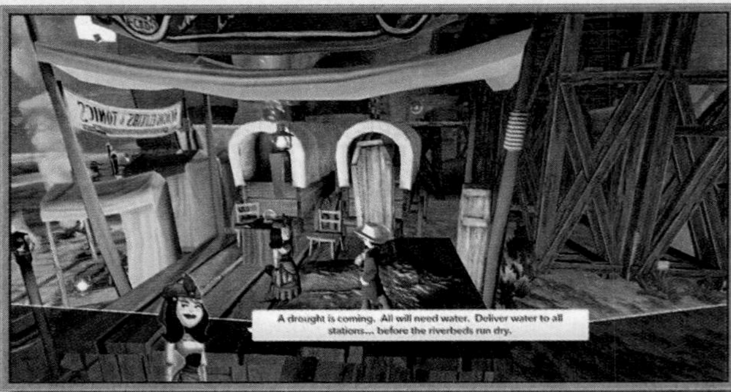

The last delivery mission is to compensate for an upcoming drought. The goal is to deliver water by train to all stations before the river bed runs dry. Keep resetting the water tower at Colby after each delivery until every station is watered.

Crow Wing Ability

Mission Giver: Automatic
Type: Platforming
Rewards: 1,000 Coins / 50 Sparks

This is sort of a hidden mission that runs throughout the adventure. There are five special totems to find in the Play Set, and once you have encountered them all you will gain the ability to fly!

The first totem should have been found when searching for the nests during the Clearin' the Lines mission. Outside of Colby you can climb up some wooden planks on the side of the mountain and go up several more planks to a high ledge.

The second totem is easy to find but also easy to overlook. The canyon near Colby had some Cavendish boys lurking around, but you probably didn't go all the way around the fire into the small alcove where it hides.

The third totem is also easy to find but is out of sight at Red's Traveling Entertainments. Next to Red is a brown building that obscures this totem to the left of it.

The next one is NOT easy to find and your only clue is that you might have noticed the planks on the left side of the wall when visiting the miner. There are a series of ledges below that hide the fourth totem as well a few boulders that lead to a little island. The planks on the side near the miner can be used to climb down to the find the totem and get back up.

The last one is also hard to notice because it is really high up. Go to the Railroad Camp and climb to the area where you went to meet the Silent Warrior and used the Gatling gun. However, instead of climbing the wooden planks, run out towards the hills to the left.

Run as far as you can along this path to a notice a tower on a ridge and a series of wooden planks you can climb.

To get to the top of this tower you need to leap up the wooden structure by climbing up boards and moving around to the sides to continue your ascension. It is not a simple climb straight up. Expect to have to maneuver around the tower as you go higher. The prize at the top is the Crow Wing Pack.

The prize was certainly worth all the effort because the Crow Wing Pack grants the ability to turn into a crow and fly across the entire Play Set to collect all capsules.

New Toy Unlocked: Crow Wing Pack

NOTE

Buying this ability unlocks new challenges.

New Challenges Available: Flight From the Elders, Water Wings, Roundin' the Ridge, Trackin' the Train, and Soarin' Through Camp

Collectibles

Red Capsules

#	Unlockable Item	Zone	Description
1	Rusty Water Car	Colby	On the side of the General Merchandise building.
2	Mustache Face	Colby	Behind the Grand Colby Saloon.
3	Metal Trim	Colby	On the roof of the Grand Colby Saloon.
4	Cowgirl Hat	Colby	On the roof of the Bank.
5	Plastic Water Car	Colby	On the top of the back staircase of the Colby Rooming House.
6	Monocle and Top Hat	Colby	On the roof of J.R. Stein, Furniture and Undertaker.
7	Corrugated Metal Lumber Car	Colby	On the roof of Samuel's Livery Stable.
8	Rusty Engine Wheels	Colby	On the roof of the Colby train station.
9	Huge Nose Face	Colby	Behind the boulder near the water tower right by the river.
10	Plastic Trim	Colby	On the river right beside a big boulder.
11	Painted Engine	Colby	At the base of the spire, near the waterfall.
12	Plastic Engine	Colby	On the ledge leading up to the spire.
13	White Trim	Colby	On the ladder leading up to the spire.
14	Cowgirl Outfit	Colby	On the railroad tracks next to the spire.
15	Patched Suit	Colby	On the ledge leading up to the spire.
16	Plastic Tarp Lumber Car	Colby	On the rock steps behind J.R. Stein, Furniture and Undertaker.
17	Plastic Wheels	Colby	On the right side of the canyon behind the Bank.
18	Elderly Female Face	Colby	On the left side of the canyon behind the Bank.
19	Rusted Metal Coal Car	Colby	Near the bridge coming up to Red's Camp.
20	Rusty Wheels	Colby	Straight behind the landing zone.
21	Dress and Apron	Colby	Behind the rocks near the Comanche Elders' Camp.
22	Wooden Wheels	Colby	Across from the Colby train station and behind a boulder on the other side of the river.
23	Camouflage Coal Car	Ranch	Behind the Ranch, near the rock and in front of the river.
24	Standard Coal Car	Ranch	In the graveyard.
25	Racecar Car	Ranch	In between the ranch house and the town.
26	Buffalo Horn Headdress	Ranch	Between the water tower and the Barn.
27	Suspenders	Ranch	On the ground near the Farmhouse.
28	Big Nose Face	Ranch	On the roof of the Farmhouse.
29	Worn Wood Car	Ranch	On the roof of the Farmhouse.
30	Rusty Engine	Ranch	Behind the water tower near the river.
31	Miner Attire	Ranch	Behind the barn, on the other side of the river.
32	Wide Nose Face	Ranch	Behind the barn, on the other side of the river and near the top of the rocks.
33	Smiling Female Face	Ranch	By a boulder across the railroad from the Comanche Elders' Camp.
34	Comanche Warrior Attire	Comanche Elders	In front of the Comanche Elders' Camp.
35	Comanche Warrior Face	Comanche Elders	In front of the Comanche Elders' Camp.
36	Railroad Worker Attire	Comanche Elders	Near the tunnel to the Silver Mine.
37	Rusty Trim	Comanche Elders	Behind the rock near the tunnel to the Silver Mine.
38	Thick Mustache	Silver Mine	Near the entrance to the Silver Mine along the wall.
39	Twisted Horned Mask	Silver Mine	In the air over the railroad.
40	Goatee and Top Hat	Silver Mine	Along the wall, in between the boulders and across from Sleeping Man.
41	Imp Mask and Cape	Silver Mine	On top of an old railroad track along the boulder wall.
42	Checkered Shirt	Silver Mine	In the air near the boulder wall.
43	Tuxedo	Silver Mine	Over a wooden platform near the mini tunnel.
44	Racecar Engine Wheels	Silver Mine	Inside mini tunnel.
45	Gypsy Attire	Silver Mine	Inside mini tunnel.
46	Floral Water Car	Silver Mine	On the elevated railroad near the mini tunnel.
47	Simple Suit	Silver Mine	Behind the wooden house near the boulder wall.
48	Floral Lumber Car	Silver Mine	On top of the wooden platform with tracks leading to the mini tunnel.
49	Plastic Coal Car	Silver Mine	On top of the wooden platform with tracks leading to the mini tunnel.
50	Stone Wheels	Silver Mine	Tucked into the wall near the Silver Mine Entrance.
51	Male Face 6	Silver Mine	Tucked into the wall near the Silver Mine Entrance.
52	Shiny Wheels	Silver Mine	Inside the tunnel that is next to the Sleeping Man.
53	Circus Water Car	Red's	On the roof of the lumber building.

#	Unlockable Item	Zone	Description
54	Floral Wheels	Red's	Near the top of the boulder near the railroad.
55	Zebra Water Car	Red's	On the roof of the shack along the railroad tracks.
56	Circus Lumber Car	Red's	In the air over the railroad.
57	Skirt and Sash	Red's	On the ground near the bridge to the Railroad Camp.
58	Metal Tile Trim	Red's	Near the top of the boulder near the railroad switcher.
59	Bearded Woman	Red's	On the ground near the railroad switcher.
60	Coiled Snake	Red's	At the top of the boulder near the railroad track.
61	Bison Head	Red's	On the ground beside the little white house near the boulder.
62	Zebra Coal Car	Red's	In the air by the bridge to Railroad Camp.
63	Male Face 3	Red's	Inside the cave.
64	Diamonds and Stripes	Red's	On the top of the wooden platform behind the wagons.
65	Suspenders and Chaps	Red's	On the wooden platform under the elevated train tracks.
66	Light Makeup Face 1	Red's	Behind the wooden house right near the entrance of Red's Camp.
67	Merchant Suit	Red's	On the top of the boulder right near the entrance of Red's Camp.
68	Frilly Dress and Corset	Red's	Behind the tents.
69	Zebra Car	Red's	Inside the tent.
70	Floral Coal Car	Red's	In the air over the tents.
71	Beak Mask	Red's	Behind the tents.
72	Leaf Mask	Red's	Beside the Palmistry and Psychic Readings.
73	Circus Car	Red's	Inside the tent.
74	Circus Trim	Red's	On top of the barrel freight of the train.
75	Visor	Red's	On top of the boulder behind the Hall of Oddities.
76	Shifty Eyed Face	Red's	Behind the tents that are near the Hall of Oddities.
77	Circus Coal Car	Red's	In the tent near the Red's Traveling Entertainments.
78	Male Face 2	Red's	In front of the Grand Colby Saloon.
79	Light Makeup Face 3	Red's	On the ground near the elevated train tracks.
80	Camouflage Car	Railroad Camp	To the side of the train tunnel.
81	Painted Coal Car	Railroad Camp	To the side of the train tunnel.
82	Carbon Fiber Wheels	Railroad Camp	In between the wagon and piles of wood.
83	Camouflage Lumber Car	Railroad Camp	Behind the tents near the fenced off area by the hay.
84	Carbon Fiber Trim	Railroad Camp	In between tents.
85	Camouflage Water Car	Railroad Camp	Near the tents by the wagon and pile of wood.
86	Beard and Hat	Railroad Camp	In between tents.
87	Camouflage Engine	Railroad Camp	In front of the wooden house behind the tents.
88	Opaque Trim	Railroad Camp	Behind the tent by the railroad tracks.
89	Painted Lumber Car	Railroad Camp	Behind the rock near the railroad track.
90	Striped Pants	Railroad Camp	Behind the tents.
91	Racecar Engine	Railroad Camp	In front of the railroad station.
92	Male Face 8	Railroad Camp	On top of the boulders across from the train station.
93	Soldier Uniform	Railroad Camp	On top of boulders across from the train station near the Gatling gun.
94	Male Face 1	Railroad Camp	Across from the train station, on top of the boulders and underneath the shed.
95	Fine Vest Suit	Railroad Camp	Behind a tent across from the train station.
96	Narrow Male Face	Railroad Camp	Across from the train station beside the rock.
97	Soldier Hat	Railroad Camp	Across from the train station tucked away along the wall.
98	Long-Nosed Mask	Railroad Camp	By the hole in the wall.
99	Full Beard and Hat	Colby	In the air behind the Grand Colby Saloon.
100	Bamboo Hat	Colby	In the air over the Sheriff building.
101	Floral Engine	Red's	In the air near the bridge to the Railroad Camp.
102	Decorative Hat	Red's	In the air over the river.
103	Zebra Lumber Car	Red's	In the air over the bridge to the Railroad Camp near the lumber yard.
104	Zebra Engine	Colby	In the air near the bridge to Red's Camp.
105	Circus Engine	Red's	In the air near the bridge to Red's Camp.
106	Painted Water Car	Railroad Camp	Behind the wooden house that is behind the tents.

Green Capsules

#	Unlockable Item	Zone	Description
107	Colby Jail House Siding	Railroad Camp	On the hill across from the train station.
108	Colby Stone Wall	Railroad Camp	In the air near the bridge to Red's Camp.
109	Colby Weathered Floorboard	Railroad Camp	Along the wall of the Railroad Camp near the entrance to the Silver Mine.
110	Colby Buildings Toy Pack 4	Colby	Over the water tower that is on the roof of the Grand Colby Saloon.
111	Colby Buildings Toy Pack 1	Colby	In the air behind the Colby Rooming House.
112	Colby Buildings Toy Pack 3	Colby	Over the water tower in front of the spire.
113	Colby General Store Siding	Colby	In the air by the water tower and spire.
114	Colby Townsperson Toy Pack 1	Colby	On the ledge near the spire wall and near the waterfall.
115	Colby Townsperson Toy Pack 2	Colby	At the top of the spire.
116	Colby Townsperson Toy Pack 5	Colby	Behind the Sheriff building.
117	Colby Bank Bricks	Colby	On the top of the rocks in the canyon behind the Bank.
118	Colby Platform Floorboard	Ranch	Under the windmill.
119	Colby Rooming House Siding	Ranch	On the far side of the river.
120	Colby Train Station Siding	Ranch	On the side of the ranch house.
121	Colby Stable Siding	Ranch	On the side of the ranch house.
122	Colby Wash House Siding	Ranch	Near the ranch house and behind the wagon.
123	Colby Buildings Toy Pack 2	Ranch	In the air behind the train station.
124	Colby Saloon Siding	Ranch	In the air in between the ranch house and the cattle barn.
125	Colby Townsperson Toy Pack 4	Ranch	On the island in the river across from the train station.
126	Vertical Sliding Walls	Ranch	In the air over the river, past the island.
127	Colby Townsperson Toy Pack 3	Ranch	On the shore, opposite from the island.
128	Colby Floorboard	Comanche Elders	Behind a rock near the Comanche Elders.
129	Colby Hardware Store Siding	Comanche Elders	In the air near the bridge to Red's Camp.
130	Red's Wooden Floorboard	Silver Mine	On the ground near the entrance to the Silver Mine.
131	Colby Worn Floorboard	Silver Mine	On the cliffside directly across from Sleeping Man.
132	Colby Decorations Toy Pack 2	Silver Mine	On the cliffside directly across from Sleeping Man.
133	Colby Large Floorboard	Silver Mine	In the air across from Sleeping Man.
134	Colby Wooden Shingles	Silver Mine	Up the path on the cliffside.
135	Colby Wooden Siding	Silver Mine	Tucked into the wall behind the dynamite.
136	Colby Decorations Toy Pack 1	Silver Mine	On the elevated train track.
137	Colby Wood Moulding	Silver Mine	In the air in between the entrance to the Silver Mine and the elevated train tracks.
138	Colby Polished Floorboard	Silver Mine	In front of Sleeping Man.
139	Colby Critter Toy Pack 1	Red's	On the roof of the red train.
140	Colby Townsperson Toy Pack 7	Red's	Inside the tent beside the Grand Colby Saloon.
141	Red's Wooden Siding	Red's	Beside the tent that is behind Red's Traveling Entertainments.
142	Colby Townsperson Toy Pack 8	Red's	Inside the tent of the Hall of Oddities.
143	Colby Large Wooden Siding	Red's	In the air behind the tents and near the elevated train track.
144	Red's Bricks	Red's	On top of the tall boulder.
145	Colby Store Vertical Siding	Red's	Along the wall near the tunnel.
146	Colby Townsperson Toy Pack 6	Red's	Near the bridge to Railroad Camp.
147	Colby Plants Toy Pack 1	Silver Mine	Inside the tunnel to Railroad Camp.
148	Colby Wooden Crate	Railroad Camp	In the hole in the wall.
149	Colby Small Siding	Railroad Camp	Over the train tunnel and underneath the wooden platform.
150	Colby Plants Toy Pack 2	Railroad Camp	In the corner of the Railroad Camp near the wooden house.

Infinity Chests/Vault

#	Unlockable Item	Zone	Description
LR1	Lone Ranger Chest 1	Ranch	In the cemetery.
LR2	Lone Ranger Chest 2	Colby	At the base of the spire.
LR3	Lone Ranger Chest 3	Railroad Camp	On the upper ledge across from the train station.
Master	Lone Ranger Avatar Vault - Reward 1	Colby	Tucked into the wall inside the canyon behind the Bank.
T1	Tonto Chest 1	Comanche Elders	On the ground near the Comanche Elders' Camp.
T2	Tonto Chest 2	Red's	At the base of the tall boulder at Red's Camp.
T3	Tonto Chest 3	Silver Mine	On the cliffside directly across from Sleeping Man.

Lone Ranger Gold Stars

#	Type	Star Names	Star Description
1	Mission	Horsing Around	Buy a horse.
2	Mission	Delivery Training	Deliver supplies by train.
3	Mission	Red's Traveling Entertainments	Get to Red's Traveling Entertainments.
4	Mission	The Railroad Camp	Get to the Railroad Camp.
5	Mission	Cavendish's Downfall	Defeat Butch Cavendish.
6	Mission	No Ordinary Round-Up	Capture all of the mystical animals.
7	Mission	All's Said and Done	Complete 50 missions.
8	Challenge	Rough Rider	Attempt all Horse Racing Challenges.
9	Challenge	Horse Master	Successfully complete the highest level of difficulty on all Horse Racing Challenges.
10	Challenge	Winging It	Attempt all Crow Flight Challenges.
11	Challenge	Flight Master	Successfully complete the highest level of difficulty on all Crow Flight Challenges.
12	Easter Egg	Sharpshooter	Hit 20 shooting gallery targets.
13	Easter Egg	Dead Eye	Hit 50 shooting gallery targets.
14	Easter Egg	Gatling Gunner	Shoot 20 Gatling gun targets.
15	Easter Egg	Cannon Master	Shoot 20 Cannon targets.
16	Easter Egg	Tailor Made	Customize townspeople 20 times.
17	Easter Egg	Gang Wrangler	Defeat 20 Cavendish Gang members.
18	Easter Egg	Gang Wrangling Legend	Defeat 75 Cavendish Gang members.
19	Easter Egg	All is Found	Collect 20 prize capsules.
20	Easter Egg	Barrel Breaker	Break 200 barrels.
21	Easter Egg	Track of All Trades	Deliver each resource at least one time.
22	Easter Egg	Track Master	Deliver five resources by train.
23	Easter Egg	Frequent Flyer	Fly as a crow 30 times.
24	Easter Egg	Surprise Attack	Summon the Silent Warrior to defeat 20 enemies.
25	Easter Egg	Dynamite Defeat	Defeat 20 enemies with dynamite from the TNT pack.
26	Purchases	Trunk Space	Purchase the Elephant.
27	Purchases	Railroad Tycoon	Purchase all of the Train Cars.
28	Purchases	On Target	Purchase all of the Target Packages.
29	Purchases	Hold Your Horses	Purchase every horse from the Toy Store.
30	Purchases	The Completist	Purchase every toy from the Toy Store.

Lone Ranger Toy List

Toys	Toy Box Export	Toy Type	Commercial
Black Horse	Yes	Vehicle/Mount	No
Black Pinto Horse	Yes	Vehicle/Mount	No
Box Car	No	Vehicle/Mount	No
Bridge to Railroad Camp	No	Unique	No
Bridge to Red's	No	Unique	No
Brown Pinto Horse	Yes	Vehicle/Mount	No
Cannon Car	No	Vehicle/Mount	No
Cannon Targets	No	Unique	No
Cattle Car	No	Vehicle/Mount	Yes
Chestnut Horse	Yes	Vehicle/Mount	No
Constitution Engine	No	Vehicle/Mount	No
Crow Wing Pack	Yes	Prop	Yes
Elephant	Yes	Vehicle/Mount	Yes
Gatling Gun Car	No	Vehicle/Mount	Yes
Gatling Gun Targets	No	Unique	No
Combo Gun Car	No	Vehicle/Mount	No

Toys	Toy Box Export	Toy Type	Commercial
Golden Horse	Yes	Vehicle/Mount	No
Lumber Car	No	Vehicle/Mount	Yes
Palomino	Yes	Vehicle/Mount	No
Dining Car	No	Vehicle/Mount	No
Scout	Yes	Vehicle/Mount	No
Silent Warrior Pack	Yes	Prop	Yes
Silver	Yes	Vehicle/Mount	Yes
Target Package 1	No	Unique	No
Target Package 2	No	Unique	No
Target Package 3	No	Unique	No
The Jupiter	No	Vehicle/Mount	No
Thundering Hooves Pack	Yes	Prop	Yes
Thundering Stallion	Yes	Vehicle/Mount	Yes
TNT Car	No	Vehicle/Mount	Yes
TNT Pack	Yes	Prop	Yes
Water Car	No	Vehicle/Mount	Yes

Lone Ranger Challenges

Name	Location	Description	Character	Requirements		
				Easy	Medium	Hard
Circlin' Colby	Near Colby	Ride a horse through all the gates before the time runs out.	Any	7 gates in 1:00	7 gates in 0:45	7 gates in 0:35
Trottin' Through Town	Near Colby	Ride a horse through all the gates before the time runs out.	Any	8 gates in 1:00	8 gates in 0:50	8 gates in 0:40
Riverbed Race	Near Colby	Ride a horse through all the gates before the time runs out.	Any	9 gates in 1:10	9 gates in 0:55	9 gates in 0:45
Railway Race	Near Red's	Ride as Lone Ranger through all the gates before the time runs out.	Lone Ranger	10 gates in 1:30	10 gates in 1:15	10 gates in 1:00
Racin' the Range	Railroad Camp	Ride a horse through all the gates before the time runs out.	Any	12 gates in 2:00	12 gates in 1:45	12 gates in 1:30
Flight from the Elders	Near Comanche Elders	Use the Crow Wing Pack to gather the collectibles before the time runs out.	Any	15 collectibles in 1:10	30 collectibles in 1:10	40 collectibles in 1:10
Water Wings	Near Ranch	Use the Crow Wing Pack to gather the collectibles before the time runs out.	Any	15 collectibles in 1:10	30 collectibles in 1:10	40 collectibles in 1:10
Roundin' the Ridge	Near Canyon by Colby	Use the Crow Wing Pack to gather the collectibles before the time runs out.	Any	20 collectibles in 1:10	35 collectibles in 1:10	50 collectibles in 1:10
Trackin' the Train	Near Red's	Using Tonto and the Crow Wing Pack, gather the collectibles before time runs out.	Tonto	15 collectibles in 1:10	30 collectibles in 1:10	45 collectibles in 1:10
Soarin' Through Camp	Near Railroad Camp	Use the Crow Wing Pack to gather the collectibles before the time runs out.	Any	20 collectibles in 1:00	35 collectibles in 1:00	45 collectibles in 1:00

Introduction to the Toy Box

Disney Infinity is a huge game with an almost infinite number of possibilities. The Toy Box is a key feature of the game, and it can be somewhat daunting at first since there is so much to do. This part of the guide focuses entirely on the Toy Box, which encompasses all parts of *Disney Infinity* that are outside of the various Play Sets.

Exploring the Toy Box

After completing the introduction to the game, you find yourself in the Toy Box Launch. While you have several options, such as getting right into one of the Play Sets, it is a good idea to take some time and explore the Toy Box. In the center of this area is the Disney Castle. Select a character and place it on your Disney Infinity Base to get started.

The Disney Infinity Hub

When you first enter the Toy Box Launch, your character is standing in the middle of the Disney Infinity Hub. The Hub has four buttons that you activate by standing on them. Use them to access different areas of the game. The red button takes you to the Travel menu, where you can select from Mastery Adventures, Adventures, Character Adventures, Prebuilt Toy Box Worlds, and the Play Set that you have placed on the Disney Infinity Base. In addition, you can also save your current Toy Box or load one you have previously saved. The yellow button opens the Disney Infinity Vault, where you can unlock new Toys to use in the Toy Box. The green button opens the Toy Store, where you can select Toys you have already unlocked. Finally, the purple button takes you to the Hall of Heroes.

NOTE

The current Toy Box will be saved automatically in a default save slot when you exit. However, it is a good idea to get in the habit of naming the Toy Box in which you are working and saving it regularly. If you don't and you open another Toy Box, it will save over the old opened one when you exit. You can have up to 100 Toy Box saves—as long as your gaming system has storage room.

Taking a Walk

The best way to explore the Toy Box Launch is to take a walk. From the hub, start moving around the left side of the castle. There is a beam of light shining up into the sky in the distance. Walk towards the light.

You need to jump up onto a small ledge to get the Toy Box Blaster. This tool is now added to your inventory in the Tools/Pack menu. The Blaster comes in handy for fighting enemies. To select the Blaster, follow the directions on the screen to open the Tools/Pack menu. Here you can select items you have unlocked to use. You can even assign an item to one of two quick slots so you can quickly access it without having to open the menu. Once you have the Blaster selected, give it a try. By this time, there may be enemies spawning in the area.

Now that you have the Blaster, head over to the other side of the castle. There is another beam of light at the top of a slope. Climb the slope to find an Autopia Car. Hop in to give it a spin.

As soon as you climb into the Autopia Car, an entire track and landscape appears magically before you. Since you are already in the driver's seat, go ahead and take the car for a spin around the track and get a feel for driving. Then you can continue driving off the course and around the Toy Box to get where you want to go faster than by walking.

Gathering Sparks and Spins

There are several capsules in the Toy Box Launch. Blue capsules are Helps. Touch them to reveal tips or other information on playing the game. Green capsules contain either Sparks or Spins. Sparks are the experience in the game. Collect them to level up your characters. You can also get Sparks by breaking barrels, crates, and other objects, by defeating enemies, and by earning medals in the Adventures.

Spins are the way you unlock new toys for the Toy Box. There are lots of Spins in green capsules in the Toy Box Launch, but this is the only place where they are in capsules. You can also earn Spins by leveling up your characters and completing Adventures. Look around the Toy Box to find as many Spins as you can. There are some inside and on top of the castle as well as hidden in groups of crates and barrels. For more information on using Spins to unlock Toys, see the Disney Infinity Vault section of the guide.

As you continue to explore the Toy Box Launch, you will run into some enemies. Use the Toy Box Blaster or just regular attacks to defeat them. Since you have the Autopia Car, you can also run into them at full speed. Continue destroying crates and fighting enemies as you explore the main land area of the Toy Box Launch. There are some more areas floating off in the air away from the main land, but don't worry about those now. Later, when you get air vehicles or have completed the Building Mastery Adventure, you will be able to get to those areas and find more green capsules.

What to do Next

Now that you have experienced the basics of the Toy Box Launch, it is time to learn more about the Toy Box. It is also a good time to learn more about how to fight and drive, which you will need to know for not only the Toy Box, but also for the Play Sets. The best place to learn this is in the Mastery Adventures. So after collecting all the Sparks and Spins you can in the Toy Box Launch, head back to the Disney Infinity Hub to continue your training and learn how to Travel to different Toy Boxes and other aspects of the game.

TIP

It is a good idea to complete all of the Mastery Adventures before continuing on. Keep reading to find more information on these in the next section.

Travel

When you want to leave a Toy Box and go somewhere else, you can step on the red button at the Disney Infinity Hub or select Travel from the Pause menu. Either way, this takes you to the Travel menu where you can choose to try out Mastery Adventures, Character Adventures, or other Adventures. You can also visit the Hall of Heroes, go to one of the Prebuilt Toy Box Worlds, or even save or load a Toy Box of your own. When you first begin *Disney Infinity*, it is a good idea to go through the Mastery Adventures to help you learn the ropes of not only playing the game, but using the many different features of the Toy Box.

Mastery Adventures

Think of the Mastery Adventures as tutorials for learning the ways to manipulate and build in the Toy Box, as well as how to play *Disney Infinity* whether you are in the Toy Box or one of the Play Sets. There are six different Mastery Adventures, but you only have access to three at the start. The other three are unlocked as you complete Building Mastery and then the other Mastery Adventures related to building in sequential order. Also be sure to do the Combat Mastery and Driving Mastery Adventures so you can learn the moves and mechanics of fighting and driving. Both of those come in handy throughout the game. Completing these two Mastery Adventures unlocks several Adventures, which are essentially challenges where you can put what you have learned to work.

Building Mastery

There be no better way to build up your world than by goin' on a treasure hunt! Place pieces in your Toy Box to help get to the gold!

The Building Mastery Adventure is a brief tutorial on using the editor for building and manipulating the Toy Box. When the Adventure begins, you must help a Captain Hook townsperson find some treasure. Follow him to the highlighted area to continue.

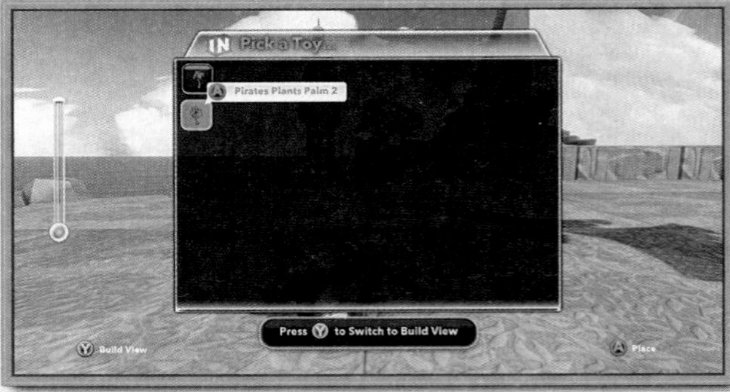

Your first task is to use the editor to place three Palm Trees in the area. Follow the on-screen instructions to open the editor and then choose from two different trees. Select one and then position it where you want to place it. Repeat this process two more times so that there are three Palm Trees.

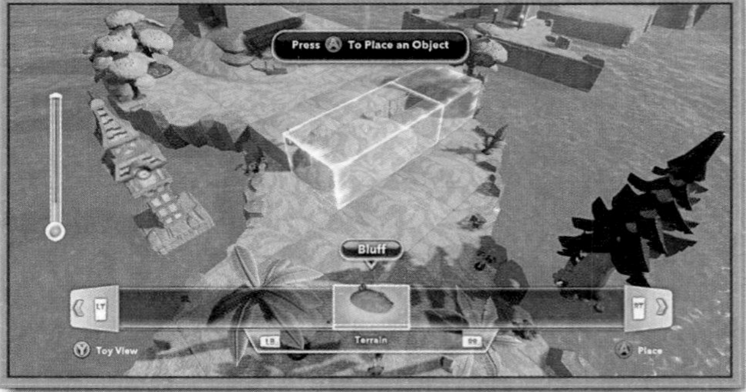

There is no way for Captain Hook to get up onto a higher level. Therefore, open the editor and select a Bluff. Line it up with the hillside so that it is within the blue box and place it. Now the Bluff can serve as a ramp for you and your friend to get up to the next area.

Once you get to the top of the level, you need to get across a gap. Bring up the editor and select the Super Cannon. Position it along the edge of the gap. However, since it is facing the wrong direction, you need to rotate it so it is facing across the gap. Once you have rotated the cannon, place it, walk into it, and launch yourself across the gap to the other side.

The bridge to the castle is missing a section. Bring up the editor and drop a Castle Bridge segment into position. Follow the on-screen directions to change the elevation of the bridge so that it lowers into the correct spot. You can also move the camera around to get a better view on your construction.

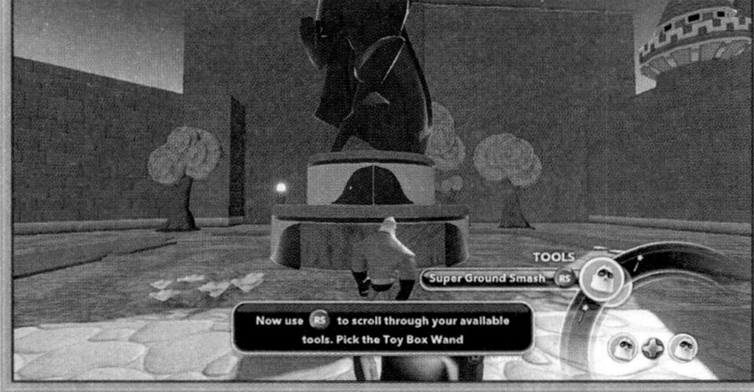

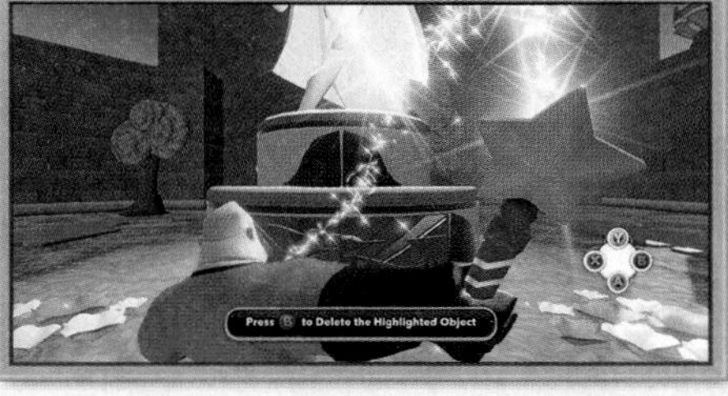

Your next task is to remove a Statue. Open up the Tools/Packs menu following the directions on the screen. Then scroll through your available tools to select the Magic Wand. Hold down the wand button to select the Statue. Finally press the delete button to send the Statue back to the inventory and get it out of your way.

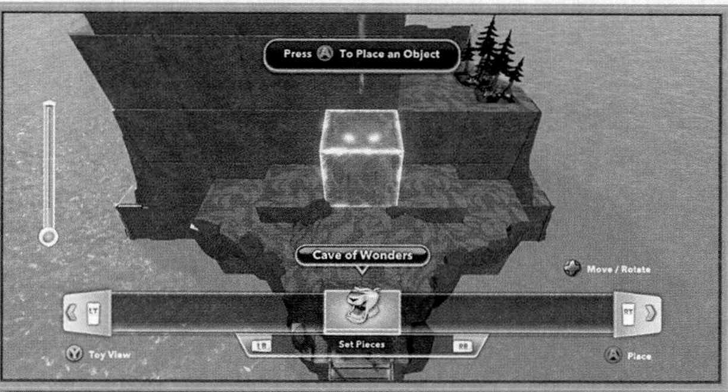

Continue to the next highlighted spot. You need to enter a cave, but there is no entry. Therefore, open the editor and place the Cave of Wonders at the indicated spot. You can then hop through the opening and enter the cave.

Follow the cave to the Treasure Grotto, however you find it is not in the correct place. Use your Magic Wand and select the Treasure Grotto. Then press the edit button. Now move the Treasure Grotto towards you so that it is adjacent to the block on which you are standing. Walk into the Treasure Grotto to complete the Adventure, earn a Spin you can use to unlock a toy from the Disney Infinity Vault, and receive a Mastery Star. This also unlocks the Dynamics Mastery and Creativi-Toy Mastery Part 1 Adventures. This also unlocks the Dynamics Mastery and Creativi-Toy Mastery Part 1 Adventures.

Combat Mastery

We'll pit you against the pros and teach you how to battle all the baddies in the Toy Box.

The Combat Mastery Adventure is a great way to learn the different ways you can fight against enemies. To get started, walk up to the wooden doors and press the attack button to knock—knock down the door that is.

Enter the training area and begin clearing out the crates and other objects by pressing the attack button. Then try using the alternate attack button to destroy several items in front of you. Finally, jump up into the air and then press the attack button to come down with a slam attack that can destroy several objects in the area around you.

Next you have to try getting a moving target. Follow after the Gaston townsperson and pick him up by pressing the action button. Then follow the directions on the screen to throw him out of the training area. In combat, picking up an enemy not only can cause damage to the enemy you pick up, but also to any enemies you throw that enemy at. Unfortunately, Gaston is not so easy to get rid of. Now that you have learned how to throw, follow the directions on the screen to kick Gaston out of the training area. During combat, you can pick up enemies and throw them for damage. You can also use them as a projectile and throw them into other enemies.

You are now ready for the battle arena. Gaston has put together a number of enemies to take you on. It starts off with a single Zurgbot. Rush forward and attack to destroy it. Then defeat two more that appear.

A Blaster appears in the middle of the area. Move over and pick it up—it will come in handy. Press the alternate attack button to fire the Blaster at enemies and hit them from longer range. Then, as they get close, finish them up with normal attacks. Gaston sends more and more enemies to attack. Defeat them all using a variety of attacks.

Now you have to knock Gaston into the arena. Take aim with the Blaster and fire at him. Once he is in the arena, he calls in a bunch of enemies. However, this time you get some allies to help you. Defeat all of the enemies to get the Mastery Star as well as a Spin. In addition, you also unlock three new Adventures—Sumo, Gladiator Arena, and Dome Defense.

Driving Mastery

Become a pro at driving and doing tricks with this driving Adventure.

One of the fun things to do in the Toy Box is racing. Complete this Mastery Adventure to earn a Mastery Star and a Spin, as well as to unlock five Adventures—Battle Race, Lap Race, Battle Race Reverse, Lap Race Reverse, and Off Road. At the start, you learn the basics of driving. Press the accelerator button to start driving and steer through the first couple of turns.

Now you need to drift through the next three turns. Follow the directions on the screen. As you drift, your car builds up energy that you can then use to activate turbo. Drifting can take some practice and, for these turns, you don't want to drift through the entire turn.

As soon as you hit the straightaway, activate the turbo for a burst of speed. Do this through the next two straightaways as well. Try hitting the jumps while using turbo to get some extra air.

There is more to the Toy Box than just driving around on tracks. You can also do stunts. In the next part of the Adventure, you must get 10 collectibles. These are yellow balloon-like spheres that you break by running into them. The driving arena is filled with ramps and other obstacles. While jumping in the air, follow the directions on the screen to do different tricks tricks. Landing a trick builds up energy, just like drifting.

Try driving up the halfpipe ramps. When you get to the top and into the air, your car will automatically rotate and come back down. This is a good time to pull off a trick as well. Play around as you try different tricks while you finish getting all of the collectibles to complete the Driving Mastery Adventure.

Dynamics Mastery

Learn how and what the Physics Blocks can do in the Toy Box.

This quick Mastery Adventure teaches you about a certain category of objects known as Physics Blocks. They are called this because they react according to the laws of physics. There are three main types of these blocks—Glass, Wood, and Steel.

Your first task is to knock down a tower made up of Glass Blocks. Move towards it and press the attack button to destroy individual blocks. As the blocks on top fall to the ground, they also break since they are made of glass.

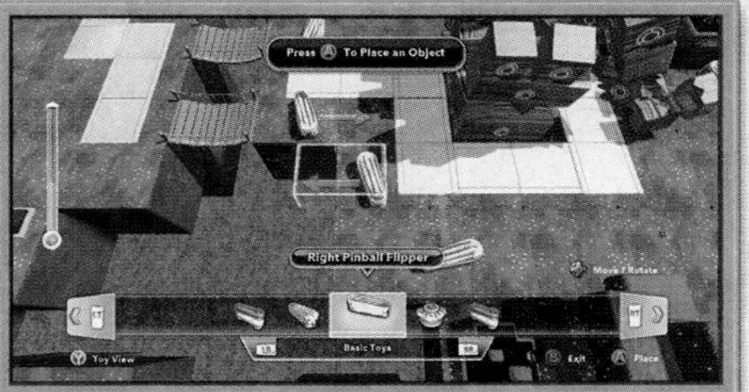

Now you must take down a tower made of Wooden Blocks. Wooden Blocks break when you attack them or they fall, however they are tougher than Glass Blocks. This time you are going to use objects to do it rather than attack it yourself. Off to one side of the tower, balls are being launched. Open the editor and use Bumpers and Flippers as found in a pinball game to hit the balls into the tower to knock it down. Try placing a bumper in the middle of the grass at the foreground end so the ball will bounce off the side of the bumper and move towards the tower. All it takes is a few hits with some balls and the tower falls.

The next task features Steel Blocks. While they will fall like Glass or Wooden Blocks, Steel Blocks are indestructible. As you approach the steel tower, it falls down. Notice that the blocks remain intact however.

To quickly reassemble the steel tower, find the Reset-O-Matic and step on it. This switch is a great way to restore a structure to its original construction.

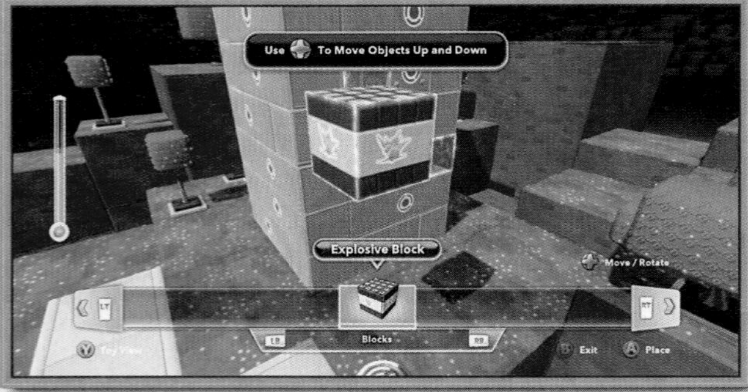

Now place an Explosive Block into one of the gaps in the steel tower. Explosive Blocks blow up when they are hit by something. This time you are going to use a Slingshot.

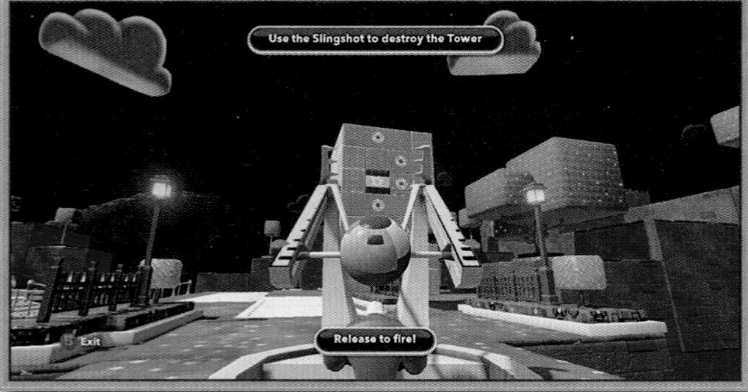

After putting the Explosive Block into position, move over to the Slingshot and take control of it. Take aim and follow the directions on the screen to fire the Slingshot. Hit the Explosive Block to knock down the steel tower and complete the Mastery Adventure. For your efforts you are awarded a Mastery Star and a Spin, and you also unlock an Adventure—Castles and Slingshots.

Creativi-Toys Mastery Part 1

Your Creativi-Toys are the key to making your own games in the Toy Box.

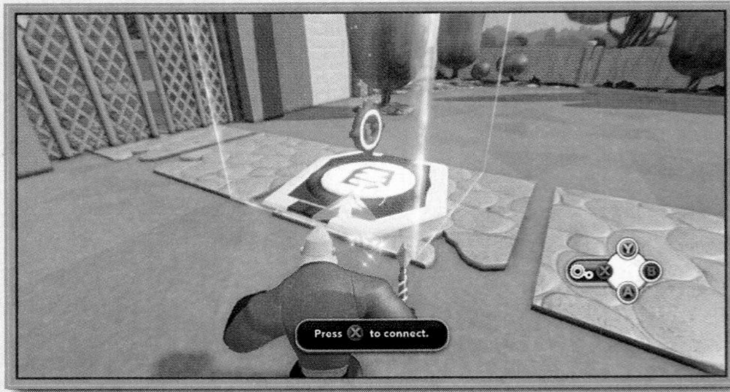

Creativi-Toys are powerful toys that you can use to create actions and reactions within the Toy Box. Start off by moving towards the stadium. Pick up the Wand and then use it to select the Step On Trigger in front of the gate. This will act as a trigger. Choose to connect the Step On Trigger, and then select "Stepped On". This sets the Step On Trigger to send a trigger signal when someone steps on it.

Now select the Stadium Gate to connect it to the Step On Trigger. From the menu, select "Open". This instructs the gate to open when someone steps on the Step On Trigger. You have just completed your first connection. Step on the plate and then move through the now open gate to enter the stadium.

TIP

While you can't do it in the Mastery Adventure now, if you wanted to, you could then use the gate as a new trigger and cause another object to react. For example, when the gate opens, it can then trigger another object by connecting it. In this way, you could create a chain of events that are all started by stepping on a single Step On Trigger.

Next you need to connect another Step On Trigger. Do the same thing you did before, however this time, connect it to the Boom Box. Now choose the song you want it to play.

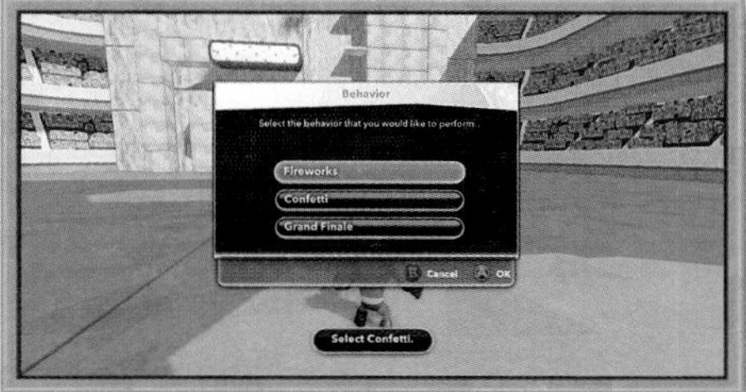

Now select the Boom Box again. We are going to use it as a trigger. Select "Started" as the trigger. Then select the Party Cannon to connect it. For the Party Cannon, choose "Confetti" as the behavior.

The Adventure then connects several more Party Cannons as well as Time Delay toys together to make an even more impressive show. Walk over to The Teleporter and step on it to travel to another Teleporter outside of the stadium.

Move back through the gate and step on the Step On Trigger. As you do, the Boom Box begins playing and the Party Cannons begin firing in succession.

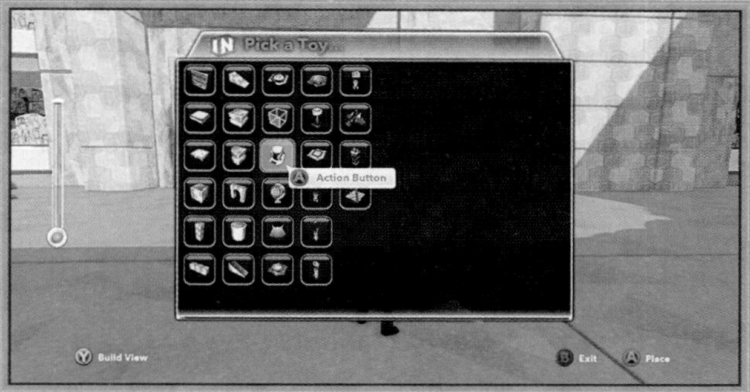

If you want, you can play around with a number of Creativi-Toys and other objects. Just open the editor to select and place them in the Toy Box, and then try connecting them. When you are done, follow the directions to a second Step-On Trigger past the Boom Box and the first Party Cannon to finish the Mastery Adventure. You not only earn a Mastery Star and a Spin, but also unlock the Creativi-Toys Mastery Part 2 Adventure.

Creativi-Toys Mastery Part 2

Even more Creativi-Toys to make your own games in the Toy Box.

Now that you have learned the basics of placing and assigning orders or behaviors to Creativi-Toys, it is time to see how you can use them to create a game. Phineas and Ferb townspeople have already built the beginnings of a platforming game. They just need you to finish it and then play it.

To get started, pull out your Magic Wand, select the Step On Trigger, and set it to "Stepped On".

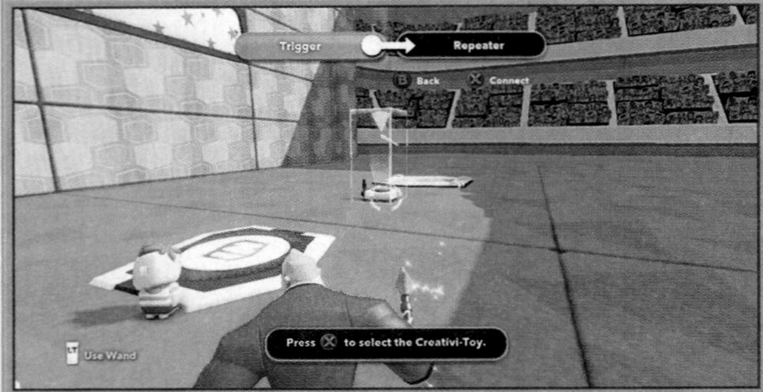

Next target the Repeater and turn it on. Now step onto the Teleporter and use it to get to the top of the game.

At the top, you can see a Falling Object Generator. Since you already have the Repeater selected, connect it to the Falling Object Generator and then select the ESPN Bowling Ball. The Step On Trigger now activates the Falling Object Generator and the Repeater causes it to drop a ball every few seconds. Take the Teleporter back down to the ground level.

To help you play this game, you have been given a Star Command Boost Pack. Press the attack button and the Boost Pack will shoot you up into the air. Move to the Step On Trigger in the game to get it started.

TIP

Notice that as soon as the game starts, the camera angle changes to a side scrolling game type. That is because the Mastery Adventure is using a Side-Step Camera behind the scenes that was activated when you stepped on the Step On Trigger. This tool allows you to create your own side scrolling games.

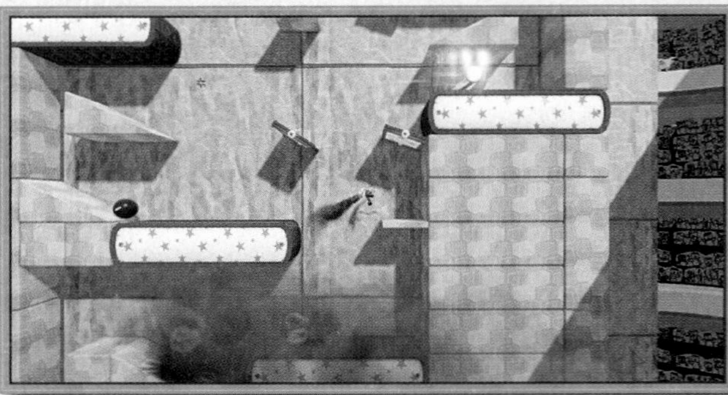

Make your way up through the game while trying to avoid being hit by the bowling balls. The key is to get to the small gray platform on the right. Then from there, boost your way up to the Flipper above. From there, boost up to another small gray platform—but you have to watch out for bowling balls here. Then move on to another Flipper, wait for a bowling ball to pass over your head, and then boost on up to the highest small gray platform to complete the game. At the end, you get a Mastery Star and a Spin.

Adventures

Adventures are like short challenges where you have to put the skills you need to know to succeed in *Disney Infinity* into action. They are unlocked by completing the Mastery Adventures. Each Adventure has three different medals you can earn—Bronze, Silver, and Gold. Each time you earn a medal for the first time in an Adventure, you receive not only Sparks but also a Spin. In addition, you can play all of the Adventures in multiplayer. Two players on the same system can play them together with a split screen, while up to four players can play together over a network connection.

TIP

Troy Johnson and Jared Bals at Disney Interactive and Avalanche were kind enough to provide some great tips for each of the Adventures and Character Adventures. Since they designed or worked on these, they know how to beat them and get gold medals and are passing their tips along to you.

Castles and Slingshots

Try to keep your spheres whole while searching out and destroying the spheres in the other castles.

Gold: 3 Spheres

Silver: 2 Spheres

Bronze: 1 Sphere

For this adventure, you have 1 minute to break down the walls of your opponents' castles, find the hidden spheres, and then destroy the spheres. To accomplish this, you have a Slingshot. The Slingshot can be rotated and elevated. Then pull back and release to fire the rocket projectiles.

As you hit the colored walls of the castles, you break them down. Keep firing until you can see one of the spheres and then shoot at it to destroy it. The key to getting a gold medal for this adventure is to immediately start pulling back on the Slingshot as soon as you release. Novices will wait to see where the first projectile hit before pulling back on the Slingshot. By pulling back as soon as you release it, you can have a second shot in the air by the time the first one hits. The faster you can fire, the more blocks you can break down and the more spheres you can destroy.

TIP

You'll have to improve your skill at using the Slingshot. Always pulling back on the Slingshot, even while you're still tuning your aim, can save you tons of time over the course of the Adventure because you'll always be ready to unleash a shot. The breakable spheres in opponents' castles always appear inside in random locations, so a little luck on your side can make the difference. Just go crazy and destroy as much of the opposing castles as possible in the time limit. In multiplayer, however, there is no time limit—it's simply "last castle standing." Under these circumstances, the winner almost invariably earns a gold medal anyway.

Sumo

Stay on solid ground as long as possible while the ground disappears out from underneath you.

Gold: Survive over 3:00 minutes

Silver: Survive over 2:10 minutes

Bronze: Survive over 1:00 minutes

This is a combat Adventure where you have to fight against several different enemies. However, the blocks on which you are standing randomly disappear. Therefore, you have to keep moving and avoid being knocked off of the blocks. Random tools such as Blasters or balls appear, which you can shoot or throw at enemies to help you keep them away from you.

As the timer progresses, blocks begin to disappear. They turn transparent a second or two before they vanish, so be quick to move to solid ground or risk falling. Also watch out for the Wooden Block with the skulls on it bouncing around. If it hits you, you take damage. Enemies are destroyed when the Wooden Block blows up near them. Shoot at it while it is near enemies to take them out. If you want to get the gold medal, try using Power Discs that increase the damage you inflict so you can more easily defeat the enemies. Also stay away from the edges since some of the enemy's attacks can push you back over the edge and end the adventure for you.

TIP

This is one of the more difficult Adventures to earn a gold medal on...unless you use Randy or Violet. By the time you last long enough to earn silver, the enemies spawn so rapidly that it's difficult to keep track of them all, and you're likely to get hit from behind and knocked off. Randy and Violet, however, have the ability to turn invisible, and enemies do not notice or attack you in this state. You can survive until the final block falls with either of them. Boring, yes, but easier. The Lone Ranger is another solid choice, and if you're using a character with weaker combat capabilities, look for Phineas's baseball gun because it has a great knock-back effect on enemies. In split-screen multiplayer, the other player's camera view can also be helpful. This is especially true if the other camera is in spectator mode because it actually shows most of the arena from a zoomed-out perspective.

Gladiator Arena

Players can use all their packs and tools to survive increasingly difficult waves of enemies in the gladiatorial arena setting.

Gold: Survive 3 enemy waves

Silver: Survive 2 enemy waves

Bronze: Survive 1 enemy wave

Think you are good at combat? Test out your skills in the arena. While it begins with just a single enemy, you then have to take on two, three, four, or even more enemies at a time. A Zurg spaceship flies around and then teleports enemies into the arena, so be sure to keep an eye on the ship once you clear out the latest batch of baddies so you are ready for more. Be sure to use all your character's different attacks.

Use Power Discs that increase your damage, increase your health, and/or give you some invincibility. Also don't forget to use the tools and packs you have collected. You should at least have the Toy Box Blaster from the Toy Box Launch. This gives you a ranged attack so you can pick off enemies before they get in close. A few of the enemies have their own ranged attacks, so be sure to keep moving to avoid getting hit.

TIP

Choose a character with awesome offensive capabilities (Violet, Lone Ranger, etc.). Being defeated one time ends the Adventure, so if you start running low on health, do your best to run away until it regenerates, and then re-enter the fray. There are plenty of waves, so your endurance will be put to the test if you want to earn the gold.

Dome Defense

Help! Stop the Disney Infinity enemies from smashing through the domes and taking the townspeople inside! One destroyed dome ends the Adventure. Use your packs and tools to keep 'em safe!

Gold: 6 enemy waves

Silver: 4 enemy waves

Bronze: 2 enemy waves

There are three domes with Princess townspeople in them. Each has a number that represents the health of the dome. If the number ever reaches 0, the Adventure is over. Omnidroid enemies come out of the towers and make their way towards the closest dome. Your job is to defeat them before they can break open a dome. Be sure to use Blasters or other tools to attack the enemies, as well as use any Power Discs you have.

At the start, the enemies come out of the towers at a slower rate. However, as you move on to subsequent waves, they come faster and from different towers. Watch the sky above the towers. A beam of light shines down on the towers that are spawning enemies. Therefore, by looking for the beam, you can set yourself up to hit the enemies as they emerge from the towers.

TIP

Use the same characters and strategies that you would for Gladiator Arena, and learn to use your camera controls to keep an eye on all possible enemy spawn locations. Towers with a beam of light are actively spawning enemies, so that should help you plan your angle of attack. Packs and tools are also available, so utilize them if your character's native abilities aren't optimal for enemy crowd control.

Battle Race

Get set...Go! Be the fastest in this three-lap race with weapons!

Gold: Finish in under 2:05

Silver: Finish in under 3:00

Bronze: Finish in under 4:30

This is a race where you can use weapons to help you get ahead—or stay in the lead. Pick up weapons by running over the surprise boxes with the "?" on them. To build up turbo, run over the blue gas cans in addition to drifting and doing tricks.

You can fire your weapons forward as well as behind you—so if you have an opponent behind you, open fire to keep them behind you. Also, be sure to look for the shortcut. It can be tough to find in this race and involves jumping up onto a blue and white striped platform to get to a higher track area. It is fairly easy to get a bronze in this race. Silver is a bit tougher. However, if you want to get gold, you need to use the shortcut and drive a perfect race without crashing into anything. While you are racing against other cars, you are also racing against the clock to earn the medals.

TIP

For all of the Battle Race and Lap Race Adventures, the key is driving skill—taking hairpin turns smoothly and finding the single true shortcut on this level (it's the same shortcut route on both regular and reverse versions). Once you pull ahead in the Battle Races, be sure to use your weapons liberally against opponents behind you—they are never too far behind and will use their own weapons on you.

Lap Race

Get set...Go! Be the fastest in this three-lap race!

Gold: Finish in under 2:05

Silver: Finish in under 3:00

Bronze: Finish in under 4:30

This race is on the same track at the Battle Race, but this time you have no weapons. Rapidly press the accelerator button while waiting to start the race to rev up. Then when the race starts, you burst from the starting line with turbo. Drift and do tricks while racing to build up power so you can use turbo on the straightaways.

As you are moving next to another car, nudge the other car off the course and hopefully into a wall or off the edge. Also try combining the Fix-It Felix Repair Power Disc with the Pieces of Eight Power Disc to create the Turbo Charge ability, which provides bonus turbo energy.

Battle Race Reverse

Get set...Go! Be the fastest in this three-lap race with weapons!

Gold: Finish in under 2:05

Silver: Finish in under 3:00

Bronze: Finish in under 4:30

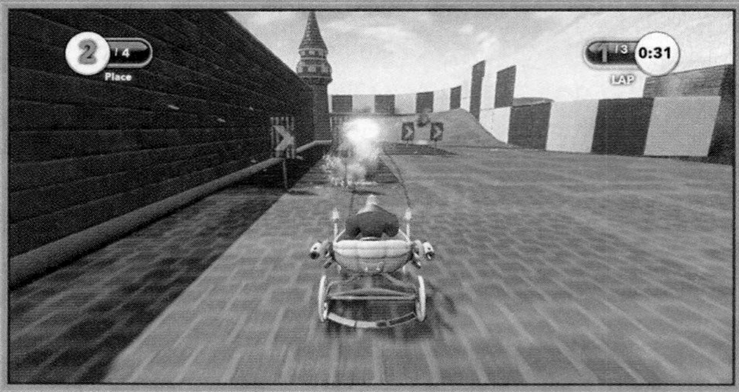

The track is the same as the Battle Race; however, this time you are driving around the track in the opposite direction. Pick up weapons and use them freely to slow down the competition.

The shortcut is in the same place as before—you just have to access it from a different spot. Once again, look for the blue and white striped platform.

Lap Race Reverse

Get set...Go! Be the fastest in this three-lap race!

Gold: Finish in under 2:05

Silver: Finish in under 3:00

Bronze: Finish in under 4:30

Use the same strategy as you did for the Lap Race, but with the reserve course. Hit the shortcut and turbo on the straightaways to get ahead and keep your time low enough to get the gold medal.

Off Road

Sure, the raceway is awesome. But how are your skills on this off-road course?

Gold: Finish in under 0:40

Silver: Finish in under 0:50

Bronze: Finish in under 1:10

The track for this race is short and has weapons you can pick up. However, it is played from a top-down view, making it a bit tougher to play. You can see exactly where your opponents are located, which makes it easier to target them—especially when they are behind you. The key to finishing the race with a good time is to avoid overcorrecting as you go around the turns. Plus when you are going down along the left side of the track, you have to remember that the controls are reversed. If you need to go to the right, you have to turn to the left.

TIP

Even though you don't see the prompt, make sure to rev it during the countdown to get your starting boost. Likewise, you won't be able to see your boost meter or load-outs because the camera is too far away, but they are available. Try to use them where you think they'll be most effective, regardless of what type might fire off.

Character Adventures

When selecting Adventures, in addition to the common Adventures, there are also Character Adventures. These appear in the Adventures menu, but only for the character you currently have on the Infinity Base. Therefore, if you have Mr. Incredible on the Base, then the "Mr. Incredible, the Hero" Adventure will be available to play. Like the other Adventures, these can be played by yourself or with 1 to 3 other players. You can also earn three levels of medals based on your performance. The more character toys you have, the more Adventures you can play.

Mr. Incredible, the Hero

You have all your packs and tools to help you smash domes to release the townspeople caught in them before the time runs out.

Gold: Release 3 townspeople

Silver: Release 2 townspeople

Bronze: Release 1 townsperson

Unlike the Dome Defense Adventure, this time you are the one trying to smash the domes. You have only 1 minute to smash as many as possible. However, it will not be easy. Syndrome has positioned Omnidroids around each one. Quickly get to the first dome and then clear out the enemies while attacking the dome as much as possible. More Omnidroids spawn in, so focus on the dome, otherwise you will spend all your time on enemies.

After the first dome is smashed, the timer resets and you get 1 minute and 30 seconds to go after the second dome. Follow the green arrow to your next objective. Watch out for turrets that fire at you along the way and try to slow you down. The Omnidroids defending the second dome are tougher. Use Mr. Incredible's alternate attack that creates a line of destruction along the ground. If you line it up correctly, you can destroy enemies and damage the dome at the same time.

You also have 1 minute and 30 seconds to smash the third dome. This time you must pass by more turrets as well as spike pads to get to it. Don't waste time trying to destroy them. Instead, rush past them and get to the dome. You can climb a Rope or use some Fans to get to the top of a ledge where the dome is located. Here you face lots of Omnidroids in all varieties and the dome is tougher to smash than the previous two. Try to keep moving so the dome is between you and the enemies as much as possible and keep attacking it. Using Power Discs can really help get the gold medal here.

TIP

You don't technically need to destroy any enemies to earn the medals, so focus almost entirely on the domes. Any time you get surrounded by enemies, your attacks will likely auto-target them instead of the domes. So peel away and around to the opposite side of the dome where you'll be more likely to be able to attack without interruption. Also, remember that any tools and packs you've obtained are available to you, so use Blasters to make quick work of the domes.

Sully's Paintball Brawl

It's time to show your rivals a victory of a different color. Put them in their place before time runs out.

Gold: 35 enemies defeated
Silver: 15 enemies defeated
Bronze: 5 enemies defeated

You have 4 minutes to defeat as many enemies as possible in this Adventure. To accomplish this, you are armed with a Paintball Gun. At the same time, you have to avoid being beaten, so watch your health. Your Paintball Gun fires several rounds and then must reload. The key to staying in the game is to keep moving—especially while reloading—otherwise you are a sitting duck. Also, when you hit an opponent, he or she is momentarily stunned, so quickly follow up with more shots to defeat the opponent before he or she can return fire. This also applies to you, so if you get hit and stunned, try to move away and get to cover before your opponents follow up with more hits.

There are teleporters along the sides that can be used to quickly get from one side of the arena to the other. A couple of balconies that run the length of the sides of the arena can be accessed by ramps at either end. This gives you a height advantage. However, since the range of the Paintball Guns is not all that long, it is usually better to stay down in the arena.

Power discs that increase your damage are useful for getting the gold medal since they can reduce the number of hits for defeating opponents and give you more time for going after others. Avoid getting surrounded by opponents or you can get into trouble. If one hits you, others can follow up with additional hits while you are momentarily stunned. That is why it is important to keep moving and use cover to avoid being ganged up on by your opponents.

TIP

Never stop pursuing the enemies. They spawn in waves of 5, so if you have trouble finding one, you're right on the cusp of a new wave of points. This one is all about persistent offense. If you start reloading your Paintball Gun before an enemy is defeated, be sure to use your shoulder charge or other attacks in the meantime.

Sparrow's Flight

Captain Jack Sparrow is on the run—to collect as much shine as he can before that scurvy time runs out. This calls for all your packs and tools.

Gold: Gather 25 collectibles
Silver: Gather 15 collectibles
Bronze: Gather 5 collectibles

Captain Jack Sparrow finds himself in a small seaside town where he needs to get as many collectibles as he can within 3 minutes. Once you gather the first 5 collectibles, then 5 more appear. Collect those and then another 5 appear. Watch out for several traps on the ground. They can either slow you down or kill you, causing you to wait while your character regenerates.

Many of the collectibles are up on top of buildings or on other elevated positions. Therefore, if you want to get gold, or even silver, having a pack with some type of boost or glide capability is helpful so you can quickly get to the tops of the buildings to grab the goodies.

For the bronze and silver medals, all of the collectibles are within the town or near it. There is no need to climb up the tall cliffs or platforms overlooking the town—that just wastes time. Instead, use the Fans to quickly get up on top of the buildings and jump from building to building to collect the yellow collectibles.

TIP

Learn the layout of the level. There are many possible spawn points for each wave of 5 collectibles, but once you start to learn where they can appear, it becomes easier to understand the quickest route to each location. Also, remember that your packs and tools are available in this Adventure. Boost packs that shoot you into the air can make this one a breeze...sort of.

Mrs. Incredible's Grab-It

Mrs. Incredible to the rescue! Use your elastic arms to take the townspeople to the safe zone and throw the criminals in prison where they belong.

Gold: Earn 40 points
Silver: Earn 20 points
Bronze: Earn 5 points

Mrs. Incredible scores 1 point for getting townspeople to the park in the middle of town and 5 points for throwing criminals into the police station. Some of these people and criminals are on the ground, but many are up on top of buildings. Get as many as you can in 4 minutes and 30 seconds.

While you can climb up the sides of the buildings, it is much quicker to use the Fans and Elevators. There are also Super Cannons to help you get from one building to another. Use Glider packs to soar down to lower buildings or to the streets. The key to earning a lot of points is to throw the citizens off the tops of the buildings towards the park. Don't worry, they have parachutes. Throw the criminals down to the street level as well, then once you have cleared the buildings, go down and throw them into the police station. If you hand deliver every person individually, you will not be able to get even a silver medal.

If you want to get gold, spend one attempt just exploring the area. Learn where the Super Cannons, Fans, and Elevators are located. Often getting part way up one building will lead to a Cannon that will shoot you up to the top of an another building. Then once you see how all the Cannons are connected, you can quickly move from building to building, throwing people and criminals down below. Make sure you leave enough time to get down to street level to put them all where they need to go.

TIP

It'll take a little practice and learning the layout of the level, but staying on the roofs for most of the Adventure is imperative. Don't hand deliver each citizen and crook one at a time. Toss all the townspeople off the roofs in the general direction of their targets, and then move directly to the next roof. Many of them will parachute down into the goal areas. Drop to the ground and deliver all the others when you have about 45 seconds left.

Violet's Stealth Mission

Avoid the Omnidroids and spotlights in Syndrome's maze! Find as many collectibles as you can.

Gold: Gather 25 collectibles

Silver: Gather 15 collectibles

Bronze: Gather 5 collectibles

Violet has to avoid spotlights and Omnidroids with lights as she moves through a maze-like canyon while gathering collectibles. There is no time limit on this Adventure, so use caution. Instead, the Adventure ends when a light beam hits you. This Adventure is played from a top-down camera view.

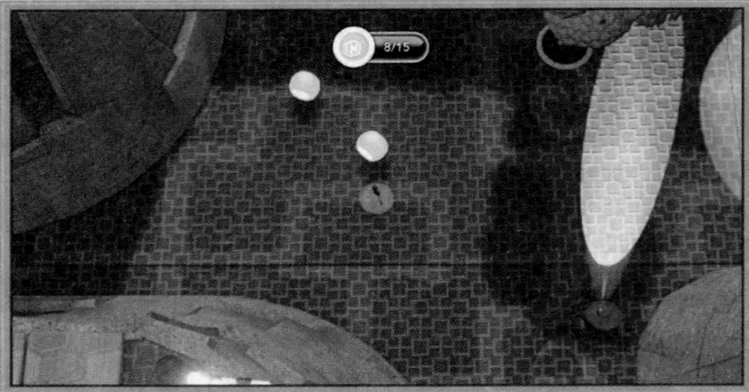

Observe the direction of motion of the spotlights and the patrol patterns of the Omnidroids before rushing into an area. A good tactic is to follow an Omnidroid through an area—just be careful it does not turn around on you. Don't try attacking them or you will get caught.

Getting bronze is fairly easy, since you can easily get the first 5 collectibles. However, the next 10 are a bit tougher and those final 10 are downright difficult to get. The best way to earn silver and gold is to play it over and over so you learn the patterns and where the safe spots are.

TIP

There's no timer on this one, so you can remain calm and wait out the searchlights until you're sure of their patterns. However, the lights subtly increase their speed over time, so waiting too long can also get you into trouble eventually. If you're caught between a couple lights closing in on you, a quick dodge roll may be able to squeeze you out of it if you just have a short distance to safety.

Dash's Data-Dart

Syndrome's at it again! You've got to gather the collectibles while avoiding the blue and red balls.

Gold: Gather 60 collectibles

Silver: Gather 40 collectibles

Bronze: Gather 10 collectibles

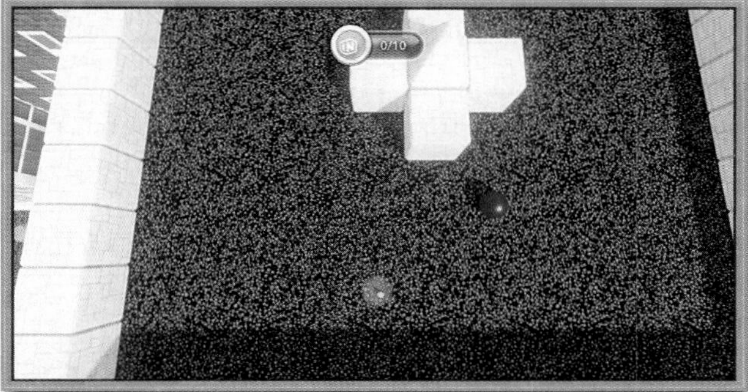

This is another top-down Adventure. While the concept is simple, mastering it is still challenging. You must move around a rooftop while avoiding blue and red balls. The blue balls drop yellow collectibles that you must collect. There is no time limit—the Adventure ends when you get hit by a ball.

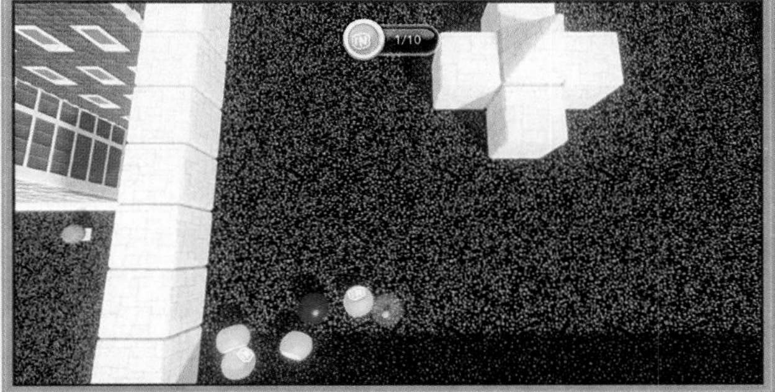

As the Adventure progresses, it gets tougher. It begins with one blue ball and then adds a second and a third. The blue balls bounce around using physics like billiard balls, so you can predict where they will go after a bounce. However, red balls are larger and follow you around, so you have to keep moving.

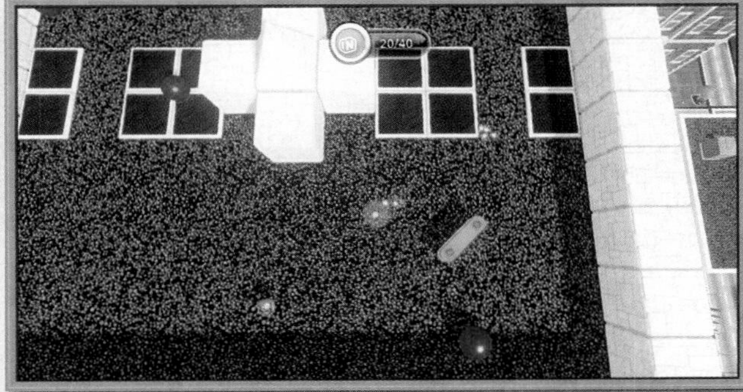

If this were not tough enough, bumpers spawn and can give the balls some unpredictable bounces. Plus tar traps slow you down—as well as the balls. Try to avoid tar traps if possible, but you will need to walk onto them to get some collectibles. Also, the collectibles disappear after a few seconds, so you have to go after them before they are gone.

TIP

Avoid taking risks. While you have to stay close enough to the dodge balls because they produce the yellow collectibles, you should have plenty of time to let the dodge balls move away before you snag the collectibles. Though you might not notice an effect at first, you can still actually jump in this Adventure, and you can double-jump over the blue dodge balls. (Don't try this with the red ones, though!) Finally, once the pinball bumpers appear, you can actually stand on top of them if you need a little time to compose yourself or wait for the balls to roll away. In split-screen multiplayer, the other player's camera view can also be helpful. This is especially true if the other camera is in spectator mode, because it actually shows most of the arena from a zoomed-out perspective.

Syndrome's Sorting Spring

You've met your match with this crazy challenge. Fling townspeople to safety with your Zero Point Energy, stop oncoming attacks, and stay alive while being pushed to your doom. Do it all before time runs out.

Gold: Earn 40 points

Silver: Earn 25 points

Bronze: Earn 5 points

This Adventure requires you to pick up townspeople on your roof and throw them onto adjacent rooftops for points. You have 5 minutes to score as many points as possible. You get 1 point for every townsperson thrown to another rooftop. Hit the targets and you score 2 points.

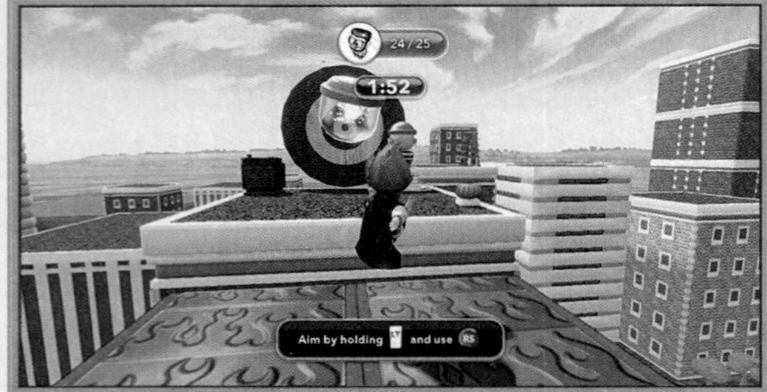

The rooftop on which you play has several conveyor belts, so you have to be careful you don't fall off the roof. While you will be taken back up to the rooftop, it wastes time. It is important to aim when you throw the townspeople since you want them to at least land on a rooftop. If they miss a roof, no points for you. For long shots, drop kick the townspeople by jumping and then pressing the alternate combat button.

Use Syndrome's Zero Point Energy to pick up and throw townspeople. This lets you grab them from a short distance and gives you a better chance of hitting the targets. As you progress, Omnidroids start appearing. Throw them off the roof with the Zero Point Energy to get them out of your way. If you want to get gold, you need to focus on hitting the targets. Take time to aim before each throw. While it may take a bit more time than just tossing them onto a rooftop, it still takes less time than picking up and throwing two different townspeople.

TIP

Quick L-stick and R-stick controls are how you'll win this one. Once you've gotten the hang of turning your character and the camera at the same time, you'll be able to find and toss the townspeople quickly. Though it's actually possible to earn gold without using aiming, if you get the hang of that skill, it becomes pretty easy to hit the center of the targets for an extra point per townsperson. That will get you to the gold in no time.

Mike's Scare Pig Dash

It's time for Mike to hog the spotlight. Race on Archie the Scare Pig around campus and collect as many points as you can!

Gold: Earn 200 points

Silver: Earn 120 points

Bronze: Earn 30 points

You have 3 minutes to score as many points as possible by gathering collectibles. Yellow collectibles are worth 1 point each, orange collectibles are 2 points, and red collectibles are 5 points. Since you have a limited amount of time, be sure to make the Scare Pig run throughout this Adventure. If you are content to get bronze, just run around the ground and pick up all of the yellow collectibles.

For those who want a silver medal, you need to get up onto the floating platforms with the orange collectibles. Jump from one platform to another without falling and get those orange collectibles. The red collectibles, which you will need to get in addition to the other colors if you want gold, are very tough to reach. You need to run and double jump to get across to the platforms where they are located or drop down from a platform to get them on your way down.

On the ground level are several scare traps. Avoid them or they will hit you and the Scare Pig and waste your precious time. These are all located near the center of the area. As with several other Adventures, spend some time exploring so you know the lay of the land and look for ways to get those red collectibles.

TIP

Practice. At first, 200 points might seem impossible, but I assure you that it can be done. First off, master controlling Archie while sprinting because that is the only way you'll reach 200. Focus on the upper-level platforms first, because you can earn more points per second up there. Learn the layout of the level, plan your lines, and be sure to explore some of the nooks and crannies for secret launcher pranks that can boost you to some valuable red collectibles.

Randy's Scavenger Hunt

Race with Randy through the scream tunnels and collect as much as you can before your time drains away.

Gold: Gather 20 collectibles

Silver: Gather 14 collectibles

Bronze: Gather 5 collectibles

While the scream tunnels are not that large, they are patrolled by enemies. Try to avoid them and grab as many yellow collectibles as you can within 3 minutes.

There are two Fear Tech Students that throw things at you down in the tunnels. When they hit, they inflict damage and slow you down a bit by the impact. Luckily you are armed with a Toilet Paper Launcher. It takes two hits to destroy an enemy and your launcher is slow to reload, however. Also, the monsters regenerate after a bit.

Once you get the first 5 collectibles, 14 more spawn in the tunnels. Get those and the final collectible number 20 spawns. Be sure to use the green arrows to help you find the collectibles as quickly as possible so you don't waste time going down tunnels where there is nothing for you to gather.

TIP

Don't worry about the enemies. Only attack them if they're directly in your way as you follow the compass to the nearest collectible. Constantly using your attack roll is actually faster than simply running. Do that and enemies won't be a problem anyway. It might make you a little dizzy, but it's definitely the best approach.

Barbossa's Blockade

There be pirates here, and you'd be wanting to gather as many collectibles as possible and stop your enemies before the time be runnin' out.

Gold: Earn 35 points

Silver: Earn 20 points

Bronze: Earn 5 points

This combat Adventure gives you 6 minutes and 20 seconds to defeat as many enemies as possible and collect the collectibles they leave behind. Follow the red arrows to get to the next enemies. When playing as a pirate, such as Barbossa or one of the others (in Multiplayer, you can be someone other than Barbossa), use your Flintlock to fire at a distance, then move in if your enemies are not defeated by the gun to finish them off with the sword.

There are several items that you can pick up and use, such as Blasters and Cherry Bombs. Or wait for an enemy to get near one of the Explosive Blocks and then shoot the block to defeat the enemy with a blast.

While most enemies only give up a yellow collectible worth 1 point, more powerful enemies give up a red collectible that scores you 4 quick points. Use any special attacks your character may have. Also use Power Discs to increase your damage or help you avoid taking damage. The key to getting gold is to use your ranged weapons to damage enemies as you approach, then get in a series of attacks. Remember to block when you are under attack, then counterattack before the enemies can block.

TIP

Never stop moving and attacking. This is one of the more difficult gold medals to achieve because it takes a while before enough enemies really start spawning with each wave. Once you earn bronze, two enemies spawn from each gate, and once you earn silver, shield-wielding enemies worth 2 points each begin to spawn. The best approach is to find a bomb-type tool, as they deal the most damage and can hit multiple enemies at once. If you still have trouble, here's a little cheat: the number of enemies scales up with the number of players, so add a second player as you start, and just play with one! You'll notice that it's much easier to defeat enough enemies to really get the points rolling in.

Davy Jones Collects Souls

Ye'll fear death with this challenge. Defeat yer enemies whilst collectin' their souls so you can send them to the Locker before time runs out.

Gold: Defeat 35 enemies
Silver: Defeat 20 enemies
Bronze: Defeat 5 enemies

This is another combat Adventure. This time you have 4 minutes to defeat as many enemies as possible. The only weapons you have are what you bring with you into the Adventure. Don't expect to find anything.

The Turtle pirates like to throw bombs at you. Plus there are some up on the pirate ship, so keep moving or you risk getting hurt by the bombs they rain down on you.

Each enemy is a bit different, so it is important to know how best to beat them. The skinny Driftwood pirates can be defeated with a single shot of the Blunderbuss. The Clam pirates are a bit tougher and like to block your attacks. Let them come at you, block their attacks, and then counterattack. Turtle pirates are best engaged up close so they can't throw bombs at you. However, their shell lets them take extra damage. If you want a chance at gold, be sure to use some Power Discs to give you an advantage.

TIP

As with Barbossa's Blockade, never stand still, and fire your Blunderbuss at enemies at every chance you get. With each wave of 5 enemies, there are 2 pirate-bomb-throwing units, 1 tough unit with a Flintlock, and 2 weak/standard units. When possible, focus on the pirate bomb throwers, as they prove to cause the most trouble. The weak units will go down with a single shot from the Blunderbuss, while the other two unit types take one shot and one fully charged strike. If you can get a rhythm down to combo that attack pair together, you should be able to pull this one off. Also, note that the hammerhead shark pirate Maccus is on the upper level of the pirate ship. He's worth 4 points, but if you go after him, be sure to have an attack strategy.

Lightning's Collector Course

It's ka-chow countdown! How many collectibles can you gather while racing around the stunt arena before times runs out?

Gold: Earn 120 points

Silver: Earn 70 points

Bronze: Earn 20 points

This car Adventure requires you to score points by running into as many collectibles as you can within 3 minutes. Yellow collectibles are worth 1 point, orange collectibles are 2 points, and red collectibles are 3 points. The red and orange are a bit tougher to collect. Right at the start, jump off the ramp and collect a row of red and orange collectibles.

In order to score points, you essentially have to perform stunts. Look for loops that are full of orange collectibles. You can score 30 points within a couple seconds. Make sure you have enough speed to get all the way around.

In order to get gold, you have to go after the red collectibles as well. Build up energy so you can use turbo, and then use ramps and tunnels to get up high enough to get those higher-point collectibles. Plus don't forget to rev up at the start.

TIP

Keep your boost meter up at all times by performing tricks at every opportunity. Many of the collectibles and a few of the areas can only be accessed by boosting off ramps and jumps. There are three key areas that can quickly and dramatically increase your score. The first is the string of collectibles right off the entry jump. Timing your jump correctly here can nab you 18 points in the first few seconds. The second area is the loop-de-loop, which is lined with orange collectibles (and, therefore, LOTS of points). The third area is on the perimeter of the level directly across from the starting line—it is a large ramp up a wall. If you boost and jump off that ramp, you can actually land on another area above that has plenty of collectibles of every color. Other than that, just explore for lines of collectibles in quick succession.

Mater's Tow'n'Go

Time's a tickin'! Can Tow Mater live up to his name and tow the tourist cars to their destination before times runs out?

Gold: 18 tourist cars

Silver: 10 tourist cars

Bronze: 3 tourist cars

There are several tourist cars stranded outside of Radiator Springs and Mater needs to tow them to the correct locations within 4 minutes. The green light beacons show you where the cars are located. Once you approach a car, press the tow button to pull it behind you. Then pull it to the beacon with the same color of light.

To save time, you can even throw the tourist cars towards their destination so you can start heading to the next car while the first is on its way. Just drive straight towards the beacon and then press the throw button. However, if you miss, you have to retrieve the car and tow it back again.

The key to getting gold on this adventure is to think ahead. Know where the locations for the three colors of cars are located. Then, as soon as you pick up a car, drive towards that location. As you are driving, look for other cars and go after those that are closest to their location or to you first. This saves time. Get good at throwing cars and you can save even more time so you can get 18 cars within the time limit.

TIP

Success on this Adventure comes down to speed and precision. The level is small and easy to memorize, so it just takes practice. A goal of 18 tourist cars delivered is a lofty goal, but it's definitely possible. Practice, practice, practice (and use your tow-to-throw ability to save a few precious seconds when you can).

Francesco's Rush

Set on a course filled with challenges and shortcuts, even Francesco will appreciate this race.

Gold: Finish in under 3:00

Silver: Finish in under 4:00

Bronze: Finish in under 6:00

Get ready to race for this Adventure. There are three different shortcuts that can help you get the gold medal. The first is when you are driving down a canyon—take a left around a stone pillar so you can then make a right turn into a cave. There are a couple of tight turns in the cave, but this can get you ahead of your opponents.

The second shortcut can't be accessed if you took the first since the first shortcut puts you past the entrance to the second. After you get through the canyon and have to make a left turn, look for a ramp on the left side. It takes you on a paved course for a short bit and cuts off a bit of time.

The third shortcut is shortly after the exits to the other two shortcuts. When the road turns to the right, and you can see the castle directly ahead, drive straight ahead, through the barriers, and jump across a gap. Then avoid swinging pendulums as you drive into the castle and out into the lead. For the quickest time, it is best to take the first and third shortcuts—if you can handle the sharp turns in the cave. Even then, you need to race clean and avoid crashes in order to earn that elusive gold medal.

TIP

Besides skill, shortcuts are the key to success on Francesco's Adventure. They are littered throughout, but in addition to the three mentioned above, there is another near the start that can give you an advantage early on. Just around the first right turn is a left turn. Instead of turning left, drive straight forward and jump up a short ledge and through the left-pointing arrow signs to enter a secret shortcut.

Holley's C.H.R.O.M.E. Course

Have what it takes to be a C.H.R.O.M.E. Agent? Eliminate the enemy targets in this combat challenge to find out.

Gold: 30 enemies defeated

Silver: 22 enemies defeated

Bronze: 10 enemies defeated

This is a combat course more than a race. While driving around an arena, you must defeat as many enemies as possible within 5 minutes. Pick up weapons from the surprise boxes to help you earn medals. The weapons only have a few shots, so you have to constantly drive over the surprise boxes to get more weapons.

The enemies spawn in the four corners of the arena. The green arrow will show you where they are in relation to your vehicle. Use weapons to eliminate them or keep up your speed and crash right into them to destroy most of the enemies.

Since you will be making lots of passes against the enemies who come in groups of three, use the 180-degree turn to quickly turn around and head back towards the enemy. Later in the adventure, the enemies that appear are tougher to defeat and just running into them once may not do the trick. Also, if you don't like the weapon you have, quickly fire it off and pick up another.

TIP

Never stop moving, and always look for the nearest surprise box when you don't have a load-out at the ready. An effective strategy with the missile load-out is to crash into an enemy at the same time that you fire the missile—it's a powerful one-two punch. Finally, don't waste bomb launcher load-outs by dropping them as mines. Search for faraway clusters of enemies and fire off your bombs—the blast radius is great for taking out several enemies at once. However, they might fly farther than you'd expect, so gauge your distance wisely!

Lone Ranger's Justice Run

Pursue the Cavendish Gang through the canyons, deserts, and ghost towns of the Old West and defeat them before they escape. Enemies on horseback are worth more points than enemies on foot.

Gold: Earn 100 points

Silver: Earn 65 points

Bronze: Earn 20 points

You have 4 minutes to ride along a course and defeat as many outlaws as possible. You get 2 points per outlaw and 10 points for an outlaw on a horse. The course makes a circuit with the same outlaws appearing during each time around.

Keep your horse riding as fast as possible as you move towards the next group of outlaws. Hit as many as you can by riding towards them until the reticle appears on them, then fire. Plus, you can also defeat an outlaw by running into them while your horse is running fast.

The key to getting gold is to go after the mounted outlaws. They spawn near the town, so it is important to try to get around the circuit as quickly as possible to go after those outlaws on horseback.

TIP

Always be firing the Blaster, and go after any mounted enemy that you see, because they're worth 10 points instead of the usual 2. Go fast, and practice accuracy. With each lap that you make around the canyons, a new batch of enemies spawns, and that means a new batch of valuable mounted enemies is in fresh supply each time.

Tonto's Flight

Race through the desert with the Crow Wing Pack, gathering collectibles before time runs out.

Gold: Earn 35 points

Silver: Earn 20 points

Bronze: Earn 5 points

This is another collection Adventure. However, this time you have Tonto and his ability to turn into a Crow. There are colored collectibles spread throughout the area. Yellow collectibles are worth 1 point, orange collectibles are worth 2 points, and red collectibles are worth 3 points. Collect as many as you can within 5 minutes.

Unlike Gliders, you can press the flap button to flap your wings and rise up into the air as you fly. There are several high-value collectibles near where you begin, so grab them quickly.

Not all of the collectibles are out in the open—check out the cave as well. If you want to earn gold, you need to play wisely. Gather all the collectibles in your immediate area before moving on to the next area. Flying to the next collectible you can see can waste time since it may be farther away than one closer to you that you cannot readily see.

TIP

Focus on the more valuables orange and red collectibles first. Travel in layers of altitude rather than simply following the compass all the time (which points you to the nearest collectible, even if it could take longer to reach it because terrain is in the way). Each wave of collectibles comes to about 27 or 28 points, so if you're having trouble finding more and your score is around that, you're close to a fresh wave of reds and oranges! Use the crow liberally (obvious, but necessary).

Hall of Heroes

The Hall of Heroes is a part of the game where you can see how your characters have progressed and keep track of all the Power Discs you have collected. At the Disney Infinity Hub, step on the purple button to travel to the Hall of Heroes. You can also access it from the Start menu when you first enter the game.

When you first begin playing *Disney Infinity*, the Hall of Heroes is very empty and consists of only a central area surrounded by pedestals. However, as you progress through the game, you not only fill in the open slots, you also build up the hall itself.

As you collect and use Power Discs, they will appear on the ground as tiles in the Hall of Heroes. The first wave consists of 20 Power Discs. However, another 35 Discs will be released in waves 2 and 3 combined for a total of 55 Power Discs. You can learn about the Power Discs you do not yet have by pressing the button indicated on the screen.

The Hall of Heroes grows as you earn stars in the Play Sets and the Toy Box—the architecture improves and you receive additional decorations. Here is a list of what you get at various levels of stars.

- **1 Star**—Stage 1 adds some details to the flooring
- **4 Stars**—Stage 2 adds some initial walls
- **9 Stars**—Stage 3 gives you some interior planters
- **16 Stars**—Stage 4 provides columns on the outside of the Hall
- **25 Stars**—Stage 5 adds plants to the lower area inside the Hall
- **37 Stars**—Stage 6 gives you inside columns and a ring around the top
- **52 Stars**—Stage 7 puts a dome over the top of the Hall
- **70 Stars**—Stage 8 adds plants outside of the Hall
- **92 Stars**—Stage 9 provides statues on the upper ring
- **118 Stars**—Stage 10 puts some plants on the dome
- **148 Stars**—Stage 11 hangs banners on the lower levels
- **183 Stars**—Stage 12 gives you an outside garden as well as a central tree and a pond
- **223 Stars**—Stage 13 adds an outside garden with Townspeople statues
- **268 Stars**—Stage 14 provides an upper ring as well as some outside plants
- **318 Stars**—The final stage hangs banners on the upper level

Once a character reaches level 1, a bronze statue of that character appears on its pedestal. Get that character to level 5 to change the statue to silver. Continue leveling up your characters to level 10 to get a gold statue. It is fun to return to the Hall of Heroes periodically to see how it is growing and what you have added through your endeavors.

The Hall of Heroes also gets buttons for interactive events as you acquire character statues. When you have 3 statues, you get a fireworks button that sets off fireworks when you step on it. At 10 character statues, a music button appears. Get 18 statues and a button appears that allows you to change the sky. Finally, if you collect all 29 characters and get them all to at least level 1 for a bronze statue, a special item will appear in the central fountain's pillar of light, and it will unlock the Ultimate Pack that can be used by all non-car characters.

Feats

While you are in a Toy Box, you can earn Feats. These are small awards that you get for a variety of actions, ranging from building things, to driving, or even defeating enemies. There are 76 Feats in all. While some are easy to earn, others will take a while. Each time you complete a Feat, you also earn some Sparks. The more difficult the Feat, the more Sparks you collect as a reward.

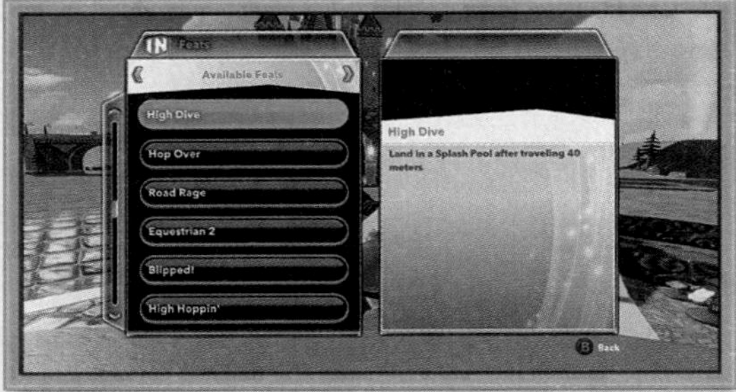

Feat	Requirement
Air Croquet	Fly through an Arch Block
Air Time	Stay up in the air for 3 seconds with one ground vehicle in one try
Backwards	Get 5 seconds of air time in reverse with one ground vehicle in one try
Barriers Not Included	Use your ground vehicle to jump over 100 objects in total
Barriers Not Included 2	Use your ground vehicle to jump over 1,000 objects in total
Bash 'n' Smash	Destroy 500 bashables
Blast Off!	Ride a ground vehicle off of a launch ramp
Blipped!	Destroy 25 Blip Blocks in one session
Bringin' Up Baddies	Use an Enemy Creator
Broken In	Travel a total distance of 100 kilometers on a mount
Clown Car	Ride in a shrunk vehicle while oversized
Crash Course	Drift into 2 bashables in one attempt
Crazy Driver	Do 2 tricks in one try in a ground vehicle
Creator Extraordinaire	Place 500 blocks in total
Destruction Zone	Destroy 5 bashables in under 5 seconds
Dodge Ball	Use a giant ball found in your editor to hit two townspeople in under 2 seconds
Double Dribble	Bounce a giant ball found in your editor off 2 enemies within 5 seconds
Drivin' You Crazy	Do 100 tricks in ground vehicles
Equestrian	Jump over 10 meters with a mount in one attempt
Equestrian 2	Jump over 50 meters with a mount in one attempt
Floatin' Along	Float for over 30 seconds
Frequent Flyin'	Travel a total distance of 25 kilometers in air vehicles
Game Maker	Place 10 Creativi-Toys in one session
Game Maker Extraordinaire	Set up 100 Creativi-Toy connections
Giddy Up!	Destroy 100 enemies while mounted in one session
Go Long!	Throw 100 townspeople
Goal!	Knock a giant ball found in your editor into a soccer goal
Green Thumb	Place 5 plants

Feat	Requirement
Havin' a Bash	Destroy 100 bashables in one session
High Dive	Land in a Splash Pool after travelling 40 meters
High Hoppin'	Jump 12 times in a single Wall Jump attempt
High Score	Score a soccer goal with an air vehicle
Hop and Spin	Jump from one Spinner to another
Hop Over	Jump directly over 10 blocks with a ground vehicle in one attempt
Hot Pursuit	Race around at top speed in your ground vehicle for 5 kilometers total
Hover Happy	Travel between 12 Fans without touching any other toys
It's Alive!	Cause 10 Creativi-Toys to react simultaneously
Just for Kicks	Punt a townsperson
Just for Kicks 2	Punt 50 townspeople
Landscapin'	Place 5 Terrain Blocks
Look Out Below!	Destroy 100 enemies with an air vehicle in one session
Look Ma, No Road!	Spend over 10 minutes in the air in a ground vehicle
Lookin' Good	Place 5 decorations
Master Builder	Place over 100 blocks in one session
Monster Mount	Ride an oversized mount while shrunk
New World	Customize 5 Terrain Blocks while in Spark Mode or with the Magic Wand
Next Floor Please	Ride an Elevator
Nifty Drifter	Drift for over 5 kilometers in total
Nifty Drifter 2	Drift for over 50 kilometers in total
Pest Control	Destroy 100 enemies
Please Stand to the Right	Stay on a Conveyor Belt for over 5 seconds
Prize Collector	Have 5 Gold Statues in your Hall of Heroes
R.O.F.	Do a trick through the Ring of Fire
Rapid Rider	Keep going as fast as you can on your mount for 30 seconds
Rapid Rider 2	Keep going as fast as you can on your mount for 60 seconds
Road Rage	Destroy 100 enemies with a ground vehicle in one session
Saddle Sore	Jump over 100 objects with your mount during the course of play

Feat	Requirement
Sharp Shooter	Shoot 1,000 objects
Sky Driving	Jump over 400 meters in one attempt in your ground vehicle
Slide Swipe	Drift into a townsperson
Speedy Steed	Ride your mount at top speed for 5 kilometers total
Spinning Shot	Shoot an enemy while on a Spinner
Straight Shooter	Shoot 5 enemies in under 5 seconds
Straight Shootin'	Shoot 10 objects in one session
Straight Shootin' 2	Shoot 500 objects in one session
Sunday Driver	Travel a total distance of 100 kilometers in a ground vehicle
Supersonic	Use 2 Super Cannons without hitting the ground
Track Changin'	Customize a track piece
Trickin'	Do a trick in reverse
Tricky	Do a trick while going boost speed in your ground vehicle
Turbo Booster	Use 25 boost pads in one session
Turbo Charged	Boost in a ground vehicle 100 times
Wrecking Crew	Destroy 25 enemies in one session
Wrecking Machine	Destroy 2 enemies in 10 seconds
Wrecking Machine 2	Destroy 3 enemies in 10 seconds
Wrecking Machine 3	Destroy 5 enemies in 10 seconds

Unlocking Toys for the Toy Box

The Toy Box is the place where you can let your creativity run wild. At the beginning of the game, you start off with only a few toys. However, you can collect many more toys as you play through the game.

Unlocking Toys in the Play Sets

One of the best ways to unlock toys for the Toy Box is to play through the Play Sets. Each Play Set has a number of types of toys themed to that Play Set that you can then take into the Toy Box once you unlock them. There are several ways to unlock toys. First, as you are playing in a Play Set, look for green capsules—these contain toys for the Toy Box. (The red capsules have toys that remain in the Play Set.) Green capsules are rarer than red capsules, so stay on the lookout for them while in the Play Sets.

Another way to unlock toys is through the Character Chests. These also appear in the Play Set. However, unlike the green capsules, the Character Chests require a specific character to unlock them. A picture of the specific character appears on the chest. Switch to that character to unlock the chest and unlock toys as well.

While exploring a Play Set, be sure to look for large Vaults. These look like large Character Chests, however you need all of the characters from the Play Set in order to open one of these Vaults. For example, in the Pirates of the Caribbean Play Set, you not only need Captain Jack Sparrow, but also Barbossa and Davy Jones. Opening these Vaults unlocks an entire Toy Box world as well as several different toys for all Toy Boxes. As you can see, it is important to have all the characters if you want to get all of the toys.

TIP

If you are missing a character from a Play Set, but your friend has it, you can always borrow your friend's character and use it as a guest to unlock Character Chests and the large Vaults. Just be sure to return the favor.

The Disney Infinity Vault

All of the toys unlocked in the Play Sets are themed or related to the specific Play Sets. However, there are also a great number of other toys that can be unlocked from within the Toy Box itself. These can be unlocked at the Disney Infinity Vault, which can be accessed through the Pause menu while in a Toy Box or at the Disney Infinity Hub by stepping on the yellow button. The Vault is like a game of chance. It offers 16 different toys or toy packs. You then spend Spins for a chance to randomly unlock one of the 16. If you don't get what you want, you can spend another Spin to get one of the remaining 15 toys. You can also shuffle the Vault to randomly get a new set of 16 toys to spin for. Some of the toys have a yellow background. That indicates that you not only get the toy shown, but also some bonus toys as well. For packs, select the toy in the Vault to see what the pack contains. Most packs consist of two or more townspeople, or groups of plants or decorations.

Spins are the currency you use in the Vault to unlock the toys. There are several ways to get Spins.

- Collect them in the Toy Box Launch where they are inside green capsules. Look for these capsules hidden in clusters of crates and barrels.
- Complete the Mastery Adventures. You get a Spin once you complete each of these for the first time.
- Earn medals in the Adventures and Character Adventures. You get a Spin for earning each medal for the first time. Therefore, you can get three Spins for each Adventure—one each for bronze, silver, and gold.
- Level up your characters. Each time you collect enough Sparks to level up a character, you get another Spin. You can level them up in the Toy Box or in the Play Sets. The Spins can only be used in the Toy Box though.

TIP

If you want to ensure you get the toys you want, make sure you have at least 16 Spins before you use the Disney Infinity Vault. Then keep shuffling the Vault until there are several Toys that you want on the same screen of 16. At that point start spending Spins. At the worst, it will cost you 16 Spins—but you are guaranteed to get that toy.

The Toy Box Worlds

Captain Jack Sparrow was kind enough to take us on a tour of the Toy Box Worlds along with Dumbo the Flying Elephant (which is one of the rare Power Discs in the first wave).

Toy Box and Toy Box Worlds can be confusing. Toy Box is the mode of play in *Disney Infinity* where you can create your own worlds. These worlds are called Toy Boxes or collectively as Toy Box Worlds. Some of them, such as the Toy Box Launch, are available right from the start. Others must be unlocked. This section covers each of these Toy Box Worlds and how to unlock them, if necessary. You can create and use all the toys you have collected or unlocked in each of these Toy Box Worlds.

NOTE

For those playing *Disney Infinity* on the Wii, the Toy Box mode and Toy Box Worlds are a bit different. Access your free eGuide (voucher code on the insert) to access this content.

Basic Toy Box Worlds

These Toy Box Worlds are all created using the Fairytale Kingdom theme and are fairly open, so you can start building right away without too much effort.

Empty Toy Box

This is one of the Toy Box Worlds available right at the start of the game. It is just a square of flat ground. You can use it for a small world or just use it as a starting block for an entire world of your own. The possibilities are endless.

Basic Toy Box

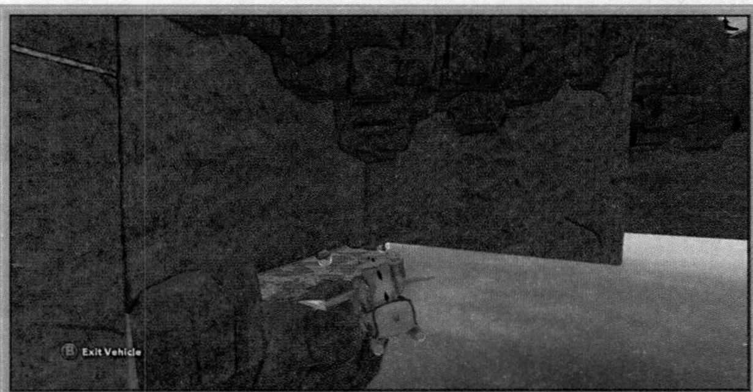

To unlock this Toy Box World, you must find a special green capsule in the Toy Box Launch world. It is located down on a small ledge between the castle and the race track. If you do not have an air vehicle, you can drop down to this ledge. Then, since you can't climb back up, go to the Pause menu and select "Reset Gameplay" to return your character to a safe location.

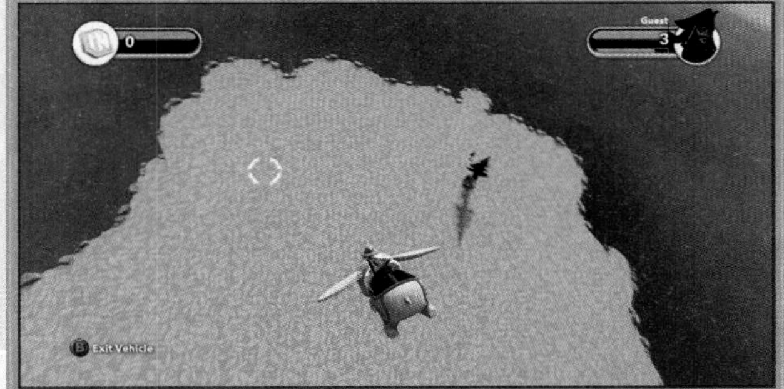

This world is flat and already has edges along with a few plants. This is a good place to start your first world of your own when you only have a limited number of toys with which to begin building. However, as you get more and more toys, you will probably want to use the Empty Toy Box instead, since it is easier to expand.

Rolling Hills

Take an air vehicle, or use Spark mode, to get to the small floating island on the side of the mainland near the River Gazebo where the Disney Infinity Hub is located. Once you get the green capsule, you unlock the Rolling Hills world.

Larger than most of the other basic Toy Box Worlds, Rolling Hills has no finished edges and has slopes that raise the land towards the center. Play around in this world to get a feel for how to create hills and other raised terrain so that it looks natural. This is a fun place to build a race track or some caves for others to explore.

World of Walkways

The green capsule that unlocks this world is on a small floating island high above the Toy Box Launch world on the opposite side of the mainland from the Rolling Hills green capsule. Again, use an air vehicle or Spark mode to get there.

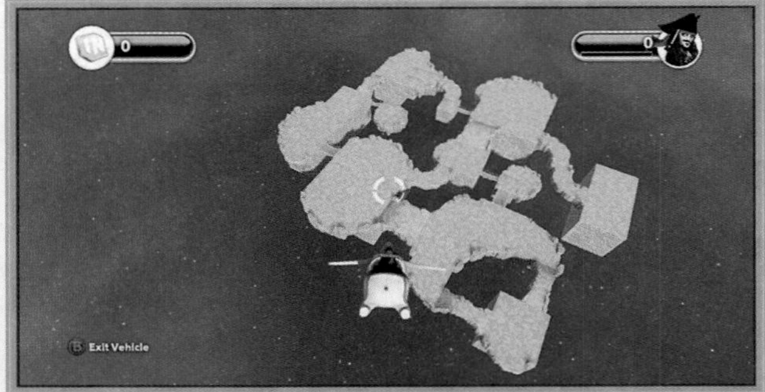

This world contains floating islands connected by walking paths and bridges. Use this world for paintball matches or horse races. It also has some larger islands on which you can easily expand. Again, this is a good place to explore to see how the designers connect larger land masses together.

The Play Set Toy Box Worlds

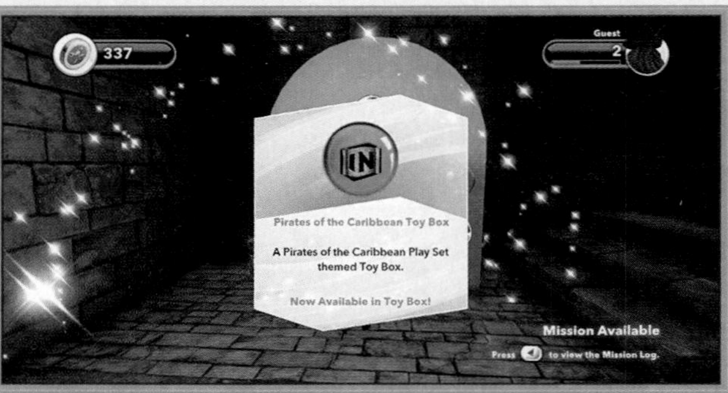

Each Play Set has a Toy Box World that you can unlock. Look for a large Vault in each Play Set. In order to open these Vaults, you need all of the characters for that Play Set. Use each character to open one of the locks. Then when the Vault is opened, you not only are rewarded with lots of toys, but also an entire Toy Box World themed after that Play Set.

In addition to providing pre-built Toy Boxes, these worlds are already themed. Take some time to study how the designers built them by taking a character with a Magic Wand and selecting different features. By studying and exploring these worlds, you can learn a lot about how to make a Toy Box World look really cool so you can impress your friends.

Metroville Toy Box

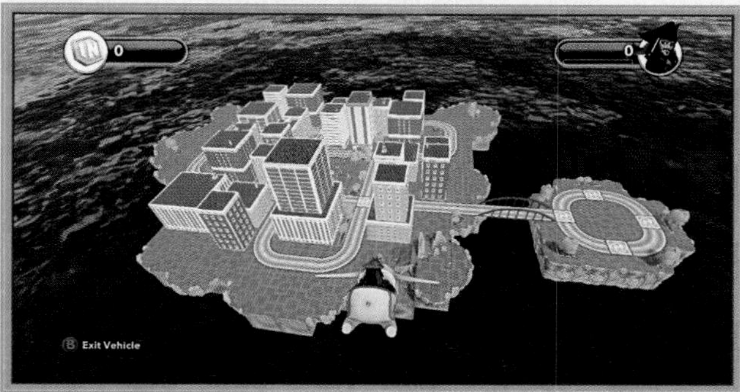

This Toy Box World is themed after The Incredibles Play Set. It features a city with tall buildings and a small island connected to the mainland by a road bridge. Explore it to learn how to build cities or just use the pre-built city for your own world.

Monsters University Toy Box

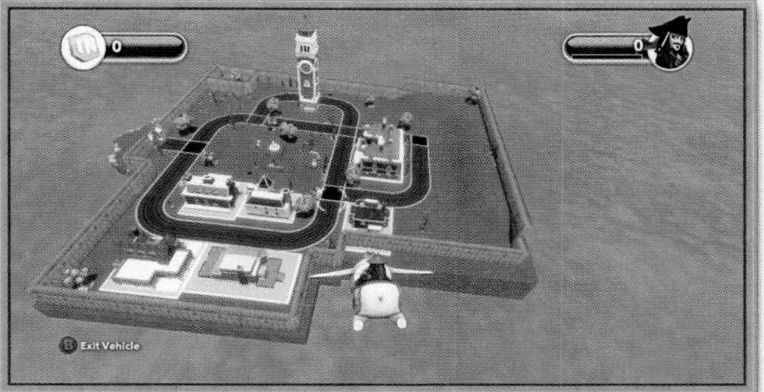

Themed after Monsters University, this world has a hedge around its border, a few buildings, and even a clock tower. There is still some open ground on which to build even more.

Pirates of the Caribbean Toy Box

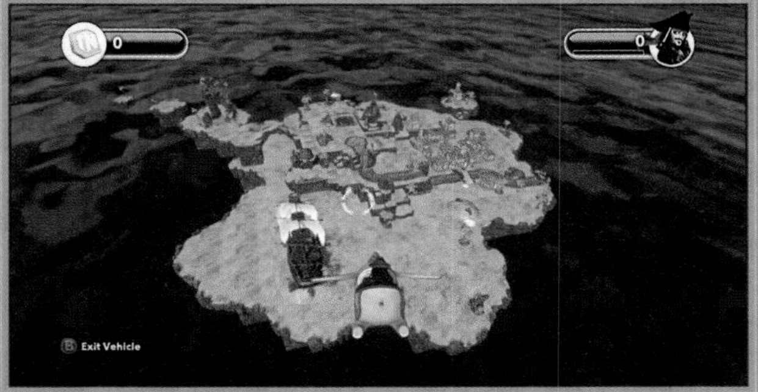

Ahoy there matey! This tropical island comes complete with a shipwreck, a small town, and even some small islands to which you can build bridges or pathways. Observe how to build waterfalls and streams so they appear natural and try building a treasure grotto under the ground, along with a cave that leads down to the gold and jewels. Maybe even put some pirate enemies to guard the treasure.

Radiator Springs Toy Box

Get ready race fans. This Cars-themed world comes complete with an awesome race track that covers most of the world. This is a good place to see how to build a great race track of your own and then theme it with landmarks and other features to make it aesthetically pleasing—or are they just obstacles you need to avoid hitting while at high speed? Once you unlock this world, be sure to invite your friends over for a race.

Colby Toy Box

Themed after the Lone Ranger Play Set, Colby has a southwestern desert feel with tall mesas, canyons, tepee villages, and much more. This world has a lot of possibilities for making shooting games where players ride horses and can use the canyons for cover or to try to lose a pursuer. Or modernize it by building a race track across the tops of the mesas with some half loops that lead down to the desert floor below.

Creating in the Toy Box

While you can do Adventures and play around in the Toy Box, the main feature of *Disney Infinity* is the ability to create within a Toy Box World a land of your very own that is only limited by your imagination—and the toys you have unlocked. After going to a Toy Box World, your main tool is the Magic Wand. Open up the Tools/Packs menu and select the Magic Wand. It will be your best friend in the Toy Box.

Changing the Theme

You can change the look of a Toy Box World with just a few steps and not even have to build anything new. The default theme for most of the Pre-Built Toy Box Worlds, with the exception of the Play Set Toy Boxes, is Fairytale Kingdom. This theme affects the ground. To change it, select the ground of any part of the world and then press the button corresponding to the art palette icon. A menu pops up along the bottom and allows you to select from all of the themes you have unlocked. Then you can either change just the theme of the block you have selected, or change the theme for the entire world. One of the ways to get new themes is to unlock them within the Play Sets so you can theme your world like those Play Sets.

You can also change the theme of some of the decorations. Select a tree or group of terrain with your Magic Wand and, if it is themed terrain, you will have the option of editing the theme. Another menu pops up and now you can change the theme of just that one piece of terrain, or all themed terrain in the entire world. Once again, this is a powerful feature and allows you to change the look of a world very easily.

The area surrounding the land of your Toy Box World is called the Skydome. It is the backdrop or background to your world. It too can be customized to fit your theme. To do this, go into the editor and, within the Basic Toys category, select the Sky Changer. Place it anywhere in the world. When you hit the large button on the side of the Sky Changer, the Skydome changes to a different theme. It can change the sky to night or make the Skydome look like it something from one of the Play Sets. Keep hitting the button on the Sky Changer to cycle through your choices. Skydomes are not only visual effects, but also have audio. The background sounds and music change with some Skydomes, thus adding even more to the experience.

Another way to change themes is through the use of Power Discs. There are two different types of Power Discs that affect theme. The Texture Set changes the ground and themed terrain to the new theme, while the Skydome changes the sky to the new theme. For example, if you want to change the theme of your world to *Alice in Wonderland*, you would need two Power Discs—one for the Texture Set and one for the Skydome. Then if you want to change it back to your original theme, just use the steps above to change the land, the terrain, and the Skydome.

TIP

In Series 1 of the Power Discs, there are four different themes you can collect. In addition to *Alice in Wonderland*, there are also themes for Sugar Rush from *Wreck-It Ralph*, the Lantern Sky and textures from *Tangled*, and an underwater theme from *Finding Nemo*. Look for even more themes in Series 2 and Series 3 of Power Discs.

Categories of Toys

Before you start building, it is important to understand that there are several different categories of toys within the Toy Box. When you first open the editor, you are presented with the "Pick a Toy..." screen. Here you can cycle through every toy that you have unlocked. However, when building in a world, it is easier to use the build view. Switch to this view by pressing the button shown on the screen. As you unlock more and more toys, the "Pick a Toy..." screen can be overwhelming. The build view, on the other hand, organizes the toys into 18 different categories. Let's take a look at each category and what you can expect from them.

Terrain

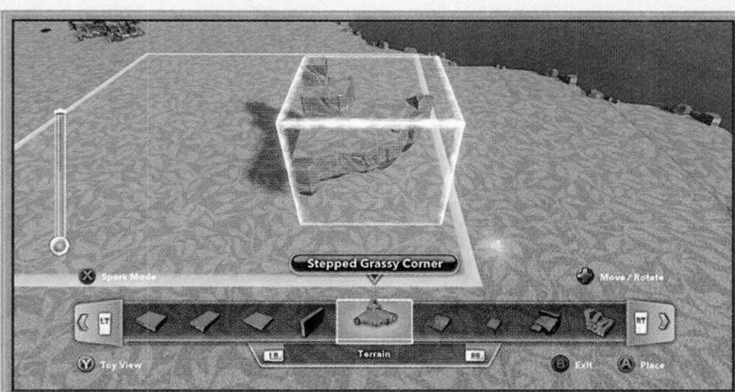

Terrain is the ground for your Toy Box Worlds. You can use it to expand the size of your worlds or to create features on your worlds. Build slopes and hills or even underground caves. When building a world, you usually want to start out with the terrain first, since it is on this terrain that you will build all your structures. Experiment with different levels of terrain to create some interesting features. For example, create a cave system or canyon through which you can have a horse race.

Building Sets

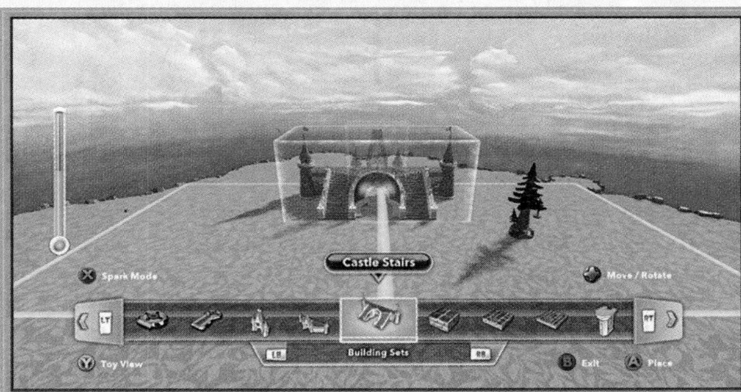

Building sets are unlocked through the Disney Infinity Vault and within the Play Sets. These toys consist of several different parts that can be put together to create one type of building. For example, you can unlock parts to build a Disney-style castle or the Agrabah Palace. There are several different parts for each, so you can really create a custom castle or palace with lots of different features. Use these toys to build stadiums or cities. If you are going to be using Building Sets toys, it is a good idea to start with them, since they can make some very large structures.

TIP

When creating your own Toy Box World, it is a good idea to start big and end small. Put out all your big terrain or buildings first, then add small details such as plants, decorations, and even townspeople or critters. If you don't, the small toys will get in the way of your larger toys.

Buildings

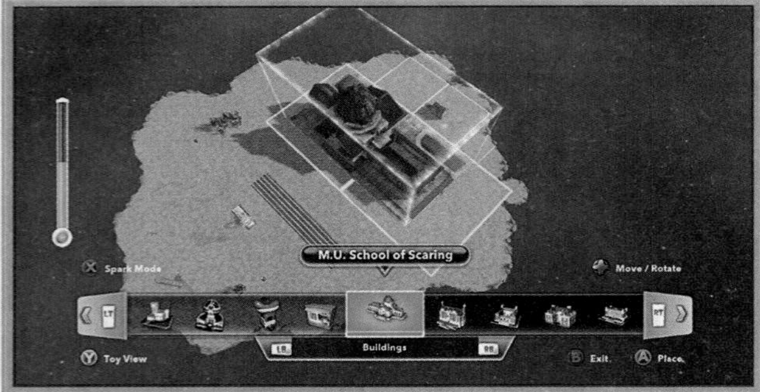

Buildings are complete structures. You pick one, place it, and you are done. You don't have to assemble a bunch of pieces like the Building Sets. Some are unlocked in the Play Sets—and have the theme of that Play Set—while others are unlocked through the Disney Infinity Vault. They range in size from the very small Hotdog Stand to the large buildings from the Monsters University Play Set.

Set Pieces

Set Pieces, for the most part, are very large toys. Many are from the sets of Disney movies, shows, or theme parks, or they have some type of interactive features. These are fun to use and can add a major talking point to your worlds when you invite your friends. Be sure to show them your very own Pride Rock, Matterhorn, or Dungeon—all right next to each other. Only in *Disney Infinity*.

Basic Toys

The Basic Toys contain a variety of different toys such as the Disney Infinity Hub, the Sky Changer, the Enemy Creator, and several other items. Many are interactive in some way and don't necessarily fit into one of the other categories. Be sure to check out these toys, since most can be fun to use in your world no matter what the theme.

Action Toys

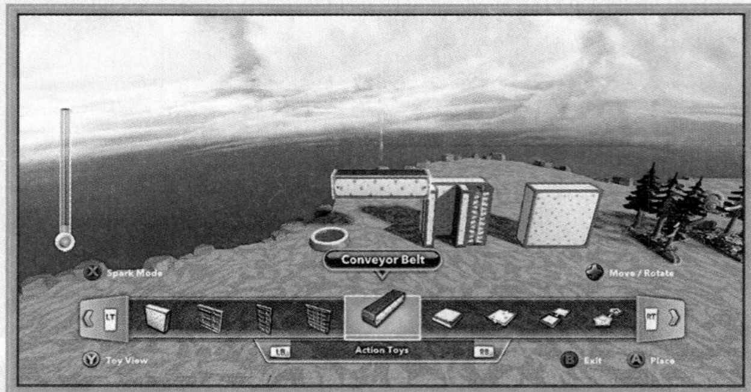

If you think the Basic Toys can be fun, wait until you try out the Action Toys. These all move or do some action—hence the name. Use Action Toys to create your own games or adventures and challenge your friends to visit your worlds and try them out. Set up a series of Action Toys and then try them out. Action Toys work great for platforming-type games. Combine them with Creativi-Toys for even more options and fun.

Creativi-Toys

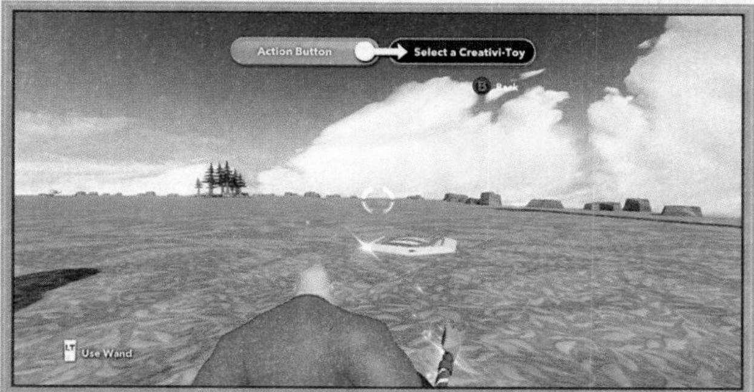

Creativi-Toys are the thinking or logic toys of the Toy Box. They can be programmed with functions to be triggers or reactions. You can even link several of these toys in series or parallel so that one action or trigger can result in several different reactions. We have included a section devoted entirely to Creativi-Toys later in this chapter. Be sure to check it out. And the best way to learn about these toys is to put them in your Toy Box Worlds and play with them. Creativi-Toys can be unlocked in the Disney Infinity Vault and by completing Creativi-Toys Mastery Adventures part 1 and 2. Creativi-Toys can interact with some toys in other categories as well.

Blocks

Blocks are just that—blocks. They come in very many different shapes and sizes. Use them to build things just like you might with a box of wooden blocks in real life. You can even change the theme of the blocks from their default stone look to a variety of themes that you can unlock. In addition to the standard blocks, there are also blip blocks that are destroyed when you hit them. Physics blocks behave following the laws of physics and some of them, such as the glass and wood ones, can be destroyed. There are even explosive blocks—which blow up when you hit them—and lava blocks.

Track Pieces

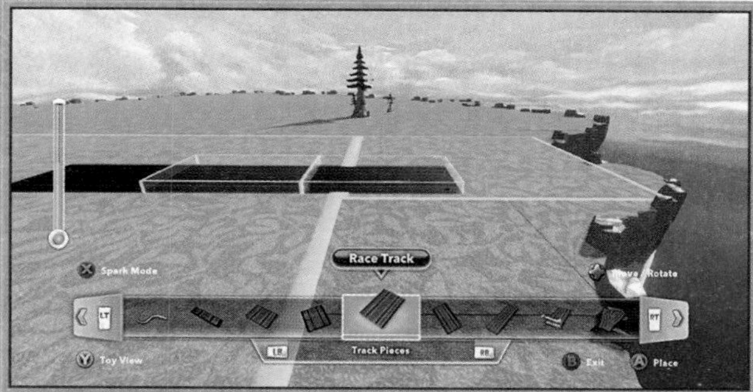

Track Pieces include road track as well as grinding rails and even barriers that you can set up around your tracks. The key to assembling a track is to ensure that each piece connects to the adjacent pieces, otherwise you have trouble racing or grinding on them. Once you have used the pieces to create a track, try changing the theme. While the slot car track is the default, there are several themes that can be unlocked in the Play Sets or the Disney Infinity Vault. You can even make your track look like a running track by using the ESPN Sports theme. Track pieces also include ramps and other toys for doing stunts.

Sports Toys

These toys are great for creating games you can play with other players. Several of the goals can be linked to Creativi-Toys to keep score or do other functions. The balls and puck all react according to the laws of physics. It is a good idea to include some barriers when building with Sports Toys. It is no fun when your soccer ball rolls off the edge of the world.

Plants

Your world can always benefit from some green and the Plants category has you covered. Pick from trees, flowers, shrubs, and even some non-organic toys such as light poles to give your world some color and flora. Some of the toys in the Plant category are themed. This can be helpful when you want to change the theme of your entire world. Select one of your plants and edit the theme for all plants and, with one action, every themed Plant toy will change to the new theme. Some plants, such as those unlocked in the Play Sets, cannot change themes.

Decorations

While you have some large toys with which to play, Decorations are much smaller. However, they can be just as important. Decorations fill in empty spaces and provide continuity for your world. Some decorations can be destroyed, while others are static and just stay there.

Vehicles and Mounts

Your characters need a way to get around the Toy Box Worlds you create. That is where Vehicles and Mounts come in. A Mount is an animal you can ride—usually a horse, mule, or even an elephant. Vehicles come in two types—ground or air. Ground vehicles can drive along the ground and stay on the ground—un-

less you drive off a cliff or do some stunts. Air vehicles, on the other hand, can fly through the air. You can use both vehicles and mounts for races as well as transportation. Some vehicles also include weapons, such as the Attack Copter or The Incredicar. You can use these for games where you have to destroy a number of targets or even for getting hits on opponents' vehicles.

Enemies

What would a Disney movie be without villains or enemies? Add some spice and conflict to your world by including Enemies. While you start out with only a few, you can unlock lots more in the Play Sets as well as at the Disney Infinity Vault. You can keep a theme for your Enemies, or mix and match them for a battle royale. In a Toy Box World, Enemies will attack any players (unless you use a Creativi-Toy to assign teams). They do this automatically and will actually seek out players as they wander around the world. Of course it is always fun to let loose a few Enemies when visiting a friend's world as well.

Cast Members

Cast Members are unlocked in the Play Sets. They are the characters in the Play Sets that give you missions to complete. Cast Members will walk around a Play Set on their own. They do not interact with you, do not attack you, and can't be harmed or defeated. They are there to add personalities to your world. Don't be shy about mixing up these toys. It is always fun to see monsters roaming the streets of an Old West town. Remember, this is your world.

Toy Box Townspeople

These little townspeople like to dress up in costumes from various Disney movies or related features. They will scoot around the world not causing any harm. They are great for populating a town in your world to give it some more personality and life. While they don't attack, you can pick them up and even throw them. Try picking them up and drop kicking them by jumping and then pressing the alternate attack button. You can make a game where you have to punt Townspeople through a goal post. (Only in your Toy Box World. Please do not attempt this in the real world.) These toys can be unlocked from the Disney Infinity Vault.

Play Set Townspeople

These Townspeople are just like the Toy Box Townspeople. The only difference is that they are unlocked through the Play Sets rather than spending Spins in the Disney Infinity Vault.

Critters

Critters are just like Townspeople—except they are not people. They are animals. While you may want to put Townspeople near your buildings and towns in your worlds, place Critters out in the forests. You can pick up Critters just like the Townspeople. However, Critters are skittish and tougher to catch. You need to move slow if you want to catch them. Rush at them and they tend to run away.

Getting Started

So you want to try your hand at building in the Toy Box? Here is a sample of the process you might go through with just the basics. You can take this and add a lot more to it, however the basic procedures are the same. Start off with a Pre-Built Toy Box World. For this we chose a blank one. Make sure you have your Wand handy, since it is the tool for building and modifying your Toy Box World. This tiny world is going to be centered around the Matterhorn. Select this toy from the Set Pieces category and place it on the terrain. You can also add some plants to the corners of the land now or later.

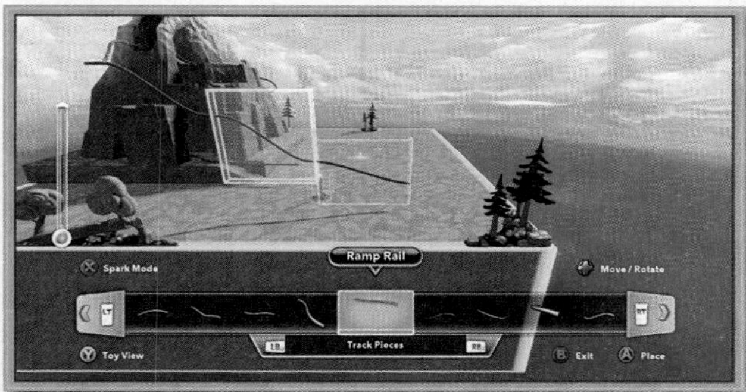

If you noticed, the Matterhorn has some grinding rails built into it. These are the tracks for the bobsleds. However, in this world, the characters can take a ride by grinding the rails going through the Matterhorn. Switch to the Track Pieces category and select rails. Be careful that they connect to the existing rails by changing the view so you can check from all angles. Add some bending rails to go down and some curved rails to make turns.

The rails are a bit high for characters to jump onto. Therefore, switch to the Blocks category and put in a couple Long Wedge Blocks to serve as ramps for your characters to get up to the rails.

Now that you have completed the rails and ramps, try it out. Walk your character up one of the ramps and jump onto the rail to begin a ride through the scenic Alpine Matterhorn. This was just a simple example of how easy it is to create in the Toy Box Worlds. You can then add more terrain and create a complete theme park of your own. Just remember, the best way to learn about building is to build. Hands-on experience is a great teacher.

Using Creativi-Toys in the Toy Box

Most of the toys are straightforward in their use. You place them in the Toy Box World and there they are. Creativi-Toys, on the other hand, require a bit more effort, since you have to program them in order to make full use of them. The key to understanding these toys is learning their two main functions. First, they can act as a trigger. Remember those "If (or when) and then" logic equations you might have learned in math? The trigger is the "when". For example, when a player steps on this pad. Or it could be something like "when the elevator reaches the top of its path". These triggers set the conditions for another action or behavior. That is the second function of a Creativi-Toy—to cause a behavior effect. This is the "then" part of the equation. It could be something like "then the door opens" or "the pad spawns a blaster". A quick setup uses a Trigger and a Falling Object Generator. Select the Trigger by pressing the connect button and choose a trigger action such as "stepped on". Then select the Falling Object Generator with the connect button and select a behavior such as "ESPN Soccer Ball". Now if your character walks onto the Trigger, a soccer ball will drop from the Falling Object Generator.

Some Creativi-Toys can only be a trigger or an effect and some can be both. Let's take a look at all of the different Creativi-Toys available in the Toy Box.

Trigger

The Trigger is a pressure pad and one of the simplest Creativi-Toys. In order for it to have an effect, it must be connected to another toy. There are four different ways you can set the Trigger.

Trigger Action	Description
Stepped On	When the Trigger is stepped on by a player or AI
Stepped Off	When a player or AI steps off of the Trigger
Player Stepped On	When the Trigger is stepped on only by a human player
Player Stepped Off	When only a human player steps off the Trigger

Trigger Area

The Trigger Area acts like a trigger. However, instead of stepping on a pad, it triggers when something walks through an area that is invisible in the Toy Box World (but visible in the editor mode). There are several different ways you can set the Trigger Area, including for specific players. This works great when creating games to play against other players.

Trigger Action	Description
Entered	When a player or AI enters the Trigger Area
Exited	When a player or AI leaves the Trigger Area
Player Entered	When any player enters the Trigger Area
Player Exited	When any player leaves the Trigger Area
Player 1 Entered	When only player 1 enters the Trigger Area
Player 2 Entered	When only player 2 enters the Trigger Area
Player 3 Entered	When only player 3 enters the Trigger Area
Player 4 Entered	When only player 4 enters the Trigger Area
Player 1 Exited	When only player 1 leaves the Trigger Area
Player 2 Exited	When only player 2 leaves the Trigger Area
Player 3 Exited	When only player 3 leaves the Trigger Area
Player 4 Exited	When only player 4 leaves the Trigger Area

Action Button

The Action Button can be a trigger as well as a behavior. You could have another trigger cause the Action Button to be pressed as the behavior, so something else could trigger the Action Button to be pressed.

Trigger Action	Description	Behavior	Description
Pressed	When the Action Button is pressed	Press Button	The Action Button's button to be pressed.

Target

This trigger device only activates when you shoot at it or throw a tool at it. Running into it or hitting it with a melee attack will not activate it. Use this for shooting games.

Trigger Action	Description
Hit	When the Target is hit by any weapon or tool

Power Switch

The Power Switch is a toggle. By stepping on the red side you turn it on. Step on the yellow side to turn it off. You can assign different triggers to both the on and off triggers. In addition, you can have it as a behavior in response to another trigger.

Trigger Action	Description	Behavior	Description
On	When the Power Switch gets stepped on and the Power Switch gets turned on (red part of switch is down), the output is supposed to happen	On	The power switch to turn on (red = down)
Off	When the Power Switch gets stepped on and the Power Switch gets turned off (red part of switch is up), the output is supposed to happen	Off	The power switch to turn off (red = up)
Output	When the Power Switch receives an "Input" behavior and the Power Switch is in the on position	Input	The Power Switch to send an "Output" action if it is in the on position

Dual Action Trigger

The Dual Action Trigger requires two inputs in order to activate the trigger function. To use it, you would first select two different triggering actions and connect them to the Dual Action Trigger as input 1 and input 2. Then select the Dual Action Trigger and select for what it will act as the trigger. An example of this could be you have to walk through a Trigger Area and hit a Target, then the Dual Action Trigger will cause a light to turn on.

Trigger Action	Description	Behavior	Description
Complete	When the Dual Action Trigger completes both inputs	Input 1	The Dual Action Trigger's input 1 to turn on
		Input 2	The Dual Action Trigger's input 2 to turn on
		Reset	The Dual Action Trigger to reset (both inputs return to off)

Racing Gate

This is similar to a Trigger Area. However, the Racing Gate works better for tracks and is also visible so players can see a visual end or finish line to a race.

Trigger Action	Description
Crossed by Player	When a player runs/drives/flies through the Racing Gate

Collection Pen

This toy acts as a trigger. However, you can distinguish different triggers depending on what you put into the pen. For example, you could cause one counter to advance if an enemy is placed into the Collection Pen and another counter to advance when a friend is put into the pen. This can be a lot of fun for creating your own games.

Trigger Action	Description
Enemy Entered	When an enemy enters the Collection Pen
Friend Entered	When an NPC/Critter enters the Collection Pen
Ball Entered	When a ESPN/Action Toy Ball enters the Collection Pen

Checkpoint

The Checkpoint is a bit different than a Trigger. It keeps track of the fact that it has been triggered and can only be used once. Use Checkpoints for races or other games where you want a player to go to different spots and so they only get one point for each Checkpoint. Once a Checkpoint is activated, it cannot send out another trigger.

Trigger Action	Description	Behavior	Description
Checkpoint Set	When the Checkpoint is set (stepping on the checkpoint can set the Checkpoint)	Set Check-point	The Checkpoint to be set

Object Generator

The Object Generator usually is the behavior as a result of another trigger. You can select from a variety of objects you want to appear on this toy. However, you can also use this as a trigger for when this toy spawns an object or for when an object that is spawned is destroyed. These can be fun for lots of different types of games. (Note: You must have already unlocked an object in order to have it generated by this toy.)

Trigger Action	Description	Behavior	Description
Spawned	When the Object Generator spawns an object	Buzz Lightyear's Jetpack	The Object Generator to spawn a Buzz Lightyear's Jetpack
Killed Spawned Toy	When the spawned object is killed	Star Command Boost Pack	The Object Generator to spawn a Star Command Boost Pack.
		Pirate Bombs	The Object Generator to spawn Pirate Bombs
		Frying Pan	The Object Generator to spawn a Frying Pan
		Mania Blaster	The Object Generator to spawn a Mania Blaster
		Toilet Paper Launcher	The Object Generator to spawn a Toilet Paper Launcher
		Paintball Gun	The Object Generator to spawn a Paintball Gun
		Zero Point Energy Gauntlet	The Object Generator to spawn a Zero Point Energy Gauntlet
		Goo Grower	The Object Generator to spawn a Goo Grower
		Goo Shrinker	The Object Generator to spawn a Goo Shrinker
		Hover Board	The Object Generator to spawn a Hover Board
		Glide Pack	The Object Generator to spawn a Glide Pack

Trigger Action	Description	Behavior	Description
		Surfboard	The Object Generator to spawn a Surfboard
		Flamingo Mallet	The Object Generator to spawn a Flamingo Mallet
		Blunderbuss	The Object Generator to spawn a Blunderbuss
		Grappling Hook	The Object Generator to spawn a Grappling Hook
		Star Command Blaster	The Object Generator to spawn a Star Command Blaster
		Elasti-Hand	The Object Generator to spawn an Elasti-Hand
		Invisibility Device	The Object Generator to spawn an Invisibility Device
		Medicine Ball	The Object Generator to spawn a Medicine Ball
		Glow Urchin	The Object Generator to spawn a Glow Urchin
		Sword	The Object Generator to spawn a Sword
		Crow Wing Pack	The Object Generator to spawn a Crow Wing Pack
		TNT Pack	The Object Generator to spawn a TNT Pack
		Thundering Hooves Pack	The Object Generator to spawn a Thundering Hooves Pack
		Silent Warrior Pack	The Object Generator to spawn a Silent Warrior Pack
		Kill All	All objects spawned by the Object Generator to be removed

Falling Object Generator

This toy drops balls or a puck down into your world. You can also set its behavior to destroy all of the objects it spawns as a behavior to a trigger. It can also act as a trigger if one of the objects it drops is killed.

Trigger Action	Description	Behavior	Description
Spawned	When the Falling Object Generator spawns an object	ESPN Bowling Ball	When the Falling Object Generator spawns a Bowling Ball
Killed Spawned Toy	When the spawned object is killed	ESPN Soccer Ball	When the Falling Object Generator spawns a Soccer Ball
		ESPN Basketball	When the Falling Object Generator spawns a Basketball
		ESPN Baseball	When the Falling Object Generator spawns a Baseball
		ESPN Football	When the Falling Object Generator spawns a Football
		ESPN Tennis Ball	When the Falling Object Generator spawns a Tennis Ball
		ESPN Golf Ball	When the Falling Object Generator spawns a Golf Ball
		ESPN Hockey Puck	When the Falling Object Generator spawns a Hockey Puck
		Kill All	All the objects spawned from the Falling Object Generator to be removed

Friend Generator

This is similar to the Object Generator except that it spawns friendly toys.

Trigger Action	Description	Behavior	Description
Spawned	When the Friend Generator spawns a Friend	Spawn Bullseye	The Friend Generator to spawn Bullseye
Killed Spawned Toy	When the spawned Friend is killed	Spawn Snow White	The Friend Generator to spawn Snow White
		Spawn Hulk	The Friend Generator to spawn Hulk
		Kill All	All the Friends spawned from the Friend Generator to be removed

Enemy Generator

This functions just like the Friend Generator, but this spawns Enemies. It also offers lots of options for the types of Enemies you can spawn. Use this toy for combat games.

Trigger Action	Description	Behavior	Description
Spawned	When the Enemy Generator spawns an Enemy	Soldier of Clubs Costume	The Enemy Generator to spawn a Soldier of Clubs Costume
Killed Spawned Toy	When the spawned Enemy is killed	Soldier of Hearts Costume	The Enemy Generator to spawn a Soldier of Hearts Costume
		Sorcerer's Broom Costume	The Enemy Generator to spawn a Sorcerer's Broom Costume
		The King's Guard	The Enemy Generator to spawn a The King's Guard
		Agrabah Guard	The Enemy Generator to spawn an Agrabah Guard
		Rhino Guard	The Enemy Generator to spawn a Rhino Guard
		Omnidroid	The Enemy Generator to spawn an Omnidroid
		Melee Omnidroid	The Enemy Generator to spawn a Melee Omnidroid
		Ranged Omnidroid	The Enemy Generator to spawn a Ranged Omnidroid
		Tank Omnidroid	The Enemy Generator to spawn a Tank Omnidroid
		Mini Zurgbot	The Enemy Generator to spawn a Mini Zurgbot
		Zurgbot	The Enemy Generator to spawn a Zurgbot
		Giant Zurgbot	The Enemy Generator to spawn a Giant Zurgbot
		Mini Blasting Zurgbot	The Enemy Generator to spawn a Mini Blasting Zurgbot
		Blasting Zurgbot	The Enemy Generator to spawn a Blasting Zurgbot
		Giant Blasting Zurgbot	The Enemy Generator to spawn a Giant Blasting Zurgbot
		Goo Bot	The Enemy Generator to spawn a Goo Bot
		Cavendish's Pistol Man	The Enemy Generator to spawn a Cavendish's Pistol Man
		Cavendish's TNT Man	The Enemy Generator to spawn a Cavendish's TNT Man
		Cavendish's Shotgun Man	The Enemy Generator to spawn a Cavendish's Shotgun Man
		Clam Pirate	The Enemy Generator to spawn a Clam Pirate
		Driftwood Pirate	The Enemy Generator to spawn a Driftwood Pirate
		Maccus	The Enemy Generator to spawn a Maccus
		Turtle Pirate	The Enemy Generator to spawn a Turtle Pirate
		Fear Tech Paintball Player 1	The Enemy Generator to spawn a Fear Tech Paintball Player 1
		Fear Tech Paintball Player 2	The Enemy Generator to spawn a Fear Tech Paintball Player 2
		Fear Tech Paintball Player 3	The Enemy Generator to spawn a Fear Tech Paintball Player 3
		Fear Tech Student 1	The Enemy Generator to spawn a Fear Tech Student 1
		Fear Tech Student 2	The Enemy Generator to spawn a Fear Tech Student 2
		Fear Tech Student 3	The Enemy Generator to spawn a Fear Tech Student 3
		Fear Tech Student Patrol 1	The Enemy Generator to spawn a Fear Tech Student Patrol 1
		Fear Tech Student Patrol 2	The Enemy Generator to spawn a Fear Tech Student Patrol 2
		Fear Tech Student Patrol 3	The Enemy Generator to spawn a Fear Tech Student Patrol 3
		Kill All	All the Enemies spawned from the Enemy Generator to be removed

Vehicle Weapon Generator

Similar to the other generator toys, this spawns random vehicle weapons. Place these on your race tracks to add a battle element to races.

Trigger Action	Description	Behavior	Description
Item Collected	When a player collects the Vehicle Weapon	Spawn Item	The Vehicle Weapon Generator to spawn a vehicle weapon
Item Spawned	When a Vehicle Weapon spawns		

Party Cannon

The Party Cannon is usually used as a behavior for another toy's trigger. However, you can also use this toy to trigger behaviors in other toys. Set these up at the end of a race or as a victory celebration at the end of a game.

Trigger Action	Description	Behavior	Description
Explode	When the Party Cannon shoots something out	Fireworks	The Party Cannon to shoot Fireworks
		Confetti	The Party Cannon to shoot Confetti
		Grand Finale	The Party Cannon to shoot Grand Finale

Safety Dome

The Safety Dome is great to use as an objective to either try to destroy or to try to defend. It can be used as both a trigger and a behavior.

Trigger Action	Description	Behavior	Description
Started	When the Safety Dome starts (need another toy to Start the Safety Dome)	Start	The Safety Dome to start (an NPC spawns in the Dome)
Destroyed	When the Safety Dome is destroyed	End	The Safety Dome to end (the NPC in the Dome disappears)

Marching Orders

This is a cool toy. It sets up an area. Any NPC or enemy that moves (or is thrown into) the area of the Marching Orders toy will begin walking in the direction the toy is pointing—even after they exit the toy area. You can position several of these toys around a world and set up patrol paths. While Marching Orders is visible in the editor, it can not be seen out in the Toy Box World. This is a fun toy to play around with.

Trigger Action	Description
Entered	When the Marching Orders is entered by an NPC/ Enemy
Exited	When an NPC/Enemy leaves the Marching Orders

Teleporter

Teleporters require two or more of this type of toy in order to work. They are a quick way to transport players around the Toy Box World. You can program them to go from one to another if you have more than two. Otherwise, they just teleport the player between the two Teleporters.

Trigger Action	Description	Behavior	Description
Teleport (can only go to another teleporter)	When a player steps on the Teleporter	Teleport Here (can only activate from another teleporter)	The player to be teleported from the starting teleporter to this destination

Stopwatch

The Stopwatch is a toy that when activated will stop all enemies and NPCs. You can hit the button to start and stop it or set is as either a trigger or even a behavior.

Trigger Action	Description	Behavior	Description
Stopwatch Started	When the Stopwatch starts	Start Stopwatch	The Stopwatch to start
Stopwatch Stopped	When the Stopwatch stops	Stop Stopwatch	The Stopwatch to stop

Replayer

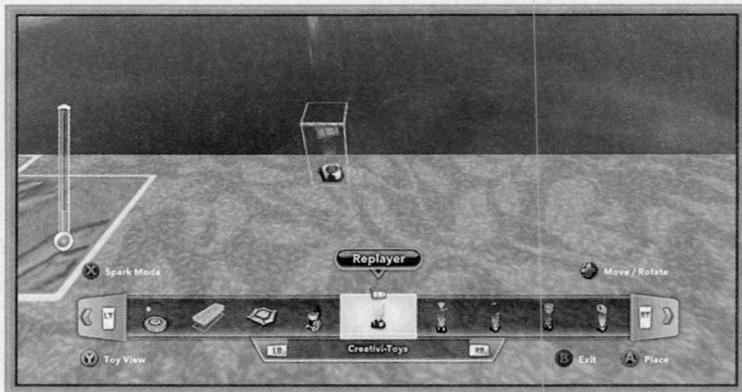

The Replayer is one of the more powerful tools you can use in the Toy Box. An easy way to use it is to connect it to several Triggers that you can then use as your buttons for recording, stopping, and playing back. When the Replayer is recording, it will save all the actions you do in the editor, such as building things. Stop the recording after you exit the editor and then play. You will then see your building efforts appear right before you. The Replayer can be used to actually create a game where the course appears before you as you move. Be sure to play around with it and you will be impressed with what you can do.

Trigger Action	Description	Behavior	Description
Recording Started	When the recording starts	Start Recording	The Replayer to start recording
Recording Stopped	When the recording stops	Stop Recording	The Replayer to stop recording
Clear	When the recording is cleared	Clear	The Replayer to clear everything it has recorded so far
Playback	When the recording is played back	Playback	The Replayer to play back everything that was placed into the world
Reverse Playback	When the recording is played back in reverse	Reverse Playback	The Replayer to play back everything that was placed into the world in reverse
Reset	When the recording is reset	Reset	The Replayer to remove all the objects it has played back into the world

Repeater

The Repeater is a toy you can use to make another toy do the same thing over and over. For example, connect it to a Falling Object Generator and it will continue to drop objects. You can even adjust the amount of time between each trigger that the Repeater sends out.

Trigger Action	Description	Behavior	Description
On	When the Repeater is turned on (the player can now repeat an action)	On	The Repeater to turn on
Off	When the Repeater is turned off (the player can no longer repeat an action)	Off	The Repeater to turn off
Repeat	Every time the Repeater repeats an action		

Time Delay

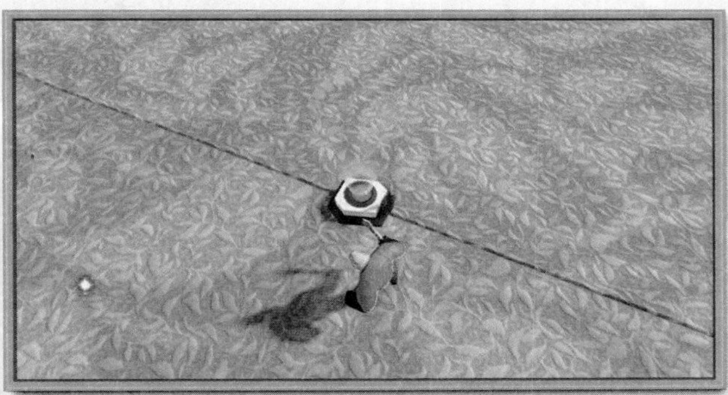

If you want to create a series of behaviors from one trigger, but do not want them all to occur at the same time, use the Time Delay. It lets you set a delay between the trigger and the behavior. Try this with a row of Party Cannons so they go off one at a time rather than all at once.

Trigger Action	Description	Behavior	Description
Delay Completed	When the amount of time the player set in the Properties to delay an action is completed	Start Delay	The Time Delay to start the delay

Timer

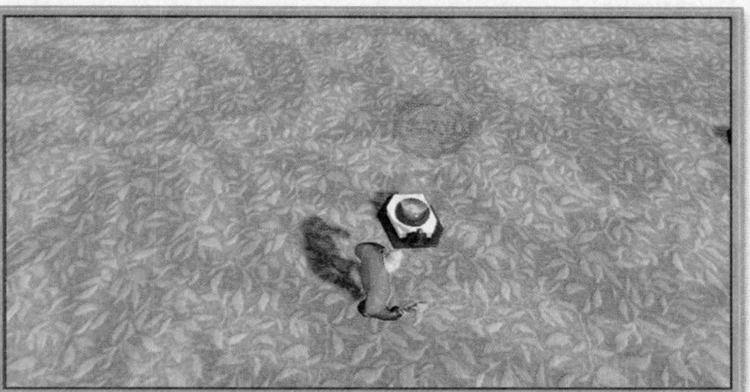

This toy actually creates a timer at the top of the screen when it is activated, so you can time players during a game. Connect it to one Racing Gate to start and another Racing Gate to stop. Or you can even set it to be a countdown timer.

Trigger Action	Description	Behavior	Description
Started	When the Timer starts timing something	Start	The Timer to start timing
Stopped	When the Timer stops timing something	Stop	The Timer to stop timing
Timer Expired	When the amount of time the player sets up in the Properties expires		

Counter

Like the Timer, this puts some numbers at the top of the screen. However, this time it counts signals from a trigger as its behavior. Connect this to a goal in the Sports toys to keep track of how many goals you score.

Trigger Action	Description	Behavior	Description
Target Reached	When the Counter reaches the limit the player sets up in the Properties	Reset	The Counter to reset (return to 0)
Zero Reached	When the Counter reaches zero	Increment	The Counter to increase by 1
		Decrement	The Counter to decrease by 1

Scoreboard

The Scoreboard is like a bit counter, except instead of counting just one action, it can keep track of scores for four different players.

Trigger Action	Description	Behavior	Description
Increment Score 1	When the scoreboard increases the score for Player 1	Increment Score 1	The Scoreboard to increase by 1
Increment Score 2	When the scoreboard increases the score for Player 2	Increment Score 2	The Scoreboard to increase by 2
Increment Score 3	When the scoreboard increases the score for Player 3	Increment Score 3	The Scoreboard to increase by 3
Increment Score 4	When the scoreboard increases the score for Player 4	Increment Score 4	The Scoreboard to increase by 4
Reset	The Scoreboard to reset the score	Reset	When the Scoreboard is reset to 0
Remove Display	The Scoreboard to remove the score at the top of the screen		
Player 1 Wins	When player 1 is declared the winner		
Player 2 Wins	When player 2 is declared the winner		
Player 3 Wins	When player 3 is declared the winner		
Player 4 Wins	When player 4 is declared the winner		

Bird's Eye Camera

When activated, the Bird's Eye Camera changes the view of the Toy Box to a top-down angle. This can be great for some types of games you can create to play against your friends.

Trigger Action	Description	Behavior	Description
Started	When the camera first becomes active	Start	The camera to become active
Ended	When the camera ends	End	The camera to stop

Side-Step Camera

This functions just like the Bird's Eye Camera, except the view is from this side. Use this when making platforming type games.

Trigger Action	Description	Behavior	Description
Started	When the camera first becomes active	Start	The camera to become active
Ended	When the camera ends	End	The camera to stop

Area Light

This toy allows you to light up an area. It can be programmed to turn on, off, or toggle in response to a trigger or even be a trigger itself.

Trigger Action	Description	Behavior	Description
Turn On	When the light turns on	Turn Light On	The light to turn on
Turn Off	When the light turns off	Turn Light Off	The light to turn off
Toggle	When the light turns on or off	Toggle Light	The light to toggle to the next state

Sound Effects

You can select from a variety of sounds that emanate from this toy as a behavior. For example, connect it to a goal for a sound effect when a player moves a ball into the goal. This just adds more fun to games.

Trigger Action	Description	Behavior	Description
Started	When the sound effects start playing	Alarm	The Sound Effects toy to play an alarm sound
		Horn	The Sound Effects toy to play a horn sound
		Cheering	The Sound Effects toy to play a crowd cheering sound
		Cash Register	The Sound Effects toy to play a cash register sound
		Charge!	The Sound Effects toy to play a trumpet playing the "Charge!" theme
		Countdown	The Sound Effects toy to play the narrator counting down from 3 to 1
		Destruction	The Sound Effects toy to play an explosion sound
		Success	The Sound Effects toy to play the narrator to say "What a performance"
		Awesome!	The Sound Effects toy to play the narrator to say "Awesome!"
		Fantastic!	The Sound Effects toy to play the narrator to say "Fantastic!"

Boom Box

This is similar to the Sound Effects toy. However, the Boom Box plays music instead of just sound effects.

Trigger Action	Description	Behavior	Description
Started	When the Boom Box is activated	Off	
Stopped	When the Boom Box becomes inactivate	Mickey Mouse	The Boom Box to play the Mickey Mouse song
		Cinderella's Castle	The Boom Box to play the Cinderella's Castle song
		Peter Pan's Flight	The Boom Box to play the Peter Pan's Flight song
		Alice in Wonderland	The Boom Box to play the Alice in Wonderland song
		Tangled	The Boom Box to play the Tangled song
		Sugar Rush	The Boom Box to play the Sugar Rush song
		Vanellope	The Boom Box to play Vanel-lope's song
		Jessie	The Boom Box to play Jes-sie's song
		Alien Emper-or Zurg	The Boom Box to play the Alien Emperor Zurg song
		Metroville	The Boom Box to play the Metroville song
		Finding Nemo	The Boom Box to play the Finding Nemo song
		WALL-E	The Boom Box to play the WALL-E song
		The Night-mare Before Christmas	The Boom Box to play The Nightmare Before Christmas song
		Frankenwee-nie	The Boom Box to play the Frankenweenie song
		Phineas and Ferb	The Boom Box to play the Phineas and Ferb song
		Recognizer	The Boom Box to play the Recognizer song
		Tron	The Boom Box to play the Tron song
		Condorman	The Boom Box to play the Condorman song

Invulnerability Beacon

Normally your characters in the Toy Box Worlds are invulnerable. However, this toy can turn on a health bar that shows how much damage a character is taking and allows them to be defeated. This can be good for combat games where a kill or defeat can be used for scoring or another reason.

Trigger Action	Description	Behavior	Description
Health Bar On	When the health bar is turned on, on the small screen	Health Bar on	The Health Bar on the screen to turn on
Health Bar Off	When the health bar is turned off, on the small screen	Health Bar off	The Health Bar on the screen to turn off

Kill Switch

The Kill Switch is a way to get rid of something in the game. It can be a trigger, but its main function is a behavior. For example, you could set it to when a player enters a Target Area over a lava block, the player dies.

Trigger Action	Description	Behavior	Description
Killed	When something is killed by the Kill Switch	Kill	The Kill Switch to kill the entity that triggered this behavior (i.e., step on a button that tells the Kill Switch to kill whatever just stepped on the button)

Blue and Orange Team Activators

These two toys are a lot of fun. They can set players and enemies into two teams. Set Marching Orders toys to move enemies into these team activators and create team fighting games. If you have also walked through the activator, you will have a color as well. Enemies on your team will not attack you. Instead they will attack players and other enemies on the opposing team. This is a lot of fun to try out.

Trigger Action	Description
Team Set	When an entity is set to the blue (or orange) team

Victory Tracker

While this toy can seem complex, it is just a trigger that is activated by players being killed, killing other players, killing enemies, or getting hit by something. You will usually connect this to a Scoreboard or Counter to keep track of the score.

Trigger Action	Description
Player 1 was Killed	When player 1 is killed
Player 2 was Killed	When player 2 is killed
Player 3 was Killed	When player 3 is killed
Player 4 was Killed	When player 4 is killed
Player 1 Killed Enemy	When player 1 kills an enemy
Player 2 Killed Enemy	When player 2 kills an enemy
Player 3 Killed Enemy	When player 3 kills an enemy
Player 4 Killed Enemy	When player 4 kills an enemy
Player 1 Killed Player	When player 1 kills another player
Player 2 Killed Player	When player 2 kills another player
Player 3 Killed Player	When player 3 kills another player
Player 4 Killed Player	When player 4 kills another player
Player 1 was Hit	When player 1 gets hit by something
Player 2 was Hit	When player 2 gets hit by something
Player 3 was Hit	When player 3 gets hit by something
Player 4 was Hit	When player 4 gets hit by something

Other Toys That Interact

In addition to the Creativi-Toys, there are also several other different toys that can be used as a trigger or a behavior. The following is a list of these toys and the trigger and/or behaviors for which they can be connected.

Toy	Trigger Action	Description	Behavior	Descritption
Automatic Door	Opened	When the Automatic Door opens	Open	The Automatic Door to open
	Closed	When the Automatic Door closes	Close	The Automatic Door to close
			Query	The Automatic Door to send an output based on the door's current state (opened if currently open and closed if currently closed)
Automatic Double Door	Opened	When the Automatic Double Door opens	Open	The Automatic Double Door to open
	Closed	When the Automatic Double Door closes	Close	The Automatic Double Door to close
			Query	The Automatic Double Door to send an output based on the door's current state (opened if currently open and closed if currently closed)
The Big Spinner	Off	When The Big Spinner turns off	Off	The Big Spinner to turn off
	On	When The Big Spinner turns on	On	The Big Spinner to turn on
	Speed Up	When The Big Spinner speeds up	Speed Up	The Big Spinner to start spinning faster
	Slow Down	When The Big Spinner slows down	Slow Down	The Big Spinner to start spinning slower
Boost Pad	Used	When the player drives over the Boost Pad	On	When something causes the Boost Pad to turn on
			Off	When something causes the Boost Pad to turn off
Cars	Entered	When the Car is entered	None	
	Exited	When the Car is exited		
	Boost	When boost is activated in the car		
	Trick Completed	When a trick is completed with a Car		
Elevator Platform	Off	When the Elevator Platform turns off	Off	The Elevator Platform to turn off
	On	When the Elevator Platform turns on	On	The Elevator Platform to turn on
	At Top	When the Elevator Platform reaches the top of the path	Move Up	The Elevator Platform to move up
	At Bottom	When the Elevator Platform reaches the bottom of the path	Move Down	The Elevator Platform to move down
Exploding Mine	Exploded	When the Exploding Mine explodes	Reset	The Exploding Mine to return to its initial state (mine is not exploded)
Fan	Stopped	When the Fan stops	Off	The Fan to turn off
	Started	When the Fan starts	On	The Fan to turn on
	Entered	When a player enters the Fan		
The Flipper	Started	When The Flipper gets started	On	The Flipper to turn on
	Stopped	When The Flipper gets stopped	Off	The Flipper to turn off
Floor Spikes	Spikes Engaged	When the Floor Spikes pop out of the pad	Activate Spikes	The Floor Spikes to pop out of the pad
	Spikes Retracted	When the Floor Spikes return to the pad		
	Killed Player	When the Floor Spikes kill a player		
Helicopters	Entered	When the Helicopter is entered	None	
	Exited	When the Helicopter is exited		
Hop Over Gate	Broken	When a player breaks the Hop Over Gate	Reset	The Hop Over Gate to return to its intial state (unbroken)
	Cleared	When a player jumps over the Hop Over Gate		
Invisinator	Invised	When the player turns invisible	Off	The Invisinator to turn off (standing on the Invisinator will not turn the player invisible)
	Expired	When the invisible turns visible	On	The Invisinator to turn on (standing on the Invisinator will turn the player invisible)

Toy	Trigger Action	Description	Behavior	Descritption
Masher	Triggered	When the Masher's stamping mechanism slams down	Action	The Masher's stamping mechanism to slam down
	Reset	When the Masher's stamping mechanism returns to the Masher		
	Killed Player	When the Masher's stamping mechanism kills a player		
Mounts	Mounted	When the player gets on the Mount	None	
	Dismounted	When the player gets off the Mount		
	Sprint	When the player uses sprint while on the Mount		
	Jump	When the player jumps while on the Mount		
Moving Wall	Off	When the Moving Wall gets turned off	Off	The Moving Wall to turn off
	On	When the Moving Wall gets turned on	On	The Moving Wall to turn on
Pendulum	Off	When the Pendulum stops swinging	Off	The Pendulum to stop swinging
	On	When the Pendulum starts swinging	On	The Pendulum to start swinging
Pop Up Turret	Activated	When the Pop Up Turret pops up and shoots	Off	The Pop Up Turret to turn off (the turret will not shoot at the player when standing near it)
	Deactivated	When the Pop Up Turret goes down and stops shooting	On	The Pop Up Turret to turn on (the turret will shoot at the player when standing near it)
Reset-o-Matic	Reset	When the toy is reset	Reset	The Reset-o-Matic to reset physics toys
	Start	When the toy starts its action	Start	The Reset-o-Matic to start
Ring of Fire	Go Through	When something goes through the ring	Stop Spinning	The Ring of Fire to stop spinning
			Start Spinning	The Ring of Fire to start spinning
The Spinner	Off	When The Spinner turns off	Off	The Spinner to turn off
	On	When The Spinner turns on	On	The Spinner to turn on
Splash Pool	Entered	When a player enters the Splash Pool	N/A	
Super Cannon	Tilted Complete	When the Super Cannon finishes a tilt	Turn Off	The Super Cannon to turn off
	Launched	When a player gets launched from the Super Cannon	Turn On	The Super Cannon to turn on
			Tilt	The Super Cannon's angle to tilt
Tall Automatic Door	Opened	When the Tall Automatic Door Opens	Open	The Tall Automatic Door to open
	Closed	When the Tall Automatic Door Closes	Close	The Tall Automatic Door to close
Tar Trap	Player Entered	When a player enters the Tar Trap	N/A	
	Player Exited	When a player leaves the Tar Trap		
	Object Entered	When on object enters the Tar Trap		
	Object Exited	When an object enters the Tar Trap		
Tripwire	Tripped	When a player trips on the Tripwire	On	The tripwire to turn on (be able to trip a player)
			Off	The tripwire to turn off (not be able to trip a player)

Tips for Designing Worlds and Games in the Toy Box

There are a lot of different things you can do in your Toy Box Worlds. This section is designed to give you some quick tips to help you create your own worlds from scratch as well as games you can play against your friends. These focus on the basics of design to help you get started with some of the more difficult aspects of creating in the Toy Box. However, once you have mastered these tips, feel free to continue adding to your world to make them even more cool and exciting.

> **TIP**
>
> **Be sure to keep track of the thermometer-like meter on the left side of the screen that appears when you are in the editor. It keeps track of how much you can add to your world. Once the meter is full, nothing else can be added to the Toy Box. Lots of things in your Toy Box can also affect multiplayer games. So if you want to invite other players over to your world, be sure to not push the meter all the way to the top, since it can slow down playing. In fact for worlds you are building for games, keep the meter in the green so there is less lag and fewer connection problems.**

Open World Builder

This part covers the steps for building in an open world and helps you avoid some pitfalls and mistakes made by new players.

1. The Terrain

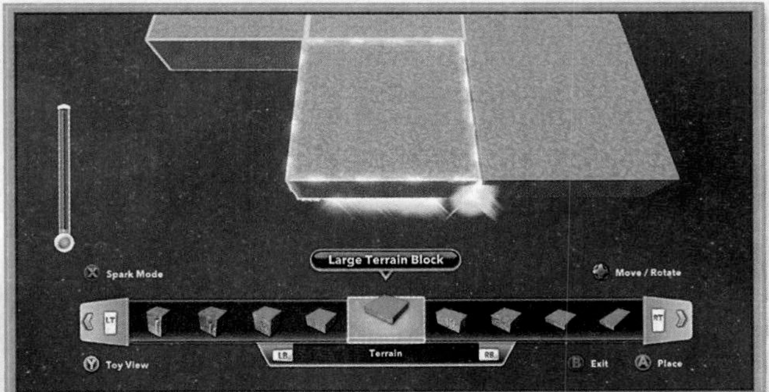

When you are starting from scratch in a world of your own, you must first be sure you have enough land on which to build and that there are no obstacles in your way. Depending on which prebuilt world you choose, you may need to add more large terrain blocks to make it large enough or clear out hills and plants that might be in your way.

2. Structures

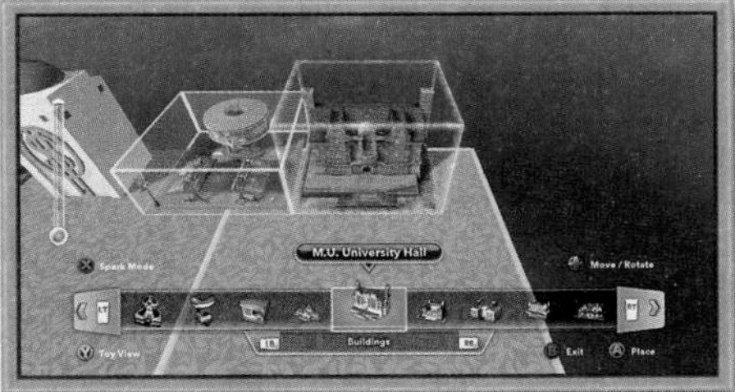

Next, start building your buildings. The Building Sets and Set Pieces are usually the largest toys, and you want to place them down on your world before adding anything else. Some of them are very large and you need to be sure you have space. Once you have the big structures in place, add other buildings.

3. Track Pieces

After you get your structures in place, put in any track pieces you want. Remember that with a Magic Wand in the hand of your character, you can change the theme of the track pieces. While they default as the slot track, you can change that to any of the themes you have already unlocked to make your track look like roads or trails. Roads are important for cities and towns since they add to the look and feel of these types of worlds.

4. Plants and Decorations

Now that you have the main part of the world completed, go in and fill it out with lots of plants and decorations. These may be small—or large in some cases—but they really add to a world. They are the details that help complete the look. In addition, you may also want to use some more terrain to finish off the land. Rather than leaving your world with square corners at the edge of the landmass, put in some edge pieces to soften the borders of your land and accent them with more plants and decorations. Adding some slopes or higher levels of terrain at the edges can give the illusion that the land goes on further but you can't see it because of the higher terrain.

5. Populate the World

The final step is to populate the world you have created. You can use enemies, townspeople, and cast members. Don't forget to throw in some vehicles or mounts for helping players get around the world quickly. This final step is another important part of a world. By adding people, you will feel like you are in a realistic world where people are going about their business instead of having players feel like they are all alone. Now that you have completed your world, play in it and have fun. Don't forget to invite some friends over to see the efforts of your labor.

Racing Game

Do you want to create the most awesome race track in the world? If so, you have come to the right place. Racing games are really quite easy to make. Just follow the step-by-step instructions included here.

1. Get the Race Track Start Toy

If you want to create a racing game, you have to have the Race Track Start track piece. It is the key to starting a race. It can be found in the Disney Infinity Vault. Save up at least 16 Spins before visiting the vault. Then shuffle the selections until you see the Race Track Start toy (and hopefully some other track pieces as well) as one of the 16. Start spending your Spins without shuffling again until you get it.

2. Lay Down Some Track

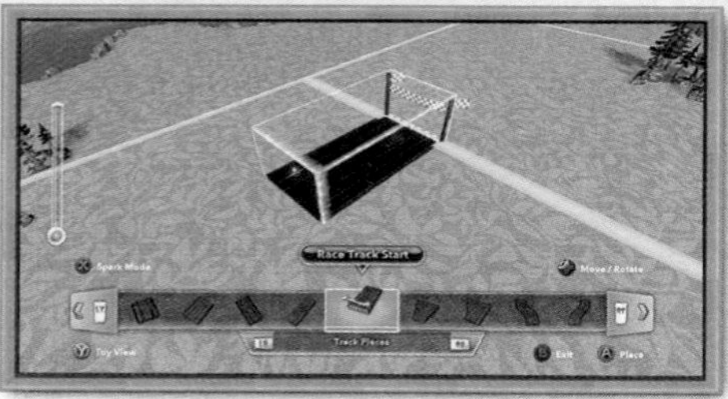

Place the Race Track Start toy down on your world. Then select other track pieces and begin connecting them. It is important that you line up the ends of the track pieces so they fit together exactly. Change the angle of your view around so you can see the track pieces from all sides to ensure they are connected. Add loops, curves, and ramps to make your track as easy or challenging as you want. You can even add some shortcuts.

3. Complete the Circuit

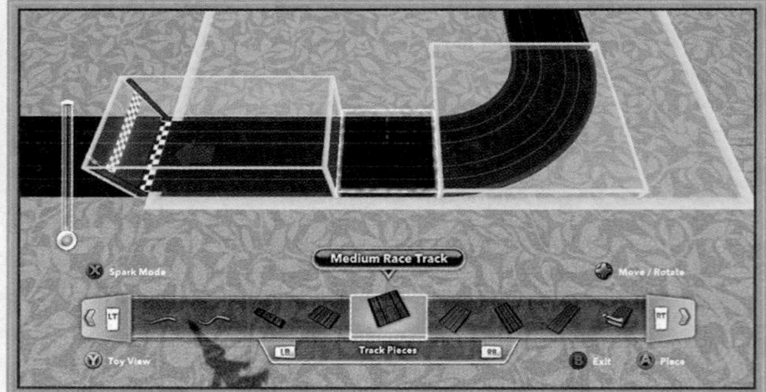

As your track continues to grow, make sure you end up at the opposite side of the Race Track Start. Again, be sure to line up the track carefully. Only when you have made a complete circuit of track connecting the two ends of the Race Track Start toy can you have race on your track. If you added shortcuts, make sure your main track is a complete circuit.

4. Add Barriers or Decorations

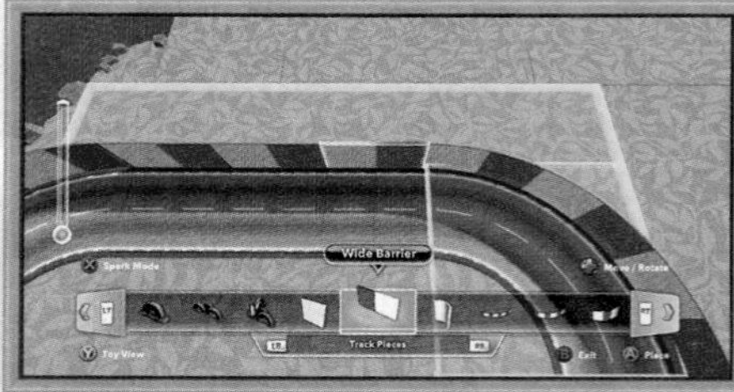

While the track is completed, add some barriers to the turns to prevent cars from driving off the road if you want and place some plants and decorations to make the race track more exciting and visually pleasing. If you want to turn this race into a battle race, be sure to include Vehicle Weapon Generators to the track to add some firepower. Try to place objects or decorations on the track that are destructible to hide or disguise your shortcuts.

5. Start Your Engines

When you are ready, drive a vehicle or ride a mount up onto the Race Track Start and a button will appear. Follow the on-screen instructions to start a race. Three opponents will automatically be provided and a three-lap race is ready to begin.

TIP

If, after completing your track, the race option does not appear when you drive onto the Race Track Start, go back and check your track connections. Often it is a couple pieces whose connection is just a little off that will prevent you from starting a race. It is a good idea to test out your track before adding barriers and decorations.

Action and Platformer Games

There are lots of action toys you can use to create some fun games. Be sure to use different cameras to provide different effects for the game.

1. Planning

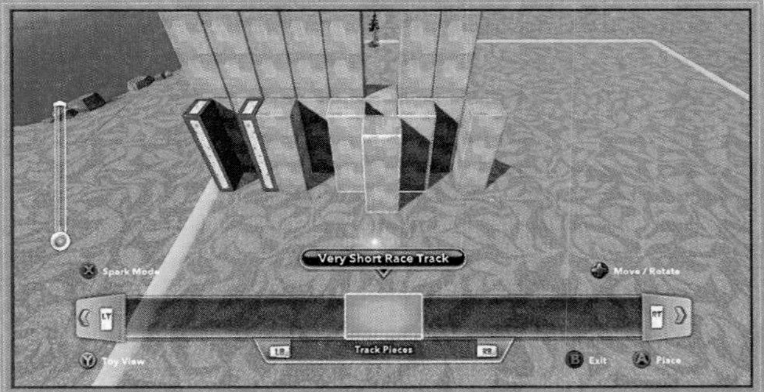

The first step in creating this type of game is planning out what you want to do. Figure out where you want to start, where you want to end, and what you want players to accomplish along the way.

2. Build the Course

Once you know what you want to do, start putting together the course. Use blocks or action toys to create the level and then add more action toys as obstacles or challenges that players must get past. As you are building it, use your character to try it out and make sure it is possible to jump across gaps or up to higher blocks.

3. Set up a Timer

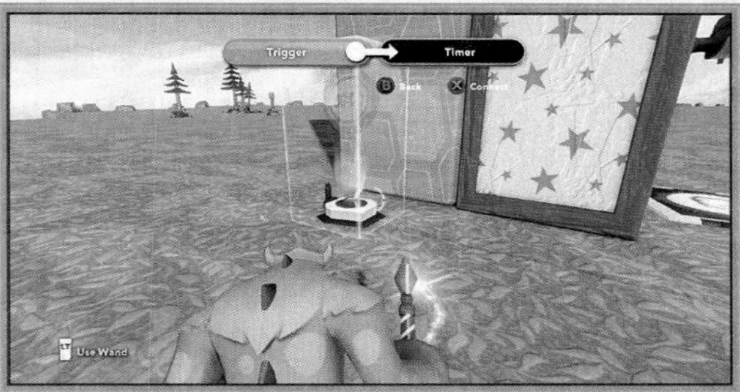

Place Triggers or Trigger Areas at the start and finish of the course. Connect them to a Timer so that the Timer starts when the player goes through the starting trigger and ends when he or she passes through the end trigger. You can also connect other toys such as Party Cannons to shoot out fireworks when the player gets to the end. Try setting Triggers along the way and connect them to Sound Effects to help cheer the player on in the middle of the game.

4. Cameras

Depending on the type of game, you may want to include a specific camera angle. For example, when making a platform game, put a Side-Step Camera to the side of the course and position it so it is facing the course. Program it to follow the player. Connect it to the start and end triggers so the camera starts up as the game starts. Or you may even want to have a starting trigger somewhere before the start so the player can get used to the camera angle before the game and timer begins.

5. Test It

As with any games, once you are done, test it out. If something is not working correctly, whip out the Magic Wand and make some corrections. Keep trying and fixing until you have everything working perfectly.

Sports Games

Sports games are a lot of fun—especially in the Toy Box Worlds. There are several different types of balls and goals that you can use to re-create real sports games or create games of your own.

Game Basics
Characters
Power Discs
Play Sets
Toy Box
Toy Box Collection
Achievements

1. Determine the Type of Game

The entire design of a sports game depends on what type of game you want to do. Do you want players to try to push a soccer ball into a goal, shoot basketballs, or put a football through the goal post? There is even a hockey puck. Don't feel constrained to re-create a real sport. This is your world so you can come up with the most outrageous sports you can think of.

2. Build the Stadium

The balls and puck are physics toys, so they will keep moving for a bit after you push or run into them. Therefore, it is usually a good idea to build some boundaries for your game. You can build a stadium with the Building Sets toys or just use some barriers from the Track Pieces. The goal is to keep the ball or puck in play.

> **TIP**
>
> **If you find your ball or puck leaving the play area or falling off the world at times, put in a Falling Object Generator that releases a new ball or puck if the ball or puck in play leaves the world. Therefore, if it goes "out of bounds" you get a new ball or puck.**

3. Goals

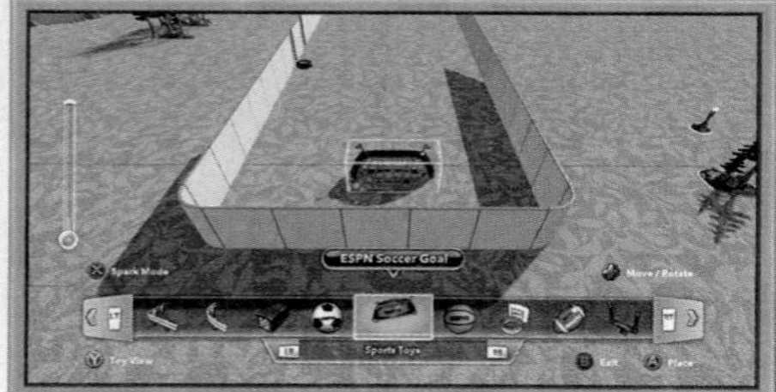

Once the stadium or playing area is set up, you need to place goals. The ESPN Soccer Goal works great for soccer or hockey. If you are using the ESPN Basketball Hoop or ESPN Goal Post, you will also need to provide a way to get the ball up into or through the goals. Try placing a Super Cannon on the field in line with the goals so players can move the balls to the cannon, which then launches them up into the air. Or you can even put several Toy Box Townspeople in the world and then drop kick them over the goals to score points.

4. Scoring

You can't have a sports game with a score. Place a Scoreboard toy from the Creativi-Toy category. Then link it to one of the goals (with the goal as the trigger and the Scoreboard as the behavior) and determine which of four possible teams gets the score. Under Properties in the Scoreboard menu, you can choose the victory requirements for the game.

5. Effects

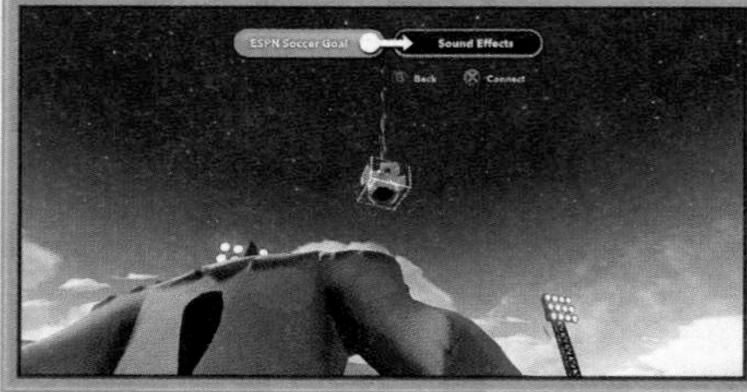

Finally, to make the game more exciting, link a Sound Effects toy to the goal so that you get cheering or other sounds when a goal is scored. Then link a Boom Box and/or Party Cannons to the Scoreboard. Use the Scoreboard as a trigger when one of the players wins to set off music or effects to show the end of the game. Once you have everything in place, be sure to test out your game to make sure it works how you want it to.

Combat or Fighting Games

Combat games can be a lot of fun. It is easy to create one that even sets teams so you can have several enemies on your team to fight against your opponent and his or her team of enemies.

1. Build the Arena

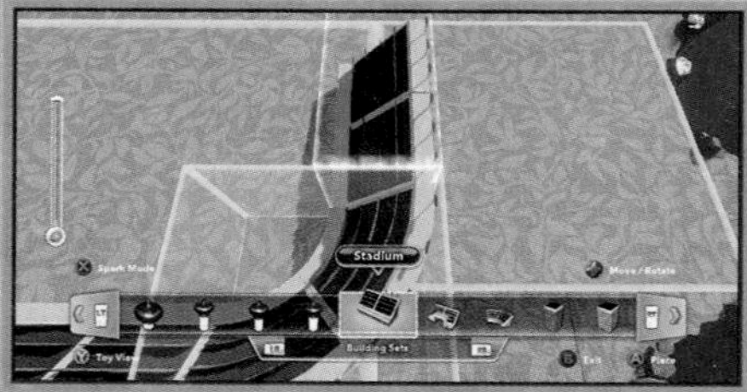

While you can just fight out in the open world, it is usually more fun to have some type of battle arena. Again, you can use the stadium toys to create a large stadium complete with a crowd or you can make your own area out of blocks. Place blocks or other objects in the arena to provide cover or to add to the challenge—especially if you will be using Blasters or other ranged weapons.

2. Weapons

If you want to use weapons, place some Object Generators around the arena and set them to spawn the tools or packs of your choice. It is a good idea to have a variety of weapon types unless you want to focus on a single type. For example, if you want a paintball match, only have the Object Generators spawn Paintball Guns.

3. Enemies

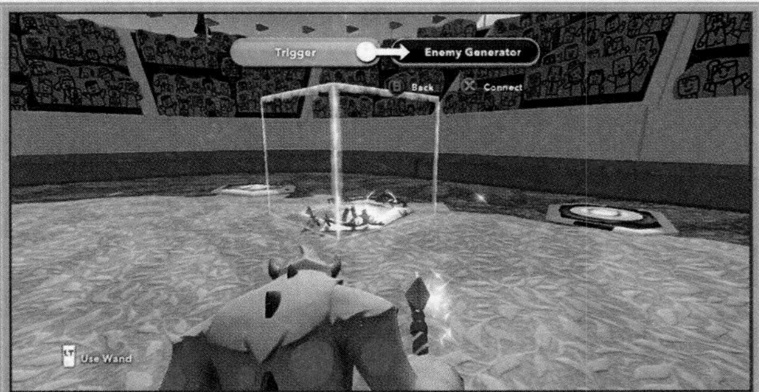

If you want to play a game where you have to defeat enemies, then you will need an Enemy Generator. Set these to spawn a specific type of enemy. You can even have several different triggers connected to one Enemy Generator to spawn different types of enemies depending on the triggering action. If playing a two-player team combat match, you can even set the enemies spawned to either a blue or orange team in the properties. Be sure to place Orange and Blue Team Activators that players can move through to designate their team color. Then enemies of your same color will not attack you, but attack other players and enemies of the opposing team's color.

4. Keeping Score

Since combat games do not have physical goals like sports games, you need to use a Victory Tracker. This acts as a trigger that you can set for a variety of actions, such as defeating an enemy, defeating another player, being defeated, or taking a hit. Connect the Victory Tracker to a Scoreboard to then keep track of the score.

5. Effects

Once you have the combat game all set up, then it is time to add the effects. As with other games, you can set sounds, music, or visual effects to occur for various aspects of the game to add more flavor and fun.

> **TIP**
>
> **Try making combat games with different camera angles for a challenge. The Bird's Eye Camera provides a top-down view that can be fun. However, try combining platforming with combat with a Side-Step Camera.**

Multiplayer Games

Any type of game you create can be played multiplayer. You can play split screen on a single console or invite up to three other friends to join you in your world and challenge them to try out the games you have created. It is usually a good idea to create a separate world for each game so that you do not have too many toys in one world, which can slow down your connection to other players. Play through the Adventures and Character Adventures to get a feel for the various types of games you can create for multiplayer games, since all of those can be played against other players.

> **TIP**
>
> While this section provides some tips and ideas to help you get started, there are many more types of games you can create. The key is to experiment and try out different combinations. The Creativi-Toys are very powerful toys that can allow you to do many different things in games in addition to keeping score and providing effects. Let your imagination run wild and be sure to share your creations with others and look at those worlds that have been built by other players to get some new ideas.

Online/Multiplayer

While there is a lot to do solo in the *Disney Infinity* Toy Box, it is even more fun to play with others and show off your hard work. There are two main ways you can interact with other players online. The first is to invite them into your worlds to explore, play games you have created, or challenge them to play the Adventures and Character Adventures with you. The second is to use the Toy Box Share to upload Toy Box Worlds that you have created.

Welcome to My Toy Box

Join up with your friends by inviting them to play with you in one of your Toy Box Worlds, or join another player's game to visit his or her worlds. Use Xbox Live, the PlayStation Network, or whatever online network you have for your gaming system. You can have a total of four players in one world at a time. Take some time to show your friends around the world that you have created.

Any player can choose to start an Adventure from those that player has unlocked. In addition, a player can also start a Character Adventure for the character they are currently playing as. To change characters, just replace the Disney Infinity Figure on your Disney Infinity Base. For example, if you are playing as Mr. Incredible, you can invite your friends to play the "Mr. Incredible, the Hero" Adventure. While you play as Mr. Incredible, your friends play as whichever character they currently have selected.

Once everyone had joined, the game is on. While you are competing against your opponents for points or to finish first with the best time, you are also competing against yourself to earn medals, if you have not already earned them during solo play. Some medals are easier to earn during multiplayer games since there may be more point earning opportunities. Multiplayer versions of some Adventures and Character Adventures have more collectibles. So if you are trying for the elusive gold, get on with some friends and have them go after low-point collectibles while you focus on the higher value ones. Then when you and your friends have gathered them all, more collectibles will appear in a second batch.

Share with the World

While you can invite three friends over to one of your Toy Box Worlds to check it out, you can also submit your worlds for the entire planet to enjoy and explore. To do this, open the Pause menu and then select Online/Multiplayer. Next select Toy Box Share. Follow the on-screen directions for uploading one of your saved Toy Box Worlds. Disney will review your submission and may feature it on their collection of user-created Toy Box Worlds for other people to try out.

In addition to submitting your Toy Box Worlds, you can also download featured Toy Box Worlds from Disney's collection. It is a lot of fun to see what other people have designed and to explore how they were able to do it. This is especially true for worlds with lots of Creativi-toys linked together. Who knows what you might find when you take millions of players' imaginations to the power of Infinity.

TIP

Some of the designers of *Disney Infinity* have created some very cool Toy Box Worlds while developing and testing the game. They have been waiting for release day to upload their worlds and to show you their creations. Be sure to check them out.

The Collection

There are over a thousand toys that you can collect and use in the Toy Box. Some are available right from the start. Others can be unlocked by spending Spins in the Disney Infinity Vault. Finally, others are collected in the Play Sets. As new Play Sets and characters are released in the future, there will be even more toys for you to use.

The following table includes information on all the toys available at the release of *Disney Infinity.* It contains the names, the type of toy, and how it is unlocked. Plus we have included a check box so you can keep track of the toys you have in your collection and what you still need to get.

The function of a toy refers to how it interacts with characters or other toys. Here is a key for these attributes:

Air Vehicle: These vehicles can fly through the air and move off the edges of the land in Toy Box Worlds.

Blip Block: These blocks can be destroyed when they are hit by characters or projectiles.

Breakable: This toy can be destroyed by attacking it or hitting it with projectiles or vehicles.

Critter: These are animals that can't be destroyed, but you can still pick them up.

Custom: This toy can be connected with other toys for interaction.

Enemy: Watch out for these toys. They can attack you.

Flying Critter: These critter toys can fly around and are not stuck on the ground.

Ground Vehicle: These toys can be driven by characters, but stay on land—unless you drive off a cliff or jump.

Mission Givers: These toys are non-player characters in the Toy Box and provide missions in the Play Sets.

Mount: These animal toys can be ridden by characters.

Pack: This toy is carried on the back of a character and activated by pressing the attack button.

Physics Ball: This ball moves and bounces according to the laws of physics.

Physics Block: These blocks obey the laws of physics. They fall and some can break.

Rail Grind: Characters, even Cars characters, can grind on these toys. Connect them together for long periods of grinding.

Static: These toys just sit there. Come back later, they are still there. They can't be destroyed.

Tool: This is a toy that can be carried by a character and activated by pressing the alternate attack button.

Towable: These toys can be towed by a Cars character.

Townspeople: These small people can be picked up, thrown, and even drop kicked. They do not attack nor can they be destroyed.

Track: Connect these toys together to create a race track.

NOTE

Themed Terrain can be changed when you use a Magic Wand to customize it. The default is Fantasy Terrain in the editor. However, by selecting a themed terrain toy, you can change the theme to any that you have unlocked. This terrain also changes when you place a texture set Power Disc on the Disney Infinity Base.

Got It?	Icon	Toy Name	Category	Function	Unlock
✓		Abu the Elephant	Vehicle/Mount	Mount	Power Disc
✓		Action Button	Creativi-Toys	Custom	Disney Infinity Vault
✓		Admiral's Daughter	Play Set Townspeople	Townspeople	Play Set (Pirates)
✓		Agrabah Guard	Enemy	Enemy	Disney Infinity Vault
✓		Agrabah Palace Base	Building Sets	Static	Disney Infinity Vault
✓		Agrabah Palace Columns	Building Sets	Static	Disney Infinity Vault
✓		Agrabah Palace Entrance	Building Sets	Static	Disney Infinity Vault
✓		Agrabah Palace Front	Building Sets	Static	Disney Infinity Vault

Got It?	Icon	Toy Name	Category	Function	Unlock
✓		Agrabah Palace Ramp	Building Sets	Static	Disney Infinity Vault
✓		Agrabah Palace Tower 1	Building Sets	Static	Disney Infinity Vault
✓		Agrabah Palace Tower 2	Building Sets	Static	Disney Infinity Vault
✓		Agrabah Palace Tower 3	Building Sets	Static	Disney Infinity Vault
✓		Agrabah Palace Tower 4	Building Sets	Static	Disney Infinity Vault
✓		Agrabah Palace Wall	Building Sets	Static	Disney Infinity Vault
✓		Agrabah Palace Wall Corner	Building Sets	Static	Disney Infinity Vault
✓		Agrabah Palace Wall Long	Building Sets	Static	Disney Infinity Vault
✓		Agrabah Palace Wall Lookout	Building Sets	Static	Disney Infinity Vault
✓		Air Conditioning Unit	Decoration	Static	Play Set (Incredibles)
✓		Angered Tiki Monument	Decoration	Static	Disney Infinity Vault
✓		Animal Costume	Toy Box Townspeople	Townspeople	Disney Infinity Vault
✓		Announcer Speakers	Decoration	Breakable	Play Set (Cars)
✓		Apogee	Play Set Townspeople	Townspeople	Play Set (Incredibles)
✓		Arch Blip Block	Block	Blip Block	Disney Infinity Vault
✓		Arch Block	Block	Static	Disney Infinity Vault
✓		Arched Race Track Ramp	Track Piece	Track	Disney Infinity Vault
✓		Archie the Scare Pig	Vehicle/Mount	Mount	Play Set (Monsters)
✓		Area Light	Creativi-Toys	Custom	Disney Infinity Vault
✓		Ariel Costume	Toy Box Townspeople	Townspeople	Disney Infinity Vault
✓		Armadillo	Critter	Critter	Play Set (Lone Ranger)
✓		Armorer	Play Set Townspeople	Townspeople	Play Set (Pirates)
✓		Art	Cast Member	Mission Giver	Play Set (Monsters)
✓		Astro Blasters Space Cruiser	Vehicle/Mount	Ground Vehicle	Power Disc
✓		Atlas Blade	Tool/Pack	Pack	Play Set (Pirates)
✓		Attack Copter	Vehicle/Mount	Air Vehicle	Disney Infinity Vault
✓		Automatic Door	Action Toy	Custom	Disney Infinity Vault
✓		Automatic Double Door	Action Toy	Custom	Disney Infinity Vault
✓		Autopia Car	Vehicle/Mount	Ground Vehicle	Starting Toy

Got It?	Icon	Toy Name	Category	Function	Unlock
✓		Awning	Building Sets	Static	Play Set (Pirates)
✓		Balcony (Block)	Block	Static	Disney Infinity Vault
✓		Balcony (Pirates)	Building Sets	Static	Play Set (Pirates)
✓		Banked Curve	Terrain	Static	Disney Infinity Vault
✓		Banked Race Track Curve	Track Piece	Track	Disney Infinity Vault
✓		Banked Race Track Turn	Track Piece	Track	Disney Infinity Vault
✓		Baron Von Ruthless	Play Set Townspeople	Townspeople	Play Set (Incredibles)
✓		Barrel	Decoration	Breakable	Disney Infinity Vault
✓		Barrel Costume	Enemy	Enemy	Disney Infinity Vault
✓		Barricade Post	Decoration	Static	Disney Infinity Vault
✓		Barrier Corner	Track Piece	Static	Disney Infinity Vault
✓		Barriers 1	Decoration	Static	Play Set (Monsters)
✓		Barriers 2	Decoration	Static	Play Set (Monsters)
✓		Barriers 3	Decoration	Static	Play Set (Monsters)
✓		Barriers and Barrel 1	Decoration	Static	Play Set (Monsters)
✓		Barriers and Barrel 2	Decoration	Static	Play Set (Monsters)
✓		Barriers and Barrel 3	Decoration	Static	Play Set (Monsters)
✓		Bayou Beauty	Play Set Townspeople	Townspeople	Play Set (Pirates)
✓		Bayou Raftman	Play Set Townspeople	Townspeople	Play Set (Pirates)
✓		Bayou Rascal	Play Set Townspeople	Townspeople	Play Set (Pirates)
✓		Beach Ball	Basic Toy	Physics Ball	Starting Toy
✓		Beagle Boy Costume	Enemy	Enemy	Disney Infinity Vault
✓		Beaked Mask	Play Set Townspeople	Townspeople	Play Set (Lone Ranger)
✓		Bear	Critter	Critter	Disney Infinity Vault
✓		Bear Topiary	Plants	Static	Disney Infinity Vault
✓		Bearded Lady	Play Set Townspeople	Townspeople	Play Set (Lone Ranger)
✓		Bee Hive	Decoration	Breakable	Disney Infinity Vault
✓		Belle Costume	Toy Box Townspeople	Townspeople	Disney Infinity Vault
✓		Bench (Incredibles)	Decoration	Static	Play Set (Incredibles)
✓		Bench (Monsters)	Decoration	Static	Play Set (Monsters)

Got It?	Icon	Toy Name	Category	Function	Unlock
✓		Bending Rail	Track Piece	Rail Grind	Disney Infinity Vault
✓		Bevel Beast	Critter	Critter	Play Set (Monsters)
✓		Bird	Critter	Critter	Disney Infinity Vault
✓		Bird's Eye Camera	Creativi-Toys	Custom	Disney Infinity Vault
✓		Bison Head	Play Set Townspeople	Townspeople	Play Set (Lone Ranger)
✓		Black Horse	Vehicle/Mount	Mount	Play Set (Lone Ranger)
✓		Black Pinto	Vehicle/Mount	Mount	Play Set (Lone Ranger)
✓		Blue Mailbox	Decoration	Breakable	Play Set (Cars)
✓		Blue Plane	Critter	Flying Critter	Play Set (Cars)
✓		Blue Shipwreck	Set Piece	Static	Play Set (Pirates)
✓		Bluff	Terrain	Static	Starting Toy
✓		Blunderbuss	Tool/Pack	Tool	Play Set (Pirates)
✓		Boatswain	Play Set Townspeople	Townspeople	Play Set (Pirates)
✓		Bone Chime	Decoration	Breakable	Play Set (Pirates)
✓		Bonny Lass	Play Set Townspeople	Townspeople	Play Set (Pirates)
✓		Boom Box	Creativi-Toys	Custom	Disney Infinity Vault
✓		Boost Pad	Track Piece	Static	Disney Infinity Vault
✓		Boulder	Basic Toy	Physics Ball	Disney Infinity Vault
✓		Bounty Hunter	Playset Townspeople	Townspeople	Play Set (Pirates)
✓		Bowed Race Track Ramp	Track Piece	Track	Disney Infinity Vault
✓		Box o' Fireworks	Decoration	Breakable	Disney Infinity Vault
✓		Box Topiary	Plants	Static	Disney Infinity Vault
✓		Boxy Monacle Monster	Critter	Critter	Play Set (Monsters)
✓		Breaking News Ender	Decoration	Custom	Play Set (Monsters)
✓		Brick Building	Building Sets	Static	Play Set (Incredibles)
✓		Broken Cement Barrier	Decoration	Breakable	Play Set (Incredibles)
✓		Broken Dinoco Crate	Decoration	Breakable	Play Set (Cars)
✓		Brontosaurus Topiary	Plants	Static	Disney Infinity Vault
✓		Brown Hair Tiki Totem	Decoration	Static	Disney Infinity Vault

Got It?	Icon	Toy Name	Category	Function	Unlock
✓		Brown Pinto	Vehicle/Mount	Mount	Play Set (Lone Ranger)
✓		Buck	Critter	Critter	Disney Infinity Vault
✓		Building Base Corner	Building Sets	Static	Play Set (Pirates)
✓		Building Base Ground Corner	Building Sets	Static	Play Set (Pirates)
✓		Building Base with Arch	Building Sets	Static	Play Set (Pirates)
✓		Building Nook	Building Sets	Static	Play Set (Pirates)
✓		Bulletin Board	Decoration	Breakable	Play Set (Monsters)
✓		Bump Rail	Track Piece	Rail Grind	Disney Infinity Vault
✓		Business Man	Play Set Townspeople	Townspeople	Play Set (Incredibles)
✓		Business Woman	Play Set Townspeople	Townspeople	Play Set (Incredibles)
✓		Cabin Boy	Play Set Townspeople	Townspeople	Play Set (Pirates)
✓		Cannon Base	Basic Toy	Custom	Disney Infinity Vault
✓		Canyon Bend	Terrain	Static	Disney Infinity Vault
✓		Canyon Curve	Terrain	Static	Disney Infinity Vault
✓		Canyon Divide	Terrain	Static	Disney Infinity Vault
✓		Canyon End	Terrain	Static	Disney Infinity Vault
✓		Canyon Gulley	Terrain	Static	Disney Infinity Vault
✓		Canyon Outer Curve	Terrain	Static	Disney Infinity Vault
✓		Canyon Split	Terrain	Static	Disney Infinity Vault
✓		Canyon Wall	Terrain	Static	Disney Infinity Vault
✓		Capsule Creator	Basic Toy	Custom	Starting Toy
✓		Captain	Play Set Townspeople	Townspeople	Play Set (Pirates)
✓		Captain Hook Costume	Toy Box Townspeople	Townspeople	Disney Infinity Vault
✓		Captured Baron von Ruthless	Decoration	Breakable	Play Set (Incredibles)
✓		Captured Snoring Gloria	Decoration	Breakable	Play Set (Incredibles)
✓		Captured The Hoarder	Decoration	Breakable	Play Set (Incredibles)
✓		Cardboard Box	Decoration	Breakable	Disney Infinity Vault
✓		Carl Fredricksen's Cane	Tool/Pack	Pack	Power Disc
✓		Carl Fredricksen's House	Set Piece	Static	Disney Infinity Vault
✓		Carpenter	Play Set Townspeople	Townspeople	Play Set (Pirates)

Got It?	Icon	Toy Name	Category	Function	Unlock
✓		Cars Crossing Sign	Decoration	Breakable	Play Set (Cars)
✓		Castle Bridge	Building Sets	Static	Disney Infinity Vault
✓		Castle Floor	Building Sets	Static	Disney Infinity Vault
✓		Castle Front Entrance	Building Sets	Static	Disney Infinity Vault
✓		Castle Front Full	Building Sets	Static	Disney Infinity Vault
✓		Castle Ladder Wall	Building Sets	Static	Disney Infinity Vault
✓		Castle Ramp	Building Sets	Static	Disney Infinity Vault
✓		Castle Rope Wall	Building Sets	Static	Disney Infinity Vault
✓		Castle Spire 1	Building Sets	Static	Disney Infinity Vault
✓		Castle Spire 2	Building Sets	Static	Disney Infinity Vault
✓		Castle Stairs	Building Sets	Static	Disney Infinity Vault
✓		Castle Top Archway	Building Sets	Static	Disney Infinity Vault
✓		Castle Tower 1	Building Sets	Static	Disney Infinity Vault
✓		Castle Tower 2	Building Sets	Static	Disney Infinity Vault
✓		Castle Tower 3	Building Sets	Static	Disney Infinity Vault
✓		Castle Tower Base	Building Sets	Static	Disney Infinity Vault
✓		Castle Tower Corner 1	Building Sets	Static	Disney Infinity Vault
✓		Castle Tower Corner 2	Building Sets	Static	Disney Infinity Vault
✓		Castle Tower Top	Building Sets	Static	Disney Infinity Vault
✓		Castle Wall	Building Sets	Static	Disney Infinity Vault
✓		Castle Wall and Bridge	Building Sets	Static	Disney Infinity Vault
✓		Castle Wall and Tower 1	Building Sets	Static	Disney Infinity Vault
✓		Castle Wall and Tower 2	Building Sets	Static	Disney Infinity Vault
✓		Castle Wall Angled Corner	Building Sets	Static	Disney Infinity Vault
✓		Castle Wall Corner	Building Sets	Static	Disney Infinity Vault
✓		Castle Wall Inside Corner	Building Sets	Static	Disney Infinity Vault
✓		Castle Wall Lookout	Building Sets	Static	Disney Infinity Vault
✓		Castle Wall Overhang	Building Sets	Static	Disney Infinity Vault
✓		Cauldron	Decoration	Breakable	Play Set (Pirates)

Got It?	Icon	Toy Name	Category	Function	Unlock
✓		Cave	Terrain	Static	Disney Infinity Vault
✓		Cave and Well	Terrain	Static	Disney Infinity Vault
✓		Cave Bend	Terrain	Static	Disney Infinity Vault
✓		Cave Cliff	Terrain	Static	Disney Infinity Vault
✓		Cave End	Terrain	Static	Disney Infinity Vault
✓		Cave Fort	Terrain	Static	Disney Infinity Vault
✓		Cave Fort Block	Terrain	Static	Disney Infinity Vault
✓		Cave Intersection	Terrain	Static	Disney Infinity Vault
✓		Cave of Wonders	Set Piece	Static	Disney Infinity Vault
✓		Cave Tunnel	Terrain	Static	Disney Infinity Vault
✓		Cave Waterfall	Terrain	Static	Disney Infinity Vault
✓		Cavendish's Pistol Man	Enemy	Enemy	Play Set (Lone Ranger)
✓		Cavendish's Shotgun Man	Enemy	Enemy	Play Set (Lone Ranger)
✓		Cavendish's TNT Man	Enemy	Enemy	Play Set (Lone Ranger)
✓		Cement Barrier	Decoration	Breakable	Play Set (Incredibles)
✓		Chair	Decoration	Static	Disney Infinity Vault
✓		Checkered Flags	Decoration	Breakable	Play Set (Cars)
✓		Checkpoint	Creativi-Toys	Custom	Disney Infinity Vault
✓		Chestnut Horse	Vehicle/Mount	Mount	Play Set (Lone Ranger)
✓		Chicane	Track Piece	Static	Disney Infinity Vault
✓		Chicane Base	Track Piece	Static	Disney Infinity Vault
✓		Chicane End	Track Piece	Static	Disney Infinity Vault
✓		Chicane Hop Over	Track Piece	Static	Disney Infinity Vault
✓		Chick Hicks	Cast Member	Mission Giver	Play Set (Cars)
✓		Chicken Coop	Decoration	Breakable	Disney Infinity Vault
✓		Cinderella Costume	Toy Box Townspeople	Townspeople	Disney Infinity Vault
✓		Cinderella's Castle	Set Piece	Static	Starting Toy
✓		Cinderella's Coach	Vehicle/Mount	Ground Vehicle	Power Disc
✓		Clam Pirate	Enemy	Enemy	Play Set (Pirates)
✓		Cliff	Terrain	Static	Disney Infinity Vault

Got It?	Icon	Toy Name	Category	Function	Unlock
✓		Cliff Corner	Terrain	Static	Disney Infinity Vault
✓		Cliff Ledge	Terrain	Static	Disney Infinity Vault
✓		Cliff Slope 1	Terrain	Static	Disney Infinity Vault
✓		Cliff Slope 2	Terrain	Static	Disney Infinity Vault
✓		Climbing Cliff	Terrain	Static	Disney Infinity Vault
✓		Climbing Ledge Wall	Terrain	Static	Disney Infinity Vault
✓		Clock Tower	Set Piece	Static	Play Set (Pirates)
✓		Colby Bush 1	Plants	Static	Play Set (Lone Ranger)
✓		Colby Cactus 1	Plants	Static	Play Set (Lone Ranger)
✓		Colby Cactus 2	Plants	Static	Play Set (Lone Ranger)
✓		Colby Cactus 3	Plants	Static	Play Set (Lone Ranger)
✓		Colby Cactus 4	Plants	Static	Play Set (Lone Ranger)
✓		Colby Terrain 1	Themed Terrain	Static	Play Set (Lone Ranger)
✓		Colby Terrain 2	Themed Terrain	Static	Play Set (Lone Ranger)
✓		Colby Terrain 3	Themed Terrain	Static	Play Set (Lone Ranger)
✓		Colby Terrain 4	Themed Terrain	Static	Play Set (Lone Ranger)
✓		Colby Terrain 5	Themed Terrain	Static	Play Set (Lone Ranger)
✓		Colby Terrain Corner 1	Themed Terrain	Static	Play Set (Lone Ranger)
✓		Colby Terrain Corner 2	Themed Terrain	Static	Play Set (Lone Ranger)
✓		Colby Terrain Strip 1	Themed Terrain	Static	Play Set (Lone Ranger)
✓		Colby Terrain Strip 2	Themed Terrain	Static	Play Set (Lone Ranger)
✓		Colby Train Station	Building	Static	Play Set (Lone Ranger)
✓		Colby Tree	Plants	Static	Play Set (Lone Ranger)
✓		Colby's General Store	Building	Static	Play Set (Lone Ranger)
✓		Colby's Hardware Store	Building	Static	Play Set (Lone Ranger)
✓		Colby's Rooming House	Building	Static	Play Set (Lone Ranger)
✓		Colby's Saddler	Building	Static	Play Set (Lone Ranger)
✓		Colby's Stable	Building	Static	Play Set (Lone Ranger)
✓		Colby's Undertaker	Building	Static	Play Set (Lone Ranger)

Got It?	Icon	Toy Name	Category	Function	Unlock
✓		Colby's Wash House	Building	Static	Play Set (Lone Ranger)
✓		Collection Pen	Creativi-Toys	Custom	Disney Infinity Vault
✓		Column	Block	Static	Disney Infinity Vault
✓		Comanche Warrior	Play Set Townspeople	Townspeople	Play Set (Lone Ranger)
✓		Combover Classmate	Play Set Townspeople	Townspeople	Play Set (Monsters)
✓		Concerned Tiki Monument	Decoration	Static	Disney Infinity Vault
✓		Cone Topiary	Plants	Static	Disney Infinity Vault
✓		Construction Pylon	Decoration	Breakable	Play Set (Cars)
✓		Construction Pylon with Reflector	Decoration	Breakable	Play Set (Cars)
✓		Construction Terrain 1	Themed Terrain	Static	Starting Toy
✓		Construction Terrain 2	Themed Terrain	Static	Starting Toy
✓		Construction Terrain 3	Themed Terrain	Static	Starting Toy
✓		Construction Terrain 4	Themed Terrain	Static	Starting Toy
✓		Construction Terrain 5	Themed Terrain	Static	Starting Toy
✓		Construction Terrain Corner 1	Themed Terrain	Static	Starting Toy
✓		Construction Terrain Corner 2	Themed Terrain	Static	Starting Toy
✓		Construction Terrain Strip 1	Themed Terrain	Static	Starting Toy
✓		Construction Terrain Strip 2	Themed Terrain	Static	Starting Toy
✓		Construction Worker	Play Set Townspeople	Townspeople	Play Set (Incredibles)
✓		Conveyor Belt	Action Toy	Custom	Disney Infinity Vault
✓		Cook	Play Set Townspeople	Townspeople	Play Set (Pirates)
✓		Corner Block with Ramps	Terrain	Static	Starting Toy
✓		Corner Hill	Terrain	Static	Starting Toy
✓		Corner Slope	Terrain	Static	Starting Toy
✓		Corporal	Play Set Townspeople	Townspeople	Play Set (Pirates)
✓		Couch	Decoration	Static	Disney Infinity Vault
✓		Counter	Creativi-Toys	Custom	Disney Infinity Vault
✓		Cow Boss	Play Set Townspeople	Townspeople	Play Set (Lone Ranger)
✓		Cowboy	Play Set Townspeople	Townspeople	Play Set (Lone Ranger)
✓		Cowman	Play Set Townspeople	Townspeople	Play Set (Lone Ranger)

Got It?	Icon	Toy Name	Category	Function	Unlock
✓		Cozy Cone Motel	Building	Static	Play Set (Cars)
✓		Cracklin' Backpack	Tool/Pack	Pack	Play Set (Monsters)
✓		Crate	Decoration	Breakable	Starting Toy
✓		Crow Wing Pack	Tool/Pack	Pack	Play Set (Lone Ranger)
✓		Cruella De Vil Costume	Toy Box Townspeople	Townspeople	Disney Infinity Vault
✓		Crystal Cavern	Terrain	Static	Disney Infinity Vault
✓		Cube Topiary	Plants	Static	Disney Infinity Vault
✓		Curved Barrier	Track Piece	Static	Disney Infinity Vault
✓		Curved Blip Block	Block	Blip Block	Disney Infinity Vault
✓		Curved Block	Block	Static	Disney Infinity Vault
✓		Curved Fence Corner	Decoration	Static	Disney Infinity Vault
✓		Curved Floating Bridge	Terrain	Static	Disney Infinity Vault
✓		Curved Rail	Track Piece	Rail Grind	Disney Infinity Vault
✓		Curved Stadium	Building Sets	Static	Disney Infinity Vault
✓		Curved Tire Fence	Track Piece	Static	Disney Infinity Vault
✓		Damaged Wood Crate	Decoration	Breakable	Play Set (Pirates)
✓		Dash Costume	Toy Box Townspeople	Townspeople	Play Set (Incredibles)
✓		Dash Statue	Decoration	Breakable	Play Set (Incredibles)
✓		Davy Jones Costume	Toy Box Townspeople	Townspeople	Play Set (Pirates)
✓		Deer	Critter	Critter	Disney Infinity Vault
✓		Devil Mask	Play Set Townspeople	Townspeople	Play Set (Lone Ranger)
✓		Dip Beam	Block	Static	Disney Infinity Vault
✓		Dipped Rail	Track Piece	Rail Grind	Disney Infinity Vault
✓		Disney Infinity Bush 1	Plants	Static	Disney Infinity Vault
✓		Disney Infinity Bush 2	Plants	Static	Disney Infinity Vault
✓		Disney Infinity Flowers 1	Plants	Static	Starting Toy
✓		Disney Infinity Flowers 2	Plants	Static	Starting Toy
✓		Disney Infinity Flowers 3	Plants	Static	Starting Toy
✓		Disney Infinity Hub	Basic Toy	Custom	Starting Toy

Got It?	Icon	Toy Name	Category	Function	Unlock
✓		Disney Infinity Leaf Patch	Plants	Static	Starting Toy
✓		Disney Infinity Pine Tree	Plants	Static	Starting Toy
✓		Disney Infinity Spruce Tree	Plants	Breakable	Starting Toy
✓		Disney Infinity Tree 1	Plants	Static	Disney Infinity Vault
✓		Disney Infinity Tree 2	Plants	Static	Disney Infinity Vault
✓		Dock	Building Sets	Static	Play Set (Pirates)
✓		Dock Balcony Corner	Building Sets	Static	Play Set (Pirates)
✓		Dock Stairs	Building Sets	Static	Play Set (Pirates)
✓		Don Carlton	Cast Member	Mission Giver	Play Set (Monsters)
✓		Dopey Costume	Toy Box Townspeople	Townspeople	Disney Infinity Vault
✓		Dragon Woman	Play Set Townspeople	Townspeople	Play Set (Pirates)
✓		Driftwood Pirate	Enemy	Enemy	Play Set (Pirates)
✓		Driving Loop	Track Piece	Track	Disney Infinity Vault
✓		Dual Action Trigger	Creativi-Toys	Custom	Disney Infinity Vault
✓		Dual Street Light	Decoration	Static	Play Set (Incredibles)
✓		Dumbo the Flying Elephant	Vehicle/Mount	Air Vehicle	Power Disc
✓		Dumpster	Decoration	Breakable	Play Set (Incredibles)
✓		Dungeon	Set Piece	Static	Disney Infinity Vault
✓		Dynaguy	Play Set Townspeople	Townspeople	Play Set (Incredibles)
✓		Edna Mode	Cast Member	Mission Giver	Play Set (Incredibles)
✓		Edna's Costume Shop	Building	Static	Play Set (Incredibles)
✓		Egg	Basic Toy	Custom	Disney Infinity Vault
✓		EKO House	Building	Static	Play Set (Monsters)
✓		Elasti-Hand	Tool/Pack	Tool	Play Set (Incredibles)
✓		Electrical Box	Decoration	Breakable	Play Set (Incredibles)
✓		Elephant (Critter)	Critter	Critter	Play Set (Incredibles)
✓		Elephant (Lone Ranger)	Vehicle/Mount	Mount	Play Set (Lone Ranger)
✓		Elephant Topiary	Plants	Static	Disney Infinity Vault
✓		Elevator Platform	Action Toy	Custom	Disney Infinity Vault
✓		Elliott Costume	Toy Box Townspeople	Townspeople	Disney Infinity Vault

Got It?	Icon	Toy Name	Category	Function	Unlock
✓		Enemy Creator	Basic Toy	Custom	Starting Toy
✓		Enemy Generator	Creativi-Toys	Custom	Disney Infinity Vault
✓		Engineer	Cast Member	Mission Giver	Play Set (Lone Ranger)
✓		Epcot's Spaceship Earth	Set Piece	Static	Disney Infinity Vault
✓		ESPN Award Podium	Sports Toy	Static	Disney Infinity Vault
✓		ESPN Banner	Sports Toy	Static	Disney Infinity Vault
✓		ESPN Baseball	Sports Toy	Physics Ball	Disney Infinity Vault
✓		ESPN Basketball	Sports Toy	Physics Ball	Disney Infinity Vault
✓		ESPN Basketball Hoop	Sports Toy	Custom	Disney Infinity Vault
✓		ESPN Bench	Sports Toy	Static	Disney Infinity Vault
✓		ESPN Bowling Ball	Sports Toy	Physics Ball	Disney Infinity Vault
✓		ESPN Corner Track Railing	Sports Toy	Static	Disney Infinity Vault
✓		ESPN Curved Track Railing	Sports Toy	Static	Disney Infinity Vault
✓		ESPN Double Banner	Sports Toy	Static	Disney Infinity Vault
✓		ESPN Flag	Sports Toy	Static	Disney Infinity Vault
✓		ESPN Football	Sports Toy	Physics Ball	Disney Infinity Vault
✓		ESPN Goal Post	Sports Toy	Custom	Disney Infinity Vault
✓		ESPN Golf Ball	Sports Toy	Physics Ball	Disney Infinity Vault
✓		ESPN Hockey Puck	Sports Toy	Physics Ball	Disney Infinity Vault
✓		ESPN Pylon	Sports Toy	Static	Disney Infinity Vault
✓		ESPN Scrolling Sign	Sports Toy	Static	Disney Infinity Vault
✓		ESPN Soccer Ball	Sports Toy	Physics Ball	Disney Infinity Vault
✓		ESPN Soccer Goal	Sports Toy	Custom	Disney Infinity Vault
✓		ESPN Stadium Lights	Sports Toy	Static	Disney Infinity Vault
✓		ESPN Tennis Ball	Sports Toy	Physics Ball	Disney Infinity Vault
✓		ESPN Track Railing	Sports Toy	Static	Disney Infinity Vault
✓		Evil Queen Costume	Toy Box Townspeople	Townspeople	Disney Infinity Vault
✓		Exploding Mine	Action Toy	Custom	Disney Infinity Vault
✓		Explosive Block	Block	Physics Block	Disney Infinity Vault

Got It?	Icon	Toy Name	Category	Function	Unlock
✓		Explosive Crate	Decoration	Breakable	Play Set (Cars)
✓		Extended Castle Wall Corner	Building Sets	Static	Disney Infinity Vault
✓		Extra Wide Canyon Wall	Terrain	Static	Disney Infinity Vault
✓		Fairy Godmother Costume	Toy Box Townspeople	Townspeople	Disney Infinity Vault
✓		Falling Object Generator	Creativi-Toys	Custom	Disney Infinity Vault
✓		Fan	Action Toy	Custom	Disney Infinity Vault
✓		Fantasy Terrain 1	Plants	Static	Starting Toy
✓		Fantasy Terrain 2	Plants	Static	Starting Toy
✓		Fantasy Terrain 3	Plants	Static	Starting Toy
✓		Fantasy Terrain 4	Plants	Static	Starting Toy
✓		Fantasy Terrain 5	Plants	Static	Starting Toy
✓		Fantasy Terrain Corner 1	Plants	Static	Starting Toy
✓		Fantasy Terrain Corner 2	Plants	Static	Starting Toy
✓		Fantasy Terrain Strip 1	Plants	Static	Starting Toy
✓		Fantasy Terrain Strip 2	Plants	Static	Starting Toy
✓		Fear Tech Fraternity Brother	Play Set Townspeople	Townspeople	Play Set (Monsters)
✓		Fear Tech Freshman	Play Set Townspeople	Townspeople	Play Set (Monsters)
✓		Fear Tech Junior	Play Set Townspeople	Townspeople	Play Set (Monsters)
✓		Fear Tech Paintball Player 1	Enemy	Enemy	Play Set (Monsters)
✓		Fear Tech Paintball Player 2	Enemy	Enemy	Play Set (Monsters)
✓		Fear Tech Paintball Player 3	Enemy	Enemy	Play Set (Monsters)
✓		Fear Tech Senior	Play Set Townspeople	Townspeople	Play Set (Monsters)
✓		Fear Tech Sophomore	Play Set Townspeople	Townspeople	Play Set (Monsters)
✓		Fear Tech Student 1	Enemy	Enemy	Play Set (Monsters)
✓		Fear Tech Student 2	Enemy	Enemy	Play Set (Monsters)
✓		Fear Tech Student 3	Enemy	Enemy	Play Set (Monsters)
✓		Fear Tech Student Patrol 1	Enemy	Enemy	Play Set (Monsters)
✓		Fear Tech Student Patrol 2	Enemy	Enemy	Play Set (Monsters)
✓		Fear Tech Student Patrol 3	Enemy	Enemy	Play Set (Monsters)
✓		Fence Corner	Decoration	Static	Disney Infinity Vault

Got It?	Icon	Toy Name	Category	Function	Unlock
✓		Ferocious Freshman	Play Set Townspeople	Townspeople	Play Set (Monsters)
✓		Fillmore	Cast Member	Mission Giver	Play Set (Cars)
✓		Fillmore's Organic Fuels	Building	Static	Play Set (Cars)
✓		Fin Fan Freshman	Play Set Townspeople	Townspeople	Play Set (Monsters)
✓		Finn McMissile	Cast Member	Mission Giver	Play Set (Cars)
✓		Finn McMissile Paint Job	Toy Box Townspeople	Townspeople	Play Set (Cars)
✓		Fire Escape	Decoration	Static	Play Set (Incredibles)
✓		Fire Hydrant	Decoration	Breakable	Play Set (Incredibles)
✓		Fix-It Felix, Jr. Costume	Toy Box Townspeople	Townspeople	Disney Infinity Vault
✓		Flapping Freshman	Play Set Townspeople	Townspeople	Play Set (Monsters)
✓		Flat Race Track Ramp	Track Piece	Track	Disney Infinity Vault
✓		Flat Terrain Block	Terrain	Static	Disney Infinity Vault
✓		Flintlock	Tool/Pack	Tool	Play Set (Pirates)
✓		Flo	Cast Member	Mission Giver	Play Set (Cars)
✓		Flo's Mailbox	Decoration	Breakable	Play Set (Cars)
✓		Floating Bridge Hill	Terrain	Static	Disney Infinity Vault
✓		Floating Rope Cliff	Terrain	Static	Starting Toy
✓		Floating Waterfall	Terrain	Static	Starting Toy
✓		Floor Spikes	Action Toy	Custom	Disney Infinity Vault
✓		Flo's V8 Café	Building	Static	Play Set (Cars)
✓		Flower Power	Decoration	Breakable	Play Set (Cars)
✓		Fly Swatter Launcher	Decoration	Custom	Play Set (Monsters)
✓		Folding Construction Barrier	Decoration	Breakable	Play Set (Cars)
✓		Foot Locker	Decoration	Breakable	Play Set (Monsters)
✓		Football Player Costume	Toy Box Townspeople	Townspeople	Disney Infinity Vault
✓		Fortune Teller	Play Set Townspeople	Townspeople	Play Set (Lone Ranger)
✓		Francesco Bernoulli Paint Job	Toy Box Townspeople	Townspeople	Play Set (Cars)
✓		Friend Generator	Creativi-Toys	Custom	Disney Infinity Vault
✓		Frog	Critter	Critter	Starting Toy

Got It?	Icon	Toy Name	Category	Function	Unlock
✓		Fuel Barrel Pile	Decoration	Breakable	Play Set (Cars)
✓		Fuel Barrel Pyramid	Decoration	Breakable	Play Set (Cars)
✓		Fuel Barrel Stack	Decoration	Breakable	Play Set (Cars)
✓		Fuel Barrel Tower	Decoration	Breakable	Play Set (Cars)
✓		Fuel Barrels	Decoration	Breakable	Play Set (Cars)
✓		Full Dome	Block	Static	Disney Infinity Vault
✓		Gal	Play Set Townspeople	Townspeople	Play Set (Lone Ranger)
✓		Garbage Can	Decoration	Static	Play Set (Incredibles)
✓		Gargoyle 1	Decoration	Static	Play Set (Monsters)
✓		Gargoyle 2	Decoration	Static	Play Set (Monsters)
✓		Gaston Costume	Toy Box Townspeople	Townspeople	Disney Infinity Vault
✓		Gator Goon Costume	Enemy	Enemy	Disney Infinity Vault
✓		Gazerbeam	Play Set Townspeople	Townspeople	Play Set (Incredibles)
✓		Genie Costume	Toy Box Townspeople	Townspeople	Disney Infinity Vault
✓		Giraffe	Critter	Critter	Play Set (Incredibles)
✓		Giraffe Topiary	Plants	Static	Disney Infinity Vault
✓		Give 'em a Hand Launcher	Decoration	Custom	Play Set (Monsters)
✓		Glass Block	Block	Physics Block	Disney Infinity Vault
✓		Glass Tower	Building Sets	Static	Play Set (Incredibles)
✓		Glide Pack	Tool/Pack	Pack	Play Set (Incredibles)
✓		Glow Urchin	Tool/Pack	Tool	Play Set (Monsters)
✓		Gold Parking Meter	Decoration	Breakable	Play Set (Cars)
✓		Golden Horse	Vehicle/Mount	Mount	Play Set (Lone Ranger)
✓		Gopher	Critter	Critter	Disney Infinity Vault
✓		Gopher (Lone Ranger)	Critter	Critter	Play Set (Lone Ranger)
✓		Graduating Growler	Play Set Townspeople	Townspeople	Play Set (Monsters)
✓		Grand Duke Costume	Toy Box Townspeople	Townspeople	Disney Infinity Vault
✓		Granny	Play Set Townspeople	Townspeople	Play Set (Lone Ranger)
✓		Grappling Hook	Tool/Pack	Tool	Play Set (Pirates)
✓		Grassy Bridge	Terrain	Static	Disney Infinity Vault

Got It?	Icon	Toy Name	Category	Function	Unlock
✓		Green Basketball Jersey Costume	Toy Box Townspeople	Townspeople	Disney Infinity Vault
✓		Green Hair Tiki Totem	Decoration	Static	Disney Infinity Vault
✓		Green Plane	Critter	Flying Critter	Play Set (Cars)
✓		Ground Vehicle Weapon Generator	Creativi-Toys	Custom	Disney Infinity Vault
✓		Grow Panel	Action Toy	Custom	Disney Infinity Vault
✓		Grumbling Tiki Monument	Decoration	Static	Disney Infinity Vault
✓		Grumpy Costume	Toy Box Townspeople	Townspeople	Disney Infinity Vault
✓		Guido	Cast Member	Mission Giver	Play Set (Cars)
✓		Guido at Work Sign	Decoration	Breakable	Play Set (Cars)
✓		Gunner	Play Set Townspeople	Townspeople	Play Set (Pirates)
✓		Hades Costume	Toy Box Townspeople	Townspeople	Disney Infinity Vault
✓		Half Dome	Block	Static	Disney Infinity Vault
✓		Half Loop	Track Piece	Track	Disney Infinity Vault
✓		Hangin' Tire	Decoration	Breakable	Play Set (Cars)
✓		Hanging Rope Cliff	Terrain	Static	Disney Infinity Vault
✓		Haunted Mansion	Set Piece	Static	Disney Infinity Vault
✓		Have a Nice Trip Launcher	Decoration	Custom	Play Set (Monsters)
✓		Hay Bale	Decoration	Breakable	Play Set (Cars)
✓		Hazard Fence	Decoration	Breakable	Play Set (Cars)
✓		Hector Barbossa Costume	Toy Box Townspeople	Townspeople	Play Set (Pirates)
✓		Hedge Arch	Plants	Static	Disney Infinity Vault
✓		Hedge Corner	Plants	Static	Disney Infinity Vault
✓		Hedge Wall	Plants	Static	Disney Infinity Vault
✓		Hillside Block	Terrain	Static	Disney Infinity Vault
✓		Hockey Player Costume	Toy Box Townspeople	Townspeople	Disney Infinity Vault
✓		Holley Shiftwell Paint Job	Toy Box Townspeople	Townspeople	Play Set (Cars)
✓		Holley's Hubcap Pinwheel	Decoration	Breakable	Play Set (Cars)
✓		Hop Over Gate	Action Toy	Custom	Disney Infinity Vault
✓		Horned Mask	Play Set Townspeople	Townspeople	Play Set (Lone Ranger)

Got It?	Icon	Toy Name	Category	Function	Unlock
✓		Hotdog Stand	Building	Static	Play Set (Incredibles)
✓		Hover Board	Tool/Pack	Pack	Play Set (Incredibles)
✓		HQ Research Station	Building	Static	Play Set (Incredibles)
✓		HSS House	Building	Static	Play Set (Monsters)
✓		Identity Disc	Tool/Pack	Pack	Disney Infinity Vault
✓		Incoming Call Ender	Decoration	Custom	Play Set (Monsters)
✓		Incredibles Antenna	Decoration	Static	Play Set (Incredibles)
✓		Inflatable Guido Balloon	Decoration	Static	Play Set (Cars)
✓		Insect Car	Critter	Flying Critter	Play Set (Cars)
✓		Insurance Sales Woman	Play Set Townspeople	Townspeople	Play Set (Incredibles)
✓		Invisibility Device	Tool/Pack	Tool	Play Set (Incredibles)
✓		Invisinator	Action Toy	Custom	Disney Infinity Vault
✓		Invulnerability Beacon	Creativi-Toys	Custom	Disney Infinity Vault
✓		Jack Sparrow Costume	Toy Box Townspeople	Townspeople	Disney Infinity Vault
✓		Jack-O-Lantern	Decoration	Breakable	Disney Infinity Vault
✓		Jack-O-Lantern in the Box Costume	Enemy	Enemy	Disney Infinity Vault
✓		Jafar Costume	Toy Box Townspeople	Townspeople	Disney Infinity Vault
✓		Jaunty Junior	Play Set Townspeople	Townspeople	Play Set (Monsters)
✓		Jiminy Cricket Costume	Toy Box Townspeople	Townspeople	Disney Infinity Vault
✓		Job Hunter	Play Set Townspeople	Townspeople	Play Set (Incredibles)
✓		Jovial Junior	Play Set Townspeople	Townspeople	Play Set (Monsters)
✓		JOX House	Building	Static	Play Set (Monsters)
✓		Joyful Junior	Play Set Townspeople	Townspeople	Play Set (Monsters)
✓		Jutting Ledge	Terrain	Static	Disney Infinity Vault
✓		Kahn	Vehicle/Mount	Mount	Power Disc
✓		Kermit the Frog Costume	Toy Box Townspeople	Townspeople	Disney Infinity Vault
✓		Kill Switch	Creativi-Toys	Custom	Disney Infinity Vault
✓		King Costume	Toy Box Townspeople	Townspeople	Disney Infinity Vault
✓		Knight Costume	Toy Box Townspeople	Townspeople	Disney Infinity Vault
✓		Lady (Incredibles)	Play Set Townspeople	Townspeople	Play Set (Incredibles)

Got It?	Icon	Toy Name	Category	Function	Unlock
✓		Lady (Lone Ranger)	Play Set Townspeople	Townspeople	Play Set (Lone Ranger)
✓		Lady Buccaneer	Play Set Townspeople	Townspeople	Play Set (Pirates)
✓		Lake	Terrain	Static	Disney Infinity Vault
✓		Lamp Post	Decoration	Static	Starting Toy
✓		Lantern Pole	Decoration	Static	Play Set (Lone Ranger)
✓		Large Brick Building	Building Sets	Static	Play Set (Incredibles)
✓		Large Canyon Curve	Terrain	Static	Disney Infinity Vault
✓		Large Canyon Outer Curve	Terrain	Static	Disney Infinity Vault
✓		Large Castle Floor	Building Sets	Static	Disney Infinity Vault
✓		Large Cliff	Terrain	Static	Disney Infinity Vault
✓		Large Cliff Ledge	Terrain	Static	Disney Infinity Vault
✓		Large Colby Tree	Plants	Static	Play Set (Lone Ranger)
✓		Large Curved Barrier	Track Piece	Static	Disney Infinity Vault
✓		Large Disney Infinity Pine Tree	Plants	Static	Starting Toy
✓		Large Flat Terrain Block	Terrain	Static	Disney Infinity Vault
✓		Large Floor	Block	Static	Disney Infinity Vault
✓		Large Lava Block	Block	Custom	Disney Infinity Vault
✓		Large Metroville Tree	Plants	Static	Play Set (Incredibles)
✓		Large Monster Tree	Plants	Static	Play Set (Monsters)
✓		Large Nose Mask	Play Set Townspeople	Townspeople	Play Set (Lone Ranger)
✓		Large Radiator Springs Bush	Plants	Static	Play Set (Cars)
✓		Large Radiator Springs Cactus	Plants	Static	Play Set (Cars)
✓		Large Roof Vent	Decoration	Static	Play Set (Incredibles)
✓		Large Rounded Cliff	Terrain	Static	Starting Toy
✓		Large Slope	Terrain	Static	Starting Toy
✓		Large Stone Wall	Block	Static	Disney Infinity Vault
✓		Large Terrain Block	Terrain	Static	Disney Infinity Vault
✓		Lass	Play Set Townspeople	Townspeople	Play Set (Lone Ranger)
✓		Launching Ramp	Track Piece	Static	Disney Infinity Vault

Got It?	Icon	Toy Name	Category	Function	Unlock
✓		Lava Block	Block	Custom	Disney Infinity Vault
✓		Leaf Mask	Play Set Townspeople	Townspeople	Play Set (Lone Ranger)
✓		Ledge Block	Block	Static	Disney Infinity Vault
✓		Left Pinball Flipper	Basic Toy	Custom	Disney Infinity Vault
✓		Left Rail	Track Piece	Rail Grind	Disney Infinity Vault
✓		Left Upward Curving Rail	Track Piece	Rail Grind	Disney Infinity Vault
✓		Light Runner	Vehicle/Mount	Ground Vehicle	Disney Infinity Vault
✓		Lightning McQueen Paint Job	Toy Box Townspeople	Townspeople	Play Set (Cars)
✓		Lion	Critter	Critter	Play Set (Incredibles)
✓		Little Boy	Play Set Townspeople	Townspeople	Play Set (Incredibles)
✓		Little Girl	Play Set Townspeople	Townspeople	Play Set (Incredibles)
✓		Little Kid	Play Set Townspeople	Townspeople	Play Set (Incredibles)
✓		Little Mad Tiki Monument	Decoration	Static	Disney Infinity Vault
✓		Little Sad Tiki Monument	Decoration	Static	Disney Infinity Vault
✓		Lizard	Critter	Critter	Play Set (Lone Ranger)
✓		Lock Costume	Enemy	Enemy	Disney Infinity Vault
✓		Log	Decoration	Static	Starting Toy
✓		Lone Ranger Costume	Toy Box Townspeople	Townspeople	Play Set (Lone Ranger)
✓		Long Awning	Building Sets	Static	Play Set (Pirates)
✓		Long Barricade	Decoration	Static	Disney Infinity Vault
✓		Long Blip Block	Block	Blip Block	Disney Infinity Vault
✓		Long Block	Block	Static	Disney Infinity Vault
✓		Long Castle Top Archway	Building Sets	Static	Disney Infinity Vault
✓		Long Flat Terrain Block	Terrain	Static	Disney Infinity Vault
✓		Long Glass Block	Block	Physics Block	Disney Infinity Vault
✓		Long Metal Block	Block	Physics Block	Disney Infinity Vault
✓		Long Race Track	Track Piece	Track	Starting Toy
✓		Long Race Track Ramp	Track Piece	Track	Starting Toy
✓		Long Roof	Building Sets	Static	Play Set (Pirates)
✓		Long Support Arch	Block	Static	Disney Infinity Vault

Got It?	Icon	Toy Name	Category	Function	Unlock
✓		Long Tiny Terrain Block	Terrain	Static	Disney Infinity Vault
✓		Long Wedge Blip Block	Block	Blip Block	Disney Infinity Vault
✓		Long Wedge Block	Block	Static	Disney Infinity Vault
✓		Long Wooden Block	Block	Physics Block	Disney Infinity Vault
✓		Long Wooden Bridge	Decoration	Static	Disney Infinity Vault
✓		Long Wooden Ladder	Decoration	Static	Disney Infinity Vault
✓		Long-Necked Critter	Critter	Critter	Play Set (Monsters)
✓		Luigi	Cast Member	Mission Giver	Play Set (Cars)
✓		Luigi's Casa Della Tires	Building	Static	Play Set (Cars)
✓		M.U. Clock Tower	Set Piece	Static	Play Set (Monsters)
✓		M.U. Dorm	Building	Static	Play Set (Monsters)
✓		M.U. Entrance Gate	Set Piece	Static	Play Set (Monsters)
✓		M.U. Founder's Fountain	Set Piece	Static	Play Set (Monsters)
✓		M.U. Groundskeeper	Play Set Townspeople	Townspeople	Play Set (Monsters)
✓		M.U. Library	Building	Static	Play Set (Monsters)
✓		M.U. Registration Hall	Building	Static	Play Set (Monsters)
✓		M.U. School of Scaring	Building	Static	Play Set (Monsters)
✓		M.U. University Hall	Building	Static	Play Set (Monsters)
✓		Maccus	Enemy	Enemy	Play Set (Pirates)
✓		Mad Hatter Costume	Toy Box Townspeople	Townspeople	Disney Infinity Vault
✓		Mad Scientist	Play Set Townspeople	Townspeople	Play Set (Incredibles)
✓		Magic Wand	Tool/Pack	Tool	Starting Toy
✓		Mail Box	Decoration	Breakable	Play Set (Incredibles)
✓		Maleficent Costume	Toy Box Townspeople	Townspeople	Disney Infinity Vault
✓		Man About Town	Play Set Townspeople	Townspeople	Play Set (Incredibles)
✓		Man on the Street	Play Set Townspeople	Townspeople	Play Set (Incredibles)
✓		Marching Orders	Creativi-Toys	Custom	Disney Infinity Vault
✓		Masher	Action Toy	Custom	Disney Infinity Vault
✓		Massive Rounded Cliff	Terrain	Static	Starting Toy

Got It?	Icon	Toy Name	Category	Function	Unlock
✓		Massive Terrain Block	Terrain	Static	Disney Infinity Vault
✓		Mater Paint Job	Toy Box Townspeople	Townspeople	Play Set (Cars)
✓		Matterhorn Yeti Costume	Toy Box Townspeople	Townspeople	Disney Infinity Vault
✓		Medium Canyon Outer Curve	Terrain	Static	Disney Infinity Vault
✓		Medium Cliff Ledge	Terrain	Static	Disney Infinity Vault
✓		Medium Fence	Decoration	Breakable	Play Set (Cars)
✓		Medium Race Track	Track Piece	Track	Starting Toy
✓		Medium Waterfall	Terrain	Static	Disney Infinity Vault
✓		Melancholy Tiki Monument	Decoration	Static	Disney Infinity Vault
✓		Melee Omnidroid	Enemy	Enemy	Play Set (Incredibles)
✓		Merlin Costume	Toy Box Townspeople	Townspeople	Disney Infinity Vault
✓		Metal Block	Block	Physics Block	Disney Infinity Vault
✓		Metroville Bush	Plants	Static	Play Set (Incredibles)
✓		Metroville Business Office	Building Sets	Static	Play Set (Incredibles)
✓		Metroville Center	Building Sets	Static	Play Set (Incredibles)
✓		Metroville Deli	Building Sets	Static	Play Set (Incredibles)
✓		Metroville Fireman	Play Set Townspeople	Townspeople	Play Set (Incredibles)
✓		Metroville Manor	Building Sets	Static	Play Set (Incredibles)
✓		Metroville Mart	Building Sets	Static	Play Set (Incredibles)
✓		Metroville Police Officer	Play Set Townspeople	Townspeople	Play Set (Incredibles)
✓		Metroville Shop	Building Sets	Static	Play Set (Incredibles)
✓		Metroville Street Light	Themed Terrain	Static	Play Set (Incredibles)
✓		Metroville Terrain 1	Themed Terrain	Static	Play Set (Incredibles)
✓		Metroville Terrain 2	Themed Terrain	Static	Play Set (Incredibles)
✓		Metroville Terrain 3	Themed Terrain	Static	Play Set (Incredibles)
✓		Metroville Terrain 4	Themed Terrain	Static	Play Set (Incredibles)
✓		Metroville Terrain Corner 1	Themed Terrain	Static	Play Set (Incredibles)
✓		Metroville Terrain Corner 2	Themed Terrain	Static	Play Set (Incredibles)
✓		Metroville Terrain Strip 1	Themed Terrain	Static	Play Set (Incredibles)
✓		Metroville Terrain Strip 2	Themed Terrain	Static	Play Set (Incredibles)

Got It?	Icon	Toy Name	Category	Function	Unlock
✓		Metroville Tree	Plants	Static	Play Set (Incredibles)
✓		Metroville Storefront	Building Sets	Static	Play Set (Incredibles)
✓		Metroville's Woman of the Year	Play Set Townspeople	Townspeople	Play Set (Incredibles)
✓		Mickey Topiary	Plants	Static	Disney Infinity Vault
✓		Mickey's Car	Vehicle/Mount	Ground Vehicle	Power Disc
✓		Mike Wazowski Costume	Toy Box Townspeople	Townspeople	Disney Infinity Vault
✓		Miner	Play Set Townspeople	Townspeople	Play Set (Lone Ranger)
✓		Mining Tunnel	Terrain	Static	Disney Infinity Vault
✓		Mirage	Cast Member	Mission Giver	Play Set (Incredibles)
✓		Miss	Play Set Townspeople	Townspeople	Play Set (Lone Ranger)
✓		Miss Piggy Costume	Toy Box Townspeople	Townspeople	Disney Infinity Vault
✓		Modern Air Conditioning Unit	Decoration	Static	Play Set (Incredibles)
✓		Monkey	Critter	Critter	Play Set (Incredibles)
✓		Monster Flowers 1	Plants	Static	Play Set (Monsters)
✓		Monster Flowers 2	Plants	Static	Play Set (Monsters)
✓		Monster Flowers 3	Plants	Static	Play Set (Monsters)
✓		Monster Tree	Plants	Static	Play Set (Monsters)
✓		Monsters University Light Post	Decoration	Static	Play Set (Monsters)
✓		Monsters University Terrain 1	Themed Terrain	Static	Play Set (Monsters)
✓		Monsters University Terrain 2	Themed Terrain	Static	Play Set (Monsters)
✓		Monsters University Terrain 3	Themed Terrain	Static	Play Set (Monsters)
✓		Monsters University Terrain 4	Themed Terrain	Static	Play Set (Monsters)
✓		Monsters University Terrain 5	Themed Terrain	Static	Plays Set (Monsters)
✓		Monsters University Terrain Corner 1	Themed Terrain	Static	Play Set (Monsters)
✓		Monsters University Terrain Corner 2	Themed Terrain	Static	Play Set (Monsters)
✓		Monsters University Terrain Strip 1	Themed Terrain	Static	Play Set (Monsters)
✓		Monsters University Terrain Strip 2	Themed Terrain	Static	Play Set (Monsters)
✓		Monstro the Whale	Set Piece	Static	Disney Infinity Vault
✓		Monstrous Citizen	Play Set Townspeople	Townspeople	Play Set (Incredibles)

Got It?	Icon	Toy Name	Category	Function	Unlock
✓		Monument of Heroes	Set Piece	Static	Play Set (Incredibles)
✓		Moose Topiary	Plants	Static	Disney Infinity Vault
✓		Morning Edition Launcher	Decoration	Custom	Play Set (Monsters)
✓		Motorin' Topiary	Decoration	Breakable	Play Set (Cars)
✓		Mountain Cave	Terrain	Static	Disney Infinity Vault
✓		Mountain Tunnel	Terrain	Static	Disney Infinity Vault
✓		Moving Wall	Action Toy	Custom	Disney Infinity Vault
✓		Mr. Gibbs	Cast Member	Mission Giver	Play Set (Pirates)
✓		Mr. Incredible Costume	Toy Box Townspeople	Townspeople	Play Set (Incredibles)
✓		Mr. Incredible Defeats Syndrome	Decoration	Breakable	Play Set (Incredibles)
✓		Mr. Incredible Statue	Decoration	Breakable	Play Set (Incredibles)
✓		Mr. Incredible's Sports Car	Vehicle/Mount	Ground Vehicle	Play Set (Incredibles)
✓		Mrs. Incredible Costume	Toy Box Townspeople	Townspeople	Play Set (Incredibles)
✓		Mrs. Incredible Statue	Decoration	Breakable	Play Set (Incredibles)
✓		Mrs. Incredible vs. Syndrome Statue	Decoration	Breakable	Play Set (Incredibles)
✓		Mule	Vehicle/Mount	Mount	Play Set (Lone Ranger)
✓		Nanny Costume	Toy Box Townspeople	Townspeople	Disney Infinity Vault
✓		Narrow Barrier	Track Piece	Static	Disney Infinity Vault
✓		Narrow Canyon Wall	Terrain	Static	Disney Infinity Vault
✓		Narrow Cliff Ledge	Terrain	Static	Disney Infinity Vault
✓		Narrow Floating Cliff	Terrain	Static	Starting Toy
✓		Navigator	Playset Townspeople	Townspeople	Play Set (Pirates)
✓		Nemo's Reef Terrain 1	Themed Terrain	Static	Power Disc
✓		Nemo's Reef Terrain 2	Themed Terrain	Static	Power Disc
✓		Nemo's Reef Terrain 3	Themed Terrain	Static	Power Disc
✓		Nemo's Reef Terrain 4	Themed Terrain	Static	Power Disc
✓		Nemo's Reef Terrain 5	Themed Terrain	Static	Power Disc
✓		Nemo's Reef Terrain Corner 1	Themed Terrain	Static	Power Disc
✓		Nemo's Reef Terrain Corner 2	Themed Terrain	Static	Power Disc
✓		Nemo's Reef Terrain Strip 1	Themed Terrain	Static	Power Disc

Got It?	Icon	Toy Name	Category	Function	Unlock
✓		Nemo's Reef Terrain Strip 2	Themed Terrain	Static	Power Disc
✓		New Holland Windmill	Set Piece	Static	Disney Infinity Vault
✓		Newspaper Stand	Building	Static	Play Set (Incredibles)
✓		Newsstand	Decoration	Breakable	Play Set (Monsters)
✓		Nurse	Play Set Townspeople	Townspeople	Play Set (Incredibles)
✓		Obelisk	Block	Static	Disney Infinity Vault
✓		Object Generator	Creativi-Toys	Custom	Disney Infinity Vault
✓		Office Building	Building Sets	Static	Play Set (Incredibles)
✓		Office Tower	Building Sets	Static	Play Set (Incredibles)
✓		Officer	Play Set Townspeople	Townspeople	Play Set (Pirates)
✓		Olaf Costume	Toy Box Townspeople	Townspeople	Disney Infinity Vault
✓		Old Barrel	Decoration	Static	Play Set (Monsters)
✓		Old Timer	Play Set Townspeople	Townspeople	Play Set (Lone Ranger)
✓		Old Woman	Play Set Townspeople	Townspeople	Play Set (Incredibles)
✓		Omnidroid	Enemy	Enemy	Play Set (Incredibles)
✓		Onion Dome	Block	Static	Disney Infinity Vault
✓		Oogie Boogie Costume	Enemy	Enemy	Disney Infinity Vault
✓		Orange Bat-Winged Pest Bush	Plants	Custom	Play Set (Monsters)
✓		Overhanging Corner	Terrain	Static	Disney Infinity Vault
✓		Overhanging Ledge	Terrain	Static	Disney Infinity Vault
✓		Paintball Gun	Tool/Pack	Tool	Play Set (Monsters)
✓		Palomino	Vehicle/Mount	Mount	Play Set (Lone Ranger)
✓		Panda	Critter	Critter	Play Set (Incredibles)
✓		Parking Meter	Decoration	Breakable	Play Set (Cars)
✓		Party Cannon	Creativi-Toys	Custom	Disney Infinity Vault
✓		Pendulum	Action Toy	Custom	Disney Infinity Vault
✓		Penguin	Critter	Critter	Play Set (Incredibles)
✓		Peter Pan Costume	Toy Box Townspeople	Townspeople	Disney Infinity Vault
✓		Phone Booth (Incredibles)	Decoration	Breakable	Play Set (Incredibles)

Got It?	Icon	Toy Name	Category	Function	Unlock
✓		Phone Booth (Monsters)	Decoration	Breakable	Play Set (Monsters)
✓		Picket Fence	Decoration	Static	Disney Infinity Vault
✓		Pig Goon Costume	Enemy	Enemy	Disney Infinity Vault
✓		Pillar Blip Block	Block	Blip Block	Disney Infinity Vault
✓		Pillar Block	Block	Static	Disney Infinity Vault
✓		Pinball Bouncer	Basic Toy	Custom	Disney Infinity Vault
✓		Pinball Bumper	Basic Toy	Custom	Disney Infinity Vault
✓		Pink Flamingo 1	Decoration	Breakable	Play Set (Cars)
✓		Pink Flamingo 2	Decoration	Breakable	Play Set (Cars)
✓		Pinocchio Costume	Toy Box Townspeople	Townspeople	Disney Infinity Vault
✓		Pintel	Cast Member	Mission Giver	Play Set (Pirates)
✓		Pipe Climb Block	Action Toy	Static	Disney Infinity Vault
✓		Pirate Bombs	Tool/Pack	Tool	Play Set (Pirates)
✓		Pirate Flag	Decoration	Static	Play Set (Pirates)
✓		Pirate Sign 1	Decoration	Static	Play Set (Pirates)
✓		Pirate Sign 2	Decoration	Static	Play Set (Pirates)
✓		Pirates Bush 1	Plants	Static	Play Set (Pirates)
✓		Pirates Bush 2	Plants	Static	Play Set (Pirates)
✓		Pirates Bush 3	Plants	Static	Play Set (Pirates)
✓		Pirates Bush 4	Plants	Static	Play Set (Pirates)
✓		Pirates Bush 5	Plants	Static	Play Set (Pirates)
✓		Pirates Dock	Decoration	Static	Play Set (Pirates)
✓		Pirates Plant Edge	Themed Terrain	Static	Play Set (Pirates)
✓		Pirates Plants Palm 1	Plants	Static	Play Set (Pirates)
✓		Pirates Plants Palm 2	Plants	Static	Play Set (Pirates)
✓		Pirates Street Lamp 1	Decoration	Static	Play Set (Pirates)
✓		Pirates Street Lamp 2	Decoration	Static	Play Set (Pirates)
✓		Pirates Terrain 1	Themed Terrain	Static	Play Set (Pirates)
✓		Pirates Terrain 2	Themed Terrain	Static	Play Set (Pirates)
✓		Pirates Terrain 3	Themed Terrain	Static	Play Set (Pirates)

Got It?	Icon	Toy Name	Category	Function	Unlock
✓		Pirates Terrain 4	Themed Terrain	Static	Play Set (Pirates)
✓		Pirates Terrain Corner 1	Themed Terrain	Static	Play Set (Pirates)
✓		Pirates Terrain Corner 2	Themed Terrain	Static	Play Set (Pirates)
✓		Pirates Terrain Strip 1	Themed Terrain	Static	Play Set (Pirates)
✓		Pirates Terrain Strip 2	Themed Terrain	Static	Play Set (Pirates)
✓		Pirates Tree	Plants	Static	Play Set (Pirates)
✓		Plasmabolt	Play Set Townspeople	Townspeople	Play Set (Incredibles)
✓		Plateau Block with Ramp	Terrain	Static	Disney Infinity Vault
✓		Plated Slug	Critter	Critter	Play Set (Monsters)
✓		Platform	Building Sets	Static	Play Set (Pirates)
✓		PNK House	Building	Static	Play Set (Monsters)
✓		Pokey Pest	Critter	Critter	Play Set (Monsters)
✓		Police Barricade	Decoration	Breakable	Play Set (Incredibles)
✓		Pond	Terrain	Static	Starting Toy
✓		Pop Up Turret	Action Toy	Custom	Disney Infinity Vault
✓		Powder Monkey	Play Set Townspeople	Townspeople	Play Set (Pirates)
✓		Power Switch	Creativi-Toys	Custom	Disney Infinity Vault
✓		Powerful Tiki Monument	Decoration	Static	Disney Infinity Vault
✓		Pride Rock	Set Piece	Static	Disney Infinity Vault
✓		Prince Charming Costume	Toy Box Townspeople	Townspeople	Disney Infinity Vault
✓		Princess Jasmine Costume	Toy Box Townspeople	Townspeople	Disney Infinity Vault
✓		Privateer	Play Set Townspeople	Townspeople	Play Set (Pirates)
✓		Purple Bat-Winged Pest Bush	Plants	Custom	Play Set (Monsters)
✓		Quarter Pipe Ramp	Track Piece	Static	Disney Infinity Vault
✓		Quartermaster	Play Set Townspeople	Townspeople	Play Set (Pirates)
✓		Rabbit	Critter	Critter	Disney Infinity Vault
✓		Rabbit (Lone Ranger)	Critter	Critter	Play Set (Lone Ranger)
✓		Race Track	Track Piece	Track	Disney Infinity Vault
✓		Race Track Bridge	Track Piece	Track	Disney Infinity Vault

Got It?	Icon	Toy Name	Category	Function	Unlock
✓		Race Track Curve	Track Piece	Track	Starting Toy
✓		Race Track Intersection	Track Piece	Track	Disney Infinity Vault
✓		Race Track Junction	Track Piece	Track	Disney Infinity Vault
✓		Race Track Left	Track Piece	Track	Disney Infinity Vault
✓		Race Track Right	Track Piece	Track	Disney Infinity Vault
✓		Race Track Split	Track Piece	Track	Disney Infinity Vault
✓		Race Track Start	Track Piece	Track	Disney Infinity Vault
✓		Racing Gate	Creativi-Toys	Custom	Disney Infinity Vault
✓		Radiator Springs Bush	Plants	Static	Play Set (Cars)
✓		Radiator Springs Cactus	Plants	Breakable	Play Set (Cars)
✓		Radiator Springs Courthouse	Building	Static	Play Set (Cars)
✓		Radiator Springs Curios	Building	Static	Play Set (Cars)
✓		Radiator Springs Farmhouse	Building	Static	Play Set (Cars)
✓		Radiator Springs Terrain 1	Themed Terrain	Static	Play Set (Cars)
✓		Radiator Springs Terrain 2	Themed Terrain	Static	Play Set (Cars)
✓		Radiator Springs Terrain 3	Themed Terrain	Static	Play Set (Cars)
✓		Radiator Springs Terrain 4	Themed Terrain	Static	Play Set (Cars)
✓		Radiator Springs Terrain 5	Themed Terrain	Static	Play Set (Cars)
✓		Radiator Springs Terrain Corner 1	Themed Terrain	Static	Play Set (Cars)
✓		Radiator Springs Terrain Corner 2	Themed Terrain	Static	Play Set (Cars)
✓		Radiator Springs Terrain Strip 1	Themed Terrain	Static	Play Set (Cars)
✓		Radiator Springs Terrain Strip 2	Themed Terrain	Static	Play Set (Cars)
✓		Radiator Springs Tree	Plants	Static	Play Set (Cars)
✓		Ragetti	Cast Member	Mission Giver	Play Set (Pirates)
✓		Railroad Camp Foreman	Play Set Townspeople	Townspeople	Play Set (Lone Ranger)
✓		Railroad Worker	Play Set Townspeople	Townspeople	Play Set (Lone Ranger)
✓		Ramone	Cast Member	Mission Giver	Play Set (Cars)
✓		Ramone's House of Body Art	Building	Static	Play Set (Cars)
✓		Ramp Cliff	Terrain	Static	Disney Infinity Vault
✓		Ramp Rail	Track Piece	Rail Grind	Disney Infinity Vault

Got It?	Icon	Toy Name	Category	Function	Unlock
✓		Ramp Vertical	Block	Static	Disney Infinity Vault
✓		Rancher	Play Set Townspeople	Townspeople	Play Set (Lone Ranger)
✓		Randy Costume	Toy Box Townspeople	Townspeople	Play Set (Monsters)
✓		Ranged Omnidroid	Enemy	Enemy	Play Set (Incredibles)
✓		Rat	Critter	Critter	Disney Infinity Vault
✓		Recognizer	Vehicle/Mount	Air Vehicle	Disney Infinity Vault
✓		Red Harrington	Cast Member	Mission Giver	Play Set (Lone Ranger)
✓		Red Mailbox	Decoration	Breakable	Play Set (Cars)
✓		Red Shipwreck	Set Piece	Static	Play Set (Pirates)
✓		Referee Costume	Toy Box Townspeople	Townspeople	Disney Infinity Vault
✓		Reformed Thug	Play Set Townspeople	Townspeople	Play Set (Incredibles)
✓		Repeater	Creativi-Toys	Custom	Disney Infinity Vault
✓		Replayer	Creativi-Toys	Custom	Disney Infinity Vault
✓		Reset-O-Matic	Basic Toy	Custom	Disney Infinity Vault
✓		Retro TV	Decoration	Breakable	Disney Infinity Vault
✓		Rhino Guard	Enemy	Enemy	Disney Infinity Vault
✓		Rhino Topiary	Plants	Static	Disney Infinity Vault
✓		Rick Dicker	Cast Member	Mission Giver	Play Set (Incredibles)
✓		Right Pinball Flipper	Basic Toy	Custom	Disney Infinity Vault
✓		Right Rail	Track Piece	Rail Grind	Disney Infinity Vault
✓		Right Upward Curving Rail	Track Piece	Rail Grind	Disney Infinity Vault
✓		Ring of Fire	Track Piece	Static	Disney Infinity Vault
✓		Ringmaster	Play Set Townspeople	Townspeople	Play Set (Lone Ranger)
✓		River	Terrain	Static	Starting Toy
✓		River Gazebo	Set Piece	Static	Starting Toy
✓		Riverbend	Terrain	Static	Disney Infinity Vault
✓		Road Closed Barrier	Decoration	Breakable	Play Set (Cars)
✓		Robin Hood Costume	Toy Box Townspeople	Townspeople	Disney Infinity Vault
✓		Rocky Climbing Block	Terrain	Static	Disney Infinity Vault

Got It?	Icon	Toy Name	Category	Function	Unlock
✓		Rocky Layered Block	Terrain	Static	Starting Toy
✓		Rocky Ramp Block	Terrain	Static	Disney Infinity Vault
✓		Rocky Terrain Block	Terrain	Static	Starting Toy
✓		Rocky Wall Jump Block	Terrain	Static	Disney Infinity Vault
✓		Roof	Building Sets	Static	Play Set (Pirates)
✓		Roof Vent	Decoration	Static	Play Set (Incredibles)
✓		Roof Wedge	Building Sets	Static	Play Set (Pirates)
✓		Roof Wedge Corner	Building Sets	Static	Play Set (Pirates)
✓		Rooftop Door	Decoration	Static	Play Set (Incredibles)
✓		Rope Bridge	Decoration	Static	Disney Infinity Vault
✓		ROR House	Building	Static	Play Set (Monsters)
✓		ROR Pledge	Play Set Townspeople	Townspeople	Play Set (Monsters)
✓		Rounded Ledge Block	Block	Static	Disney Infinity Vault
✓		Rounded Topiary	Plants	Static	Disney Infinity Vault
✓		Interstate Sign	Decoration	Static	Play Set (Cars)
✓		Safety Dome	Creativi-Toys	Custom	Disney Infinity Vault
✓		Sally Costume	Toy Box Townspeople	Townspeople	Disney Infinity Vault
✓		Sandbag Barricade	Decoration	Breakable	Play Set (Cars)
✓		Sandstone Building	Building Sets	Static	Play Set (Incredibles)
✓		Sarge's Antique Cannon	Decoration	Breakable	Play Set (Cars)
✓		Sarge's Surplus Hut	Building	Static	Play Set (Cars)
✓		Satellite Dish	Decoration	Static	Play Set (Incredibles)
✓		School Colors Ender	Decoration	Custom	Play Set (Monsters)
✓		Scoreboard	Creativi-Toys	Custom	Disney Infinity Vault
✓		Scottish Stone Circle	Set Piece	Static	Disney Infinity Vault
✓		Scout	Vehicle/Mount	Mount	Play Set (Lone Ranger)
✓		Scream Energy Launcher	Decoration	Custom	Play Set (Monsters)
✓		Scream Tunnel Cover	Decoration	Breakable	Play Set (Monsters)
✓		Scream Tunnel Sludge Ender	Decoration	Custom	Play Set (Monsters)
✓		Scrooge McDuck Costume	Toy Box Townspeople	Townspeople	Disney Infinity Vault

Got It?	Icon	Toy Name	Category	Function	Unlock
✓		Scrooge's Money Bin	Set Piece	Custom	Disney Infinity Vault
✓		Sea Dog	Play Set Townspeople	Townspeople	Play Set (Pirates)
✓		Sharp Shooter	Play Set Townspeople	Townspeople	Play Set (Lone Ranger)
✓		Shed	Building Sets	Static	Play Set (Pirates)
✓		Sheriff	Cast Member	Mission Giver	Play Set (Lone Ranger)
✓		Shipping Crate	Decoration	Breakable	Play Set (Incredibles)
✓		Shock Costume	Enemy	Enemy	Disney Infinity Vault
✓		Shopkeeper	Play Set Townspeople	Townspeople	Play Set (Lone Ranger)
✓		Short Barricade	Decoration	Static	Disney Infinity Vault
✓		Short Castle Ladder Wall	Building Sets	Static	Disney Infinity Vault
✓		Short Castle Rope Wall	Building Sets	Static	Disney Infinity Vault
✓		Short Castle Top Archway	Building Sets	Static	Disney Infinity Vault
✓		Short Castle Wall	Building Sets	Static	Disney Infinity Vault
✓		Short Castle Wall Angled Corner	Building Sets	Static	Disney Infinity Vault
✓		Short Castle Wall Corner	Building Sets	Static	Disney Infinity Vault
✓		Short Castle Wall Double Arch	Building Sets	Static	Disney Infinity Vault
✓		Short Castle Wall Inside Corner	Building Sets	Static	Disney Infinity Vault
✓		Short Cave Block	Terrain	Static	Disney Infinity Vault
✓		Short Race Track	Track Piece	Track	Disney Infinity Vault
✓		Short Race Track Curve	Track Piece	Track	Starting Toy
✓		Short Sandstone Building	Building Sets	Static	Play Set (Incredibles)
✓		Short Straight Rail	Track Piece	Rail Grind	Disney Infinity Vault
✓		Short Support Arch	Block	Static	Disney Infinity Vault
✓		Short Tiki Torch	Decoration	Static	Disney Infinity Vault
✓		Short Wooden Bridge	Decoration	Static	Disney Infinity Vault
✓		Short Wooden Ladder	Decoration	Static	Disney Infinity Vault
✓		Shrink Panel	Action Toy	Custom	Disney Infinity Vault
✓		Side-Step Camera	Creativi-Toys	Custom	Disney Infinity Vault
✓		Sidewalk Corner Piece	Decoration	Static	Play Set (Incredibles)

Got It?	Icon	Toy Name	Category	Function	Unlock
✓		Sidewalk Piece	Decoration	Static	Play Set (Incredibles)
✓		Sight Crawler	Critter	Critter	Play Set (Monsters)
✓		Silent Warrior Pack	Tool/Pack	Pack	Play Set (Lone Ranger)
✓		Silver	Vehicle/Mount	Mount	Play Set (Lone Ranger)
✓		Simple Topiary	Plants	Static	Disney Infinity Vault
✓		Single Tire Fence	Track Piece	Static	Disney Infinity Vault
✓		Six Shooter	Tool/Pack	Tool	Play Set (Lone Ranger)
✓		Skittery Critter	Critter	Critter	Play Set (Monsters)
✓		Skull Idol	Decoration	Breakable	Play Set (Pirates)
✓		Skunk	Critter	Critter	Play Set (Lone Ranger)
✓		Sky Changer	Basic Toy	Custom	Starting Toy
✓		Slingshot	Basic Toy	Custom	Disney Infinity Vault
✓		Slithering Senior	Play Set Townspeople	Townspeople	Play Set (Monsters)
✓		Slope	Terrain	Static	Disney Infinity Vault
✓		Sloping Hill	Terrain	Static	Disney Infinity Vault
✓		Small Bridge Cliff	Terrain	Static	Starting Toy
✓		Small Canyon Curve	Terrain	Static	Disney Infinity Vault
✓		Small Canyon Outer Curve	Terrain	Static	Disney Infinity Vault
✓		Small Castle Floor	Building Sets	Static	Disney Infinity Vault
✓		Small Cliff Ledge	Terrain	Static	Disney Infinity Vault
✓		Small Curved Barrier	Track Piece	Static	Disney Infinity Vault
✓		Small Disney Infinity Pine Tree	Plants	Static	Starting Toy
✓		Small Disney Infinity Spruce Tree	Plants	Breakable	Starting Toy
✓		Small Fence	Decoration	Breakable	Play Set (Cars)
✓		Small Flat Terrain Block	Terrain	Static	Disney Infinity Vault
✓		Small Floating Cliff	Terrain	Static	Disney Infinity Vault
✓		Small Floor	Block	Static	Disney Infinity Vault
✓		Small Jutting Ledge	Terrain	Static	Disney Infinity Vault
✓		Small Monster Tree 1	Plants	Static	Play Set (Monsters)
✓		Small Monster Tree 2	Plants	Static	Play Set (Monsters)

Got It?	Icon	Toy Name	Category	Function	Unlock
✓		Small Radiator Springs Cactus	Plants	Static	Play Set (Cars)
✓		Small Ramp Cliff	Terrain	Static	Disney Infinity Vault
✓		Small Rocky Terrain Block 1	Terrain	Static	Starting Toy
✓		Small Rocky Terrain Block 2	Terrain	Static	Disney Infinity Vault
✓		Small Rocky Terrain Block 3	Terrain	Static	Disney Infinity Vault
✓		Small Slope	Terrain	Static	Disney Infinity Vault
✓		Small Terrain Block	Terrain	Static	Disney Infinity Vault
✓		Snake Lady	Play Set Townspeople	Townspeople	Play Set (Lone Ranger)
✓		Sneaking Sophomore	Play Set Townspeople	Townspeople	Play Set (Monsters)
✓		Snoring Gloria	Play Set Townspeople	Townspeople	Play Set (Incredibles)
✓		Snow White Costume	Toy Box Townspeople	Townspeople	Disney Infinity Vault
✓		Soaring Senior	Play Set Townspeople	Townspeople	Play Set (Monsters)
✓		Soldier of Clubs Costume	Enemy	Enemy	Starting Toy
✓		Soldier of Hearts Costume	Enemy	Enemy	Starting Toy
✓		Sorcerer's Apprentice Mickey Costume	Toy Box Townspeople	Townspeople	Disney Infinity Vault
✓		Sorcerer's Broom Costume	Enemy	Enemy	Disney Infinity Vault
✓		Sound Effects	Creativi-Toys	Custom	Disney Infinity Vault
✓		Spare Parts Windmill	Decoration	Breakable	Play Set (Cars)
✓		Spare Tire	Basic Toy	Towable	Disney Infinity Vault
✓		Speed Bump	Track Piece	Static	Disney Infinity Vault
✓		Spiral Topiary	Plants	Static	Disney Infinity Vault
✓		Spirited Sophomore	Play Set Townspeople	Townspeople	Play Set (Monsters)
✓		Splash Pool	Action Toy	Custom	Disney Infinity Vault
✓		Sports Car Topiary	Decoration	Breakable	Play Set (Cars)
✓		Sports Fan Senior	Play Set Townspeople	Townspeople	Play Set (Monsters)
✓		Square Blip Block	Block	Blip Block	Disney Infinity Vault
✓		Square Block	Block	Static	Disney Infinity Vault
✓		Square Castle Tower	Building Sets	Static	Disney Infinity Vault
✓		Square Rocky Terrain Block	Terrain	Static	Disney Infinity Vault

Got It?	Icon	Toy Name	Category	Function	Unlock
✓		Squid-Legged Sophomore	Play Set Townspeople	Townspeople	Play Set (Monsters)
✓		Squishy	Cast Member	Mission Giver	Play Set (Monsters)
✓		Stacked Boxes	Decoration	Breakable	Play Set (Cars)
✓		Stacked Cube Topiary	Plants	Static	Disney Infinity Vault
✓		Stadium	Building Sets	Static	Disney Infinity Vault
✓		Stadium Gate	Building Sets	Static	Disney Infinity Vault
✓		Stage Coach	Vehicle/Mount	Ground Vehicle	Play Set (Lone Ranger)
✓		Stairs	Block	Static	Disney Infinity Vault
✓		Starting Gate Lights	Decoration	Breakable	Play Set (Cars)
✓		Stately Metroville Tower	Building Sets	Static	Play Set (Incredibles)
✓		Steep Arched Race Track Ramp	Track Piece	Track	Disney Infinity Vault
✓		Steep Bending Rail	Track Piece	Rail Grind	Disney Infinity Vault
✓		Steep Bowed Race Track Ramp	Track Piece	Track	Disney Infinity Vault
✓		Steep Flat Race Track Ramp	Track Piece	Track	Disney Infinity Vault
✓		Steep Ramp Rail	Track Piece	Rail Grind	Disney Infinity Vault
✓		Step Cliff	Terrain	Static	Starting Toy
✓		Stepped Grassy Corner	Terrain	Static	Starting Toy
✓		Stitch's Blaster	Tool/Pack	Tool	Power Disc
✓		Stone Arch Fort	Set Piece	Static	Play Set (Pirates)
✓		Stone Wall	Block	Static	Disney Infinity Vault
✓		Stone Wall Corner	Block	Static	Disney Infinity Vault
✓		Stopwatch	Creativi-Toys	Custom	Disney Infinity Vault
✓		Straight Dock Balcony	Building Sets	Static	Play Set (Pirates)
✓		Straight Rail	Track Piece	Rail Grind	Disney Infinity Vault
✓		Straight Tire Fence	Track Piece	Static	Disney Infinity Vault
✓		Street Light	Decoration	Static	Play Set (Incredibles)
✓		Street Light	Decoration	Static	Play Set (Cars)
✓		Street Rubble	Decoration	Breakable	Play Set (Incredibles)
✓		Street Thug	Play Set Townspeople	Townspeople	Play Set (Incredibles)
✓		Stunt Buggy	Vehicle/Mount	Ground Vehicle	Disney Infinity Vault

Got It?	Icon	Toy Name	Category	Function	Unlock
✓		Stunt Park Clover Pool	Track Piece	Static	Play Set (Cars)
✓		Stunt Park Hill	Track Piece	Static	Play Set (Cars)
✓		Stunt Park Ridge Ramp	Track Piece	Static	Play Set (Cars)
✓		Sugar Rush Terrain 1	Themed Terrain	Static	Power Disc
✓		Sugar Rush Terrain 2	Themed Terrain	Static	Power Disc
✓		Sugar Rush Terrain 3	Themed Terrain	Static	Power Disc
✓		Sugar Rush Terrain 4	Themed Terrain	Static	Power Disc
✓		Sugar Rush Terrain 5	Themed Terrain	Static	Power Disc
✓		Sugar Rush Terrain Corner 1	Themed Terrain	Static	Power Disc
✓		Sugar Rush Terrain Corner 2	Themed Terrain	Static	Power Disc
✓		Sugar Rush Terrain Strip 1	Themed Terrain	Static	Power Disc
✓		Sugar Rush Terrain Strip 2	Themed Terrain	Static	Power Disc
✓		Sulley Costume	Toy Box Townspeople	Townspeople	Disney Infinity Vault
✓		Super Cannon	Action Toy	Custom	Disney Infinity Vault
✓		Super Pipe	Track Piece	Static	Play Set (Cars)
✓		SuperMax Prison	Building	Static	Play Set (Incredibles)
✓		Surgeon	Play Set Townspeople	Townspeople	Play Set (Incredibles)
✓		Swabbie	Play Set Townspeople	Townspeople	Play Set (Pirates)
✓		Sword	Tool/Pack	Pack	Play Set (Pirates)
✓		Syndrome Costume	Toy Box Townspeople	Townspeople	Play Set (Incredibles)
✓		Syndrome Statue	Decoration	Breakable	Play Set (Incredibles)
✓		Tail Light Flower Planter	Plants	Static	Play Set (Cars)
✓		Tail Light Flowers	Plants	Static	Play Set (Cars)
✓		Tall Automatic Door	Action Toy	Custom	Disney Infinity Vault
✓		Tall Blip Block	Block	Blip Block	Disney Infinity Vault
✓		Tall Block	Block	Static	Disney Infinity Vault
✓		Tall Building Base	Building Sets	Static	Play Set (Pirates)
✓		Tall Fence	Decoration	Breakable	Play Set (Cars)
✓		Tall Glass Block	Block	Physics Block	Disney Infinity Vault

Got It?	Icon	Toy Name	Category	Function	Unlock
✓		Tall Metal Block	Block	Physics Block	Disney Infinity Vault
✓		Tall Monster Tree	Plants	Static	Play Set (Monsters)
✓		Tall Narrow Terrain Block	Terrain	Static	Disney Infinity Vault
✓		Tall Terrain Block	Terrain	Static	Disney Infinity Vault
✓		Tall Tiki Torch	Decoration	Static	Disney Infinity Vault
✓		Tall Vaulted Platform	Block	Static	Disney Infinity Vault
✓		Tall Wooden Block	Block	Physics Block	Disney Infinity Vault
✓		Tangled Terrain 1	Themed Terrain	Static	Power Disc
✓		Tangled Terrain 2	Themed Terrain	Static	Power Disc
✓		Tangled Terrain 3	Themed Terrain	Static	Power Disc
✓		Tangled Terrain 4	Themed Terrain	Static	Power Disc
✓		Tangled Terrain 5	Themed Terrain	Static	Power Disc
✓		Tangled Terrain Corner 1	Themed Terrain	Static	Power Disc
✓		Tangled Terrain Corner 2	Themed Terrain	Static	Power Disc
✓		Tangled Terrain Strip 1	Themed Terrain	Static	Power Disc
✓		Tangled Terrain Strip 2	Themed Terrain	Static	Power Disc
✓		Tank Omnidroid	Enemy	Enemy	Play Set (Incredibles)
✓		Tantor	Vehicle/Mount	Mount	Power Disc
✓		Tar Trap	Action Toy	Custom	Disney Infinity Vault
✓		Target	Creativi-Toys	Custom	Disney Infinity Vault
✓		Team 1 Base	Creativi-Toys	Custom	Disney Infinity Vault
✓		Team 2 Base	Creativi-Toys	Custom	Disney Infinity Vault
✓		Tear Drop Topiary	Plants	Static	Disney Infinity Vault
✓		TeePee	Decoration	Static	Play Set (Lone Ranger)
✓		Teleporter	Creativi-Toys	Custom	Disney Infinity Vault
✓		Tennis Player Costume	Toy Box Townspeople	Townspeople	Disney Infinity Vault
✓		Tent	Decoration	Static	Play Set (Lone Ranger)
✓		Terrain Block	Terrain	Static	Starting Toy
✓		Terry and Terri Perry	Cast Member	Mission Giver	Play Set (Monsters)
✓		The Big Spinner	Action Toy	Custom	Disney Infinity Vault

Got It?	Icon	Toy Name	Category	Function	Unlock
✓		The Boss	Play Set Townspeople	Townspeople	Play Set (Incredibles)
✓		The CEO	Play Set Townspeople	Townspeople	Play Set (Incredibles)
✓		The Colby Bank	Building	Static	Play Set (Lone Ranger)
✓		The Colby Jail	Building	Static	Play Set (Lone Ranger)
✓		The Colby Saloon	Building	Static	Play Set (Lone Ranger)
✓		The Flipper	Action Toy	Custom	Disney Infinity Vault
✓		The Hoarder	Play Set Townspeople	Townspeople	Play Set (Incredibles)
✓		The Incredicar	Vehicle/Mount	Ground Vehicle	Play Set (Incredibles)
✓		The Incredicopter	Vehicle/Mount	Air Vehicle	Play Set (Incredibles)
✓		The King's Guard	Enemy	Enemy	Disney Infinity Vault
✓		The Matterhorn	Terrain	Static	Disney Infinity Vault
✓		The Mayor of Metroville	Play Set Townspeople	Townspeople	Play Set (Incredibles)
✓		The Radiator Cap	Set Piece	Static	Play Set (Cars)
✓		The Ranch	Building	Static	Play Set (Lone Ranger)
✓		The Spinner	Action Toy	Custom	Disney Infinity Vault
✓		The Sword in the Stone	Set Piece	Custom	Disney Infinity Vault
✓		Thin Metroville Tree	Plants	Static	Play Set (Incredibles)
✓		Thin Radiator Springs Tree	Plants	Static	Play Set (Cars)
✓		Thunderhead	Play Set Townspeople	Townspeople	Play Set (Incredibles)
✓		Thundering Hooves Pack	Tool/Pack	Pack	Play Set (Lone Ranger)
✓		Thundering Stallion	Vehicle/Mount	Mount	Play Set (Lone Ranger)
✓		Tia Dalma	Cast Member	Mission Giver	Play Set (Pirates)
✓		Tigger Costume	Toy Box Townspeople	Townspeople	Disney Infinity Vault
✓		Tiki Torch	Decoration	Static	Disney Infinity Vault
✓		Time Delayer	Creativi-Toys	Custom	Disney Infinity Vault
✓		Timer	Creativi-Toys	Custom	Disney Infinity Vault
✓		Tinker Bell Costume	Toy Box Townspeople	Townspeople	Disney Infinity Vault
✓		Tiny Slope	Terrain	Static	Disney Infinity Vault
✓		Tiny Tall Terrain Block	Terrain	Static	Disney Infinity Vault

Got It?	Icon	Toy Name	Category	Function	Unlock
✓		Tiny Terrain Block	Terrain	Static	Starting Toy
✓		Tire Shrub	Decoration	Breakable	Play Set (Cars)
✓		Tire Stack 1	Decoration	Static	Play Set (Cars)
✓		Tire Stack 2	Decoration	Static	Play Set (Cars)
✓		Tire Tree	Decoration	Breakable	Play Set (Cars)
✓		TNT Pack	Tool/Pack	Pack	Play Set (Lone Ranger)
✓		Toilet Paper Launcher	Tool/Pack	Tool	Play Set (Monsters)
✓		Tomahawk	Tool/Pack	Tool	Play Set (Lone Ranger)
✓		Tonto Costume	Toy Box Townspeople	Townspeople	Play Set (Lone Ranger)
✓		Torus Topiary	Plants	Static	Disney Infinity Vault
✓		Tourist Sedan	Play Set Townspeople	Townspeople	Play Set (Cars)
✓		Tourist Truck	Play Set Townspeople	Townspeople	Play Set (Cars)
✓		Tourist Van	Play Set Townspeople	Townspeople	Play Set (Cars)
✓		Tow Mater Impound Lot	Building	Static	Play Set (Cars)
✓		Towable Ramp	Basic Toy	Towable	Play Set (Cars)
✓		Towable Wrecking Ball	Basic Toy	Towable	Play Set (Cars)
✓		Tower	Building Sets	Static	Play Set (Pirates)
✓		Tower Fort	Set Piece	Static	Disney Infinity Vault
✓		Toy Box Blaster	Tool/Pack	Tool	Starting Toy
✓		Tractor	Play Set Townspeople	Townspeople	Play Set (Cars)
✓		Tractor Crossing Sign	Decoration	Breakable	Play Set (Cars)
✓		Traffic Barrel	Decoration	Breakable	Play Set (Incredibles)
✓		Traffic Cone	Decoration	Breakable	Play Set (Incredibles)
✓		Traffic Cone	Decoration	Breakable	Play Set (Cars)
✓		Traffic Light	Decoration	Static	Play Set (Incredibles)
✓		Traffic Sign 1	Decoration	Static	Play Set (Cars)
✓		Traffic Sign 2	Decoration	Static	Play Set (Cars)
✓		Train Engine	Vehicle/Mount	Ground Vehicle	Play Set (Lone Ranger)
✓		Training Facility	Building	Static	Play Set (Incredibles)
✓		Trash Pile	Decoration	Breakable	Play Set (Incredibles)

Got It?	Icon	Toy Name	Category	Function	Unlock
✓		Trash Receptacle	Decoration	Breakable	Play Set (Incredibles)
✓		Treasure Grotto	Terrain	Static	Disney Infinity Vault
✓		Triangle Blip Block	Block	Blip Block	Disney Infinity Vault
✓		Triangle Block	Block	Static	Disney Infinity Vault
✓		Tri-Eye	Critter	Critter	Play Set (Monsters)
✓		Trigger	Creativi-Toys	Custom	Disney Infinity Vault
✓		Trigger Area	Creativi-Toys	Custom	Disney Infinity Vault
✓		Trim	Block	Static	Disney Infinity Vault
✓		Triple Barriers	Decoration	Static	Play Set (Monsters)
✓		Tripwire	Action Toy	Custom	Disney Infinity Vault
✓		TRON Costume	Toy Box Townspeople	Townspeople	Disney Infinity Vault
✓		Trunk	Decoration	Static	Disney Infinity Vault
✓		T-Shaped Barriers	Decoration	Static	Play Set (Monsters)
✓		Turtle Pirate	Enemy	Enemy	Play Set (Pirates)
✓		Underground Pipe Bend	Terrain	Static	Disney Infinity Vault
✓		Underground Pipe Branch	Terrain	Static	Disney Infinity Vault
✓		Underground Pipe End	Terrain	Static	Disney Infinity Vault
✓		Underground Pipe Entrance/Exit	Terrain	Static	Disney Infinity Vault
✓		Underground Pipe Intersection	Terrain	Static	Disney Infinity Vault
✓		Underground Pipe Tunnel	Terrain	Static	Disney Infinity Vault
✓		Vampire Teddy Costume	Enemy	Enemy	Disney Infinity Vault
✓		Vaulted Platform	Block	Static	Disney Infinity Vault
✓		Very Long Race Track	Track Piece	Track	Disney Infinity Vault
✓		Very Short Race Track	Track Piece	Track	Disney Infinity Vault
✓		Victory Tracker	Creativi-Toys	Custom	Disney Infinity Vault
✓		Violet Costume	Toy Box Townspeople	Townspeople	Play Set (Incredibles)
✓		Violet Statue	Decoration	Breakable	Play Set (Incredibles)
✓		Volleyball Player Costume	Toy Box Townspeople	Townspeople	Disney Infinity Vault
✓		Vulture	Critter	Flying Critter	Play Set (Lone Ranger)

Got It?	Icon	Toy Name	Category	Function	Unlock
✓		Vulture Goon Costume	Enemy	Enemy	Disney Infinity Vault
✓		Wagon	Decoration	Static	Play Set (Lone Ranger)
✓		Wall Jump Block	Action Toy	Static	Disney Infinity Vault
✓		Water Tower	Decoration	Static	Play Set (Incredibles)
✓		Waterfall	Terrain	Static	Disney Infinity Vault
✓		Weasel Costume	Enemy	Enemy	Disney Infinity Vault
✓		Wedge Blip Block	Block	Blip Block	Disney Infinity Vault
✓		Wedge Block	Block	Static	Disney Infinity Vault
✓		Which Way Sign	Decoration	Breakable	Play Set (Cars)
✓		Wide Barrier	Track Piece	Static	Disney Infinity Vault
✓		Wide Building Base	Building Sets	Static	Play Set (Pirates)
✓		Wide Canyon Wall	Terrain	Static	Disney Infinity Vault
✓		Wide Castle Wall and Tower	Building Sets	Static	Disney Infinity Vault
✓		Wide Floating Bridge Hill	Terrain	Static	Disney Infinity Vault
✓		Wide Floating Cliff	Terrain	Static	Starting Toy
✓		Wide Rope Bridge	Decoration	Static	Disney Infinity Vault
✓		Willy's Butte	Set Piece	Static	Play Set (Cars)
✓		Wind Chime	Decoration	Breakable	Play Set (Cars)
✓		Winding Floating Bridge 1	Terrain	Static	Disney Infinity Vault
✓		Winding Floating Bridge 2	Terrain	Static	Disney Infinity Vault
✓		Winner's Circle	Decoration	Breakable	Play Set (Cars)
✓		Winnie the Pooh Costume	Toy Box Townspeople	Townspeople	Disney Infinity Vault
✓		Wolf	Critter	Critter	Disney Infinity Vault
✓		Woman	Play Set Townspeople	Townspeople	Play Set (Lone Ranger)
✓		Wonderland Terrain 1	Themed Terrain	Static	Power Disc
✓		Wonderland Terrain 2	Themed Terrain	Static	Power Disc
✓		Wonderland Terrain 3	Themed Terrain	Static	Power Disc
✓		Wonderland Terrain 4	Themed Terrain	Static	Power Disc
✓		Wonderland Terrain 5	Themed Terrain	Static	Power Disc
✓		Wonderland Terrain Corner 1	Themed Terrain	Static	Power Disc

Got It?	Icon	Toy Name	Category	Function	Unlock
✓		Wonderland Terrain Corner 2	Themed Terrain	Static	Power Disc
✓		Wonderland Terrain Strip 1	Themed Terrain	Static	Power Disc
✓		Wonderland Terrain Strip 2	Themed Terrain	Static	Power Disc
✓		Wood Crate	Decoration	Breakable	Play Set (Pirates)
✓		Wooden Barrel	Decoration	Breakable	Play Set (Pirates)
✓		Wooden Block	Block	Physics Block	Disney Infinity Vault
✓		Wooden Bridge	Decoration	Static	Disney Infinity Vault
✓		Wooden Bridge Platform	Decoration	Static	Disney Infinity Vault
✓		Wooden Ladder	Decoration	Static	Disney Infinity Vault
✓		Wrangler	Play Set Townspeople	Townspeople	Play Set (Lone Ranger)
✓		X Games Barrier	Sports Toy	Static	Disney Infinity Vault
✓		X Games Rolling Stunt Ramp	Track Piece	Static	Disney Infinity Vault
✓		X Games Stunt Pipe Corner	Track Piece	Static	Disney Infinity Vault
✓		X Games Stunt Platform	Track Piece	Static	Disney Infinity Vault
✓		X Games Stunt Quarter Pipe	Track Piece	Static	Disney Infinity Vault
✓		X Games Stunt Ramp	Track Piece	Static	Disney Infinity Vault
✓		Yellow Basketball Jersey Costume	Toy Box Townspeople	Townspeople	Disney Infinity Vault
✓		Zero Point Energy Gauntlet	Tool/Pack	Tool	Play Set (Incredibles)

Achievements & Trophies

Got It?	#	Name	Location	Category	Criteria	Xbox 360 Achievements	PS3 Trophies
✓	1	Star Extractor	Global	Stars	Collect 15 stars in a Play Set	5	Bronze (15)
✓	2	1 More to Go	Global	Stars	Collect 15 stars in 2 Play Sets	10	Bronze (15)
✓	3	All Star	Global	Stars	Collect 15 stars in 3 Play Sets	25	Bronze (15)
✓	4	It's a Start	Global	Stars	Collect 50 stars	10	Bronze (15)
✓	5	Wish Upon a Star	Global	Stars	Collect 70 stars in the Disney Infinity Starter Pack	100	Gold (90)
✓	6	New Friends	Global	In Game Progression	Play a 2-player game using two different characters	10	Bronze (15)
✓	7	Character Plunder	Global	In Game Progression	Unlock 3 Character Chests	4	Bronze (15)
✓	8	Character Elite Force	Global	In Game Progression	Level up 3 Characters to level 15	100	Gold (90)
✓	9	Character Elite Set	Global	In Game Progression	Level up 2 Characters to level 15	25	Bronze (15)
✓	10	Character Elite	Global	In Game Progression	Level up 1 Character to level 15	10	Bronze (15)
✓	11	Visit the Hall	Global	General	Visit the Hall of Heroes	4	Bronze (15)
✓	12	Infinity and Beyond	Global	General	Play 3 Play Sets and the Toy Box	10	Bronze (15)
✓	13	All Modes	Global	General	Drive a car, pilot a helicopter, and a ride a mount	10	Bronze (15)
✓	14	Power Up!	Global	Toys	Place one Power Disc on the Disney Infinity Base	4	Bronze (15)
✓	15	Great Communicator	Global	A.I. Interactions	Talk to mission givers 20 times throughout Disney Infinity	10	Bronze (15)
✓	16	Defender of the Universe	Global	A.I. Interactions	Defeat 100 enemies throughout Disney Infinity	10	Bronze (15)
✓	17	It's a Party	Toy Box	Multiplayer	Play a 4 player game	10	Bronze (15)
✓	18	Sorry?	Toy Box	Multiplayer	Defeat another player's Character	4	Bronze (15)
✓	19	Not Sorry?	Toy Box	Multiplayer	Defeat 40 player Characters	10	Bronze (15)
✓	20	Acrobat	Toy Box	Multiplayer	Stand on top of a stack of 4 Characters	5	Bronze (15)
✓	21	The Champion	Toy Box	Multiplayer	Win First Place in a Multiplayer Adventure	10	Bronze (15)
✓	22	Creator	Toy Box	General	Save 4 different Toy Box worlds	5	Bronze (15)
✓	23	Graduate	Toy Box	General	Complete all Mastery Adventures	10	Bronze (15)
✓	24	Import Master	Toy Box	General	Place a toy from a Play Set in a Toy Box you are hosting	10	Bronze (15)
✓	25	Spin Start	Toy Box	Toy Maker	Take 10 turns in the Disney Infinity Vault	10	Bronze (15)
✓	26	Spin Master	Toy Box	Toy Maker	Take 20 turns in the Disney Infinity Vault	15	Bronze (15)
✓	27	Bonus Bank	Toy Box	Toy Maker	Win 5 bonuses in the Disney Infinity Vault	10	Bronze (15)
✓	28	Toy Maker Extreme	Toy Box	Toy Maker	Take 30 turns in the Disney Infinity Vault	15	Silver (30)
✓	29	Star Hunter	Toy Box	Stars	Get 18 stars from Adventures	10	Bronze (15)
✓	30	Feat Novice	Toy Box	Feats	Complete 25 feats	10	Bronze (15)
✓	31	Feat Master	Toy Box	Feats	Complete 75 feats	15	Bronze (15)
✓	32	Not Last!	Toy Box	Adventures	Complete 3 Adventures to bronze standard	10	Bronze (15)
✓	33	Almost There	Toy Box	Adventures	Complete 3 Adventures to silver standard	25	Silver (30)
✓	34	It's All Gold!	Toy Box	Adventures	Complete 3 Adventures to gold standard	100	Silver (30)
✓	35	Team Work	Play Sets	Multiplayer	Complete a Story Mission in a multiplayer game	5	Bronze (15)
✓	36	Getting It Started	Play Sets	Story Missions	Complete a Story Mission	4	Bronze (15)
✓	37	Journey Complete	Play Sets	Story Missions	Complete the story in a Play Set	10	Bronze (15)
✓	38	Another Happy Outcome	Play Sets	Story Missions	Complete the story in 2 Play Sets	25	Bronze (15)
✓	39	There Is No "End" in Infinity!	Play Sets	Story Missions	Complete the story in 3 Play Sets	100	Gold (90)
✓	40	Full of Toys	Play Sets	PS Specific Toys	Unlock 10 toys from Play Sets	10	Bronze (15)
✓	41	Power Pack!	Play Sets	PS Specific Toys	Buy 2 Packs from one Play Set	10	Bronze (15)
✓	42	Multi-Tool!	Play Sets	PS Specific Toys	Buy 2 Tools from one play set	10	Bronze (15)
✓	43	City Planner	Play Sets	PS Specific Toys	Buy 4 Play Set buildings and place them in the Toy Box	10	Bronze (15)
✓	44	Doesn't This Look Better?	Play Sets	PS Specific Toys	Customize 6 buildings in the Play Sets	10	Bronze (15)
✓	45	Challenger	Play Sets	Challenges	Complete the "Easy" level on all Challenges in a single Play Set	5	Bronze (15)
✓	46	Challenging	Play Sets	Challenges	Complete the "Medium" level on all Challenges in a single Play Set	10	Bronze (15)
✓	47	Challenges Conquered	Play Sets	Challenges	Complete the "Hard" level on all Challenges in a single Play Set	25	Silver (30)
✓	48	That Was Easy	Play Sets	Challenges	Complete 5 Challenges on Easy	10	Bronze (15)
✓	49	That Was Rough	Play Sets	Challenges	Complete 5 Challenges on Medium	25	Bronze (15)
✓	50	That Was a Challenge	Play Sets	Challenges	Complete 5 Challenges on Hard	100	Silver (30)
✓		Platinum Challenge	Global (PS3 only)	PS3	Complete all Trophies		Platinum

INFINITY

PRIMA Official Game Guide

Written by:

Howard Grossman & Michael Knight

Prima Games
An Imprint of Random House, Inc.
3000 Lava Ridge Court, Suite 100
Roseville, CA 95661
www.primagames.com/DI

Senior Product Marketing Manager: Donato Tica
Design and Layout: Ryan Zagar & Jody Seltzer
Copyeditor: Julia Mascardo
Gameplay/Maps Dudes: Josef Frech, Connor Knight and Tanner Knight

ISBN: 978-0804-16237-1

Printed in the United States of America

Prima Games would like to thank the following people for their support:

Michael Schneider, Mathew Solie, Greg Hayes, Cyril Bornette, Phil Knight, Manfred Neber, Chad Liddell, David White, Troy Johnson, Troy Leavitt, Mark McArther, Kevin Pulley, Mike Thompson, Jeff Byers, Vince Bracken, John Blackburn, John Vignocchi, Kristin Yee, Aaron King, Stephanie Martinelli, Stephen Lewis, Vince Griffin, Rick Gusa, Mary Galligan, Disney Interactive QA team, "The team at Avalanche Software"